MAKING BLACK LIVES MATTER

MAKING BLACK LIVES MATTER

CONFRONTING ANTI-BLACK RACISM

KEVIN COKLEY, EDITOR

cognella®
SAN DIEGO

Bassim Hamadeh, CEO and Publisher
Amy Smith, Senior Project Editor
Abbey Hastings, Production Editor
Emely Villavicencio, Senior Graphic Designer
Alexa Lucido, Licensing Manager
Ursina Kilburn, Interior Designer
Tiffany Mok, Senior Content Writer
Natalie Piccotti, Director of Marketing
Kassie Graves, Senior Vice President of Editorial
Jamie Giganti, Director of Academic Publishing

3970 Sorrento Valley Blvd., Ste. 500, San Diego, CA 92121

A LETTER FROM THE PUBLISHER

Dear Reader,

We are pleased to share with you *Making Black Lives Matter: Confronting Anti-Black Racism*, edited by Kevin Cokley.

This book is extremely important to all of us at Cognella. The idea for it was borne in the summer of 2020 in the wake of the murders of George Floyd, Breonna Taylor, and Ahmaud Arbery. As a company and as individuals, we were enraged and heartbroken by the senseless violence, the lives lost, and the horrific reminders that systemic racism is alive and well in our communities and our institutions.

While it has always been important for us as a publisher to give a voice to historically underrepresented authors in academia, we knew we could do even more. We wanted to leverage what we do best—publishing—and also make a difference in a meaningful way. We decided we could make a significant impact by publishing a free ebook that highlights the contemporary battle for equity and the lived experiences of those in the Black community.

We asked renowned scholar and psychologist Kevin Cokley, Ph.D., if he'd be interested in editing the book. We were elated when he said yes, and his vision and partnership have been invaluable. *Making Black Lives Matter* has transformed from a kernel of an idea into a timely and essential book that features chapters written by Black scholars, practitioners, activists, and students. It explores the history and contemporary circumstances of anti-Black racism, offers powerful personal anecdotes, and provides recommendations and solutions to challenge anti-Black racism in its various manifestations. In short, it's the book we all need, here and now.

Making Black Lives Matter is a book that is meant to be shared. Our goals in publishing this book were to amplify the voices of those who need to be heard and to provide readers free access to critical scholarship on a topic that affects their everyday lives. We're proud to provide free digital copies of the book to anyone who wants to read it.

In the spirit of sharing knowledge, send *Making Black Lives Matter* to your friends, family, and colleagues. Discuss it in your next book club. Read the book to deepen your personal understanding of anti-Black racism in America and to cultivate or nurture your own anti-racist practices.

If you're an educator, use this material in your courses. There's no permission needed; start using it today if you're so inclined. Share copies with peers at your institution. Leverage the material to support your institution's diversity, equity, and inclusion initiatives.

The only restrictions imposed upon this content are as follows: 1) no person or entity has the right to sell this book, or any portion of it, for profit; and 2) if you are a professor and using the book in your courses, the chapters are intended to be used in full. Please refrain from cutting and pasting or excerpting to ensure the integrity of the material is maintained.

We can't express enough gratitude to Kevin Cokley and the phenomenal contributors who were willing to share their experiences, expertise, and unique viewpoints to bring this book to life. Additionally, this project has been fueled and championed by the passion of the Cognella team, who have worked hard to publish a project that we hope will support the greater good. A special thank you to Emely Villavicencio for designing a gorgeous, award-winning cover and Kassie Graves for her editorial leadership.

And while this book is an exceptional achievement for all involved, and we couldn't be more optimistic about its potential impact on educators, institutions, individuals, and champions for change, we know that the work is not done. The fight for true equity is a marathon, not a sprint, and we will continue to do our part to promote justice and change at Cognella for all underrepresented and marginalized groups, today and every day.

Bassim Hamadeh
Founder and CEO

Brief Contents

Detailed Contents

INTRODUCTION

I n June 2020 Professor of African American Studies kihana ross wrote a powerful op-ed in *The New York Times* about the tremendous suffering and death being faced by African Americans. She argued that *racism*, while a useful term, did not fully capture what Black people were going through. She was specifically responding to the murder of George Floyd by officer Derek Chauvin, which had dominated U.S. news coverage and had captured the attention of much of the world. Professor ross argued that the right term to describe what was happening to African Americans was "anti-Blackness." She said that anti-Blackness is more than just racism against Black people. Using her exact words, she said, "That oversimplifies and defangs it. It's a theoretical framework that illuminates society's inability to recognize our humanity—the disdain, disregard and disgust for our existence."

This notion of anti-Blackness is both easy to understand yet difficult to fully comprehend. On the one hand, it conveys the idea that at the level of individual racism, Black people have long been the object of derision and indeed hatred. However, anti-Blackness goes well beyond acts of individual racism. It is embedded within our institutions, culture, and the social fabric of our nation. It is an attitude that is sometimes explicitly spoken but often is left unspoken. Anti-Blackness is part of the unspoken conventional wisdom held by many people about the inferior status of Black people. It is important to note that anti-Blackness is not beholden to skin color. While anti-Blackness is deeply entrenched in most White communities, members of BIPOC (Black, Indigenous, and people of color) communities are not immune from anti-Blackness. While anti-Blackness may be assumed to be predominantly affiliated with one political party, it is certainly not relegated to any one political party. Both Republicans and Democrats (and all other political affiliations) can exhibit and perpetuate anti-Blackness.

The willingness to acknowledge and finally talk openly about anti-Blackness can be largely credited to the success of the Black Lives Matter (BLM) movement, a largely decentralized social and political movement formed to protest police brutality and all forms of racially motivated violence against Black people. We owe a debt of gratitude to Alicia Garza, Patrisse Cullors, and Opal Tometi, who had the foresight to create the hashtag #BlackLivesMatter, which would capture the imagination and passion of activists and eventually grow into a worldwide movement. With an estimated 15 to 26 million people participating in the 2020 Black Lives Matter protests, the BLM movement became perhaps the largest movement in the history of the United States.

Similar to previous political and social protests, the BLM movement has generated a lot of scholarly attention. Accordingly, several books inspired by the movement have been written. In the 2016 book *From #BlackLivesMatter to Black Liberation*, activist and scholar Keeanga-Yamahtta Taylor surveys the historical and contemporary consequences of racism and the persistence of structural inequality such as mass incarceration and Black unemployment. In the 2016 book *They Can't Kill Us All: The Story of Black Lives Matter*, author Wesley Lowery offers a historically informed examination of the standoff between the police and those they are sworn to protect and shows that civil unrest is only one tool of resistance in the struggle for justice. In the 2017 book *The Making of Black Lives Matter: A Brief History of An Idea*, Associate Professor of Philosophy Christopher Lebron presents a brief and accessible intellectual history that traces the origins of the ideas of the BLM movement. In the 2017 book *Have Black Lives Ever Mattered?*, political activist and journalist Mumia provides a collection of his radio commentaries that give voice to the many people of color who have been victims of police bullets or racist abuses. In the 2018 book *Making All Black Lives Matter: Reimagining Freedom in the Twenty-First Century*, historian and activist Barbara Ransby outlines the scope, genealogy, and challenges of the movement, documents its role in Black feminist politics, and situates it within a Black radical tradition.

Each of these books is an important contribution to the ongoing story of the BLM movement. So why is there a need for yet another BLM-related book? It is important to provide the context of how this edited book came to fruition. I was contacted by Dr. Miguel Gallardo, one of a group of editors who oversee Cognella's Advances in Culture, Race, and Ethnicity book series. Dr. Gallardo indicated that as a result of the current social movement to address racism and anti-Black racism, Cognella was supporting the creation of a book or collection of books that would highlight important themes and voices in Black/African American communities. They approached me to gauge my interest in being an editor for the book. I was very honored to be asked, especially given that there are so many people who could do an incredible job being an editor for this book. One of the details that I found particularly attractive about this opportunity was the fact that Cognella is giving the book away free of charge because they are committed to the dissemination of knowledge to those who need it and want it but may not always have access to it. This is in line with the public scholarship work I engage in through the writing of op-eds, because that has been a way for me to reach audiences who would otherwise never have the opportunity to read my articles published in academic journals or hear my opinions about important social issues related to race. Giving the book away for free is a radical departure from the traditional way that knowledge is accessed and disseminated in this country.

The aforementioned BLM-related books are traditional, single-authored books. Three of the authors are professors and two are journalists, with three of the authors also self-identifying as activists. I highlight these details to make the point that the books offer the singular perspectives of the authors. This book, *Making Black Lives Matter*, is the first edited BLM-related book that I am aware of. One of the most exciting aspects of this book is that it will represent a diversity of voices from the Black community. Far from being a traditional academic book, *Making Black Lives Matter* contains chapters from scholars, practitioners, activists, and students. Several of the chapters are written in traditional scholarly prose and supported by the requisite academic citations. However, one of the unique features of this book is that some of the chapters are written from the positionality of the contributors based on their lived and/or professional work experiences. The book focuses on the ways that anti-Black racism manifests and has been confronted across various domains of Black life using research, activism, social media, and therapy. The book is divided into four sections: Activism, Public Policy, Community Voices, and Student Voices.

Part 1: Activism

Chapter 1 examines how the consequences of long-term suppressed trauma within the African American community have fostered activism as the logical vehicle toward rectifying these inequities. The authors situate contemporary activism within the centuries-long trauma that Black people have experienced. From the activism of enslaved Africans during the transatlantic slave trade and on plantations, to the 19th- and 20th-century activism that challenged racist codes, segregationist laws, bigoted practices, eugenic driven science, and racist domestic terrorism by White hate groups, to the 21st-century BLM movement and calls for defunding or abolishing the police, activism has been essential to create change and obtain human and civil rights for African Americans.

Chapter 2 addresses how scholar-activism focused on Black liberation can facilitate Black survival and wellness. The first part of the chapter explores anti-Black racism across personal, relational, and collective domains of wellness and provides an overview of the relationship between academic and anti-Black racism. The potential of scholar-activism as an intervention against anti-Black racism is examined, while risks of Black scholar-activism are explored. The second part of the chapter discusses how to develop a scholar-activism agenda for Black liberation and provides guiding questions to assist readers in developing their own agendas. The chapter ends with the idea that liberation work must go beyond the confines of academia.

Chapter 3 focuses on the impacts of anti-Black racism on mental health and describes how social media contributes to promoting social justice. Applications for confronting anti-Black racism through social media use are offered. A focus on social media is important given that it has been reported that Black people use some social networking sites at a higher rate than White people. Among other things, these social networking sites are used to start hashtags to highlight racial injustice, promote social justice, and promote healing through the use of offering psychoeducation on racial stress and mental health. #BlackLivesMatter was one of the first to capitalize on social media platforms to fight racial injustice. The chapter also addresses implications for social media use among therapists, noting some of the ethical dilemmas that can arise.

Chapter 4 examines the historical and contemporary context of racism within feminist movements and sexism with Black liberation movements experienced by Black women.

Despite the significance of the substantial contributions Black women have made to sociopolitical movements, the impact of gendered racism and misogynoir continues to be overlooked. The purpose of this chapter is to apply Black feminist thought and an intersectionality lens to highlight Black women's experiences of intersectional oppression, the impact of systemic gendered racism and misogynoir on Black women's mental health and well-being, and how Black women continue to engage in resistance. The chapter ends with specific strategies for Black women to engage in radical healing as a form of resistance against intersectional oppression.

Part 2: Public Policy

Chapter 5 examines the historical context and current state of education for Black students by looking at how decisions made by city leaders limited the equitable treatment of Black students and their families. Anti-Blackness is highlighted in the policies and practices of White leaders and families. White flight, increased enrollment in private schools, and an increase in segregation reflected the reality that White people held deep-seeded racist beliefs that Black children and families were inferior because of negative beliefs about African Americans. Additionally, concentrated poverty continues to be a serious barrier to education for many Black students who are often in under-resourced schools. The chapter calls for a direct confrontation of anti-Black policies in schools, with an emphasis on confronting and challenging White parents to care about public schools in their community.

Chapter 6 examines policing and carceral punishment through the context of global Black struggle. The purpose of the chapter is to inform how Black populations in formerly colonized nations and metropoles are similarly criminalized due in large part to shared colonial histories. Police killings in countries like Brazil, France, and Nigeria are examined to provide context in understanding the mechanisms of police brutality. The history of modern-day policing is traced back to slave codes and colonial laws enforced by European imperialists. Solutions related to both the reform and abolition positions are proposed, and examples of specific strategies that have been implemented in societies across the world are provided. The author argues that racial equity cannot be achieved in criminal law without confronting the impact of colonial legacies on contemporary modes of policing and carceral punishment.

Chapter 7 provides a review of the scant literature that focuses on Black young people with lived experiences of homelessness. There is a disproportionate prevalence of homelessness among Black young people. Given the fact that race is not a lens through which the construction of homelessness is understood, benefits and limitations of definitions of homelessness for Black young people and their implications are discussed. Little is known about how anti-Black racism affects the lives of Black young people with lived experience of homelessness because race-related factors are not examined in research and are rarely addressed in policy and services.

Chapter 8 examines the history of housing discrimination for Black people within the context of four major U.S. cities: Chicago, Los Angeles, Dallas, and Austin. A timeline of historical events at the state and national level is provided. A description of how covert structural and systematic racism shaped the persistent housing segregation that exists today in metropolitan areas across America is provided. Racial deed restrictions, racial covenants, restrictive lending practices, redlining, and the expansion of highway systems were examples of how anti-Blackness was used to maintain segregation within cities, displace Black residents, and prevent Black people from accessing home loans. The current implications of past discriminatory housing practices are discussed with considerations provided for addressing the disproportionate effects of housing discrimination on African Americans for generations.

Part 3: Community Voices

Chapter 9 examines the work of the Austin Justice Coalition (AJC), a Black-led group of activists that emerged in 2015 amidst the BLM movement in response to the killings of Black men, women, and children by the hands of police in the United States. The chapter articulates how a model for Black-led advocacy in the pursuit of justice in Austin has shaped the AJC over the past 5 years. The AJC has grown from its early days of organizing mass protests, town halls, and vigils to combat racism and anti-Blackness. The AJC launched a legislative advocacy team and has grown into a political force that has successfully fought for police reform and policy changes (e.g., improved independent civilian oversight office; a police labor contract that was informed by the priorities of the public; updated use of force policy; development of a body-worn camera policy and body-worn camera footage release policy; divestment of $20 million from the police budget). The AJC's activism is not limited to policing; it is also involved in issues related to housing, mental health, and education policy.

Chapter 10 focuses on the history of the Texas Empowerment Academy (TxEA), a charter school in east Austin that serves students from vulnerable populations, 95% of whom are African American. The school has demanded excellence from its students and is a story of extraordinary success (e.g., 100% of students who took the U.S. history, English, and biology exit test passed, while 98% passed the algebra test). The school started with only five grades (fifth through ninth) and seven students, whom other public schools had rejected, and has grown to serving 377 students from kindergarten through 12th grade on two campuses. The chapter tells the story of TxEA's origins in the words of the three people who continue to be instrumental in the success of the school. The importance of being taught Black history and the implications of not being taught about Black culture are addressed. Most importantly, believing in children who schools have said couldn't behave or learn is central to the approach of the school.

Chapter 11 uses Yorùbá ontology (metaphysical ways of being), to impart lessons for women as they navigate intersectional labyrinths of anti-Black and misogynoir oppression to build psychological well-being. Grounded in a womanist worldview, the chapter uses a definition of womanism offered by the foundational work of Layli Maparyan (Phillips), the womanist reader, and is grounded in the everyday experiences and problem-solving methods used by women of African ancestry. By centering the focus of the chapter on female Òrìṣà that are sources of guidance, healing, and protection, women of African ancestry are provided a resource for navigating intersectional patterns of oppression while seeing themselves as a reflection of the divine. Several stories are shared that highlight how Ifá can be used to address all forms of oppression while demonstrating our ongoing connection to nature.

Chapter 12 reviews a therapeutic practice, The Victorious Mind, a mental health and empowerment services clinic that focuses on those who have struggled to find or who mistrust the notion of real mental health assistance. Black males have historically underutilized mental health services, yet an impressive 37% of the patient population at The Victorious Mind have been Black male adults. With the killings of Black men and women during the summer of 2020 and the COVID-19 pandemic came feelings of rage, anger, and despair. It is important to have a safe space to express these emotions in a healthy, effective manner for the emotional and physical well-being of Black men. Additionally, Black male clients commonly experience the pressure to be perfect in the workplace, feeling like they have to work twice as hard as others in the workplace, and feeling the need to outperform their coworkers to keep their jobs. Noting that common stressors of racism, discrimination, and poverty are experienced at a higher rate among Black men than other groups, the author addresses the effective management of the deep levels of Black males' distress.

Part 4: Student Voices

Chapter 14 describes some of the ways the Black graduate experience is different from other campus populations. Black students only account for approximately 6% of incoming doctoral students enrolled at schools designated with the Carnegie classification of "Very High Research Activities" universities. The low numbers of Black graduate students place additional and undue burden on them and requires an institutional commitment to recruitment and retention. The chapter delineates some of the specific nuances of anti-Blackness in academic and social contexts and explains some of the ways Black students have responded to those problems. The chapter also identifies several individual, systemic, and sociopolitical barriers that impede the success of Black graduate students, including the impostor phenomenon and race-related stress.

Chapter 14 highlights the unique experiences of four Black undergraduate students in an academic system that was not designed for them. Despite the odds stacked against them, they tell stories of self-love against anti-Blackness, overcoming impostor syndrome, leadership development in the midst of adversity, and the healing power of solidarity. These stories are powerful and diverse. One student brings to light her struggles against anti-Blackness among her family, White friends, and in the classroom (e.g., being told that scientifically Black women were considered the ugliest group). Another student discusses the challenges of organizing student activism to advocate for Rodney Reed, a Black man on Death Row believed to have been falsely accused of murdering a White woman. Another student discusses her struggle with being detached from her Blackness because of internalizing anti-Black sentiments and how she overcame this along her journey of self-discovery. Another student talks about the importance of how immersing herself in Black student organizations was like a home away from home. Collectively these students tell a larger story of the true struggles and triumphs of going to a predominantly White college while being Black.

Chapter 15 highlights the sometimes painful and traumatizing experience Black students experience in pursuing a doctoral degree. Two doctoral students share personal anecdotes about their tumultuous journey to obtain a PhD. The eagerness and excitement that these students had for pursuing a doctoral degree slowly diminished as they encountered racist experiences that marked the beginning of their uphill battle. The racist experiences included (but were not limited to) (a) lack of support for research projects (compared to their White peers), (b) not being given authorship credit for their scientific or professional contributions and being labeled as "lazy," and (c) not being supported to attend the Association of Black Psychologists conference while White students were given much support to attend the American Psychological Association conference. Interspersed throughout the chapter are references to constructs (e.g., microaggressions, racial battle fatigue, race-based trauma) that have changed them forever. The authors challenge graduate programs to evaluate their implicit biases and provide support to Black students so they can graduate.

Each of these chapters tell a unique and powerful story about the impact of anti-Blackness and how it has been (or needs to be) confronted. It is my hope that the book will provide a blueprint for readers that will empower them to actively confront anti-Blackness wherever it exists, because this is the only way we will progress toward making Black lives matter.

Part I

ACTIVISM

CHAPTER ONE

Historical Overview of the Black Struggle

Factors Affecting African American Activism

Benson G. Cooke, Edwin J. Nichols, Schuyler C. Webb, Steven J. Jones, and Nia N. Williams

> History is not the past. It is the present. We carry our history with us. We are our history. If we pretend otherwise, we are literally criminals. I attest to this: the world is not white; it never was white, cannot be white. White is a metaphor for power, and that is simply a way of describing Chase Manhattan Bank.
>
> —James Baldwin,
> *I Am Not Your Negro*

Activism is the scaffolding around the grievances of citizens in a democratic society. The First Amendment of the U.S. Constitution guarantees this civil expression. Epigenomic studies have shown significant intergenerational trauma caused by enslavement, Jim Crow law and segregation, and the civil rights struggles during the 20th century. However, 21st-century oppression continues to sanction these behaviors. Systemic institutional racism precludes inclusion, equity, and diversity within American society. The uninterrupted and egregious racism examples are inadequate educational resources, inequitable employment opportunities, subjective judicial processes, and indefensible police aggression and brutality.

When African Americans voice their legitimate grievances, the dominant society denies the validity and neutralizes the African American issues and concerns. When pressed with visual reality, the dominant culture takes exception to the interpretation of the event. Often, they express unapologetic, unabashed, and hostile violence toward African Americans for the audacity of confronting their understanding of reality. Consequently, these factors influence the social, psychological, and health care outcomes of African Americans. The continuation of these systemic institutional racist practices exacerbates long-standing violence and trauma within the African American community. This chapter aims to demonstrate the consequences of long-term suppressed trauma within the African American community and that activism has been the logical vehicle toward rectifying these inequities.

Confronting Anti-Black Racism

The African diasporic experience in the Americas is characterized by persistent resistance to systemic and government-sanctioned anti-Black violence. This type of sanctioned violence is defined as legitimate because it is in the national interest; violence is prohibited except when used by state agents (Cairns & Sears, 2012). Specifically, African Americans encounter this assaultive behavior on multiple levels (i.e., physical, psychological, epistemic, spiritual) as well as various forms of racism—individual, systemic, and institutional. Critical race psychology is an essential tool for understanding how African Americans experience and resist myriad forms of violence. Critical race psychology approaches racism as systemic, illuminates how neoliberalism perpetuates and reproduces racial hierarchies, emphasizes the majority (and other privileged identities) philosophy and mentality, and proposes counter-narratives as a method of resisting the dominant majority narratives (Nichols, personal communication, November 30, 2020; Salter & Adams, 2017). Influenced by Black liberation psychology and critical race theory, this perspective is more than appropriate for understanding Black activism movements in response to systemic anti-Black violence. This chapter's perspective, examination, and explication broadens the scope to view racism as a systemic entity, not just individual prejudice or bias, and to properly center Black people's activist perspectives and history.

Activism Defined

The etymology of the term *activism* became a part of the common language expression in the early 20th century. The early usage of this term in 1920 was used in the political sense of "advocating energetic action" (Online Oxford Etymology, 2020). In comparison, the Oxford English Dictionary defines activism as "the use of vigorous campaigning to bring about political or social change" (Soanes & Stevenson, 2008, p. 13). According to Merriam-Webster (2007), activism is "a doctrine or practice that emphasizes direct vigorous action especially in support of or opposition to one side of a controversial issue" (p. 13). Consequently, this term's use suggests that activism is the act of human engagement through vocally and physically advocating for social change designed to ensure fundamental liberties that enhance one's survival. Predating the term *activism*, citizens collectively organized, revolted, engaged in social disobedience, and even fought for their rights to acquire liberty, fundamental human rights, and dignity.

Consequently, it is not uncharacteristic that activism in judicial principle is the aspirational liberty written into the First Amendment of the Bill of Rights ratified on December 15, 1791, stating that "Congress shall make no law respecting an establishment of religion or prohibiting the free exercise thereof; or abridging the freedom of speech, or the press; or the right of the people peaceably to assemble, and to petition the Government for the redress of grievances." Activism is the most constructive and direct action taken by the African American community to address grievances and advocate against divisive and inhumane treatment and laws designed to sustain systemic and institutional racism. Activism has given a voice of collective courage to a community of people previously enslaved and then constrained by law. Activism in this context counters the fear from systemic and institutional racism that often sanctioned abuse and death. Consequently, African American activism is probably most recognizable in street and city marches, sit-ins, crowd protests, nonviolent demonstrations, and boycotts. Activism has leveraged the written word in newspapers and pamphlets as well as used the visual images of photos and videos.

Additionally, activists have addressed community grievances by providing factual data concerning the impact of long-standing injustices using multiple media platforms. However, when advocating for civil rights or human rights is not possible, then riots or violent clashes erupt. As examined within this chapter, activism ascribes to the idea that African Americans have fought for, rebelled against, and spoken out as activists for their rights to exist as free women and men. After more than 400 years, many of the systems established to marginalize, control, and dominate African American populations continue to endure. We believe that understanding contemporary activism requires a knowledge of the impact of centuries-long trauma. Moreover, this chapter addresses historical issues, psychological trauma, and levels of change necessary to reverse the cultural conditioning resulting from acts of systemic and institutional racism that devalues, "co-opts," and undermines African American activism efforts.

A Brief Historical Account of African American Activism

> History is a clock that people use to tell their political and cultural time of day. It is also a compass that people use to find themselves on the map of human geography. The role of history is to tell a people what they have been, and where they have been, what they are, and where they are. The most important role that history plays is that it has the function of telling a people where they still must go and what they still must be.
>
> —John Henrik Clarke

More than 2 centuries of the physical and psychological trauma and protracted enslavement compelled some Africans to give in to their fears that they could be subjugated into a lifetime of harsh servitude and forced captivity. Colonial legislatures after 1660 legislated a "range of punishments that whites could mete out to blacks to support the view of master-slave relations" (Morgan, 2005, p. 5). Thus, slave owners enforced transgenerational obedience under legislative policies, laws, slave codes, the force of the master's cruel punishments, and their words. Embedded within the master's actions was a belief that their slaves had no humanity and no God-given rights to be free. So, enslavement became both an enforced tool to deprive enslaved Africans of their humanity and their freedom. Within each generation of enslavement, the hope and desire for liberty would incite activism. African activism varied from plantation to plantation and geographical region. For some enslaved Africans, their survival involved creating a reduction in work productivity by intentionally sabotaging work tools. For others, survival involved mimicking the slave stereotypes of slow-moving actions and inattentive behaviors. Yet for others their survival depended on acting out a recurrent illness. However, some men and women decided to rebel at the cost of their life to achieve their freedom. For these individuals, their calculated activism and planning of a resistance movement were designed with one purpose only: to revolt and disrupt the enslavement system of oppression and captivity by meeting brute force with brute force. With the latter, the ultimate goal of resistance was to escape and seek freedom "up north."

"Three of the largest revolts took place in South Carolina and Virginia: The Stono rebellion (1739) and the Denmark Vesey revolt (1822) in South Carolina, and the Nat Turner insurrection (1831) in Virginia" (Hadden, 2001, p. 139). To reduce and eventually crush slave rebellions, slave patrols were created to become the new White citizen enforcement. Citizens armed with weapons extended into their arsenal with legal authority to interrogate any plantations' enslaved captives at will. Any man, woman, or child deemed as an insurrection suspect could be apprehended, jailed, tried without a jury, and sentenced to death by lynching (Hadden, 2001). These punitive tactics were designed to intimidate, frighten, and warn anyone thinking of resistance. This behavioral conditioning played a significant role in consolidating White authority over an enslaved captive's hope of liberation and activism. These unspeakable actions added to rationing, food deprivation, scarcity of shelter, sexual assaults, merciless beatings, and mutilations. This indoctrination would challenge any spark of activism to secure freedom.

Following the Civil War (1861–1865), the cause of freedom would lead former enslaved African Americans to begin their exodus from southern plantations to the so-called "promised lands" of America's northern and western regions. However, those who remained in the South during and following the Reconstruction periods found themselves free without a plan. While the 13th Amendment of the Constitution (1865) formally abolished slavery, it did permit involuntary servitude as a punishment for "duly convicted" criminals (Blackmon, 2008). Consequently, "The attitudes among southern whites that a re-subjugation of African Americans was an acceptable-even-essential-element of solving the 'Negro question' couldn't have been more explicit. The desire of White farmers to recapture their former slaves through new civil laws was transparent. In the immediate wake of emancipation, the Alabama legislature swiftly passed a measure under which the orphans of freed slaves, or the children of Blacks deemed inadequate parents, were to be 'apprenticed' to their former masters. The South Carolina planter Henry Williams Ravenel wrote in September 1865, there must ... be stringent laws to control the Negroes & require them to fulfill their contracts of labor on the farms" (Blackmon, 2008, p. 53). As a consequence of this and subsequent mass political infringements, a new form of bondage took root. Although no longer called slavery, it took away personal freedoms using racially crafted laws that identified former enslaved African Americans as being indebted for life to former plantations.

Additionally, a system of peonage began to grow in the southern states (Blackmon, 2008). This system would capture and imprison African Americans who were considered to violate laws outlawing vagrancy. Although banned in 1867, peonage codes or the statutes requiring prison debts to be paid off with servitude from an employer would become the new bondage supply using convicts. For city or rural industries in the 19th and 20th centuries seeking cheap or even free labor force, peonage was the cornerstone of America's prison industrial complex and, in some ways, the justification for the disproportionate and unjustified incarceration of thousands of African Americans (Blackmon, 2008).

Throughout the 19th and 20th centuries, activism would be triggered to challenge racist codes, segregationist laws, bigoted practices, eugenic-driven science, abhorrent religious doctrines, and other forms of oppression manifested by systemic and institutional racism against African Americans. Throughout this period, activist voices would amplify the Black community's desire to attain reciprocity for the injustices for the present and future for all of those who suffered. At the same time in history, White hate groups like the Klu Klux Klan (KKK) proliferated to maintain White privilege, control, and power. With their growth and proliferation throughout America came the brutalization of innocent human beings, namely African Americans. The terrorists' arsenal included beatings, burnings, shootings, lynchings, and riots that destroyed whole Black towns (Blackmon, 2008).

Consequently, during the 20th century activism had also reversed the deliberate misinformation or disinformation of African and African Americans' history, which has been lost, stolen, and allowed to stray from the truth. This effort would have two fronts. The first was to reawaken the value of African and African American cultural heritage used to exploit African Americans' identity. The second was to reverse the stereotypes and misinformation of African and African American cultural heritage used to marginalize and minimize the humanity and value of African American culture. During this period of American history, there was a burgeoning of numerous Black societies and organizations (e.g., the National Negro Business League, the Niagara Movement, the National League for Protection of Colored Women, the National Association for the Advancement of Colored People, the Universal Negro Improvement Association, the National Council of Negro Women, the Southern Christian Leadership Conference, the Congress of Racial Equality, the Student Non-Violent Coordinating Committee, and the Black Panther Party; Harley, 1995). Activism would become the force behind individuals and groups holding institutional systems accountable to fulfill the U.S. Constitution's aspirational intent and sustain the 20th-century civil rights movements of the 1950s through the 1970s and to the 21st-century Black Lives Matter (BLM) movement and others.

The Orwellian Prophecy

The historical account of African American history in chronicling activism is crucial in accurately contextualizing the adverse psychological, physiological, and epigenomic effects of centuries-long oppression. The protracted exploitation of African American people who experienced cultural, economic, educational, political, and legal powerlessness would profoundly impact future generations. In George Orwell's (2003) novel

1984, he explores a dystopian and totalitarian society where oppression is sustained by the leadership's propaganda, surveillance, authoritarian politics, or perversions of truth. Specifically, Orwell predicts and illustrates a nightmarish society where managing the truth rather than telling the truth is a mass control tactic. Unfortunately, the tactic of employing deliberate prevarications for populace control breeds raw emotions of contempt, fear, and hatred within the oppressor, while the oppressed manifest feelings of despair and trepidation. Orwell's perspective on this notion can explain the importance of considering a historical context for examining how the struggle for freedom through activism began and continues by reclaiming one's consciousness and one's historical memory.

> If the party could thrust its hand into the past and say of this or that event, it never happened—that, surely, was more terrifying than mere torture and death.... But where did that knowledge exist? Only in his own consciousness, which in any case must soon be annihilated. And if all others accepted the lie which the Party imposed—if all records told the same tale—then the lie passed into history and became truth. "Who controls the past ... controls the future: who controls the present controls the past." (Orwell, 2003, p. 119)

History of Trauma

Trauma represents a bodily injury caused by an "extrinsic agent," or "a disordered psychic or behavioral state resulting from severe mental or emotional stress or physical injury" (Merriam-Webster, 2007, p. 1331). In the Concise Oxford English Dictionary, trauma represents "a deeply distressing experience" or "emotional shock following a stressful event" (Soanes & Stevenson, 2008, p. 1534). Factual historical accounts detail the legacy of how brutal physical assault, emotional and sexual trauma, political disenfranchisement, unemployment, economic discrimination, legal injustice, and spiritual intolerance inflicted upon generations of enslaved African descendants trafficked to America have shaped the nation's history for centuries. Unfortunately, it has been a history that the dominant society has been unwilling to engage in reconciliation along with its fear of acknowledging restitution or reparation claims (Winbush, 2003; Wittmann, 2012). It has been the dominant society suggesting that the legacy of slavery in the Americas was no worse than that imposed by human civilizations during classical antiquity. Historical accounts during classical antiquity speak of victors from battles taking their defeated captives into bondage. Researchers who study slavery have noted that the practice of slavery/indentured servitude is as long as human history. Some researchers and scholars have also pointed out that a distinctive difference can be identified between slavery and indentured servitude, as "the term slavery should be reserved for those falling permanently into this condition, and that indentured labor, of possession that has a limit should not be called slavery ... Slavery is a social and economic relationship in which a person is controlled through violence or threat of violence, is paid nothing, and is economically exploited" (Bales & Cornell, 2008, p. 9). Consequently, a distinct difference between America's "racialized slavery" (duBois, 2009), and that of classical antiquity was that racialized slavery believed that Europeans were masters over a racially darker skinned human being, whom they considered soulless. In classical antiquity, slavery was a byproduct of defeated soldiers who were considered "payment for a war tax" (Finley, 1968, p. 187) and often referred to as barbarians.

Consequently, while slavery during the periods of antiquity also held views devaluing the humanity of those enslaved with ideas explained by Plato as "natural slavery" (Finley, 1968, p. 118), it was not based exclusively on African racial characteristics. In Greek society during the time of Plato, there was a code of conduct requiring that "slaves are not to be treated cruelly or flippantly, but firmly and in a dignified manner by such behavior, the character of the master himself is improved" (Finley, 1968, p. 119). The differentiation of captives for enslavement was more often predetermined by a person's membership within their society or caste. They also determined these differences by positioning slaves at the lower end of a social scale, caste, or class. Those enslaved were from foreign lands, represented different national backgrounds, or held distinctive religious beliefs. Many choose to reeducate their slaves when possible and acculturate them to minimize their need for resistance and rebellion (duBois, 2009).

Additionally, under King Louis XIV (1685), the French government created the Code Noir in 1668 to establish guidelines for captives' enslavement. In contrast, America's racialized chattel slavery protocol seemed to be grounded in justifying European racial superiority infused with moral and religious beliefs and an attitude of being destined by God's power to dismiss any human virtues from persons of African descent. As a result, every effort was made to systematically eradicate any vestiges of cultural ideas, values, habits, language, customs, traditions, beliefs, rituals, or ceremonies that shaped human characteristics or traits of persons of African descent. Conclusively, the family structure's dismantling was a final effort to consider Africans, in general, not only less than human but less than animals.

This latter belief represents the ideas and attitudes of early Europeans entering Africa to capture and claim the bodies of children, women, and men, many of whom died during the notorious Middle Passage journey. Consequently, within the timeframe between the first arrival of enslaved Africans in 1619, the 13th Amendment to the Constitution abolished slavery, which did not occur until 1865. Unfortunately, Civil War reconstruction practices, including Jim Crow laws sanctioned by the U.S. government, perpetuated segregation and discrimination policies until the Civil Rights Act of 1964. Unfortunately, once released from human trafficking, millions of African Americans were victims of another century of the brutal killing spawned by White fear, anger, and racial hatred. In other words, there remained the perpetration of inhumane treatment and nationwide inequities that enculturated an idea of inferior human status 100 years after the ratification of the 13th Amendment of the U.S. Constitution.

Activism Through Resistance

As early as 1435, the Portuguese government engaged in trafficking captive Africans to Europe under the guise of converting West African tribal groups to Christianity. They referred to African captives as "armed captives," "Moorish infidels," "Guineas," and "Negros" (Rae, 2018, pp. 26–32). Throughout these early Portuguese incursions, indigenous Africans would fight to protect and defend their villages. The native African's successful defensive engagement would eventually result in a Portuguese policy to capture Africans for human trafficking. In 1454, the new policy of "trading and bargaining" rather than "bravery and force of arms'" was in place by the time a young Venetian named Alvise da Ca' da Mosto, also known as Luigi Cadamosto, entered the service of Portugal's Prince Henry" (Rae, 2018, p. 32). The success of this new policy change would open Africa to other European exploitation powers. These powers were invested in dividing and conquering kingdoms with the promise of trading weapons and other goods in return for Africans. The goal of this policy was to increase the European workforce. This practice included capturing and exploiting children, women, and men. Consequently, by the 16th century, the method of human trafficking implemented by European countries would involve captives being kidnapped, traded, purchased, and sold throughout Europe and beyond. Still, it would also support the expansion of their New World settlements in North, Central, and South America as well as the Caribbean Islands.

The testimonies from women and men enslaved is one record that cannot be romanticized to convey slavery as a benevolent or benign antebellum institution (Albert, 2005; Berlin et al., 1998; Brent, 1973; Eversley, 2004; Hurmence, 1984; Lester, 1968; McLaurin, 1991). Consequently, to understand the unhealed trauma inflicted on generations of people of African descent, it is crucial to understand the issues of racial colorism, self-hate, and internalized anger (Everett, 1996; Horton & Horton, 2005; White & White, 2005). These acts of degradation have created an aversion for any cultural pride or desire to reconnect with anything African. The novelist, folklorist, and anthropologist Zora Neale Hurston (2018) provided an account of one of the last known kidnapped Africans shipped to America in 1858. In her book titled, *Barracoon: The Story of the Last "Black Cargo,"* Cudjo Lewis conveyed his deep emotional struggles, human misery, and family tragedy as a record of the legacy of slavery in America. During an interview in 1928, Hurston shared the following account:

> On the Tuesday after the New Year, I found Cudjo in a backward-looking mood. He was with his departed family in the land to the west. He talked about his boys; he grew tearful over his wife.
>
> "I so lonely. I los' my wife de 15 November 1908. We been together long time. I marry her Chris'mas day, 1865. She a good wife to me."
>
> There was a long, feeling silence, then he turned to me and spoke, "Ole Charlie, he de oldest one come from Afficky, came one Sunday after my wife lef' me and say, 'Uncle Cudjo, make us a parable.'

> "Den I axed dem, 'How many limbs God give de body so it ken be active?'
>
> "Dey say six; to arms two feet two eyes.
>
> "I say dey cut off de feet, he got hands to fend hisself. Dey cut off de hands he wiggle out de way when he see danger come. But when he lose de eye, den he can't see nothin' come upon him. He finish. My boys is my feet. My daughter is my hands. My wife she my eye. She left, Cudjo finish."

Numerous historical accounts record the brutality of human trafficking and the captivity of Africans to either Europe or the so-called New World (i.e., the Americas) (Albert, 2005; Berlin et al., 1998; Horton & Horton, 2005; King, 2011; Ogot, 1992; Rae, 2018; White & White, 2005). These accounts by those held captive and those engaged in captivity also recorded the fact that those captured and enslaved resisted and became activists to secure their freedom through escape or death. Similarly, throughout the transatlantic slave trade, countless captives refused nourishment, defiantly jumped into the ocean to end their captivity (Burnside & Robotham, 1997; Carretta, 2005; Eversley, 2004) and fought and died to avert their captivity (Eversley, 2004; Hadden, 2001; Lester, 1968; McLaurin, 1991; Rae, 2018). The brutality of human trafficking and enslavement were factors enough for many to give their life, to put an end to their torture and to secure some promise of a better life for future generations (Carroll, 2004; Hall, 2005; Horne, 2014; Horton & Horton, 2006). While historical accounts of the enslavement and captivity of humans by others is recorded throughout antiquity (duBois, 2009; Finley, 1968; Ogot, 1992), the accounts of African enslavement from the 15th century through the 19th century were far less accommodating to sustaining any semblance of humanity (Bennett, 1993; Morgan, 2005; Ogot, 1992). Throughout the transatlantic slave trade, extreme dehumanizing tactics included stripping away the African captive's language, name, culture, beliefs, practices, ritual ceremonies, habits, biological relationships and bonds, and every sense of physical and emotional safety (Albert, 2005; Baptist, 2014; Horton & Horton, 2006; Tisby, 2019). It was a calculated dehumanization, stripping down every captured man and woman's humanity to remove any sense of human character that sustained their African identity. This was intentional to create a disconnect for African people from the land they and their ancestors originated. Therefore, they perpetuated the negative behavioral conditioning of those who would become the victims of their race-based human trafficking. Consequently, the wholesale attempt to destroy African civilizations fueled by racial hatred and capitalist greed set the stage for resistance and activism occurring before Africans' arrival to the Americas (Guasco, 2014).

Transgenerational Trauma and Epigenomics

Transgenerational trauma represents the historical aftermath responsible for creating generations of suffering for its survivors and their descendants. This trauma reaches into genetics as part of the human epigenome (i.e., gene expression) of surviving the systematic stressors of genocidal-like oppression (Kellerman, 2009). Correspondingly, it is part of the human psychology of oppression in its manifestation, as noted in the book *Post-Traumatic Slave Syndrome* (DeGruy, 2005). In each case, generations of African Americans could not effectively escape the cumulative impact of historical trauma inflicted upon the body, mind, and soul of the descendants of millions of children, women, and men who were kidnapped, trafficked, and enslaved for centuries.

Understanding the full psychological and epigenomic impact of victimization, trauma, and re-traumatization beginning with the first "twenty Africans," who arrived "in Jamestown, Virginia on a Dutch ship … as a forerunner to slavery in English colonies" (Harley, 1995, pp. 9–10) represents the beginning and the continuation of generational trauma that African Americans endure in contemporary America.

It is essential to know that the impact of these traumas and subsequent retraumatization impacted the body and mind and the biology down to the DNA. The continuous victimization through the 20th century created stressors that would influence the epigenome and thus account for challenged physiological responses of the offspring of those beyond the real-life experience of these eras of United States history. However, the ongoing trauma imposed by 21st-century systemic and institutional racism underscores health and mental health workers' impact to understand the effects of transgenerational trauma on African Americans' epigenomic constitution. This is essential if strategies effectively provide successful epigenomic interventions that recognize the scope of racism and oppression.

Researchers use the term *epigenomics* to denote transgenerational transmission of traits without a change in DNA sequence (Cooke et al., 2019; National Institutes of Health [NIH], 2016). For African Americans, things like nutrition and stress early in life will have lingering effects—not changing the genes themselves but changing the chromosomes in a way that silences or amplifies genes. "We not only inherit genes from our parents; we also inherit the epigenome. It seems, then, that genes can remember the environmental impacts of prior generations" (Roberts, 2011, p. 142). This genetic condition, in turn, could affect hereditary illnesses aggravated by chronic anxiety of the level generated by living day to day under oppressive circumstances. The extension of this knowledge has been explored in animal research more so than human research. However, the data from these studies support "an intergenerational epigenetic priming of the physiological response to stress in offspring of highly traumatized individuals" (Yehuda et al., 2016, p. 379).

Rethinking a More Culturally Competent Policing Policy

Historically, the police force was established to protect the citizenry from violence and property from theft and destruction. Then, in the 18th and 19th centuries, slave patrols were organized by White Southerners "for maintaining dominance over the black slaves among them" (Hadden, 2001, p. 6). This action changed policing in the historical sense as it became systematized to protect the capital investment of the slave owners in the South. As a systemic and institutional racism tool, it became a method of enforcing White supremacy and White privilege. With close ties to many southern militias, slave patrols sustained the creed of maintaining dominance and control over African American populations' movement. With the end of slavery and the beginning of the Jim Crow segregation laws, the attitude of dominance over African Americans became a part of policing. While instances with the police and the criminal justice system affect all races, we know that Black people have a higher interaction rate than Whites.

Further, these interactions lead to higher rates of deaths among Blacks. While most victims were allegedly armed, the research found that Blacks who were killed were more likely to be unarmed than Whites or Hispanics. Their interaction rate leads to less finite ends, such as disproportionately higher incarceration rates (Shannon et al., 2017).

Following the increase of African American deaths at the hands of police, the belief that two Americas exist (one Black and one White) has resulted in activism that is calling into question the implementation of excessive force disproportionately implemented against African Americans. Activists have raised concerns about the city finances appropriated to purchase urban tanks, military armament, and the building of more jails and prisons. Consequently, recent high-profile deaths of Black citizens have raised questions about the psychological and tactical training and preparation of police. Additional questions have even been raised about the attitude, character, and records of police officers' behavior. One issue raised by activists is how police departments redelegate resources to meet the police better. Some have referred to this issue around the call for "defunding the police." It is important to note that this does not mean eliminating police departments that are balanced in their efforts to protect and serve urban and rural communities. Instead, the request is to refocus financial resources to improve training and education programs that can stop unnecessary use of force when it is not needed. It also means recruiting police to live in urban communities where they police. This action could deepen their commitment to protecting the urban and rural spaces where they live. The activist organization Black Lives Matter recently called for a national defunding of police and demanded an investment of funding to address people's safety. However, in urban and rural communities where racial profiling and excessive force has become a way of dominating people of color for nonpolice matters, activism that is pushing for the defunding of police converts into a request of the impacted community to abolish the police, or a call to eliminate policing in total. According to the Urban Institute (Auxier, 2020) and data from the U.S. Census (2017), state and local governments spent $115 billion on police, excluding federal grants and other resources. This money was not used to improve Black Americans' lives who live within these communities, but instead, two thirds of police spending is on payroll (Auxier, 2020). This excessive expenditure, coupled with the continued abuse and harm to Black and Brown people, forms a disconnect between what taxpayers' money is being used for by people living outside of the very community they are sworn to protect.

Recently, the New York Civil Liberties Union (Rosado et al., 2020) suggested that communities take the $115 billion used in policing and invest it in unarmed professionals and law enforcement services training. In other words, activists have recommended identifying and training committed citizens capable of meeting the community's needs safely and productively to be embedded within local agencies. This includes redirecting funds to support mental health services (e.g., a person experiencing a mental health crisis, someone suicidal, or drug usage). Additionally, funding social workers addressing domestic violence (e.g., removing a woman and their children from their home where it is violent and placing them into a battered women's shelter). Police have marginal training to deal with these situations, and they often approach them with brute force. Further, they suggest that the money is used directly in the community, in the form of "free education, free or at least affordable physical and mental health care, affordable housing, infrastructure and public transportation, youth programs, elder services, and assistance for disabled people" (Rosado et al., 2020). Further, they suggest that we limit police contact with Black and Brown communities, demilitarize the police and end police surveillance, flood schools with counselors, and put culturally competent Black and Brown people in charge.

While these suggestions are progressive steps toward stemming the tide of harm committed on Black people by police, if we are to *defund the police* and move toward a different system, we must know what strategies and actions effectively reduce crime. The United Kingdom College of Policing (What Works Network, n.d.), which collates and shares research evidence on crime reduction and supports its use in practice, suggests interventions such as cognitive behavioral therapy, restorative justice, drug courts, therapeutic communities, therapeutic foster care, mediation, mental health courts, and problem-oriented policing. In comparison, interventions such as boot camps and scared-straight programs do not produce a high success rate (What Works Network, n.d.).

Problem-oriented policing is defined as an approach to tackling crime and disorder that involves identifying a specific problem, thorough analysis to understand the problem, developing a tailored response, and assessing the effects of the response. Further, whatever the result, we suggest that it starts with research. The examples presented are research-based examples that work and should be included in any conversation involving the police's defunding or abolishing.

Homegrown Terrorism

Noted theologian Howard Thurman dissected the "anatomy" of segregation with chilling precision in his classic 1965 book, *The Luminous Darkness*. A white supremacist society must not only "array all the forces of legislation and law enforcement ... it must falsify the facts of history, tamper with the insights of religion and religious doctrine, editorialize and slant news and the printed word. On top of that it must keep separate schools, separate churches, separate graveyards, and separate public accommodations—all this in order to freeze the place of the Negro in society and guarantee his basic immobility." Yet this was "but a partial indication of the high estimate" that the white South placed upon African Americans. "Once again, to state it categorically," Thurman concludes, "the measure of a man's estimate of your strength is the kind of weapons he feels that he must use in order to hold you fast in a prescribed place." (as cited in Chafe et al., 2001, p. 1)

The 2014 Ferguson uprisings sparked national protests and activism exposing longstanding police brutality, systemic and institutional racism, injustice, and civil rights denial (CrimethInc, n.d.). The despair and heartbreak within the Black community following the fatal shooting of Michael Brown in Ferguson, Missouri, incited activism that would extend up through 2020. The persistent use of excessive force by the police against the African American community has evolved into an act of domestic terrorism committed by those who are sworn to *serve and protect*.

The Federal Bureau of Investigation (FBI, 2020) defines domestic terrorism as "involving acts dangerous to human life that are a violation of the criminal laws of the United States or of any State; Appearing to be intended to intimidate or coerce a civilian population, influence the policy of government by intimidation or coercion, or affect the conduct of a government by mass destruction, assassination or kidnapping and occurring primarily within the territorial jurisdiction of the United States" (Federal Bureau of Investigation, 2020). We are made more aware of trauma's infliction via the broadcast of acts of terrorism as viewed on multiple media platforms that can range from TV to YouTube or from Twitter to Facebook. Consequently, access to instantaneous acts of terrorism is now made available through our cell phones or electronic tablets. No longer is it necessary to wait for the news broadcast on TV, as the latest events are accessible instantaneously.

With 20th-century internet connectivity and device technology, the public has infinite access to events. Consequently, as activism keeps up with the pace of acts of homegrown terrorism, nonviolent community rallies, protests, or marches have just as quickly highlighted acts of intolerance, bigotry, bias, systemic and institutional racism. The past 2 decades have more instantly revealed both increasing and sustained acts of racially motivated hate, ignorance, and fanaticism against African Americans at the risk of profoundly dividing America (Poon & Patino, 2020). Equally, activism has become the language of revealing the inequity in policing systems (Poon & Patino, 2020). Many violent reactions have surfaced due to the African American community's overwhelming frustrations and allies (Poon & Patino, 2020). According to the Associated Press, "More than 10,000 people have been arrested in protests decrying racism and police brutality in the wake of George Floyd's death (Snow, 2020). The most recent fatality at the hands of law enforcement is Andre Hill, who was fatally shot walking out of a garage holding a cell phone (Longbottom, 2021). His untimely death occurred around the same time another unarmed Black man in the same area was also killed by law enforcement (Longbottom, 2021).

According to a report from *The Washington Post*'s (2020) Fatal Force Database, 1,502 people have been shot and killed by on-duty police officers since 2015; 732 were White, 381 were Black, and 382 were of another race. At face value, the data suggests White people are killed more by police. But if you consider the ratio of White versus Black people in the population, you see the disproportionate rate at which Black men and women are killed (Lowery, 2019). White people make up approximately 62% of the U.S. population, but only about 49% of those are killed by police officers (Lowery, 2019). African Americans, however, account for 24% of those fatally shot and killed by the police despite being 13% of the U.S. population (Lowery, 2019). As *The Washington Post* noted, that means African Americans are 2.5 times more likely than White Americans to be fatally shot by police officers (Lowery, 2019). Due to the growing use and future dependence on technology, more police encounters are being recorded and shown worldwide.

These acts of trauma continue to retraumatize a community beset with centuries of persistent oppression. Thus, the visual reminders played out on social media platforms from cell phones or police body cams only sustain the African American community's high anxiety levels. Unfortunately, even when visual records exist that identify excessive force, the justice system is either slow to act or chooses not to act at all. Regrettably, when an unarmed Black person is killed (Ray, 2020), the routine of delay tactics to bring impartial resolution is long and questionable. The accused officer(s) are placed on administrative duty or leave; the charge may or may not be brought against them (Ray, 2020). If there are charges, the police officers will often be acquitted of the accused crimes (Ray, 2020). With domestic terrorism, such as the incident of the Emanuel African Methodist Episcopal Church in Charleston, South Carolina, in 2015, the terrorist (a White male), was apprehended and then tended to with greater care than African American counterparts arrested for minor offenses or no illegal offense (Fite et al., 2009). Many were stunned by the police taking a terrorist within the African American community to purchase a sandwich after his killing spree within a historically Black church following an invitation to enter for prayer (Osei-Opare, 2016). Therefore, it is not surprising that many in the African American community recognize the predominately White *insurrectionary* mob that attempted a coup at the U.S. Capitol on January 6, 2021, did not face any police retaliation involving excessive force. Even though it is a crime to trespass on federal property with weapons and especially intending to stage a coup (Hoffman, 2021), few arrests occurred, and police shot one member of the mob. Although the event was a blatant display of disrespect for laws and lawmakers, the same group was politely escorted from the property (Hoffman, 2021). There were approximately five deaths and more than 100 arrests made of a crowd consisting of thousands of people who invaded the U.S. Capitol building (CBS Baltimore Staff, 2021). Both factors of continual subjectivity to police violence of its own community and lack of accountability of treatment with police agencies directly contribute to the African American community's frustrations articulated by protests and activism.

We know that the continuous perpetuation of trauma and traumatization over centuries adds to the preexisting conditions contributing to physical and mental illness disparities. For many, activism has been and continues to be the way to create a climate for change. While change may evolve slowly, it has been the choice approach that gives a community a voice for resistance. By analyzing FBI and hospital data from 2014 to 2017, it was anecdotally noted that rates of violent crimes, suicides, emergency room admissions/

visits, drug usage/abuse positively correlated with an increase in violence as well as health and mental health challenges resulting from trauma (Centers for Disease Control and Prevention [CDC], 2019; FBI, 2020; World Bank Group, 2020).

The Ferguson Effect, Drug Use, Incarceration, and Health Issues Related to Activism

"The Ferguson effect" was established as a potential theory into rising crime rates in African American communities (Gross & Mann, 2017). The Ferguson effect is the notion that increased scrutiny of police following the 2014 fatal shooting of Michael Brown in Ferguson, Missouri, has led to an increased murder rate in major U.S. cities (Gross & Mann, 2017). These communities were potential high-crime and usually low-income or poverty-stricken areas (Gross & Mann, 2017). According to a Ferguson effect study, it was concluded there was no direct effect on the upward trend of violent crime in those high activism locations like Ferguson (Gross & Mann, 2017). Multiple studies disputed each other as some supported this phenomenon, and others did not find evidence to support it (Gross & Mann, 2017). In this analysis, the data suggests previous researchers collected data based on factors that seemed relevant during the period. Unfortunately, those factors were minimal and rushed. The current data suggests previous researchers were looking in the wrong areas and did not include the effects over a period of time (Lartey & Li, 2019).

According to Dr. Edwin Nichols (personal communication, November 30, 2020), activism reverberates beyond the event. He posits that the internalized anger caused by retraumatization is activated throughout the community and region. It can be quantified by observing any spike in drug use, incarceration rates, and health issues. Concerning drug use rates, data from the CDC reported that 4.1% of the African American population were already binge drinking in 2016. This increased to 4.3% of the population in 2017 (CDC, 2019). In 2016, 12.5% of the African American population engaged in illicit drug use. In the following year, illegal drug use increased to 13.7% (CDC, 2019). Between 2016 and 2017, the use of marijuana increased among the African American population from 11.1 to 11.6%. Consequently, this data shows substance use trends increasing with African Americans between 2014–2017.

The Death Penalty Information Center created and updated a database for murder rates by year and state. Although the overall crime rate has decreased, the national murder rate from 2014 to 2017 increased from 4.5 to 5.32%, equaling half of the 1991 violent crime rate. According to the Agency for Healthcare Research and Quality (AHRQ, n.d.), there was a steep and positive trend for suicide ideations or suicide attempts, especially in 2016 and 2017 among those 15–19 years old. For adults over 25, the trend is not as high as it is for young adults. Drug overdose death rates for African American women increased from 7 to 11.2% between 2014 and 2017; death rates for African American men increased from 13.8 to 29.7%. In 2015, the largest increase of drug overdose among Black men started at 16.8%. In 2016 this rate increased to 24%, and in the following year, the rate increased to 29.7% of the population. This data set reflects the cumulative effect of internalized anger. Even as African Americans engage in activism, the longstanding collective unconscious pain and anxiety resulting from generational injustices manifests itself as a crisis of health (e.g., addiction and suicide) and abuse issues more often resulting in incarceration than treatment.

Psychologists and health care workers should understand the impact of sustained acts of homegrown terrorism and historical trauma in the African American community. These are alarming upward trends that future researchers should examine closely (MedCircle, 2020).

These biases impact evidence-based treatment and research (Washington, 2006). Additionally, it is important to recognize that some Ferguson effect' studies specifically focused on states with similar police brutality issues (Gross & Mann, 2017). Studies should be geared toward the physical and mental health, stability, and trends of crime violence within those specific cities and the African American community. As mentioned, generations of African Americans could not completely escape the cumulative impact of historical trauma inflicted upon the body, mind, and soul of the descendants of millions of men, women, and children kidnapped, trafficked, enslaved, and then forced into bondage for centuries.

The analysis also revealed the positive trend in suicide and drug usage within other minority groups such as Native Americana and Hispanic/Latinx communities. Consequently, as more police-induced brutality and homicide continued to ravage the African American community in the way it has from 2014 to the present, these trends can continue to increase in the near term.

The Ferguson effect is concerning on multiple levels as "urban school environments often mirror the harsh stressful environments students of African descent live in, marked by cyber violence, physical violence, high teacher turnover, and the absence of caring supportive classroom environments (Shockley & Lomotey, 2020, p. 102). Consequently, Black youth living in underserved, harsh, and stressful environments fraught with low wealth and health disparities increases the likelihood of transgenerational health and mental health issues. Given epigenomic research outcomes of living in a high-stress environment, these conditions must be examined to understand better both its long-term effects and culturally salient generational healing strategies. Thus, activism continues to be the demonstrative tactic that confronts the trauma born out of centuries-long inequities. The COVID-19 pandemic has exhumed the long-standing achievement gap, which, if not addressed, decreases employment opportunities and higher education, both of which burden any hope of a bright future (Shockley & Lomotey, 2020). The 2019 Report to Congress from the Congressional Black Caucus: Emergency Taskforce on Black Youth Suicide and Mental Health studies "indicated that suicide attempts rose by 73 percent between 1991-2017 for Black adolescents, while injury by attempt rose by 122 percent for adolescent Black boys during that time period." This study also examined several key risks and protective factors for suicide in Black youth that included the presence of a preexisting mental illness (e.g., depression, anxiety), sex, LGBTQA+ identity, bullying, socioeconomic factors, impaired family functioning, exposure to suicide (including a family member or celebrity) and access to lethal means." The role of trauma, also impacted by racism, was another key risk factor. These studies speak to the importance of knowing, understanding, and addressing trauma through activism that accesses institutional plans to address long-term suppressed trauma within the African American community.

According to the CDC, National Center for Health Statistics, FBI, and Department of Justice, recent data sets were analyzed for trends, and potential spikes were identified (Stone et al., 2018). The analysis reviewed the years 2014–2017. The results are important for future research to examine "potential spikes" caused directly by trauma.

Contemporary American History in the Making

On January 6, 2021, an insurrection televised internationally occurred on the grounds of the U.S. Capitol. Spurred on by President Donald J. Trump's 11th-hour effort to overturn the 2020 presidential election, which he lost to Joseph (Joe) Biden. Following his remarks to "stop the steal," he extolled those gathered to breach the U.S. Senate to stop the Electoral College count guaranteed by the U.S. Constitution. Americans observed a disturbing contradiction regarding the limited number of police to manage thousands of a predominately White mob of riotous insurrectionists. The riotous insurrectionists included some police officers and ex-military from around the nation. Additionally, the FBI reported participation from members of White hate groups including the Proud Boys and White supremacist militia groups.

The world watched in terror as the insurrectionist brutalized the Capitol police force. They forced the members of the Congress to go into hiding, which stopped the Electoral College count. Ironically, the insurrectionists were not met with mounted police, armored military vehicles, and armed National Guard units. In comparison, the peaceful BLM marches were engaged by local police, the National Guard, and even the Southern Border Patrol officers who used gratuitous force against them. Insightfully, international and national reporters acknowledged this hypocrisy toward protesters of color.

The relationship between the police and the Black community is fractured. During enslavement and seamlessly followed by Jim Crow, Northern segregation, and disparate legal treatment, the police have been dispatched to the Black community to oppress Blacks. Moreover, the police have enforced their interpretation of the "law" upon Blacks. Traditionally, individuals in the Black community who felt oppressed, hopeless, and without justice acted in a passive-aggressive behavior toward the White power structure. However, this millennial generation of Black youth vents their anger and hostility openly and outwardly. Paradoxically, the venting is upon themselves within the Black community—Black-on-Black homicide; however, future behavior will be different when the tipping point is realized.

On daily television news broadcasts, we see youth from disenfranchised communities that have taken matters into their own hands. The shift from killing for respect within the Black community to killing for respect outside the community is not too significant.

Dr. Martin Luther King, Jr. engaged in activism consisting of boycotts, sit-ins, public speeches, and nonviolent marches. While demonstrating in Chicago in 1966, he reported his activism philosophy with the following statement, "We also come here today to affirm that we will no longer sit idly by in agonizing deprivation and wait on others to provide our freedom. We will be sadly mistaken if we think freedom is some lavish dish that the federal government and the white man will pass out on a silver platter while the Negro merely furnishes the appetite. Freedom is never voluntarily granted by the oppressor. It must be demanded by the oppressed" (Carson, 1998, p. 303).

Consequently, activism is the constant struggle to secure both human and civil rights. We believe that we must continue to examine the myriad of ways activism impacts Black experiences related to fear, powerlessness, humiliation, and anger. While the Black religious experience has fortified the spirituality that African descendants transported with them to America, Europeans compromised and established church doctrines of complicity in White supremacy and racism to control and pacify the desire for freedom (Tisby, 2019).

The Revolution Will Be Digitized: New World Activism

Supported by 21st-century technology, activism has witnessed a proliferation of exposure. It is not uncommon that platforms like Facebook, Twitter, Instagram, and blogs and podcasts facilitate conversations regarding the myriad of issues facing the African American community. These platforms, coupled with major news outlets posting electronically on cell phones, tablets, and computers, and networks' instantaneously broadcast with an interactive video feed from cell phones and transit the events that shape our news media and the information environment. We are each informing the information environment while simultaneously trending key issues and concerns that must be addressed.

The 21st-century activist leadership must understand the underpinnings of mainstream media's propensity to prioritize and secure ratings and market values to ensure their financial gains over and above their omission of facts and their misinformation of truths that can heal the nation. There must be interviews and interventions that push back against the nation's founding and evolution's purist narrative. There must be a reckoning with the fact that our educational systems have acted as if Black history is lost, stolen, or allowed to go so far astray that it becomes whitewashed with contrary narratives. Many would argue that this nation has been motivated by propaganda concepts such as the

European's westward land acquisition under their narcissistic Manifest Destiny[1] doctrine. Another example is the Confederate states' convictions that their defeat was a lost cause in their efforts to fight for states' rights. Even in their own words, their heritage, according to the famous Cornerstone Speech, conveys the following belief:

> The negro is not equal to the white man ... that slavery subordination to the superior race is his natural and normal condition ... Our system commits no such violation of nature's laws, with us, all of the white race, however high or low, rich or poor, are equal in the eye of the law. Not so with the negro. Subordination is his place. It is, indeed, in conformity with the ordinance of the Creator (Stephens, 1861).

Activism Persistence Against Inequity: Closing Thoughts

The purpose of this chapter was to provide a responsible historical overview of how African American activism became a necessary Black struggle strategy and tactic to achieve human and civil rights and examine the forces opposing those rights. There are compelling stories worth recanting and lives worth remembering. This chapter reflects an ongoing exercise in examining historical facts and narratives that give voice to the past to engage with the present.

Indeed, African activism was a calculated and deliberate response to the severe and systematic abuses of African men, women, and children associated with transatlantic slavery. In summary, slavery was a collective European effort of sanctioned human trafficking, kidnapping, and enslavement to achieve total power and control over generations of African descendants' minds and bodies. Centuries before and after 1619, European philosophy, religion, science, and laws were explicitly designed to decree African descent people as subhuman. However, the psychological, spiritual, and physical constitution of African people had no other recourse other than resisting, opposing, and fighting captivity and slavery. In early American history, enslaved Africans engaged in pro-activism to

---

1   "Manifest Destiny" is a phrase coined in a January 3, 1846, speech in the House of Representatives by Representative Robert C. Winthrop of Massachusetts 2 decades before the Civil War. His speech was opposing the resolution for the termination of the joint occupation of Oregon. In his speech he spoke the following: "There is one element in our title [to Oregon], however, which I confess that I have not named, and to which I may not have done entire justice. I mean that new revelation of right which has been designated as the right of our manifest destiny to spread over this whole continent" (Pratt, 1927, p. 795). Manifest Destiny is the idea that the United States is destined—by God, its advocates believed—to expand its dominion and spread democracy and capitalism across the entire North American continent. The philosophy drove 19th-century U.S. territorial expansion and was used to justify the forced removal of Native Americans and other groups from their homes. The rapid expansion of the United States intensified the issue of slavery as new states were added to the Union, leading to the outbreak of the Civil War.

claim their freedom and respect through rebellions, revolts, and insurrections. Following the American Civil War and the end of state-sanctioned enslavement, Reconstruction's destruction in the South resulted in Jim Crow laws that enforced a new subjugation type nationwide. This restructured oppression system leveraged laws, statutes, and codes to continue depriving African Americans of their civil and human rights and freedoms.

Additionally, America's majority members instituted more perfidious controls to deny constitutional liberties to citizens of African descent. Simultaneously, they worked through an array of systemic institutional racism that devalued African American identity, history, culture, and heritage. Through socialization, they overvalued Whiteness, culture, and history. As a result of the generational victimization of African Americans moving through enslavement abuses, trauma persisted, and activism focused on undoing the longstanding legal, economic, educational, health, and emotional challenges impacting African Americans. In the 20th century, activism focused on addressing African American citizens' civil and constitutional rights while combating the false ideas supporting White supremacy and privilege. Regrettably, these ideas persist in the 21st century, resulting in continuous activism to vigorously denounce racism, colorism, and terrorism by the excessive police force and killings often sanctioned by systemic institutional racism.

These complex issues do not exist in a historical vacuum or exist in a segmented, compartmentalized reality but represent the most recent phase in the evolving activism in early American history with the emergence of uprisings and protests. While it is essential to know African American struggles, it is equally necessary to understand the need for activism in dealing with the health and mental health impact of a more than 4-century struggle. Through this awareness, activism can better prepare the Black community for the effects of retraumatization. Our historical research findings in this area reveal that activism can and must work on multiple levels and platforms to secure liberation and healing while also sharing information on the impact of activists' health, wellness, and mental health.

A Call to Black Parents: Activism Begins at Home

Activism must not delimit itself to the streets of this country. Instead, activism must take hold in social media, churches, organizations, social societies, educational institutions, communities, barbershops, beauty salons, neighborhoods, and within our homes. We must educate ourselves and our children. This racial socialization can serve as a counternarrative to mainstream misinformation and representations. They may engage in cultural socialization that educates African American youth regarding their history, culture, and heritage unique and specific to our race. Parents may also prepare their children for future racial barriers and bias. African Americans and other marginalized Americans must come to terms with the reality that Africans brought to America were not slaves, but human beings enslaved against their will. Ostensibly, African American parents should prepare their children for participation in various forms and degrees of activism. The way to ensure this is to research and digitally document assiduously, as well as perpetually teach lessons and the narratives of Black activists' resistance and resilience who were and continue to be in direct opposition to systemic racism and who are audaciously committed to eradicating this insidious problem at its deepest roots.

> If there is no struggle, there is no progress. Those who profess to favor freedom, and yet depreciate agitation, are men who want crops without plowing up the ground. They want rain without thunder and lightning. They want the ocean without the awful roar of its many waters. This struggle may be a moral one; or it may be a physical one; or it may be both moral and physical; but it must be a struggle. Power concedes nothing without a demand. It never did and it never will.
>
> —Frederick Douglas, *African American Quotations*
> (Newman, 2000, p. 346)

References

Agency for Healthcare Research and Quality. (n.d.). *HCUPnet*. https://hcupnet.ahrq.gov/#setup

Albert, O. V. R. (2005). *American slaves tell their stories: Six interviews*. Dover.

Auxier, R. (2020, June 9). *What police spending data can (and cannot) explain amid calls to defund the police*. Urban Institute. https://www.urban.org/urban-wire/what-police-spending-data-can-and-cannot-explain-amid-calls-defund-police

Bales, K., & Cornell, B. (2008). *Slavery today*. Groundwood and House of Anansi Press.

Baptist, E. E. (2014). *The half has never been told: Slavery and the making of American capitalism*. Perseus.

Bennett, L. (1993). *Before the Mayflower: A history of Black America* (6th ed.). Penguin.

Berlin, I., Favreau, M., & Miller, S. F. (Eds.). (1998). *Remembering slavery: African Americans task about their personal experiences of slavery and emancipation*. The New Press.

Berman, M., Sullivan, J., Tate, J., & Jenkins, J. (2020, October 26). Protests spread over police shootings. Police promised reforms. Every year, they still shoot and kill nearly 1,000 people. *The Washington Post*. https://www.washingtonpost.com/investigations/protests-spread-over-police-shootings-police-promised-reforms-every-year-they-still-shoot-nearly-1000-people/2020/06/08/5c204f0c-a67c-11ea-b473-04905b1af82b_story.html

Black Lives Matter. (2020). *#DefundthePolice*. https://blacklivesmatter.com/defundthepolice/

Blackmon, D. A. (2008). *Slavery by another name: The re-enslavement of Black Americans from the Civil War to World War II*. Doubleday.

Brent, L. (1973). *Incidents in the life of a slave girl*. Harvest.

Browder, A. T. (1992). *Nile Valley contributions to civilization: Exploding the myths* (Vol. 1). Institute of Karmic Guidance.

Burnside, M., & Robotham, R. (1997). *Spirits of the passage: The transatlantic slave trade in the seventeenth century*. Simon & Schuster.

Cairns, J., & Sears, A. (2012). *The democratic imagination: Envisioning popular power in the 21st century*. University of Toronto Press.

Carretta, V. (2005). *Equiano the African: Biography of a self-made man*. University of Georgia Press.

Carroll, J. C. (2004). *Slave insurrections in the United States 1800–1865*. Dover.

Carson, C. (Ed.). (1998). *The autobiography of Martin Luther King, Jr.* Warner Books.

CBS Baltimore Staff. (2021, January 8). *5 dead, 82 arrested in total including 11 Marylanders after U.S. Capitol riot.* https://baltimore.cbslocal.com/2021/01/08/us-capitol-riot-dead-injured-arrested-dc-police-maryland-latest/

Centers for Disease Control and Prevention. (2019, October 30). *Health, United States, 2018—Data Finder.* https://www.cdc.gov/nchs/hus/contents2018.htm? search=Hospital_use

Chafe, W. H., Gavins, R., & Korstad, R. (Eds.). (2001). *Remembering Jim Crow: African Americans Tell about Life in the Segregated South.* The New Press.

Ciment, J. (2001). *Atlas of African-American History.* Checkmark Books.

Congressional Black Caucus Emergency Task Force on Black Youth Suicide and Mental Health. (2019). *Ring the alarm: The crisis of Black youth suicide in America.* https://watsoncoleman.house.gov/uploadedfiles/full_taskforce_report.pdf

Cooke, B. G., Webb, S. C., Bell, K. A., Mbilishaka, A., LeVere, M., Talley, W. B., & Mizelle, N. (2019). *All about depression: Issues, treatment and resources* (2nd ed.). Kendall Hunt.

CrimethInc. (n.d.). *Timeline: The Ferguson rebellion of 2014.* https://crimethinc.com/2020/08/09/timeline-the-ferguson-rebellion-of-2014-chronology-of-an-uprising

DeGruy, L. J. (2005). *Post traumatic slave syndrome: America's legacy of enduring injury and healing.* Uptone.

duBois, P. (2009). *Slavery: Antiquity and its legacy.* Oxford University Press.

Everett, S. (1996). *History of slavery.* Chartwell.

Eversley, S. (Ed). (2004). *The interesting narrative of the life of Olaudah Equiano, or Gustavus Vassa, the African.* The Modern Library.

Federal Bureau of Investigations. (2020, November 12). *Domestic terrorism: Definitions, terminology, and methodology.* https://www.fbi.gov/file-repository/fbi-dhs-domestic-terrorism-definitions-terminology-methodology.pdf/view

Fite, P.J., Raine, A., Stouthamer-Loeber, M., Loeber, R., & Pardini, D. A. (2009). Reactive and Proactive Aggression in Adolescent Males: Examining Differential Outcomes 10 Years Later in Early Adulthood. *Criminal justice and behavior, 37(2),* 141–157. https://doi.org/10.1177/0093854809353051

Finley, M. I. (Ed.). (1968). *Slavery in classical antiquity: Views and controversies.* W. Heffer & Sons.

Gross, N., & Mann, M. (2017). Is there a "Ferguson effect?" Google searches, concern about police violence, and crime in U.S. cities, 2014–2016. *Socius, 3.* https://doi.org/10.1177/2378023117703122

Guasco, M. (2014). *Slaves and Englishmen: Human bondage in the modern Atlantic world.* University of Pennsylvania Press.

Hadden, S. E. (2001). *Slave patrols: Law and violence in Virginia and the Carolinas.* Harvard University Press.

Hall, G. M. (2005). *Slavery and African ethnicities in the Americas: Restoring the links.* University of North Carolina Press.

Harley, S. (1995). *The timetables of African-American history: A chronology of the most important people and events in African-American history.* Simon & Schuster.

Hoffman, B. (2021, January 7). *Domestic terrorism strikes U.S. Capitol, and democracy.* Council on Foreign Relations. https://www.cfr.org/in-brief/domestic-terrorism-strikes-us-capitol-and-democracy

Horne, G. (2014). *The counter-revolution of 1776: Slave resistance and the origins of the United States of America.* New York University Press.

Horton, J. O., & Horton, L. E. (Eds.) (2006). *Slavery and public history: The tough stuff of America memory.* University North Carolina Press.

Hurmence, B. (Ed.). (1984). *My folks don't want me to talk about Slavery.* John F. Blair.

Hurston, Z. N. (2018). *Barracoon: The story of the last "Black Cargo."* Amistad.

Johnson, C., Smith, P., & the WGBH Series Research Team. (1998). *Africans in America: America's journey through slavery.* Harcourt.

Kellermann, N. P. F. (2009). *Holocaust trauma: Psychological effects and treatment.* iUniverse.

King, W. (2011). *Stolen childhood: Slave youth in nineteenth-century America* (2nd ed.). Indiana University Press.

Lartey, J., & Li, W. (2019, September 30). *New FBI data shows violent crime still falling, except rapes*. The Marshall Project. https://www.themarshallproject.org/2019/09/30/new-fbi-data-violent-crime-still-falling

Laughland, O., Epstein, K., & Glenza, J. (2014, December 5). Eric Garner protests continue in cities across America through the second night. *The Guardian*. https://www.theguardian.com/us-news/2014/dec/05/eric-garner-case-new-york-protests-continue-through-second-night

Lester, J. (1968). *To be a slave*. Scholastic.

Longbottom, W. (2021, January 1). *Andre Hill shooting: US officers stood by and failed to help as black man lay dying following police shooting*. Sky News. https://news.sky.com/story/andre-hill-shooting-us-officers-stood-by-and-failed-to-help-as-black-man-lay-dying-following-police-shooting-12176574

Louis XIV. (1685). *The Code Noir*. (J. Garrigus, Trans.) http://www2.latech.edu/~bmagee/louisiana_anthology/texts/louis_xiv/louis_xiv--code_noir_english.html

Lowery, W. (2019, April 28). Aren't more White people than Black people killed by police? Yes, but no. *The Washington Post*. https://www.washingtonpost.com/news/post-nation/wp/2016/07/11/arent-more-white-people-than-black-people-killed-by-police-yes-but-no/

McLaurin, M. A. (1991). *Celia a slave*. Avon.

MedCircle. (2020, June 30). *The mental health risks of discrimination & racism [What you should know]* [Video]. https://www.youtube.com/watch?v=nQOMBxpf8as

Merriam-Webster. (2007). *Collegiate dictionary* (11th ed.). Author.

Morgan, K. A. (2005). *Slavery in America: A reader and guide*. University of Georgia Press.

National Institute of Health. (2016). *Help me understand genetics: How genes work*. https://medlineplus.gov/genetics/understanding/

Newman, R. (2000). *African American quotations*. Checkmark Books.

Ogot, B. A. (Ed.). (1992). *General history of Africa-V: Africa from the sixteenth to the eighteenth century*. Heinemann.

Orwell, G. (2003). *1984*. Houghton Mifflin Harcourt.

Osei-Opare, N. (2016). Terrorism and racism, Twin sisters? *Ufahamu: A Journal of African Studies*, *39*(1), 33–40. https://escholarship.org/uc/item/7t96h7hf

Oxford Online Etymology Dictionary. (n.d.). *Activism*. https://www.etymonline.com/search?q=activism

Poon, L., & Patino, M. (2020). *CityLab University: A timeline of U.S. police protests*. Bloomberg. https://www.bloomberg.com/news/articles/2020-06-09/a-history-of-protests-against-police-brutality

Pratt, J. (1927). The origin of "Manifest Destiny." *The American Historical Review*, *32*(4), 795–798. https://doi.org/10.2307/1837859.

Rae, N. (2018). *The great stain: Witnessing American slavery*. The Overlook Press.

Ray, R. (2020, August 25). *How can we enhance police accountability in the United States?* Brookings. https://www.brookings.edu/policy2020/votervital/how-can-we-enhance-police-accountability-in-the-united-states/

Roberts, D. (2011). *Fatal invention: How science, politics, and big business re-create in the twenty-first century*. The New Press.

Rosado, L., Abid, I., & Abdul-Qadir, Y. (2020, October 13). *What could defunding the police look like?* New York Civil Liberties Union. https://www.nyclu.org/en/news/what-could-defunding-the-police-look

Salter, P. S., & Adams, G. (2017). Racism in the structure of everyday worlds: A cultural-psychological perspective. *Current Directions in Psychological Science*, *27*(3), 150–155. https://doi.org/10:1177/0963721417724239

Shannon, S. K. S., Uggen, C., Schnittker, J., Thompson, M., Wakefield, S., & Massoglia, M. (2017). The growth, scope, and spatial distribution of people with felony records in the United States, 1948–2010. *Demography*, *54*(5), 1795–1818. https://doi.org/10.1007/ s13524-017-0611-1

Shockley, K. G., & Lomotey, K. (Eds.). (2020). *African-centered education: Theory and practice*. Myers Education.

Snow, A. (2020, June 04). *AP tally: Arrests at widespread US protests hit 10,000*. AP News. https://apnews.com/article/bb2404f9b13c8b53b94c73f818f6a0b7

Soanes, C., & Stevenson, A. (Eds.). (2008). *Concise Oxford English dictionary* (11th ed. rev.). Oxford University Press.

Stephens, A. (1861, March 21). *Cornerstone.* Teaching American History. http://teachingamericanhistory.org/library/document/cornerstone-speech/

Stephenson, A., & Crosby, A.E. (2018). Vital signs: Trends in State suicide rates— United States, 1999–2016 and circumstances contributing to suicide—27 states, 2015. *Morbidity and Mortality Weekly Report, 67*(22), 617–624. https://doi.org/10.15585/mmwr.mm6722a1

Stone, D. M., Simon, T. R., Fowler, K. A., Kegler, S. R., Yuan, K., Holland, K. M., Ivey-Stephenson, A. Z., & Crosby, A. E. (2018). Vital Signs: Trends in State Suicide Rates - United States, 1999-2016 and Circumstances Contributing to Suicide - 27 States, 2015. *MMWR. Morbidity and mortality weekly report, 67*(22), 617–624. https://doi.org/10.15585/mmwr.mm6722a1

Tisby, J. (2019). *The color of compromise: The truth about the American church's complicity in racism.* Zondervan.

U.S. Census. (2017). *2017 state & local government finance historical datasets and tables.* https://www.census.gov/data/datasets/2017/econ/local/public-use-datasets.html

Washington, H. A. (2006). The Black stork: The eugenic control of African American reproduction. In *Medical apartheid: The dark history of medical experimentation on black Americans from colonial times to the present* (pp. 189–215). Doubleday.

The Washington Post. (2020). *Fatal force: Police shootings database.* https://www.washingtonpost.com/graphics/investigations/police-shootings-database/

What Works Network. (n.d.). *Welcome to the crime reduction toolkit* [Infographic]. https://whatworks.college.police.uk/toolkit/Pages/Welcome.aspx

White, S., & White, F. (2005). *The sounds of slavery.* Beacon.

Wikipedia. (2021a). *Ferguson unrest.* https://en.wikipedia.org/wiki/Ferguson_unrest#:~:text=

Wikipedia. (2021b). *List of George Floyd protests in the United States.* https://en.wikipedia.org/wiki/List_of_George_Floyd_protests_in_the_United_States

Winbush, R. A. (Ed.). (2003). *Should America pay? Slavery and the raging debate on reparations.* Amistad.

Wittmann, N. (2012). *Slavery reparations time is now: Exposing lies, claiming justice for global survival.* Power of the Trinity.

World Bank Group (2021). *World Development Indicators, United States, 2014–2017 (Hospital Beds, Intentional Homicides)* [Data set]. World Bank DataBank. https://databank.worldbank.org/source/world-development-indicators

Yehuda, R., Daskalakis, N. P., Bierer, L. M., Bader, H. N., Klengel, T., Holsboer, F., & Binder, E. B. (2016). Holocaust exposure induced intergenerational effects on FKBP5 methylation. *Biological Psychiatry, 80*(5), 372–380. http://dx.doi.org/10.1016/j.biopsych.2015.08.005

CHAPTER TWO

Facilitating Black Survival and Wellness Through Scholar-Activism

Della V. Mosley, Pearis Bellamy, Garrett Ross, Jeannette Mejia, LaNya Lee, Carla Prieto, and Sunshine Adam

Black people in institutions of higher education, or *Blackademics*, face personal, relational, and collective barriers to wellness because of the violence of the systems of white supremacy and anti-Blackness outside and within the academy. Outside the academy, anti-Blackness is evident in the failure to indict the Louisville police officers who killed Breonna Taylor, the disproportionate direct and indirect impacts of the COVID-19 pandemic on the Black community, and the murders of Black transgender folx like Tony McDade, Nina Pop, and Dior H. Ova (Human Rights Campaign, 2020; H. Taylor, 2020; Wood, 2020). In academia, anti-Blackness is the police being called on Lolade Syonbola, a Black graduate student at Yale who was found sleeping in a common area of a dormitory (Griggs, 2018). It is university students, faculty, and staff at Oxford University being asked to surveil the campus and call campus security should they find Black alumna Femi Nylander, who was working on writing his book on campus, walking on the university grounds (Joseph-Salisbury, 2019). Anti-Blackness within academia is being given a mop or broom on your 1st day on the job as assistant professor (Baxter, 2020) or being asked to take out the trash as a Black faculty member (Fitzhough, 2020). It is gaps in access to higher education because of white supremacist entrance requirements, devaluation of Black faculty work, tokenization, erasure, inequitable compensation, and barriers to achieving job security through tenure. In the words of Pearl Agyakwa (2020), "Being #Blackintheivory tower is to be hypervisible yet invisible, to be loud yet unheard, and to be continually infantilized regardless of your age, expertise, or experience."

In this chapter, the authors posit that scholar-activism focused on Black liberation can facilitate Black survival and wellness. While folx outside the academy engage in scholar-activism and may benefit from the history, theory, recommendations, and examples provided in this chapter, our desire for more academics to use the privileges of the academy to advance a scholar-activist agenda for Black survival and wellness led us to center this chapter on scholar activism undertaken by individuals within academia. Before describing how to develop this agenda, we will provide (a) an exploration of anti-Black racism across personal, relational, and collective domains of wellness; (b) an overview of the relationship between academia and anti-Black racism; (c) a literature review highlighting the powerful history and potential of scholar-activism as an intervention against anti-Black racism; and (d) an exploration of some risks and contentions of Black scholar-activism and having a Black scholar activist identity. Then, in the second part of the chapter, we will discuss how to develop a scholar-activist agenda for Black liberation. In doing so, we will describe our relationship to scholar-activism as a healing and research collective, present an overview of our scholar-activism work, and offer guiding questions to assist readers in developing their own agendas.

Part I: Anti-Black Racism, Academia, and Scholar-Activism as a Pathway toward Black Survival and Wellness

In this section, we discuss anti-Black racism and how it manifests in academia. Further, we analyze the ways in which academia inhibits the wellness of Black people. We offer scholar-activism as a pathway but not a solution to Black survival and Wellness.

Exploring Anti-Black Racism

Ecological frameworks that recognize how power operates and influences wellness are useful when analyzing both oppression and liberation. For example, Camara Jones (2000) theorizes that racism and subsequently all other -isms (e.g., sexism, heterosexism, colorism) manifest at three levels: institutional, personally mediated, and internalized. Similarly, Isaac Prilleltensky (2012) conceptualizes wellness actualizing at the collective, relational, and personal level. In these ecological models, racism at each of these levels is not siloed. Rather, the three levels operate simultaneously and intersectionally (Crenshaw, 1990; Jones, 2000) such that holistic wellness is not achieved unless it is achieved across all three levels. There is extensive and vital work that outlines how systems of oppression and their process influence the material (Li & Koedel, 2017; Lomax, 2015), psychological and physical (Essed & Carberry, 2020; Louis et al., 2016), and spiritual wellness (Johnson & Bryan, 2017; Young & Hines, 2018) of Black people both within and outside the academy (Bell et al., 2020; Dancy et al., 2018; Echols, 2020; Mustaffa, 2017; Neville & Pieterse, 2009; Quaye et al., 2020; Sue et al., 2008). Some of this work will be reviewed in the sections that follow.

Anti-Black Racism and Collective Harms

Material well-being is achieved when one has access to resources like housing, food, and/or finances. White supremacy advantages white people by enabling access to such resources and disadvantages Black people by perpetuating institutional anti-Blackness, subsequently preventing Black people from accessing and attaining material well-being (Jones, 2000; Menon et al., 2015). The collective costs of anti-Black racism are evident across various systems and contexts. For example, health disparities, the prevalence of dominant anti-Black stereotypes and narratives in media, and the disproportionate surveillance and incarceration of Black folx are collective experiences and vulnerabilities.

As a result of institutional anti-Blackness, Black people—specifically Black womxn—are at higher risk of poverty, placing Black people in a particularly perilous position regarding their access to basic human rights (Lomax, 2015). Further, anti-Blackness divides the Black community through its failure to acknowledge the diversity and multiplicity of identities inherent to the Black experience. By defining the boundaries and "acceptable" manifestations of Blackness, Black people within Black spaces may lose a sense of safety and confront the same psychosocial and relational consequences experienced in non-Black spaces (Mosley et al., 2021).

Within the academy, the costs of institutional anti-Black racism are numerous. For example, Black women hold only 2% of full-time professorships, are among the least likely to hold tenure-track professorship appointments, and often face exploitation as the "only one" (i.e., only Black person or only person with multicultural awareness and competence) systemically burdened with working through any issues related to race and diversity, regardless of their expertise (Chancellor, 2019; Croom, 2017; Lomax, 2015; Parker, 2017; U.S. Department of Education, 2015). Li and Koedel (2017) reported that there is a significant wage gap of about $10,000 to $15,000 between Black and Latinx faculty and their white counterparts. This persistent wage gap underscores how institutional anti-Blackness continues to impact the material well-being of Blackademics, especially those who identify as women or who enter the academy as poor and/or working class. For instance, Blackademics within academia who are poor earn less money for more work than their nonpoor counterparts and are often encumbered by additional financial responsibilities like loan repayment and redistributing their earnings throughout their families and communities (Lomax, 2015). As such, working-class Blackademics are prevented from attaining the financial wellness and freedom that the academy otherwise grants to white academics and academics from higher social classes (Lomax, 2015).

Anti-Black Racism and Relational Harms

In addition to systemic oppression harming the material wellness of Black people, this racial group continues to face the threat of physical violence (e.g., police brutality; Grundy, 2017; Johnson & Bryan, 2017) and the deleterious tolls that emerge as a result of unrelenting experiences of anti-Black racism. Anti-Black racism is perpetuated relationally (i.e., between persons) through everyday acts of violence that include, but are not limited to, micro- and macroaggressions (e.g., Black faculty having their expertise and qualifications challenged; Arnold et al., 2016; DeCuir-Gunby et al., 2020; Louis et al., 2016; McCoy-Wilson, 2020), erasure (e.g., Black academics existence ignored and/or only acknowledged when needed; Lomax, 2015; Louis et al., 2016), harassment (Grundy, 2017), hypervigilance (Grundy, 2017; Lomax, 2015), and theft of intellectual property. Black people have described discovering theft of intellectual property in the academy. In response to an incident, Queen_ yacinee (2018) tweeted: "yall make a bad habit of stealing black women's ideas in academia and its really annoying and disheartening. Like I'm about to just stop talking at this point cuz im tired of my ideas being regurgitated to me like they weren't mine in the first place." Finally, relational consequences of anti-Blackness include withdrawal from others (Chancellor, 2019), struggling to find and form connections with others (Reddick et al., 2020), and ending relationships with others because of tolerance or perpetuation of anti-Blackness (Mosley et al., 2021).

Anti-Black Racism and Intrapersonal Harms

Given the pervasiveness of white supremacy and anti-Blackness, anti-Black racism has intrapersonal—or internal—psychological, emotional, and physical consequences (Jones, 2000; Speight, 2007). Internalized anti-Blackness manifests when Black folx internalize the baleful beliefs of the oppressor. For example, some Black folx may succumb to and enact *respectability politics*, the idea that Black people will be treated "better" by the oppressor if they behave "respectably" (Higginbotham, 1993; Madusa, 2020; Speight, 2007). For Black people who navigate intersecting identities that are systemically marginalized, these experiences are compounded. For example, misogynoir (Bailey & Trudy, 2018; Chancellor, 2019; Grundy, 2017; Lewis et al., 2013) and homonegativity (McInnis, 2017) may lead to more dire consequences for a dark-skinned queer woman given the interlocking systems of anti-Blackness, racism, sexism, and heterosexism (McInnis, 2017).

Anti-Blackness can lead to psychological symptoms, such as intense fear, avoidance, and nightmares, that are consistent with posttraumatic stress disorder (PTSD; Bryant-Davis & Ocampo, 2005a). The psychological consequences that resemble PTSD and occur in response to anti-Black racism have been dubbed "racist incident-based trauma" or racial trauma (Bryant-Davis & Ocampo, 2005a). Racial trauma also manifests as burnout (Arnold et al., 2016; Chancellor, 2019; Quaye et al., 2020), soul wounds (Young et al., 2018), depression, stress and/or anxiety (Donavan et al., 2012), isolation (Croom, 2017), struggling to find physical and psychological safety, and feeling disempowered and/or helpless (Mosley et al., 2021). Other personal costs of anti-Blackness include physical symptoms like headaches, insomnia, and fatigue (Chancellor, 2019; Mosley et al., 2021). Shay-Akil McLean (2020), a nonbinary queer Black person who studies racism, biology, genetics, and health, wrote of the systemic racism evident in the COVID-19 pandemic on Twitter,

> It is a SPECIAL KIND OF HELL for me to know, in painstaking detail, how racism affects people's health & then spend my life knowing exactly how people I love are dying while simultaneously, I can't do anything to prevent it. (Hood_Biologist, 2020)

Here McLean (2020) implies the helplessness that he feels because of his professional engagement on the topic of racism and health and the unrelenting systemic barrier to Black health, wellness, and life, especially in the midst of a pandemic during which Black people have fallen ill and died—and still do—at disproportionately higher rates than white people (Centers for Disease Control and Prevention [CDC], 2020; Keating et al., 2020; Wood, 2020).

Taken together with the empirical data, news, and social media findings reviewed, Jones (2000) and Prilleltensky's (2012) models help us understand how Black folx' agency, self-esteem, community, political life, relationships, and equitable access to necessary means to live (e.g., housing) have been compromised. These ecological perspectives of anti-Black racism also help guide visions for scholar-activist interventions. The authors argue that scholar-activism for Black survival and wellness can and should be undertaken by individuals and collectives outside of academia. However, for those within academia, where there is a sordid history of anti-Black racism and promise for liberation through education and scholarship, it is important to understand the historic and current relationship between anti-Black racism and academia.

Academia and Anti-Black Racism

The system of academia has an inextricable relationship with anti-Black racism that is traceable to anti-Black and anti-Indigenous settler colonialism and sustains systems of oppression (Mills, 1997; Smith, 2013). This oppressive and harmful relationship, along with the simultaneous processes of learning that take place within academia, identifies the academy as a site in which the liberation and wellness of Black people might be actualized. Mia Mingus has articulated that bridging restorative and transformative justice approaches to address harm has the possibility of both (a) repairing harm caused and (b) transforming the conditions that cause harm to prevent it (Petru, 2018). The combination of both restorative and transformative justice approaches can elucidate how to promote Black survival and wellness for those within the academy. In the following section, we will ground the academy as a system rooted in anti-Blackness, review the extensive current and historical perpetuation of anti-Black racism and violence that the academy has inflicted, and unlock the possibilities of moving toward justice.

Western societies, and specifically the United States, have been founded on imperialism, colonialism, anti-Blackness, racism, and the genocide of Indigenous people (Mills, 1997). The Oxford Language Dictionary (Stevenson, 2010) defines the *academy* as a place "concerned with the pursuit of research, education, and scholarship." It has been often described as a microcosm of broader society given that academia was developed to teach and maintain colonialism (Dancy et al., 2018; Mills, 1997; Thelin, 2004). In the United States, academia has deep historical roots that are embedded in anti-Blackness and the enslavement of Black people. As such, academia was created to serve anti-Black settler colonials and their state (Dancy et al., 2018; Thelin, 2004). For example, the first colleges and universities enslaved Black people as cooks and cleaners for white people in dormitories (Dancy et al., 2018; Stein, 2016). Academia's early—and ongoing—dependence on anti-Blackness and white supremacy results in a system that engenders anti-Black violence and subjugates Black people (Dancy et al., 2018). The authors of this chapter will center the experiences of Blackademics while acknowledging that Black people within academia are inherently tied to an oppressive system that simultaneously benefits them (e.g., access to grants and material resources) and oppresses the neighboring communities located outside the boundaries of the academy (e.g., poor communities of color from which academic institutions extract).

While the academy is a system of power meant to sustain white supremacism, and oppress and harm Black people (Bell et al., 2020), it concurrently holds the necessary resources and access to tools to facilitate the survival and wellness of all Black people through research, community impact, executive boards (e.g., endowments), and education (i.e., mentorship and teaching). Nevertheless, academia has traditionally used and presently uses its power to oppress, extract, mistreat, and suppress Black, Indigenous, and other People of Color (BIPOC; Quon, 2020). This intentional misuse of power can be understood through Linda Tuhiwai Smith's (2013) understanding of research as a tool of the academic colonial project. She defines research as "one of the ways in which the underlying code of imperialism and colonialism is both regulated and realized" (Smith, 2013, p. 8. In other words, research has been used as a method to enact anti-Indigenous and anti-Black colonial rule.

As a tool of colonialism, research has facilitated white supremacist projects deeply rooted in anti-Blackness. The scientific racism of academics like physicist William Shockley, who hypothesized that Black people are genetically predisposed to lower IQs, the Tuskegee syphilis study (Brandt, 1978), and the dehumanization and exploitation of Henrietta Lacks and her family (Skloot, 2017) are notable examples. Yet Harriet A. Washington, a Black medical ethicist, said, "Tuskegee ... is the example that the government has admitted to and acknowledged. It's so famous that people think it was the worst, but it was relatively mild compared to other stuff" (Rothman, 2017), thereby acknowledging a long and violent tradition of academic anti-Blackness. Moreover, while education has been identified as a method to liberate communities that are oppressed (Fanon et al., 1963), it has often served as another medium of perpetuating anti-Black rhetoric and white supremacist ideologies. Examples of this include the erasure of Black history (Caldera, 2020), the school-to-prison pipeline (Morris, 2016), the deficit model undergirding perspectives and treatment of Black students (Williams et al., 2019), and oppressive classrooms in which instructors constantly mispronounce Black students' names or accuse Black students of misconduct, such as stealing (Hargrove, 2020). Anti-Blackness also manifests as a lack of mentorship for Black students (Louis et al., 2016) and policing of Black bodies within the classroom, evident when a white professor at the University of San Antonio called the police on a Black student for propping her feet on the chair in front of her (Machado, 2018). Anti-Blackness and white supremacy are synonymous with higher education. At the same time, colonialism prevents Black people from access to and representation within academia.

Colonial myths of scarcity and meritocracy posit that education is a privilege rather than a right (Mehl, 1969). Access to the academy is a process that is rooted in the pursuit of gatekeeping the social power (i.e., class privilege and cultural capital) gained from any association with the academy. Such gatekeeping creates a hierarchy of individuals and groups deemed more "worthy" of access and survival than others. The standardization, institutionalization, and socialization of academic disciplines can also delegitimize knowledge that is incongruent with this hegemonic formula (Shih, 2010).

Alatas (2000) notes that the "political and economic structure of imperialism generated a parallel structure in the way of thinking of the subjugated people" (p. 24) and has thus been used as a tool to colonize. Various mechanisms of institutional academic colonialism have been constructed, such as acceptance of papers at international conferences or articles in journals as well as direct control of schools, universities, and publishing houses by colonial powers (e.g., white and wealthy people) in order to maintain coloniality and white supremacy (Alatas, 2000; Shih, 2010). Value accumulates from the collection of and participation in opportunities and experiences that are hidden away from or forbidden to Blackademics. That is, academia "unfairly disadvantages certain individuals and communities and unfairly advantages other individuals and communities and undermines the realization of the full potential of the whole society through the waste of human resources" (Jones, 2003, p. 10). Standardized tests, for example, and the testing movement are driven largely by eugenics and steeped in Darwinist concepts and Western middle-class values (Clayton, 2016). Assessment of IQ and academic performance sort people for various purposes based on performance on these tests—disadvantaging and excluding Black people, by being "yet another genocidal act in that it can destroy the intellectual capacities and productivity of a people inequitably impacted by the biased tests" (Council of National Psychological Associations for the Advancement of Ethnic Minority Interests, 2016).

Furthermore, although the academy is positioned to be a conduit for Black survival and wellness, it—and the individuals who comprise the academy—often cause harm in the community. In 2017 it was discovered that the University of Florida widely utilized prison labor—a legacy of slavery—to hand-pick, produce, and mow lawns for its Institute of Food and Agricultural Sciences (IFAS; Divest UF, n.d.). Only in October 2020 did the university finally agree to divest from the Department of Corrections, yet many other universities (e.g., the University of Virginia, the City College of New York, the University of Wisconsin), still reap the benefits of the mass incarceration and forced unpaid or underpaid labor of Black people (Delegal, 2020). While universities fail to divest from legacies of slavery, many simultaneously fail to invest in the communities in which they are embedded, a large number which are low-income, Black, and Brown, and instead contribute to problems like houselessness. For example, far from being a unique condition, gentrification spurred by Lehigh University's development of South Bethlehem, Pennsylvania, a low-income community that is comprised of mostly Black, Latinx, American Indian, and Asian residents—only 37% of residents are white—created a housing crisis for its residents who now struggle to pay rent (Zhou, 2019). Should the academy continue to maneuver itself in its current state, it will inevitably continue to take from and maltreat Black people. A radical re-imagining of academia is needed if we are to facilitate survival, wellness, and liberation for Black people and communities.

Black Survival and Wellness Through Restorative and Transformative Justice in Academia

The harm, abuse, and violence that the academy has inflicted on Black and other BIPOC communities cannot be erased or undone. Nonetheless, academia holds the power and potential to take accountability, repair, resist, prevent, and engage in the processes of both restorative and transformative justice with these communities. Restorative justice (RJ) is an approach to address harm by working to restore the relationship to the condition it was in before harm occurred (Eglash, 1977). This idea is reflected in the Association of Black Psychologists' (ABPsi) core value of Serudja Ta, or "making secure, setting right a wrong, providing and fulfilling a contract to restore and make grow ... engaging in the process of the restoration of human wellness and wholeness" (Association of Black Pyschologists, 2006, pp. 8–9). RJ (a) repairs harm, (b) requires all parties involved to work in collective, and (c) opens the possibility of transformational change (Center for Justice & Reconciliation, n.d.). By contrast, transformative justice (TJ) is a liberatory approach to addressing and preventing violence by acknowledging that oppression is at the root of any form of harm. TJ thus seeks to prevent violence and harm by addressing the root cause of violence (i.e., systemic oppression) and moving away from punitive or systemic violence (Generation Five, 2007). It is a political framework that approaches violence through (a) refusing reliance on the state (e.g., prison), (b) resisting the reinforcement of violence (e.g., alienation), and (c) engaging in violence prevention (e.g., accountability; Mingus, n.d.).

The use of RJ and TJ frameworks within the academy has the potential to promote Black survival, wellness, and liberation (Petru, 2018). For instance, scholar-activists and community organizers have fought for universities and colleges to acknowledge, be accountable to, and work to right the harm and violence they have caused Black communities (The Demands, 2016). As a case in point, the Black Liberation Collective is a collective of Black students across the nation who aim to dismantle anti-Black institutions. The Black Liberation Collective (n.d.) demands, "at the minimum, Black students and Black faculty to be reflected by the national percentage of Black folx in the state and the country ... free tuition for Black and Indigenous students and ... a divestment from prisons and an investment in communities." Their statement combines principles of both RJ and TJ. Specifically, the Collective's demands express the desire for accountability for harm done through investment in prison labor and institutional discriminatory policies and norms that limit access for Black faculty and students, in addition to proactively working toward investing in surrounding communities. Understanding how research is used to colonize and oppress Black and Indigenous people and committing to dismantling colonial methods of inquiry, engaging in Black and Indigenous methods of resisting (e.g., implementing Indigenous methods of inquiry; Smith, 2013) and enacting anticolonial approaches to research (e.g., collaborative community-based social science research; Glass et al., 2018) are additional examples of how universities may employ an RJ approach to address and be accountable for institutional harms.

Black scholar-activists have long fought for Black liberation, healing, wellness and survival through their activism, research, teaching, mentorship, policy work, initiatives, and community work (Chapman-Hilliard et al., 2020; Combahee River Collective, 1995; Crenshaw, 1990; Fanon et al., 1963; Lewis & Neville, 2015; Lorde, 1984; Mosley et al., 2021). Within the field of psychology, in which the authors of this chapter are situated, scholar-activists have developed and implemented revolutionary work (e.g., Bryant-Davis, 2005b; Cokley, 2007; Helms, 1990; Neville et al., 2000; Speight, 2007; Singh, 2020) that facilitates the survival and wellness of all Black people. Notably, two authors of this chapter, Pearis Bellamy and Della V. Mosley, coconstructed the Academics for Black Survival and Wellness (A4BL) initiative, a transnational anti-oppressive and antiracist training undergirded by a TJ approach that sought to prevent anti-Black racism in the summer of 2020 (along with other colleagues Alex Colson, Amber Lewis, Anneliese Singh, Arielle Nicole Wallace, Ashley Garcia, Bryana French, Candice Hargons, Carla Prieto, Carlton E. Green, Chris Busey, Dan Walinsky, Delia Steverson, Garrett Ross, Gerry Altamirano, Grace Chen, Gregory Samarnez-Larkin, Hannah Bayne, Hector Y. Adames, Helen Neville, Jeannette Mejia, Jess Trochez, Jioni Lewis, Kate Ratliff, Lisa Scott, Kevin Nadal, Kimberly Burdine, Kirsten Gonzalez, LaNya Lee, Lisa S. Scott, Maddie Crowley, Madison Martin, Maggie Moskal, Maria Saldana, Mariah Emerson, Natalie Malone, Nayeli Chavez, Nicole Gravina, Ollie Trac, Reuben Faloughi, Roberto L. Abreu, Sade Abiodun, Sunshine Adam, Teagan Murphy, Valene Whittaker, Whitney Wheeler and Zoe Pestana). This initiative, which the entirety of our counseling psychology–focused authorship team contributed to, represents one contemporary example of how scholar-activism can be used to facilitate Black futures. Black scholar-activism, however, is immemorial and transdisciplinary.

Black Scholar Activism: Contributions and Concerns

Black scholar activism involves "engaging in activism informed by scholarship and/or contributing to scholarship informed by activism that is focused on Black liberation" (Mosley et al., 2021, p. 9). This definition was coconstructed by Black racial justice activists and scholars of Black activism through a constructivist grounded theory method (Charmaz, 2014). Importantly, this definition underscores the bidirectional relationship between scholarship and activism that is critical to the process and outcome of Black liberation. Mosley and colleagues' (2021) frame of scholar-activism is fitting for this chapter, as it encourages readers who may be drawn toward scholarship to consider activism, and vice versa, while centering Black liberation. The many contributions of Black scholar activism fall under two overarching categories of (a) speaking truth and (b) access and representation. The former category involves Black scholar activism broadly and the latter narrowly focuses on specific contributions and benefits within the academy. Finally, Black scholar-activism can be contentious work. We will review some of the concerns and risks associated with Black scholar activism.

Speaking Truth to Power and Truth to the People

Black scholar-activists have pioneered approaches to empower those who have been marginalized by systems of oppression as well as to seek accountability from oppressive systems. Scholar-activism is well suited to empower and seek accountability by speaking truth to power and truth to the people. When speaking truth to power, one "harnesses the power of ideas toward the specific goal of confronting existing power relations" (Collins, 2013, p. xii) and therefore undermining power. Speaking truth to the people is a strategy of scholar-activism that emphasizes truth telling to people who are affected by oppression in order to empower and instigate everyday change. The acts of speaking truth to power and to the people within scholar-activist projects has brought about change by (a) exposing oppressive realities, (b) facilitating resistance, and (c) fostering the development of healing spaces within academia.

Exposing Oppressive Realities

Many scholars have significantly contributed to Black survival and wellness in academia by exposing systems of oppression and the realities that are fomented by their existence. As previously noted, Janet Helms, Camara Jones, and Kimberlé Crenshaw are scholar-activists who have exposed whiteness, defined levels of racism, and exposed how interlocking systems of oppression inform the experience of individuals with multiple intersecting identities that are marginalized. These Black women's work speaks both truth to power and truth to the people because the act of exposing systems of oppression, their function, and manifestations inherently confronts the oppressive power structures. Additionally, their works make explicit what was previously implicit, invisible, and unnamed, therefore making space for individuals to understand and articulate their experiences and heal (French et al., 2020). By exposing the ways in which white supremacy ascribes value, access, and resources based in anti-Blackness, one can see how the legitimacy of experience defined by whiteness creates and perpetuates anti-Black environments (e.g., Who defines intellectualism, and who is to say intellectualism gives more legitimacy to existence?).

Mariame Kaba (2017), a community organizer, educator, and curator, has organized projects rooted in TJ centered on abolition of the prison industrial complex and has laid bare the realities facing Black girls' heightened targeting by misogynoir contributing to their integration to the school-to-prison pipeline. This Black feminist analysis is fundamental to understanding why the unveiling of oppressive realities is necessary to achieving Black survival and wellness. Specifically, when one speaks truth to power, the experiences of those who are most commonly intentionally erased are heard and honored, and systems of oppression that perpetuate violence toward Black womxn (e.g., misogynoir) move closer toward dismantling.

More recently, Black in the Ivory, a Twitter campaign cofounded by Joy Melody Woods and Shardé M. Davis, encouraged Blackademics to post about their experiences of racism and anti-Blackness during their time in academia (Calma, 2020). This sharing of experience helped expose the deep-seeded and ever-present anti-Blackness within the academy. This speaking of truth to power catalyzed specific demands for universities and other institutions and engendered structural, radical change for other institutions that perpetuate white supremacy.

Resistance

Black scholar-activists utilize resistance to facilitate the survival and wellness of Black people. For example, in centering the liberation of Black womxn from white cishet patriarchy, the Combahee River Collective (1995) spoke both truth to power (e.g., challenging hegemonic power dynamics embedded in the collective and relational erasure of Black womxn from liberation movements) and truth to the people (e.g., allowing Black womxn to be seen and affirmed in their experiences) in their activism rooted in resistance. Further, virtual takeovers, silent protests, demands to create Black Studies departments, and calls to increase funding for the hire of Black faculty are approaches to resisting anti-Blackness and speaking truth to power, as they hold power accountable to act in ways that promote well-being and liberation for Black people (Quaye et al., 2017; T'Shaka, 2012). Black scholar activism has also facilitated resistance beyond the academy. A prominent example of this is Kenneth and Mamie Clark's scholarship (e.g., the Doll Test) and their work alongside the National Association for the Advancement of Colored People, Legal Defense and Education Fund (NAACP-LDEF), which resisted the anti-Black policy of racial segregation in the 1950s (see *Brown v. Board of Education, 1954*; Jackson, 2001). The Institute for Urban Policy Research and Analysis (IUPRA), directed by Kevin Cokley, and its efforts to apply research to inform legislative policies that shape the experiences of BIPOC is another example of how Black scholar activism has moved beyond the academy to promote wellness for BIPOC in and out of academia. Resistance as a method of speaking truth to power and truth to the people has allowed Black scholar activism to hold those in power accountable, combat anti-Black racial violence, and work in collective with love, care, and honesty to advance wellness and survival beyond academic boundaries.

Healing Spaces

As Helms (2017) described, intentional effort toward healing from racial trauma is imperative for psychologists, and the provision of healing spaces informed by scholarship as an act of resisting anti-Blackness and centering Black wellness is necessary for Black liberation. Violence experienced by Black students and the lack of resources for them (e.g., getting turned away from counseling services; harmful counseling services) yield a lack of spaces for Black students to be safe. To address this, a Black graduate student support group (e.g., Black in Community) at the University of Florida was created and cofacilitated by one of the authors of this chapter, Garrett Ross, along with Milan Raiford-Savoury, in response to the lack of safe campus spaces for Black students following the killings of Ahmaud Arbery, George Floyd, Breonna Taylor, and others in spring and summer 2020.

Facilitating Black survival and wellness necessitates the two-pronged approach outlined by Collins (2013) of speaking both truth to power and truth to the people. Resistance, healing spaces, and exposing anti-Blackness operate as potential means to realize this goal.

Access and Representation

Black scholar-activism has facilitated access and representation in the academy. W.E.B Du Bois was a formative leader in the push for access and representation. In his work *The Talented Tenth*, he critiques Booker T. Washington's notion that Black people should focus on industrial training. Du Bois (1903) asserted that African Americans needed a classical education to be able to reach their potential and become leaders of the race, and that the approach to educate the most promising Black youth would lead to Black liberation. Similar to *The Talented Tenth*'s central proposition of increased access and representation within academia, Daniel (1973) summarized the efforts of Black scholar-activists who had called on academic institutions to combat systemic racism through acts such as giving power to Black folx, taking accountability for harm toward Black communities through research, divesting from racist employers, and redistributing wealth and access equitably to Black students and faculty within the university. Subsequently, universities experienced an increase in enrollment of Black graduate students admitted with financial aid to Historically White Institutions, the hiring of Black faculty members, and the development of new curriculums for college courses. This access to the academy has provided a path toward financial wellness (College Board, 2017), and the increase of representation (NewsOne Staff, 2011) of Black faculty and students has spurred racial consciousness raising, a sense of belonging, and greater responsibility to minority and campus communities through the creation of safe spaces, accessibility, and advocacy (Genheimer, 2016; Vandelinder, 2016). Additionally, the demands of the Black Student Association during the San Francisco State strike resulted in the creation of a Black Studies department with funding for 12 new faculty (T'Shaka, 2012). The representation following the creation of a Black Studies department served as a subversion to whiteness (e.g., white value-oriented courses) through the implementation of a rigorous, Afro-centric intellectual curriculum across disciplines (T'Shaka, 2012). Progress toward increased access prompted by the work of Black scholar-activists is evident in how various community resources, organizing, and community work are attained through academic grants and redistributed to the community.

Concerns Surrounding Black Scholar Activism for Academics

Although the work of Black scholar-activists has positively impacted the wellness and survival of Black people, there are also contentions and risks involved in this work. Gumbs (2012) reminds us that institutions know "Black feminists are a trouble more useful as dead invocation than as live troublemakers" and will continue to profit from their dead faculty members. Gumbs' (2012) re-interpretive analysis of Audre Lorde reminds us that survival is not guaranteed through or because of the academy.

For Black scholar-activists in academia, our identity has a nuanced meaning due to the very nature of the dissonance between what we are fighting for and motivated by and what we are upholding and benefiting from. Our identity is inherently contentious and who we are is constantly competing with what we want to facilitate. We as Black academics can be both oppressed as well as the oppressors (through horizontal violence). This dialectic can be understood through the lens of internalized coloniality wherein the oppressed can in turn become the co-oppressor (Fanon, 1952/2008; Gaztambide, 2020). Black scholar-activists are positioned in a catch 22 between (a) using the academy and our scholarship as a means to facilitate Black survival and wellness and (b) being aware of how the academy thwarts Black survival and wellness. In order to survive the structures we exist within, we perpetuate systems of oppression (e.g., elitism) that intentionally devalue the humanity of Black folx despite our awareness of the academy's harm. Continuing to perpetuate the assignment of value undergirded by racism and anti-Blackness exemplifies what Jones (2003) described as a waste of human resources that ultimately undermines the potential of the society as a whole.

Another contention that Black scholar-activists face involves the experience of epistemic exclusion. Epistemic exclusion has been defined by Settles et al. (2020) as the devaluation of scholars of color (specifically Black scholars) and the research they do as illegitimate, lacking value, and outside of disciplinary norms established and maintained by those who hold power and prestige due to their success working within the dominant discourses. Thus, Black scholar-activists exist in a system that perpetuates the delegitimization of non-Western knowledge/approaches in research, clinical application, and teaching. For example, (a) quantitative methods courses are required for the department of psychology (despite whether the student is utilizing quantitative methodologies), (b) Black feminist and liberation-focused theories are critiqued and devalued from a white supremacist lens, and finally (c) instructors perpetuate a banking model of education and hesitate to interrogate new or opposing perspectives. This is because, ultimately, worth and validity are ascribed with settler-colonial values. For example, Griffin et al. (2013) underlined that the very definition of being "successful" was different for Black scholars, which further pressured Black faculty to produce in ways that leave them less vulnerable to doubts for promotion due to the "myth of meritocracy embedded within tenure review" (p. 505). Griffin et al. (2013) note this experience is more harmful for Black womxn who hold intersecting identities that are marginalized. They highlighted how greater scrutiny is placed on Black womxn professors' tenure application, resulting in inequitable expectations. For example, Black womxn are expected to mentor students of color (Griffin et al., 2013; Harley, 2008; Matthew, 2016) and provide resources related to antiracism and anti-Blackness (e.g., scholar strike, teach-in). The inequitable distribution of labor is rooted in the fact that Black womxn are put in the role of being the "maids" of the academy (Griffin et al., 2013; Harley, 2008). Given how colorism and misogynoir intertwine as oppressive systems, the extraction, delegitimization, and burdening of labor looks differently for a Black man who has light skin. Because our identity as academics inherently perpetuates elitism, classism, and anti-Blackness, we are faced with complicated existential questions regarding this duality while also experiencing risk to our job security and wellness.

Risks of Being a Black Scholar-Activist in Academia

Academics hold power and privilege in part because classism and elitism protect the ruling class. Consequently, our proximity to whiteness means that we are afforded access to wellness and protection often denied to people outside academia (Mehl, 1969; TEDx Talks, 2016). Collins (2013) claimed that activist communities outside academia regard academics with suspicion, as they are perceived to be insufficiently committed to the frontlines of the very political and social movements they may study. Therefore, as outsiders, Collins (2013) posits that academics can misinterpret academic politics as real politics. Despite this power and privilege, Blackademic scholar-activists face risks in terms of job security, threats to physical and psychological safety, delegitimization, and negative evaluations due to anti-Black stereotypes.

Examples and Consequences of Negative Evaluations and Why This Is a Risk
Because much of the labor in scholar activism does not get recognized by the current incentive structures within academia, this work is often extracurricular and disadvantages us compared to colleagues who instead allocate their time toward the activities deemed "valuable" by the academy. Suzuki and Mayorga (2014) suggested that institutions of higher education don't "count" their activism because it lies outside doctoral coursework and dissertation. The authors continued to describe "the fact that activism in scholarship becomes the focus of a journal issue itself represents the paralysis that plagues our education academy today. It not only reveals the insufficiency of activism in scholarship but also speaks to the false separation of the two" (p. 17).

The metrics for tenure, promotion, or graduation requirements do not account for the risks and benefits of scholar activism, and the reflection of the labor invested (although we admit that we are examining this from a white lens, because that is the culture we are surviving in) will not be rewarded. Given this, racial inequities in salaries and funding exist and may be expected to further widen (Li & Koedel, 2017; Murakami, 2020). Colleagues and students may also directly evaluate and devalue the advocacy of Black scholar activists. For example, when advocating for dismantling anti-Blackness (which goes against the status quo) within the classroom setting, Black womxn are evaluated based on the anti-Black stereotypes of being "aggressive" and "angry." Not only does going against the status quo risk evaluations related to job security, but there are also psychosocial and physical wellness risks that arise from this work. For example, Angela Davis's outing as a communist and member of the Black Panther party in the mainstream media was followed by threats and attempts on her life (Davis, 1974).

Duality of Being a Black Scholar-Activist: Reflections for Self- and Collective Preservation
Although a necessity for Black survival and wellness, Black scholar activism results in the institutional and relational exploitation of Black people's labor and impacts our wellness, despite simultaneous efforts to facilitate wellness. The intentional disregard of centering Black survival and wellness by people who are not Black scholar-activists (e.g., lacking desire and/or accountability to do this work) has left the majority of the labor of dismantling anti-Blackness to Black people. As such, the costs to our wellness are evident and borne of this necessity. Academic strikes at historically White institutions during 2020 have challenged white supremacy and anti-Blackness through educational initiatives (e.g., via trainings, talks, assigning non-Black academics to attend courses led by Black faculty on critical race theory). Not only is there an inclination for Blackademics to do this work for survival and wellness (i.e., feeling the need to lead organizing/educating efforts), but there also exists institutional pressure (Griffin et al., 2013; Harley, 2008) for Blackademics to take on significantly more labor compared to other academics. The Black in Community support group for Black graduate students at the University of Florida was formed with the intention of facilitating Black wellness

and survival; however, in acting with love, the organizers sacrifice their own wellness (e.g., being consistently spread thin in regard to emotional capacity and wellness) and progression within their academic program. We asked ourselves, "If we don't do it, who will?" and proceeded intentionally, highlighting the duality of fighting for wellness and survival at the cost of our own.

Adapting (or Internalizing White Supremacy) to Survive the Violence of the Academy

Blackademics hold a contentious relationship with the academy and are pressured to adapt and internalize the colonizers' views in order to survive whiteness. Within higher education, the socialization process prompts academics to conform to existing structures, programs, and institutional norms (Winkle-Wagner et al., 2020). Although this type of socialization may help one progress within institutions of higher learning, scholars have shown the detrimental effects that this has on students' identities and ability to find a sense of belonging in higher education institutions (Antony, 2002; McCoy, 2007; Winkle-Wagner, 2009). The duality of needing to ultimately internalize and perpetuate norms of white supremacy within academia to adapt and survive while fighting for Black liberation as Black scholar-activists can be a source of cognitive dissonance.

Reckoning With the Duality

Grappling with these realities is work. Exploring them may lead one to ask whether it is even possible to achieve Black liberation without Black people being overworked, exhausted, and extracted from. The duality of the experience of being a Black scholar-activist reveals the complexity of the identity, and that as Black scholar-activists we are acutely aware of the ways in which power is intimately intertwined with our identity. Collins (2013) described that power monopolizes truth through being co-opted and repackaged to suit the interests of those in power. As we think about the nuances of what systems and people our work is benefitting, perpetuating, and oppressing, despite our best interests to strive for Black liberation, we need to interrogate the processes by which this is getting repackaged to maintain anti-Blackness. For example, while the Havasupai case (see *Havasupai Tribe v. Arizona Bd. of Regents*, 2008) is an example of how white scholars have utilized their power to extract from BIPOC communities, it is important to acknowledge that Black scholar activists are not exempt from utilizing power in similar ways—as stated previously, by nature of being in academia, we perpetuate its oppressive anti-Blackness. Black scholar-activists have one foot in, one foot out, but not fully in either. That is, we will never be accepted by the academy, and because we're in the academy, we pay the price for leaving the community (Suzuki & Mayorga, 2014). For example, Collins (2013) described her struggles around the dialectic of writing a book about Black womxn's experiences that would be accepted by scholarly audiences that had long excluded and derogated this group or writing a book that spoke directly to Black womxn yet risked being dismissed by scholarly audiences. "Is it worth it?" has been an ontological question that many scholar-activists face given all the tradeoffs with family, graduate/job security, wellness, and potential value misalignments (Suzuki & Mayorga, 2014).

Why a Scholar-Activist Agenda for Black Survival and Wellness Is Necessary

As Black scholar-activists, we strive to unsettle the very same academic power relations that are used for our legitimacy. Collins (2013) described that "some changes are best initiated from within the belly of the beast" (p. xiii), suggesting that we can fight for incremental change of power structures from within the academy. Black scholar-activists can use their access to academia to speak truth to the people, "produce oppositional knowledge that assists in [our] survival" (Collins, 2013, p. xv), and hold systems of oppression accountable. A critique of the "belly of the beast" approach is that truth to power and truth to the people both rely on the validation of truth within a system that oppresses certain forms of knowing and certain people's worthiness. The root of the issue is that academia is needed for our legitimacy, yet the same legitimacy gained through academia delegitimizes and oppresses those outside academia.

Scholar-activists who have sat with the dualities inherent within their identity may approach their work by resisting the ableist, misogynoir roots of academia and orienting toward the work that aligns with their values. In other words, a complement to the "working within the system approach" requires the divestment from components of racist/capitalist/colonial notions of "value" and an investment in committing to Black liberation outside the settler-colonial state. For example, by viewing academia's allocation of funding, Aminah Pilgrim cofounded the Student Ambassadors Bonded Under Recreation and Achievement (SABURA) with Anita "Leny" Monteiro by using academic funding to support community organizing with Black youth. Together they created a program for youth to feel empowered through self-awareness and increased cultural connection, with the ultimate goal of encouraging youth to raise the social consciousness of their communities on a local and global level and learn the skills to participate in service and civic engagement in our contemporary world. Her work highlights the power that academics have to divest from academia through redistributing wealth within communities.

We use Gumbs's (2012) closing remarks of her essay entitled "The Shape of My Impact" to invite readers to consider developing or updating their own scholar-activist agenda for Black survival and wellness. Gumbs (2012) offers the following reminders related to reclaiming the term *survival*: "May we never sell our legacy for a mess of ego and scholar-styled swag. May we refuse to exploit our legacy in order to earn more exploitation. May we remember who we are." The following sections provide reflections and directions that can help guide scholar-activists in their Black liberation efforts.

Part II: Developing a Scholar-Activist Agenda for Black Survival and Wellness: Reflections From the WELLS Collective

Building from Gumbs's (2012) powerful call for Black scholars to remember who they are, we invite all readers to consider developing or updating a scholar-activist agenda that does not exploit or harm Black folx, but instead enhances our survival and wellness. While we certainly have a scholar-activism agenda that we invite others to work toward alongside us, we do not recommend a singular agenda. Rather, we intend to describe how we are positioned to enhance Black survival and wellness and how that positioning influences our process in developing and executing scholar activism efforts centered on Black liberation. Based on our experiences and engagement with other Black scholar-activists and scholar activism (e.g., manuscripts, policy, initiatives) we will share some considerations that may help readers to determine how they can develop a personal agenda for Black survival and wellness through scholar activism.

Positionality: Getting in Formation for Black Scholar Activism

This authorship team is a part of the Wellness, Equity, Love, Liberation, and Sexuality (WELLS) Healing and Research Collective, founded by Della V. Mosley in the summer of 2018. WELLS explores how to promote wellness, particularly among Black people and/ or queer and transgender People of Color (QTPOC). Our collective operates within Black feminist and liberation frameworks. Through research, community events centered around healing and wellness, and outreach and education efforts across our various social media platforms, we strive to facilitate wellness and liberation for people experiencing oppression.

Being a part of a collective has allowed us to come to our interventions in community with one another, often in really organic ways. Most of us writing this chapter are Black, some are multiracial Black (GR, SA), and one is a white Latina (CP). The impact of anti-Black racism shows up differently for each of us, and we each have different skills for, beliefs about, and experiences in resisting the many manifestations of oppression. We have varying degrees of privilege based on our class backgrounds (ranging from poor working class to middle class), skin tone (ranging from white to darker complexioned Black), and homeplace (ranging from suburban to urban, East to West Coast, from the United States to Brazil). We have different relationships to disability (inclusive of psychological and educational disabilities), different access based on our educational privilege (ranging from undergraduate student to 3rd-year tenure-track faculty member), and diverse gender and sexualities (ranging from nonbinary and queer to cisgender and straight). What we have in common is that we are all committed to using Black feminist and liberatory approaches to promoting wellness and resisting oppression.

We write, organize, teach, create, engage in healing work, rest, self-reflect, mentor, love, learn, and fight, all in an effort to achieve liberation. Showing up in this way is self-love. It's self-preservation. We see self as united with and inseparable from the collective groups with whom we identify. The self is collective. And we work for our collective, for ourselves to get free from oppression using the tools and skills and resources we have access to, including scholar activism.

Our authorship team and broader collective is constantly working with, learning about, and practicing various applications of Black feminist and liberation psychology approaches. We believe that having a foundation in and commitment to these theories and their core principles has enhanced our ability to engage in Black scholar activism. Black feminism is a theory that recognizes how systems of oppression such as white supremacy, patriarchy, and capitalism coalesce to shape a unique experience for Black womxn and unapologetically uses an awareness of those everyday experiences for theorizing and creating change (Collins, 2000).

Within a Black feminist framework, we uphold the principles of intersectionality and equity, relationality and mutual respect, and healing justice. When working on scholar activism, tasks are typically not divided equally but rather based on who may have more capacity (e.g., personal wellness, time available), and on who should be inputting more labor based on positionality to the work. As a collective that values wellness and transparent communication, the group continues to check in throughout the duration of our projects, and we shift tasks or roles when necessary. Each member holds an understanding that capacities often shift, we can all lead and follow, and working as a unit toward our shared goals is most important.

True to Black feminism, we merge our academic and embodied knowledge to facilitate liberation. WELLS strives to center the most marginalized voices when making decisions and makes a point to value the embodied knowledge of the members of our collective to uphold Black feminism and ensure we are working toward Black liberation. Our projects are led by those who hold the identity of and/or work closely with those we are advocating and creating an intervention with and for. In the rare cases where someone of that identity is unable to lead the project, we consult and work alongside someone who does. WELLS includes values and honors the ideas and input of everyone, including those without academic credentials or positions.

A Black queer feminist social justice movement framework also guides our work (brown, 2017; Carruthers, 2018). We have spent time in deep reflection on the five questions that Carruthers (2018) deems "critical to determining the health and success of our movements: Who am I? Who are my people? What do we want? What are we building? Are we ready to win?" (p. 92). Like brown's (2017) concept of "emergent strategy," we have homed in on the localized, small-scale, and relational practices as a collective that have allowed us to "create complex patterns, systems, and transformations—including adaptation, interdependence and decentralization, fractal awareness, resilience and transformative justice, nonlinear and iterative change, creating more possibilities" (brown, 2017, p. 22).

We invite readers to consider the extent to which Black feminism as an interdisciplinary theory and social justice organizing framework is—or could be—a guidepost for their scholar-activist agenda. Whether or not Black feminism is the framework you utilize, we encourage you to ground your scholar activism on an applied theory that fits well with your positionality. Importantly, you may use different theories in your scholarship and activism. What we are advocating for here is that you clarify which frameworks and principles will guide your overarching agenda, whether you engage in scholar activism as an individual or as part of a collective. By describing one scholar-activist effort our collective engaged in, Academics for Black Survival and Wellness, we aim to demonstrate how our positionality, commitment to Black feminist praxis as a collective, and intentionality around merging scholarship and activism for Black liberation served us. We will (a) integrate a number of questions (*in italics*) throughout this example to help readers define their scholar-activist agenda for Black survival and wellness and (b) describe in detail how scholarship informed our activism and how activism informed (and continues to inform) our scholarship.

Academics for Black Survival and Wellness: Examples of Black Scholar Activism

WELLS values keep us attuned to the news and relevant media as we seek to be responsive to global and local events that impact the Black community. In the midst of a global pandemic in 2020, there was no respite from the deadly consequences of white supremacy and anti-Black racism. George Floyd was murdered by a police officer, and this was video-recorded, leading to global protests and calls for justice (D.B. Taylor, 2020). Breonna Taylor was murdered by the police in Louisville using a no-knock warrant (Oppel & Taylor, 2020). We saw the commodification of Breonna Taylor's death and the stark difference in how Black womxn who are murdered at the hands of white supremacy are treated compared to others. The summer of 2020 was a summer that many called "America's racial reckoning." In reality, summer 2020 was a syndemic between the COVID-19 pandemic and the sins of America's legacy of white supremacy and anti-Black racism (Poteat et al., 2020).

To what extent are you concerned with the current and historical manifestations of anti-Black racism? How can history, current events, and other temporal realities help you situate and contextualize your scholar activism efforts? How will you prioritize your actions based on the urgency of the sociopolitical moment? To what extent will you engage with and center historical analyses and consider future impacts?

In May 2020, while surviving the COVID-19 pandemic, Pearis Bellamy and Della V. Mosley were also navigating anti-Black academic systems and being exposed to repeated tragic murders of Black people. Pearis, a counseling psychology doctoral student, felt overwhelmed by the expectation that she show up in virtual academic spaces after repeated Black murders while her non-Black peers seemed either unaware or not impacted by current events. Della, an assistant professor and principal investigator of the WELLS Healing and Research Collective, felt similarly to Pearis and was facilitating dialogue in the collective about how they were feeling. Pearis recalls asking, "How are you supposed to be productive? How are you supposed to focus? And why does no one who does not look like you care?"

From that conversation, Della and Pearis dreamed up Academics for Black Survival and Wellness (A4BL). The idea was simple: Non-Black (i.e., white and non-Black POC) academics would take a full week away from work to decenter themselves and to recognize the toll of continued racial trauma on their Black colleagues and the Black community. We called this the "training" track. During this time, training track participants would educate themselves on anti-Black racism, be accountable to the ways they perpetuate ABR, and take action to support Black liberation. At the same time, Blackademics, educators, and healers outside academia would participate in wellness workshops to provide them with the rest, healing, and tools for resistance to navigate and thrive in academia and other spaces. This was referred to as the Black wellness track.

In what ways would it be useful for you to utilize your embodied experiences as a guide for the scholar-activist initiatives you undertake? Do you have a community with whom you can share your embodied experiences and discuss their potential as catalysts for scholar activism? If you are a Black person engaging Black scholar activism in response to anti-Black racism or racial trauma, how will you prioritize and navigate your own need for healing in the process? If you are a not a dark-skinned Black person, how will you mitigate the impact of your race or color-related privilege as you engage in Black scholar activism?

The events of the summer called for swift but intentional planning. Della intentionally created a team through her networks of Black scholars, activists, and healers as well as non-Black allies, advocates, and activists. This collective was brought together with the specific aims of creating training to enhance critical consciousness of anti-Black racism (Mosley et al., 2021) for the training track, and conceptualizing and facilitating interventions that would facilitate radical healing (French et al., 2020) for the Black wellness track. By basing both tracks on relevant theories and scholarship related to Black wellness, we were able to provide a clear framework to the A4BL collective from the start. These guiding frameworks (critical consciousness of anti-Black racism and radical healing) were informative, yet still allowed spaciousness for these team members to meaningfully integrate their own knowledge, skills, ideas, and Black liberation dreams.

Are there individuals or collectives you can collaborate with on your efforts? How do you determine who you can fight for Black liberation with? What frameworks and collective agreements might best guide your work and foster a culture that works well for you and your Black survival and wellness efforts? To what extent will your agenda allow for an integration of you and your team members' knowledge, skills, ideas, and Black liberation dreams?

Conclusion

The authors' personal experiences in academia have highlighted the deeply rooted nature of anti-Black racism and colonialism within academia. Torres Rivera (2020) stated, "To liberate someone, psychologists themselves need to be liberated at a personal level" (p. 48). In this way, liberation starts with the personal actions of academics rather than the reliance on the systems within academia to create liberation. However, in the pursuit of facilitating Black liberation for all Black people, which our work is purported to do, the ways in which we are doing this work given the oppressive confines of the system of academia in fact perpetuates our lack of freedom and the inability to actualize Black liberation via self-determination. Within the system of academia, we are still choosing between our wellness and using the colonial tools of academia in hopes of benefiting and supporting healing for Black people. Because of this dichotomy between our own wellness and participating in academia, which as a system actively harms us, we cannot truly be free. Thus, our own "work" is actually getting in the way of our liberation. In other words, Black liberation is in contention with our enmeshment with academic colonialism.

Could Black futures be built outside the confines of settler colonialism, white supremacy, and capitalism? Our dream is that scholar-activism won't be necessary because Black liberation of all Black people will be realized. In this dream, the ascription of worth and what is valued are fundamentally shifted such that access is equitably distributed. For this to become actualized, we would need to (a) live in a world that does not necessitate and rely on killing Black people and systemic inequities to function, (b) divest from capitalist/colonial notions of what provides "value" in order to be seen as worthy (e.g., elitism), and (c) because Black self-determination is in contention with coloniality, we must interrogate how we are perpetuating academic colonialism and how to navigate being the beneficiaries of a system aimed to maintain the subjugation of Black people (Dancy et al., 2018). For reasons stated throughout the chapter, scholar-activism thus is not and cannot be our final solution to Black liberation. Rather, it is merely a pathway to which we function in systems that are oppressive with the knowledge that these systems will never free us and our liberation work must go beyond the confines of academia.

References

Agyakwa, P. [DrMaterialsMum]. (2020, June 8). *Being #Blackintheivory tower is to be hypervisible yet invisible, to be loud yet unheard, and to be continually infantilized regardless* [Tweet]. Twitter. https://twitter.com/DrMaterialsMum/status/1269918841452273667?s=20

Alatas, S. F. (2003). Academic dependency and the global division of labour in the social sciences. *Current sociology, 51*(6), 599–613. https://doi.org/10.1177/00113921030516003

Antony, J. S. (2002). Reexamining doctoral student socialization and professional development: Moving beyond the congruence and assimilation orientation. In J.C. Smart & W.G. Tierney (Eds), *Higher education: Handbook of theory and research* (pp. 349–380). Springer. https://doi.org/10.1007/978-94-010-0245-5_8

Arnold, N. W., Crawford, E. R., & Khalifa, M. (2016). Psychological heuristics and faculty of color: Racial battle fatigue and tenure/promotion. *The Journal of Higher Education, 87*(6), 890–919. https://doi.org/10.1080/00221546.2016.11780891

Association of Black Psychologists. (2020). *The pandemics of COVID 1619 - COVID 19 - The complexities of racial trauma.* https://www.facebook.com/watch/live/?v=672263073641952&ref=watch_permalink

Association of Black Psychologists (2006). *Licensure Certification Proficiency Program Standards: The ABPsi Ethical Standards.*

Bailey, M., & Trudy. (2018). On misogynoir: Citation, erasure, and plagiarism. *Feminist Media Studies, 18*(4), 762–768. https://doi.org/10.1080/14680777.2018.1447395

Bell, M. P., Berry, D., Leopold, J., & Nkomo, S. (2020). Making Black lives matter in academia: A Black feminist call for collective action against anti-blackness in the academy. *Gender, Work & Organization, 29* (39–57) https://doi.org/10.1111/gwao.12555

The Black Liberation Collective. (n.d.). *Our demands.* http://www.blackliberationcollective.org/our-demands

Brandt, A. M. (1978). *Racism and research: The case of the Tuskegee Syphilis Study.* Hastings Center, 21–29. https://dash.harvard.edu/bitstream/handle/1/3372911/Brandt_Racism.pdf

brown, A. M. (2017). *Emergent strategy: Shaping change, changing worlds.* A. K. Press.

Bryant-Davis, T., & Ocampo, C. (2005a). Racist incident–based trauma. *The Counseling Psychologist, 33*(4), 479–500. https://doi.org/10.1177/0011000005276465

Bryant-Davis, T., & Ocampo, C. (2005b). The trauma of racism: Implications for counseling, research, and education. *The Counseling Psychologist, 33*(4), 574–578. https://doi.org/10.1177/0011000005276581

Caldera, A. L. (2020). Eradicating anti-Black racism in US schools: A call-to-action for school leaders. *Diversity, Social Justice, and the Educational Leader, 4*(1), 3, 12–25. https://scholarworks.uttyler.edu/dsjel/vol4/iss1/3?utm_source=scholarworks.uttyler.edu%2Fdsjel%2Fvol4%2Fiss1%2F3&utm_medium=PDF&utm_campaign=PDFCoverPages

Calma, J. (2020, June 11). *Black scientists call out racism in their institutions.* The Verge. https://www.theverge.com/21286924/science-racism-strike-stem-black-lives-matter-protests

Carruthers, C. (2018). *Unapologetic: A Black, queer, and feminist mandate for radical movements.* Beacon.

Center for Justice & Reconciliation. (n.d.). *Restorative Justice.* http://restorativejustice.org/restorative-justice/#sthash.AhsZ8JTI.dpbs

Centers for Disease Control and Prevention. (2021). *COVID-19 hospitalization and death by race/ethnicity.* https://www.cdc.gov/coronavirus/2019-ncov/covid-data/investigations-discovery/hospitalization-death-by-race-ethnicity.html

Chancellor, R. L. (2019). Racial battle fatigue: The unspoken burden of Black women faculty in LIS. *Journal of Education for Library and Information Science, 60*(3), 182–189. https://doi.org/10.3138/jelis.2019-0007

Chapman-Hilliard, C., Abdullah, T., Denton, E. G., Holman, A., & Awad, G. (2020). The index of race-related stress-brief: Further validation, cross-validation, and item response theory-based evidence. *Journal of Black Psychology,46(6–7),* 550–580. https://doi.org/10.1177/0095798420947508

Charmaz, K. (2014). *Constructing grounded theory: A practical guide through qualitative analysis.* SAGE.

Clayton, V. (2016, March 1). The problem with the GRE: The exam "is a proxy for asking 'Are you rich?' 'Are you White?' 'Are you male?'" *The Atlantic.* https://www.theatlantic.com/education/archive/2016/03/the-problem-with-the-gre/471633/

Cokley, K. (2007). Critical issues in the measurement of ethnic and racial identity: A referendum on the state of the field. *Journal of Counseling Psychology, 54*(3), 224–234. https://doi.org/10.1037/0022-0167.54.3.224

Combahee River Collective (1983). *Home girls: A Black Feminist Anthology,* 264–274.

Combahee River Collective. (1995). Combahee River Collective statement. In B. Guy-Sheftall (Ed.), *Words of fire: An anthology of African American feminist thought* (pp. 232–240). The New Press. (Original work published 1977).

College Board. (2017, January 9). *College education linked to higher pay, job security, healthier behaviors and more civic involvement: New college board report.* https://newsroom.collegeboard.org/college-education-linked-higher-pay-job-security-healthier-behaviors-and-more-civic-involvement-new

Collins, P. H. (2000). *Black feminist thought: Knowledge, consciousness, and the politics of empowerment.* Routledge New York.

Collins, P. H. (2013). *On intellectual activism.* Temple University Press.

Council of National Psychological Associations for the Advancement of Ethnic Minority Interests. (2016). *Testing and assessment with persons & communities of color.* American Psychological Association. https://www.apa.org/pi/oema/resources/testing-assessment-monograph.pdf

Crenshaw, K. (1990). Mapping the margins: Intersectionality, identity politics, and violence against women of color. *Stanford Law Review, 43,* 1241–1279. https://doi.org/10.2307/1229039

Crenshaw, K., Ritchie, A., Anspach, R., Gilmer, R., & Harris, L. (2015). *Say her name: Resisting police brutality against Black women.* African American Policy Forum. http://static1.squarespace.com/static/53f20d90e4b0b80451158d8c/t/560c068ee4b0af26f72741df/1443628686535/AAPF_SMN_Brief_Full_singles-min.pdf

Croom, N. N. (2017). Promotion beyond tenure: Unpacking racism and sexism in the experiences of Black womyn professors. *The Review of Higher Education, 40*(4), 557–583. https://doi.org/10.1353/rhe.2017.0022

Dancy, T. E., Edwards, K. T., & Earl Davis, J. (2018). Historically White universities and plantation politics: Anti-Blackness and higher education in the Black Lives Matter era. *Urban Education, 53*(2), 176–195. https://doi.org/10.1177/0042085918754328

Daniel, J. L. (1973). Black academic activism. *The Black Scholar, 4*(4), 44–52. https://doi.org/10.1080/00064246.1973.11431294

Davis, A.Y. (1974). *Angela Davis: An autobiography.* Women's Press.

DeCuir-Gunby, J. T., Johnson, O. T., Womble Edwards, C., McCoy, W. N., & White, A. M. (2020). African American professionals in higher education: Experiencing and coping with racial microaggressions. *Race Ethnicity and Education, 23*(4), 492–508. https://doi.org/10.1080/13613324.2019.1579706

Delegal, C. (2020, July 6). *The use of prison labor in universities.* Uloop. https://www.uloop.com/news/view.php/282894/The-Use-of-Prison-Labor-in-Universities-#:~:text=The

The Demands. (2016). *Home page.* https://www.thedemands.org/

Divest UF. (n.d.). *Home page.* https://divestuf.org/#:~:text=In

Donovan, R. A., Galban, D. J., Grace, R. K., Bennett, J. K., & Felicié, S. Z. (2013). Impact of racial macro-and microaggressions in Black women's lives: A preliminary analysis. *Journal of Black Psychology, 39*(2), 185–196. https://doi.org/10.1177/0095798412443259

Du Bois, W. E. B. (1903). *The talented tenth.* James Pott and CompanyEchols, C. M. (2020). *Anti-Blackness is the American way: An integrative assessment of the direct and indirect effects of racially violent histories* [Doctoral dissertation, University of California, Irvine]. Retrieved from https://escholarship.org/uc/item/0r05b7pgd

Eglash, A. (1977). *Beyond restitution: Creative restitution.* In J. Hudson & B. Galaway (Eds.), *Restitution in criminal justice* (pp. 91–129. Lexington.

Essed, P., & Carberry, K. (2020). In the name of our humanity: Challenging academic racism and its effects on the emotional wellbeing of women of colour professors. In R. Majors, K. Carberry, & T.S. Ransaw (Eds.), *The international handbook of Black community mental health* (pp. 61-81. Emerald. https://doi.org/10.1108/978-1-83909-964-920201005

Fanon, F., Sartre, J. P., & Farrington, C. (1963). *The wretched of the earth* (Vol. 36). Grove Press.

Fanon, F. (2008). *Black skin, white masks* (C. L. Markham, Trans.). Pluto Press. (Original work published 1952)

Fitzhough, V. [@DrFNA].freedomtothrive (2019, April 10). *Students demand their universities divest endowments from prisons + re-invest in community initiatives, end labor contracts w. inmates + ensure greater rights for campus workers, defund campus police + invest in mental health. Here's to students re-defining safety! #FreedomCampus* [Twitter post]. https://twitter.com/freedomtothrive/status/1115985817837740032

Freire, P. (1970). *Pedagogy of the oppressed* (M. Bergman Ramos, Trans.). Continuum.

French, B. H., Lewis, J. A., Mosley, D. V., Adames, H. Y., Chavez-Dueñas, N. Y., Chen, G. A., & Neville, H. A. (2020). Toward a psychological framework of radical healing in communities of color. *The Counseling Psychologist*, *48*(1), 14–46. https://doi.org/10.1177/0011000019843506

Gaztambide, D. (2020). From Freud to Fanon to Freire. In L. C. Comas-Díaz & E. Torres Rivera (Eds.) *Liberation psychology: Theory, method, practice, and social justice* (pp. 71–90). American Psychological Association.

Generation Five. (2007, June). *Toward transformative justice: A liberatory approach to child sexual abuse and other forms of intimate and community violence*. http://www.usprisonculture.com/blog/wp-content/uploads/2012/03/G5_Toward_Transformative_Justice.pdf

Genheimer, E. (2016). The impact of minority faculty and staff involvement on minority student experiences. [Master's thesis, Taylor University]. Master of Arts in Higher Education Thesis Collection. http://pillars.taylor.edu/mahe/23?utm_source=pillars.taylor.edu%2Fmahe%2F23&utm_medium=PDF&utm_campaign=PDFCoverPages

Glass, R. D., Morton, J. M., King, J. E., Krueger-Henney, P., Moses, M. S., Sabati, S., & Richardson, T. (2018). The ethical stakes of collaborative community-based social science research. *Urban Education*, *53*(4), 503–531. https://doi.org/10.1177/0042085918762522

Griffin, K. A., Bennett, J. C., & Harris, J. (2013). Marginalizing merit?: Gender differences in Black faculty discourses on tenure, advancement, and professional success. *The Review of Higher Education*, *36*(4), 489–512. https://doi.org/10.1353/rhe.2013.0040

Griggs, B. (2018, May 12). A Black Yale graduate student took a nap in her dorm's common room. So a white student called police. *CNN*. https://www.cnn.com/2018/05/09/us/yale-student-napping-black-trnd/index.html

Grundy, S. (2017). A history of White violence tells us attacks on Black academics are not ending (I know because it happened to me). *Ethnic and Racial Studies*, *40*(11), 1864–1871. https://doi.org/10.1080/01419870.2017.1334933

Gumbs, A. P. (2012, October 29). The shape of my impact. *The Feminist Wire*. https://thefeministwire.com/2012/10/the-shape-of-my-impact/

Hargrove, N. (2020, June 13). Making stories of struggle a thing of the past. *The New York Times*. https://www.nytimes.com/2020/06/13/well/family/family-stories-race-lgbtq.html

Harley, D. A. (2008). Maids of academe: African American women faculty at predominately White institutions. *Journal of African American Studies*, *12*(1), 19–36. https://doi.org/10.1007/s12111-007-9030-5

Havasupai Tribe v. Arizona Bd. of Regents, 204 P.3d 1063, 220 Ariz. 214 (Ct. App. 2008)

Helms, J. E. (1990). *Black and White racial identity: Theory, research, and practice*. Greenwood.

Helms, J. E. (2017). The challenge of making Whiteness visible: Reactions to four Whiteness articles. *The Counseling Psychologist*, *45*(5), 717–726. http://dx.doi.org/10.1177/0011000017718943

Higginbotham, E. B. (1993). *Righteous discontent: The women's movement in the Black Baptist church, 1880–1920*. Harvard University Press.

Hood_Biologist (2020, November 5). *It is a SPECIAL KIND OF HELL for me to know, in painstaking detail, how racism affects people's health & then spend my life knowing exactly how people I love are dying while simultaneously, I can't do anything to prevent it* [Twitter post]. https://twitter.com/Hood_Biologist/status/1324497189943607296

Human Rights Campaign. (2020. *Fatal violence against the transgender community in 2020*. https://www.hrc.org/resources/violence-against-the-trans-and-gender-non-conforming-community-in-2020

Jackson, J. P., Jr. (2001). *Social scientists for social justice: Making the case against segregation* (Vol. 85). New York University Press.

Johnson, L., & Bryan, N. (2017). Using our voices, losing our bodies: Michael Brown, Trayvon Martin, and the spirit murders of Black male professors in the academy. *Race Ethnicity and Education*, *20*(2), 163–177. https://doi.org/10.1080/13613324.2016.1248831

Jones, C. P. (2000). Levels of racism: A theoretic framework and a gardener's tale. *American Journal of Public Health, 90*(8), 1212–1215. https://www.ncbi.nlm.nih.gov/pmc/articles/PMC1446334/pdf/10936998.pdf

Jones, C. P. (2003). Confronting institutionalized racism. *Phylon, 50*, 7–22. https://doi.org/10.2307/4149999

Joseph-Salisbury, R. (2019). Institutionalised Whiteness, racial microaggressions and Black bodies out of place in Higher Education. *Whiteness and Education, 4*(1), 1–17. https://doi.org/10.1080/23793406.2019.1620629

Kaba, M. (2017, October 10). How the school-to-prison pipeline works and why Black girls are particularly at risk. *Teen Vogue*. https://www.teenvogue.com/story/how-the-school-to-prison-pipeline-works

Keating, D., Cha, A. E., & Florit, G. (2020, November 20). "I just pray God will help me": Racial, ethnic minorities reel from higher covid-19 death rates. *The Washington Post*. https://www.washingtonpost.com/graphics/2020/health/covid-race-mortality-rate/

Lewis, J. A., Mendenhall, R., Harwood, S. A., & Huntt, M. B. (2013). Coping with gendered racial microaggressions among Black women college students. *Journal of African American Studies, 17*(1), 51–73. https://doi.org/10.1007/s12111-012-9219-0

Lewis, J. A., & Neville, H. A. (2015). Construction and initial validation of the Gendered Racial Microaggressions Scale for Black women. *Journal of Counseling Psychology, 62*(2), 289–301. http://dx.doi.org/10.1037/cou0000062

Li, D., & Koedel, C. (2017). Representation and salary gaps by race-ethnicity and gender at selective public universities. *Educational Researcher, 46*(7), 343–354. https://doi.org/10.3102/0013189X17726535

Lomax, T. (2015, May 18). Black women's lives don't matter in academia either, or why I quit academic spaces that don't value Black women's lives. *The Feminist Wire*. https://thefeministwire.com/2015/05/black-womens-lives-dont-matter-in-academia-either-or-why-i-quit-academic-spaces-that-dont-value-black-womens-life/

Lorde, A. (1984). The master's tools will never dismantle the master's house. *Sister outsider: Essays and Speeches, 1*, 10–14.

Louis, D. A., Rawls, G. J., Jackson-Smith, D., Chambers, G. A., Phillips, L. L., & Louis, S. L. (2016). Listening to our voices: Experiences of Black faculty at predominantly White research universities with microaggression. *Journal of Black Studies, 47*(5), 454–474. https://doi.org/10.1177/0021934716632983

Machado, J. (2018, November 14). *Professor calls police on Black student who put her feet up in class*. Daily Dot. https://www.dailydot.com/irl/professors-are-policing-black-bodies-in-classrooms-too/

Madusa, S. (2020, June 5). *We need to let go of respectability politics in the fight for Black liberation*. HNHH. https://www.hotnewhiphop.com/we-need-to-let-go-of-respectability-politics-in-the-fight-for-black-liberation-news.111905.html

Matthew, P. (2016, November 23). What is faculty diversity worth to a university?: The "invisible labor" done by professors of color is not usually rewarded with tenure and promotion. But it is more important now than ever. *The Atlantic*. https://www.theatlantic.com/education/archive/2016/11/what-is-faculty-diversity-worth-to-a-university/508334/

McCoy, D. L. (2006). Entering the academy: Exploring the socialization experiences of African American male faculty. (Doctoral dissertation, Louisiana State University). Retrieved from http://etd.lsu.edu/docs/available/ etd04052006-143046/

McCoy-Wilson, S. (2020). "We have a Black professor?" Rejecting African Americans as disseminators of knowledge. *Journal of Black Studies, 51*(6),545-564 https://doi.org/10.1177%2F0021934720925777

McInnis, T. D. (2017, February 10). *On being a queer Black woman in academia*. For Harriet. http://www.forharriet.com/2017/02/on-being-queen-black-woman-in-academia.html

Mehl, B. (1969). Academic colonialism: A new look. *Educational Leadership, 27*(3), 243–246.

Menon, M., Pendakur, R., & Perali, F. (2015). All in the family: How do social capital and material wellbeing affect relational wellbeing? *Social Indicators Research, 124*(3), 889–910. https://doi.org/10.1007/s11205-014-0816-2

Mills, C. (1997). *The racial contract*. Cornell University Press.

Mingus, M. (n.d.). *Transformative justice: A brief description*. https://transformharm.org/transformative-justice/

Morris, M. (2016). *Pushout: The criminalization of Black girls in schools*. The New Press.

Mosley, D. V., Hargons, C. N., Meiller, C., Angyal, B., Wheeler, P., Davis, C., & Stevens-Watkins, D. (2021). Critical consciousness of anti-Black racism: A practical model to prevent and resist racial trauma. *Journal of Counseling Psychology, 68*(1), 1–16. https://doi.org/10.1037/cou0000430

Mosley, D. V., Neville, H. A., Chavez-Dueñas, N. Y., Adames, H. Y., Lewis, J. A., & French, B. H. (2020). Radical hope in revolting times: Proposing a culturally relevant psychological framework. *Social and Personality Psychology Compass, 14*(1). https://doi.org/10.1111/spc3.12512.

Murakami, K. (2020, October). Racial equity in funding for higher ed. *Inside Higher Ed*. https://www.insidehighered.com/news/2020/10/29/racial-disparities-higher-education-funding-could-widen-during-economic-downturn

Mustaffa, J. B. (2017). Mapping violence, naming life: A history of anti-Black oppression in the higher education system. *International Journal of Qualitative Studies in Education, 30*(8), 711–727. https://doi.org/10.1080/09518398.2017.1350299

Neville, H. A., Lilly, R. L., Duran, G., Lee, R. M., & Browne, L. (2000). Construction and initial validation of the color-blind racial attitudes scale (CoBRAS). *Journal of Counseling Psychology, 47*(1), 59–70. https://doi.org/10.1037/0022-0167.47.1.59

Neville, H. A., & Pieterse, A. L. (2009). *Racism, White supremacy, and resistance: Contextualizing Black American experiences*. In H. A. Neville, B. M. Tynes, & S. O. Utsey (Eds.), *Handbook of African American Psychology* (pp. 159–172). SAGE.

NewsOne Staff. (2011, August 17). *Black college students need Black professors*. NewsOne. https://newsone.com/1466745/black-college-students-need-black-professors/

Oppel, R. A., Jr. & Taylor, D. B. (2020). Here's what you need to know about Breonna Taylor's death. *The New York Times*. https://www.nytimes.com/article/breonna-taylor-police.html

Parker, V. E. (2017). *How I got over: A study of the tenure experiences of Black female professors at predominantly White institutions* [Doctoral dissertations, Louisiana State University]. https://digitalcommons.lsu.edu/gradschool_dissertations/4381

Petru, C. (Host). (2018, June). Mia Mingus of the Bay Area Transformative Justice Collective [Audio podcast episode]. *KPFA*. https://kpfa.org/area941/episode/ep-5-mia-mingus-of-the-bay-area-transformative-justice-collective/

Poteat, T., Millett, G., Nelson, L. E., & Beyrer, C. (2020). Understanding COVID-19 risks and vulnerabilities among Black communities in America: The lethal force of syndemics. *Annals of Epidemiology*. 47, 1–3. https://doi.org/10.1016/j.annepidem.2020.05.004

Prilleltensky I. (2012). Wellness as fairness. *American Journal of Community Psychology, 49*(1–2), 1–21. https://doi.org/10.1007/s10464-011-9448-8

Quaye, S. J., Karikari, S. N., Carter, K. D., Okello, W. K., & Allen, C. (2020). "Why can't I just chill?": The visceral nature of racial battle fatigue. *Journal of College Student Development, 61*(5), 609–623. https://doi.org/10.1353/csd.2020.0058

Quaye, S. J., Shaw, M. D., & Hill, D. C. (2017). Blending scholar and activist identities: Establishing the need for scholar activism. *Journal of Diversity in Higher Education, 10*(4), 381–399. https://doi.org/10.1037/dhe0000060

Queen_yacinee (2018, January 23). *yall make a bad habit of stealing black women's ideas in academia and its really annoying and disheartening. Like I'm about to just stop talking at this point cuz im tired of my ideas being regurgitated to me like they weren't mine in the first place* [Twitter post]. https://twitter.com/queen_yacinee/status/955817307326074880

Quon, V. (2020, November 10). *Academia alienates BIPOC knowledge*. The Eye Opener. https://theeyeopener.com/2020/11/ivory-tinted-glasses-how-westernized-academia-alienates-bipoc-knowledge/

Reddick, R. J., Taylor, B. J., Nagbe, M., & Taylor, Z. W. (2020). Professor beware: Liberating faculty voices of color working in predominantly White institutions and geographic settings. *Education and Urban Society, 53*(5), 536–560. https://doi.org/10.1177/0013124520933349

Rothman, L. (2017, March 07). The disturbing history of African-Americans and medican research goes beyond Henrietta Lacks. *Time*. https://time.com/4746297/henrietta-lacks-movie-history-research-oprah/

Settles, I. H., Jones, M. K., Buchanan, N. T., & Dotson, K. (2020). Epistemic exclusion: Scholar(ly) devaluation that marginalizes faculty of color. *Journal of Diversity in Higher Education*. https://doi.org/10.1037/dhe0000174

Shih, C. F. (2010). Academic colonialism and the struggle for indigenous knowledge systems in Taiwan. *Social Alternatives*, *29*(1), 44–47. http://faculty.ndhu.edu.tw/~cfshih/journal-articles/201003-1.pdf

Singh, A. (2020). Building a counseling psychology of liberation: The path behind us, under us, and before us. *The Counseling Psychologist*, *48*(8), 1109–1130. https://doi.org/10.1177/0011000020959007

Skloot, R. (2017). *The immortal life of Henrietta Lacks*. Broadway Paperbacks.

Smith, L. T. (2013). *Decolonizing methodologies: Research and Indigenous peoples*. Zed.

Speight, S. L. (2007). Internalized racism: One more piece of the puzzle. *The Counseling Psychologist*, *35*(1), 126–134. https://doi.org/10.1177/0011000006295119

Stein, S. (2016). Universities, slavery, and the unthought of anti-Blackness. *Cultural Dynamics*, *28*(2), 169–187. https://doi.org/10.1177/0921374016634379

Stevenson, A. (Ed.). (2010). *Oxford Dictionary of English*. Oxford University Press.

Sue, D. W., Nadal, K. L., Capodilupo, C. M., Lin, A. I., Torino, G. C., & Rivera, D. P. (2008). Racial microaggressions against Black Americans: Implications for counseling. *Journal of Counseling & Development*, *86*(3), 330–338. https://doi.org/10.1002/j.1556-6678.2008.tb00517.x

Suzuki, D., & Mayorga, E. (2014). Scholar-activism: A twice told tale. *Multicultural Perspectives*, *16*(1), 16–20. https://doi.org/10.1080/15210960.2013.867405

T'Shaka, O. (2012). Africana Studies Department history: San Francisco State University. *The Journal of Pan African Studies*, *5*(7), 13–32. https://link.gale.com/apps/doc/A316072914/AONE?u=tall22798&sid=googleScholar&xid=250e08db

Taylor, D. B. (2020). George Floyd protests: A timeline. *The New York Times*. https://www.nytimes.com/article/george-floyd-protests-timeline.html

Taylor, H., Jr. (2020, July 22). Breonna Taylor's death and racist police violence highlight danger of gentrification. NBC News. https://www.nbcnews.com/think/opinion/breonna-taylor-s-death-racist-police-violence-highlight-danger-gentrification-ncna1234472

TEDx Talks (2016, March 21). *Let's get to the root of racial injustice | Megan Ming Francis | TEDxRainier* [Video]. https://www.youtube.com/watch?v=-aCn72iX09s&t=464s&ab_channel=TEDxTalks

Thelin, J. (2004). *A history of American higher education*. Johns Hopkins University Press.

Torres Rivera, E. (2020). Concepts of liberation psychology. In L. C. Comas-Díaz & E. Torres Rivera (Eds.), *Liberation psychology: Theory, method, practice, and social justice* (pp. 41–51). American Psychological Association. https://psycnet.apa.org/doi/10.1037/0000198-000

U.S. Department of Education. (2016, July). *The state of racial diversity in the educator workforce*. https://www2.ed.gov/rschstat/eval/highered/racial-diversity/state-racial-diversity-workforce.pdf

Vandelinder, E. (2016, March 21). Mentorship, promotion among challenges of keeping Black faculty. *Missourian*. https://www.columbiamissourian.com/news/higher_education/mentorship-promotion-among-challenges-of-keeping-black-faculty/article_8ce54bfa-e494-11e5-a5eb-b33315c55989.html

Warren, C. J. E. (1954). Brown v. board of education. *United States Reports*, *347*(1954), 483. https://www.whatsoproudlywehail.org/wp-content/uploads/2013/01/Warren_Brown-v-Board-of-Education.pdf

Williams, K. L., Burt, B. A., Clay, K. L., & Bridges, B. K. (2019). Stories untold: Counter-narratives to anti-Blackness and deficit-oriented discourse concerning HBCUs. *American Educational Research Journal*, *56*(2), 556–599. https://doi.org/10.3102/0002831218802776

Winkle-Wagner R., McCoy D. L., Lee-Johnson J. (2020). Creating porous ivory towers: Two-way socialization processes that embrace Black students' identities in Academia. In J. Weidman & L. DeAngelo (Eds.), *Socialization in higher education and the early career* (pp. 73–89). Springer. https://doi.org/10.1007/978-3-030-33350-8_5.

Winkle-Wagner, R. (2009). *The unchosen me: Race, gender, and identity among Black women in college.* Johns Hopkins University Press.

Wood, D. (2020, September 23). *As pandemic deaths add up, racial disparities persist—and in some cases worsen.* NPR. https://www.npr.org/sections/health-shots/2020/09/23/914427907/as-pandemic-deaths-add-up-racial-disparities-persist-and-in-some-cases-worsen

Young, J. L., & Hines, D. E. (2018). Killing my spirit, renewing my soul: Black female professors' critical reflections on spirit killings while teaching. *Women, Gender, and Families of Color, 6*(1), 18–25. https://doi.org/10.5406/womgenfamcol.6.1.0018

Zhou, L. (2019, October 21). Low-income community members forgotten. *The Brown and White.* https://thebrownandwhite.com/2019/10/20/a-better-bethlehem-needed-low-income-community-members-forgotten-in-fastest-growing-market/

CHAPTER THREE

Confronting Anti-Black Racism and Promoting Social Justice

Applications Through Social Media

Erlanger A. Turner, Maryam Jernigan-Noesi, and Isha Metzger

D iscrimination, oppression, and injustice in America have a significant impact on the mental health functioning among Black people in America. Decades of research indicate the deleterious effects of anti-Black racism on mental health among Black Americans, including both youth and adults (Franklin-Jackson & Carter, 2007; Metzger et al., 2018; Turner, 2019). According to some scholars, racism and oppression are chronic sources of stress among Black people (Belgrave & Allison, 2014; Helms et al., 2012; Utsey & Payne, 2000; Williams et al., 2014). More recently, police brutality against Black people and injustice related to police violence continue to be an increasing concern. Given increased use of social media (e.g., Instagram and Twitter), awareness of dehumanization has increased through content being shared on social networking sites, resulting in additional concerns about racial stress and mental health difficulties (Turner & Turner, 2021). Literature on police brutality and anti-Black racism have shown that both indirect and direct exposure can result in poor mental health outcomes (Bor et al., 2018; Bryant-Davis et al., 2017; Turner, 2019). For example, Bor et al. (2018) found that Black people reported significantly worse mental health compared to their White counterparts after events of police killings regardless of if the incident was in their community.

Anti-Black Racism and Mental Health

In the 21st century, anti-Black racism and racial injustice contribute to mental health difficulties among Black people. Scholars have long contended that experiences of racism, racial discrimination, and racial harassment have deleterious effects on mental health and well-being (Bryant-Davis & Ocampo, 2005; Carter 2007; Cavanagh & Obasi, 2020; Harrell, 2010; Helms et al., 2012; Jernigan & Daniel, 2011; Turner & Turner, 2021). More specifically, experiences of racism have been found to predict psychobiological responses, including hypervigilance, disruptions to cognitive processing, headaches, memory impairment, decision-making, and sleep difficulty, among other symptoms (Bryant-Davis & Ocampo, 2005; Carlson, 1997; Carter, 2007). Carter and Pieterse (2020) proposed that certain race-related encounters can lead to significant levels of stress responses, based on the subjective experience of the individual, and thus potentially indicate a racially traumatic response. Racially stressful encounters can be categorized as those that are hostile (e.g., racialized interpersonal conflict), avoidant-hostile (e.g., being perceived as threatening due to one's race), or avoidant (e.g., being denied service). For Black people who report regular experiences of racism, encounters of racial discrimination are likely blatant and symbolic, direct and indirect, overt and covert, and micro and macro experiences. Moreover, negative race-related encounters often begin early in childhood and continue over the course of the life span (Morris, 2007; Quintana, 1998). Given that approximately 75% of Black people report that they experience racial discrimination, the recent declarations of racism as a public health issue are long overdue (Anderson, 2019).

Although there is a tendency to focus on interpersonal experiences of racism, James Jones's (1972), seminal scholarship defined racism relative to multiple domains, which also included cultural and systemic domains. Systemic racism embodies laws, policies, practices, and protocols that serve to underscore a system of racial social hierarchy, which favors one racial group over others, thus furthering racial inequities (Ajwani, 2020; Tourse et al., 2019). In addition to direct experiences of racism and racial discrimination, for many Black individuals vicarious experiences of racism, which they may witness or learn of indirectly through family members, friends, or peers, also contribute to the cumulative effects of racial stress and trauma. As such, the witnessing of racial violence against Black bodies as reported by national media, viewed and reshared on social media outlets, and the stories that may be communicated within Black communities (who likely identify with victims on the basis of race) can be retriggering. Despite these challenges and risks, many Black people continue to survive and thrive. One of the methods that may help the Black community navigate these psychological risks is through engaging with using social networking sites. The focus of this chapter will be to discuss the impacts of anti-Black racism on mental health, describe how social media contributes to promoting social justice, and offer applications for confronting anti-Black racism through social media use.

Using Social Media to Promote Social Justice

According to data from the Pew Research Center (2021), social media use has significantly increased over time. In 2010, approximately 45% of Americans reported using social networking platforms, and use increased to 73% by 2019. Furthermore, the Pew Research Center (2021) notes that Black people reportedly use some social networking sites at a higher rate than White people (see Table 3.1). This increased use can serve as an avenue to confront anti-Black racism and promote social justice efforts to benefit the Black community. Many individuals have used social networking sites to start hashtags to promote social justice, to highlight racial injustice, and to promote healing through the use of offering psychoeducation on racial stress and mental health. For example, Jones and Anderson (2020) discussed how social networking platforms can be used to

(a) reduce stigma about mental health in the Black community; (b) provide resources in access, utilization, and quality of mental health care; and (c) increase mental health literacy. Later in this chapter, applications of social media platforms to confront anti-Black racism and promote social justice will be discussed in detail.

Over the last 15 years, the emergence of using hashtags on social networking platforms to engage in social justice efforts has drastically increased. This has resulted in more scholarship on social media use and activism (e.g., Mundt et al., 2018; Wilkins et al., 2019; Yang, 2016). Some have emphasized how hashtags on social media allow for individuals to engage in collective action, mobilize movements, and build coalitions (Mundt et al., 2018; Wilkins et al., 2019). Furthermore, social media hashtags are an important component of successful activism because they allow minoritized groups to garner support of allies (Wilkins et al., 2019). With respect to Black people, the use of #BlackLivesMatter has been one of the earliest to capitalize on social media platforms to fight racial injustice.

TABLE 3.1 USE OF SOCIAL NETWORKING PLATFORMS BY RACE

Race	Social Networking Platform			
	YouTube	Facebook	Instagram	Twitter
Black	84%	74%	49%	29%
White	79%	67%	35%	22%

Note: Data obtained from the Pew Research Center (2019).

During summer 2013, three Black women activists (Alicia Garza, Patrisse Cullors, and Opal Tometi) created the Black Lives Matter hashtag after the killing of Trayvon Martin— an unarmed Black teen whose murderer was acquitted. Since going viral in 2014, the Black Lives Matter (BLM) movement has continued to thrive and expand, with chapters being formed around the globe (www.blacklivesmatter.com). During summer 2020, the BLM movement played a critical role in galvanizing people to fight for justice after the police killings of Breonna Taylor (an African American woman killed in her home in Louisville, Kentucky) and George Floyd (an African American man killed in Minneapolis, Minnesota). BLM activists helped create protests and peaceful rallies around the world. The use of hashtags on social media platforms provided a quick approach to organizing events, mobilizing activists, and generating donations. Over the years, numerous hashtag movements have emerged such as #CiteBlackScholars, #Academics4BlackLives, and #BlackInTheIvory. These social media campaigns and movements have served critical roles in fighting injustice, being community, and raising awareness to structural racism. For example, #Academics4BlackLives hosted a series of webinars to support survival and wellness among Black people and offered training for White allies on anti-Black racism, as well as understanding the toll of racial stress (www.academics4blacklives).

The Role of the BLM Movement in Promoting Social Justice

There is a long history of systemic racism and oppression against African Americans in America that includes the transatlantic slave trade, the Jim Crow era, mass incarceration, and police-sanctioned violence. As such, African Americans continue to heal from the residual effects of slavery and oppression, struggle for human equality in the United States, and fight to restore and retain our history and strengths. BLM, which has been referred to as the new civil rights movement of the 21st century (Clayton, 2018; Thompson & Thurston, 2017), initially began as a hashtag (#BlackLivesMatter) on social media in 2013 after Trayvon Martin was murdered by a White volunteer neighborhood watchman who was later acquitted. The BLM movement began to gain traction in 2014 when Michael Brown was murdered in Ferguson, Missouri, and the White police officer involved in his death was not indicted (i.e., formally charged for a crime). After organizing the "Black Life Matters Ride," similar to the freedom rides during the civil rights movement, to Ferguson for over 600 people, BLM has since evolved to a rally cry, social movement, and global network with more than 40 chapters (Watson et al., 2020).

Among BLM's mission is "combatting and countering acts of violence, creating space for Black imagination and innovation, and centering Black joy." To date, BLM has been active in organizing peaceful protests in response to numerous deaths of African Americans by the hands of the police, including Tamir Rice, Tanisha Anderson, Laquan McDonald, Freddie Gray, Sandra Bland, Botham Jean, Alton Sterling, Mya Hall, Eric Garner, Philando Castile, George Floyd, Breonna Taylor, and more. BLM continues to fight for many of the issues of previous Black liberation movements while using the same technique that the civil rights movement used, nonviolent direct action, to bring attention to these issues (Clayton, 2018). Although BLM is focused on fighting police brutality and racially motivated violence against Black people, many of these protests are being met with armed resistance from local and state police departments. In addition to illuminating the deeply entrenched issue of racism in the United States, the movement also emphasizes that *all* Black lives matter, including those who have often been marginalized in previous Black liberation movements, such as women, transgender, and queer Blacks, which "differs from past activism that challenged racism as a singular issue" (Scott & Brown, 2016). In addition, BLM supports the development of new Black leaders, specifically leadership from women, queer, and trans people in the movement, many of whom coordinate their movements on social media and online.

Applications for Using Social Media

As social media use has increased, more individuals and organizations have joined to disseminate information to the public. In the following sections, we discuss several applications for using social media to address anti-Black racism.

Social Media as a Social Justice Tool

According to Carney (2016), "With rapidly developing technology and the rise of social media, the public sphere today looks very different than it did even 10 years ago" (p. 183). Historically, individuals have had to mobilize and organize social justice efforts through in-person meetings and protests. Given the use of technology and social media platforms people can now engage in activism and confronting anti-Black racism through platforms such as Twitter. Despite the potential for fake news and censorship, many continue to use Twitter as an outlet to engage in activism and confront racism. Twitter is a microblogging platform that allows users to post messages up to 280 characters. The social media platform offers opportunities for engaging in activism, but because of limitations on word count users must carefully craft their messages (Carney, 2016). This often results in people stringing together threads or linking content using hashtags. Furthermore, hashtags such as #BlackLivesMatter creates easily searchable posts and promotes discourse around racial injustice.

Over the last 10 years, Twitter has been one of the most commonly used social media platforms for engaging in activism. For example, since the BLM movement many have used Twitter to discuss police brutality and organize protests. Following numerous incidents of police killings of Black people hashtags with victims' names have brought awareness to racial injustice. In examining the research on Twitter and social justice, many articles describe ways the platform has been helpful to create community and promote policy change at the local and national levels. One qualitative textual analysis of Twitter posts following the nonindictments of officers in the murders of Michael Brown and Eric Garner found that Black people frequently used Twitter to call out structural racism and confront those who attempted to undermine the BLM movement by posting using #AllLivesMatter (Carney, 2016). Another study examined Twitter posts during 2014 and found that BLM or #BlackLivesMatter was mentioned over 660,000 times during the 11-month search period (Ince et al., 2017). Ince et al. (2017) note that "when hashtags are extremely successful, such as #BlackLivesMatter, they can create a community of like-minded people who can sustain a conversation and even mobilize offline" (p. 1818).

During summer 2020, the world witnessed the firsthand benefit of social media platforms such as Twitter. In the midst of a global coronavirus pandemic and a racism pandemic, hashtags including #BlackLivesMatter, #BlackInTheIvory, and #Academics-4BlackLives were trending on Twitter. Black people and other minoritized communities joined together to confront anti-Black racism in communities and within university settings. After the killings of George Floyd and Breonna Taylor, individuals around the globe engaged in protests and peaceful rallies to push for justice and systemic change within the justice system. #Academics4BlackLives was created by a group of Black counseling psychologists and their non-Black colleagues (www.academics4blacklives.com/). The group known as Academics for Black Survival and Wellness was formed to address racial trauma experienced by Black people in academia and to resist anti-Blackness and White supremacy. The group quickly mobilized and offered a series of workshops and events to support Black people in academic settings and to foster accountability among non-Black allies. Twitter and other social media platforms provided a critical role in these social justice efforts. Whereas most people may use social media platforms for personal use, it has also played an important role in confronting anti-Black racism and social justice efforts.

Social Media as an Academic Tool

An important aspect of social justice is a person's ability to recognize their own potential to impact change in the context of their proximal and distal societal environment (Russell, 2015). This aspect of social justice has not been a strong focal point within the traditional research community; however, there have been a few advancements in how research has been used to advance social justice initiatives targeting specific communities. For example, the GenerationPulse Project utilized social media coupled with relational-cultural and positive youth development theories to increase youth awareness of social justice and humanitarian issues in a safe and empathetic environment online (Liang et al., 2010). This section will provide an overview of several possible applications for using social media to confront anti-Black racism and to promote social justice.

Social media is frequently utilized by private citizens to advocate for and educate others about historical and current social justice issues. In academia, issues of race, gender, and intersectional disparities in social justice are also regularly researched in clinical and community psychology through studies such as "inequality, distress and harm-reduction: a social justice approach to self-injury" (Inckle, 2020) and "social work, social justice, and the causes to which we are called: Attitudes, ally behavior, and activism" (Ash, 2020). Notedly, the field of psychology sits atop a history of violating the trust of citizens, gate keeping, and cultural exploitation in order to uphold a status quo of dominance and subordination (Vasquez, 2012). This is evidenced by issues such as racist themes present in early psychological testing, the Tuskegee syphilis study, and eugenic philosophies as described in Robert Guthrie's (2004) *Even the Rat Was White: A Historical View of Psychology* (Turner, 2019; Vasquez, 2012). Although progress has been made in the relationship between the psychological sciences and the public, we recognize that researchers, practitioners, and community organizations have the responsibility to rebuild trust and provide care to at-risk marginalized communities. One way that this has been recently achieved is through utilizing social media as an academic tool for social justice.

Another example is The EMPOWER lab at the University of Georgia (UGA), which focuses on engaging minorities in prevention, outreach, wellness, education, and research (directed by the third author, Dr. Isha Metzger). The EMPOWER lab operates its social media as a platform for sharing scientific information and facilitating conversations about race and ethnicity. Of its social media initiatives, research spotlights regularly feature summaries of peer-reviewed articles that convey the importance of understanding and treating racial trauma. Furthermore, the lab's social media publicize research-based infographics regarding the negative health outcomes caused by racial discrimination. One such post presents conclusions from the Center on the Developing Child at Harvard University about chronic stress among minority children who experience or witness discrimination. These snippets of knowledge attend to fundamental values of fairness and equity among psychological researchers and mental health care providers striving toward social justice (Constantine et al., 2007; Vera & Speight, 2003). As the demographics and sociopolitical trends change in the United States, diversity and inclusion in psychological research and practice are more imperative than ever (American Psychological Association, 2003). The EMPOWER lab also promotes civil rights such as voting in elections as a remedy for historical disenfranchisement (Walton & Dweck, 2009). Posts outlining calls to action following the loss of Breonna Taylor and those celebrating Kwanzaa facilitated critical incident analysis that helped to emphasize racial and cultural awareness across social media platforms. The Black & EMPOWERed podcast is another initiative of the EMPOWER lab wherein the most recent episode addresses the presence of people of color in academia and provides details about how to succeed in a competitive field like clinical psychology. By sharing personal stories about their own academic trajectories, the hosts create a "brave space" that is honest to their own values and capable of exploring controversy with civility (Arao & Clemens, 2013). In addition, the EMPOWER lab created an online learning tool, the CARE (Cultivating Awareness and Resilience through Empowerment) package, that can be distributed throughout social media platforms to teach self-directed cognitive, emotional, and behavioral skills for overcoming racial stressors to practice individually or with family, friends, and community (Metzger, 2020). Efforts like these must increase in order for the utilization of social media to reach its full potential to help others through the psychology community.

Societal events, both historical and current, necessitate conversations about race and heritage, but such topics have been difficult to discuss for many. Even in spaces that encourage comfortable self-expression, participants report a variety of negative emotions when engaged in evidence-based cognitive and behavioral strategies for confronting potential involvement in oppressive acts, listening to stories of the oppressed, and responding to challenges to their worldview (Arao & Clemens, 2013). Yet psychologists utilize research to uncover underlying psychological mechanisms behind social phenomena and develop psychological interventions to help solve individual and social problems (Walton & Dweck, 2009). Psychology, as a social science, was called on to deliver unbiased evidence for documenting the psychological and social barriers to equality during the civil rights movement (King, 1968). Today, guidelines are implemented for psychologists to educate, train, research, and practice with multicultural competence (American Psychological Association, 2003; Constantine et al., 2007; Vera & Speight, 2003), which includes standards for culturally informed care.

Social justice–related research is in high demand, and clinical and community graduate training programs are particularly situated to fulfill the needs of marginalized populations. As such, a letter signed by 43 graduate students in the clinical psychology PhD program at UGA expressed dissatisfaction with the program's lack of racial literacy and diversity efforts. The students urged institutional action to engage the community in social justice dialogue, mandate multicultural competence training, and diversify the faculty and staff. Most importantly, the letter highlighted areas in UGA's policy that could infringe on the students' free speech by prohibiting or retaliating against nonviolent protests. A similar letter signed by 17 graduate students commended the EMPOWER lab's use of social media to reach out to the UGA and surrounding community, and as such these 17 students collaborated with the Clinical Psychology Clinic at UGA to develop a racial trauma guide in the summer of the "racism pandemic" (Racism Pandemic Task Force, 2020). Through these efforts and others, the EMPOWER lab provides an excellent example of the ways academia can positively impact behavioral and mental health for people of color through using social media platforms.

Social Media as a Tool for Psychoeducation and Healing

Social media can be a powerful tool to disseminate information to the general public to inform them about the psychological and related health consequences of racism, as well as other issues pertaining to the Black community. It is reported that social media outlets, such as Facebook and Instagram, have the capacity to reach large audiences from the convenience of their phones, computers, or other digital devices (Delfino, 2020). Facebook Live continues to increase in popularity, climbing to 2 billion viewers in 2020. In 2018, some estimates included up to 3.5 billion views of Facebook Live content, which is said to produce six times as many interactions as traditional videos and yield larger engagement from audience members for longer periods of time (Zuckerberg, 2019).

In the summer of 2020, the Institute for the Study and Promotion of Race and Culture curated a series of presentations in response to national Black Live Matter protests and increased calls for discourse about race, racism, antiracism, and anti-Blackness. Four separate videos dedicated to supporting Black communities, confronting anti-Blackness, and working toward antiracist identities among non-Black people of color and White individuals, and modeling positive Black racial identity development were streamed over the course of 2 months. Topics included "Racism Recovery: Racial Wellness Toolkit" (8,400 views), "White Folx and Anti-Racism" (1,900 views), "AAPI/APIDAS Navigating Anti-Blackness" (2,100 views), and "Unapologetically Black: Black Racial Identity Development" (1,800 views). Panelists were predominantly mental health professionals and those in related human service industries. With minimal marketing outside of social media announcements prior to the events, the reach of the videos, which included high engagement from live audiences, as well as post-live commentary, and shares continues to increase. The goal of disseminating information to the public in an effort to address anti-Black racism and offer support to those navigating the impacts of racism was met at an arguably higher rate than would have been the case using individual (e.g., therapeutic setting) or in-person (e.g., training) methods.

Instagram, a social media company acquired by Facebook, also has a mechanism for live streaming video content through its IGTV mechanism, as well as digital content in the form of pictures and short video clips. Instagram is the third most populated social media channel and is known to attract younger generations of followers interested in digital content. As such, Instagram is another mechanism frequently used to offer content that confronts anti-Black racism. The aforementioned @theEMPOWERLab has been documenting its community-based research and social justice work on Instagram;

however, it is not the first of its kind. For example, the @theEMPOWERLab follows in the footsteps of other social media pages like the @mindfield_drj Instagram page that features infographics, historical content, and videos that facilitate awareness of issues related to the Black community and offer guidance on how to access resources to navigate a range of topics. The @mindfield_drj Instagram page is curated by a licensed psychologist with expertise in race and culture, racial trauma, and researchers' racial health disparities among Black girls and women. As such, videos, shared stories, images, and quotes are created to engage the audience by highlighting common misperceptions, providing factual knowledge about the experiences of Black people and communities, sharing research findings to increase dissemination of science to the public, and offer video content featuring experts who offer guidance on health-related topics impacting the Black community toward the goal of discussing healing and coping strategies.

Podcasting is another method used by psychologists and mental health therapists to shed light on social injustice and coping strategies. For example, podcasts hosted by two Black Los Angeles–based licensed psychologists offer science-based information and wellness strategies on mental health. The *Homecoming* podcast with Dr. Thema Bryant-Davis and *The Breakdown* with Dr. Earl Mental Health, hosted by Dr. Erlanger Turner, offer their audience psychoeducation on topics such as racial trauma, recognizing your strengths, racial battle fatigue, and racial trauma during COVID. Given that many Black people may be reluctant to seek mental health treatment, podcasts offer opportunities to break stigma around mental health and encourage individuals to consider active coping strategies in the midst of everyday anti-Black racism. As podcasting continues to grow, more individuals may use the information as a source of identifying self-help strategies.

Social media offers the opportunity to engage a wide range of people. As is the case with any public forum, a large audience is accompanied by a multitude of perspectives. This may include those who espouse anti-Black sentiment, racist views, or are generally dedicated to negative commentary. Race is a topic that permeates all aspects of society; however, explicit discourse that names anti-Black racism and its consequences is more rare. Therefore, it is likely that efforts to highlight race-related topics may generate some support *and* negative feedback. Those who choose to use social media as a public platform are wise to consider their personal stance with regard to when and what content they will share. Additionally, professionals such as psychologists, academics, mental health professionals, or activists can become targeted by those who oppose their views. This may include coworkers in places of employment, administrations within academic institutions, and peers and family members. There are a number of cases of academics, for example, who were placed on leave or left institutions due to backlash from commentary related to race. Lisa Durden, an adjunct faculty member, reportedly offered comments in support of the Black Lives Matter movement in an interview. She later stated that she was wrongfully fired after defending the movement publicly (Adely, 2018). Any professional choosing to use social media in an attempt to confront antiracism and anti-Blackness would be remiss to not consider the potential implications of their actions. This is likely why many professionals using Facebook, Instagram, or Twitter have opted to verbally include or write statements indicating that their views and opinions shared are their own and do not represent a reflection of their institution.

Ethical Considerations for Mental Health Professionals

Numerous organizations have a code of ethical conduct to help guide professional activities in research, practice, training, and consultation. For example, the ethics code by the American Psychological Association describes the ethical guidelines that apply to psychologist activities across a variety of settings including scientific, educational, and professional roles (APA, 2002). The current version of the APA ethics code applies to settings such as in-person therapy, telephone, internet, and other electronic forms of communication. However, to our knowledge there are few professional organizations that identify ethical guidelines regarding social media use by mental health professionals. As a result, mental health professionals must be prepared to interpret existing ethics codes and apply them to social networking sites such as Facebook, Twitter, and Instagram (Lannin & Scott, 2013).

Ethical guidelines are extremely important for providing guidance on how to navigate professional behavior. Kolmes (2012) suggested that mental health training programs should offer education and guidance on integrating ethical use of social media into their curriculum. However, it appears that few programs discuss issues around professional use of social media or limits of social media use on therapeutic relationships (Kolmes, 2012; Lannin & Scott, 2013). According to the APA (2017) Code of Ethics,

> When psychologists provide public advice or comment via print, Internet, or other electronic transmission, they take precautions to ensure that statements (1) are based on their professional knowledge, training, or experience in accord with appropriate psychological literature and practice; (2) are otherwise consistent with this Ethics Code; and (3) do not indicate that a professional relationship has been established with the recipient. (Section 5.04)

However, one of the challenges with offering mental health psychoeducation (e.g., Twitter town hall or Instagram Live) on social media platforms is that the public may not understand the limitations and many professionals have limited guidance on the risk involved with their professional license or liability insurance. It is important that professional organizations begin to grapple with ethical use of social networking sites and identify guidance on specific ethical principles to aid training programs in developing competence in using emerging technologies.

Information posted on social networking sites by mental health professionals may have potential to be harmful regardless of when the information is posted. Baier (2019) noted that content may adversely affect the client-therapist alliance or relationships with professional colleagues (p. 343). This should not prevent you from being authentic, but it should make you approach using social media platforms with caution and intentionality.

Given the potential ethical dilemmas, professional organizations should offer guidelines for mental health professionals and training programs should provide education, as well as supervision, to graduate students to prepare them to apply a code of ethics in their use of social media platforms. Currently, few organizations explicitly address social media use among licensed mental health professionals or academics. The American Counseling Association's (ACA, 2014) Code of Ethics identifies several considerations for technology and social media. As articulated in Section H, "Counselors actively attempt to understand the evolving nature of the profession with regards to distance counseling, technology, and social media" (p. 17). Furthermore, ethical obligations are specified regarding social media, such as that professionals should develop knowledge and skills regarding techni-cal, ethical, and legal considerations, which may include additional course work; clearly distinguish their professional versus personal virtual presence; discuss social media as part of informed consent; and respect the clients' presence on social media by avoiding viewing content unless given consent (ACA, 2014).

Given the increasing use of social media by mental health professionals, this is a call to action for more professional associations and organizations to develop ethical guidelines and training around using social media platforms. Baier (2019) notes some important considerations when developing ethical guidelines:

- **Increase anonymity:** Providers should examine the extent to which they can increase their online anonymity such as through the use of pseudonyms and blocking personal information from public view including friend lists, birthday, hometown, educational background, and relatives.
- **Decrease social networks:** Clinicians should aim to decrease their social networks by being selective when accepting friend requests and limiting the visibility of posts to others. Friending individuals prematurely could lead to ethical complications in the future (e.g., if that individual seeks therapy services through your practice).
- **Hide profiles from search engines:** Social media profiles should be hidden from search engines (e.g., Google) to remove profiles from public previews on search returns. Enabling such privacy options will ensure that social media profiles are less easily accessible to curious clients who may Google their therapist.
- **Search your online persona:** Clinicians should Google themselves regularly to under-stand what information is available on the internet and social media platforms and consider what is unavoidable (e.g., professional awards, profile on university or hospital website) and what could be altered or taken down (e.g., a friend's old photographs from college publicly viewable on Facebook).
- **Discuss policies with clients:** Clinicians should consider the potential need and ben-efit of having explicit discussions with clients about their expectations and policies regarding social media use. Such discussions might lend themselves particularly well during early conversations with clients regarding routine matters such as confidentiality, client rights, and other policies of the therapy practice.

These practices can be helpful to reduce the risk of ethical dilemmas. It is necessary for mental health professions to make a shift requiring professionals to adapt and learn about social networking platforms and how to engage in ethical use in the digital age. Lannin and Scott (2013) note that "adapting to the new culture wisely will necessarily involve both understanding the ethical principles themselves as well as developing competence in the technology of the burgeoning digital culture" (p. 135). It is our hope that professional organizations such as the American Psychological Association will offer more guidance around ethical use of social media in future updates of the APA Code of Ethics.

Finally, graduate education and training need to be intentional about providing courses and supervision on ethical use of social media platforms. With the emergence of platforms like TikTok and Clubhouse, many graduate students and trainees are utilizing these platforms with limited guidance, and often their mentors or supervisors lack knowledge about their profession or personal use. Additionally, data indicate that individuals between ages 18–29 use social media at higher rates compared to those ages 30 and over (Pew Research Center, 2019). Therefore, graduate students and trainees may have more experience using these sites than their supervisors or mentors. This poses a challenge with teaching ethical responsibility if supervisors and professors are not familiar with various social media platforms. At a minimum, graduate training programs should offer seminars or workshops on the ethical use of social media. It is also important to add a topic on technology and social media in ethics courses.

Conclusion

This chapter discussed ways to apply social media use to benefit Black people through multiple approaches. Historically, anti-Black racism and racial injustice have contributed to poor mental health and health risks among Black people (e.g., Belgrave & Allison, 2014; Cavanagh & Obasi, 2020; Turner & Turner, 2021; Utsey et al., 2002). As discussed in this chapter, systemic racism embodied in laws, policies, practices, and protocols serves to underscore a system of racial social hierarchy, which sustains racial inequities (Ajwani, 2020; Tourse et al., 2019). Black people have begun to use social media platforms more intentionally to fight oppressive systems. Furthermore, the use of social media platforms (e.g., Facebook, Instagram, Twitter, and YouTube) by psychologists, counselors, and other mental health professionals are increasingly common and arguably now ubiquitous (as cited in Baier, 2019). This provides a unique opportunity to use these platforms for confronting anti-Black racism and promoting social justice. Existing research indicates that social media can help shape discourse on relevant political issues, build coalitions, and create opportunities for increasing turnout at peaceful protests (Mundt et al., 2018). It is now time for scholars and the field of psychology to create ethical practices for mental health professionals who use these emerging technologies to help them navigate both their personal and professional life.

References

Adely, H. (2018). Professor who was fired after defending Black Lives Matter on Fox News sues NJ college. *North Jersey*. https://www.northjersey.com/story/news/2018/04/16/fired-professor-sues-college-claiming-her-free-speech-violationshttps-presto-gannettdigital/521563002

Ajwani, N. (2020) Systemic racism in the United States: Scaffolding as social construction. *Smith College Studies in Social Work, 90*(4), 237–239, https://doi.org/10.1080/00377317.2020.1800551

American Counseling Association (2014). *2014 ACA Code of Ethics*. https://www.counseling.org/knowledge-center/ethics

American Psychological Association (2017). *Ethical principles of psychologists and code of conduct*. https://www.apa.org/ethics/code

Anderson, M. (2019). *For Black Americans, experiences of racial discrimination vary by education level, gender*. Pew Research Center. https://www.pewresearch.org/fact-tank

Arao, B., & Clemens, K. (2013). From safe spaces to brave spaces. *The art of effective facilitation: Reflections from Social Justice Educators*, 135–150.

Ash, B. A. (2020). *Social work, social justice, and the causes to which we are called: Attitudes, ally behavior, and activism* [Doctoral dissertation, University of Denver].

Baier, A. L. (2019). The ethical implications of social media: Issues and recommendations for clinical practice. *Ethics & Behavior, 29*(5), 341–351. https://doi.org/10.1080/10508422.2018.1516148

Belgrave, F. Z., & Allison, K. W. (2018). *African American psychology: From Africa to America*. SAGE.

Bor, J., Venkataramani, A. S., Williams, D. R., & Tsai, A. C. (2018). Police killings and their spillover effects on the mental health of Black Americans: A population-based, quasi-experimental study. *The Lancet, 392*(10144), 302–310.

Bryant-Davis, T., & Ocampo, C. (2005). The trauma of racism: Implications for counseling, research, and education. *The Counseling Psychologist, 33*(4), 574–578. https://doi.org/10.1177/0011000005276581

Bryant-Davis, T., Adams, T., Alejandre, A., & Gray, A. A. (2017). The trauma lens of police violence against racial and ethnic minorities. *Journal of Social Issues, 73*(4), 852–871. https://doi.org/10.1111/josi.12251

Carney, N. (2016). All lives matter, but so does race: Black lives matter and the evolving role of social media. *Humanity & Society, 40*(2), 180–199. https://doi.org/10.1177/0160597616643868

Carlson, E. B. (1997). Trauma assessments: Clinician's guide. New York: The Gilford Press

Carter, R. (2007). Racism and psychological and emotional injury: Recognizing and assessing race-based traumatic stress. *The Counseling Psychologist, 35*(1), 13–105. https://doi.org/10.1177/0011000006292033.

Carter, R. T. & Pieterse, A. L. (2020). *Measuring the effects of racism: Guidelines for the assessment and treatment of race-based traumatic stress injury*. Columbia University Press.

Cavanagh, L., & Obasi, E. M. (2020). The moderating role of coping style on chronic stress exposure and cardiovascular reactivity among African American emerging adults. *Prevention Science, 22*, 357–366. https://doi.org/10.1007/s11121-020-01141-3

Clayton, D. M. (2018). Black Lives Matter and the civil rights movement: A comparative analysis of two social movements in the United States. *Journal of Black Studies, 49*(5), 448–480. https://doi.org/10.1177/0021934718764099

Constantine, M. G., Hage, S. M., Kindaichi, M. M., & Bryant, R. M. (2007). Social justice and multicultural issues: Implications for the practice and training of counselors and counseling psychologists. *Journal of Counseling & Development, 85*(1), 24–29. https://doi.org/10.1002/j.1556-6678.2007.tb00440.x

Delfino, D. (2020, October 14). How to advertise on Facebook, and help your business or brand reach new audiences. *Business Insider*. https://www.businessinsider.com/how-to-advertise-on-facebook

Franklin-Jackson, D., & Carter, R. T. (2007). The relationships between race-related stress, racial identity, and mental health for Black Americans. *Journal of Black Psychology, 33*(1), 5–26. https://doi.org/10.1177/0095798406295092

Guthrie, R. (2004). *Even the rat was White: A historical view of psychology* (2nd ed.). Allyn & Bacon.

Harrell, S. P. (2000). A multidimensional conceptualization of racism-related stress: Implications for the well-being of people of color. *American Journal of Orthopsychiatry, 70*(1), 42–57. https://doi.org/10.1037/h0087722

Helms, J. E., Nicolas, G., & Green, C. E. (2012). Racism and ethnoviolence as trauma: Enhancing professional and research training. *Traumatology, 18*(1), 65–74. https://doi.org/10.1177/1534765610396728

Ince, J., Rojas, F., & Davis, C. A. (2017). The social media response to Black Lives Matter: How Twitter users interact with Black Lives Matter through hashtag use. *Ethnic and Racial Studies, 40*(11), 1814–1830.

Inckle, K. (2020). Inequality, distress and harm-reduction: A social justice approach to self-injury. *Social Theory & Health, 18*(3), 224–239. https://doi.org/10.1057/s41285-020-00146-w

Jernigan, M. M., & Daniel, J. H. (2011). Racial trauma in the lives of Black children and adolescents: Challenges and clinical implications. *Journal of Child & Adolescent Trauma, 4*(2), 123–141. https://doi.org/10.1080/19361521.2011.574678

Jones, J. (1972). *Prejudice and racism*. McGraw-Hill.

Jones, S. C., & Anderson, R. E. (2020). "One minute for your mind": The development, implementation, and application of our mental health minute. *Journal of Black Psychology, 46*(5), 351–363.

King, M. L., Jr. (1968). The role of the behavioral scientist in the civil rights movement. *American Psychologist, 23*(3), 180–186. https://doi.org/10.1037/h0025715

Kolmes, K. (2012). Social media in the future of professional psychology. *Professional Psychology: Research and Practice, 43*(6), 606–612. https://doi.org/10.1037/a0028678

Lannin, D. G., & Scott, N. A. (2013). Social networking ethics: Developing best practices for the new small world. *Professional Psychology: Research and Practice, 44*(3), 135–141. https://doi.org/10.1037/a0031794

Liang, B., Commins, M., & Duffy, N. (2010). Using social media to engage youth: Education, social justice, and humanitarianism. *he Prevention Researcher, 17*(1), 13–17.

Metzger, I. W., Salami, T., Carter, S., Halliday-Boykins, C., Anderson, R. E., Jernigan, M. M., & Ritchwood, T. (2018). African American emerging adults' experiences with racial discrimination and drinking habits: The moderating roles of perceived stress. *Cultural Diversity and Ethnic Minority Psychology, 24*(4), 489–497.

Morris, E. W. (2007). "Ladies" or "Loudies"?: Perceptions and experience of Black girls in classrooms. *Youth and Society, 38*, 490–515. https://doi/org/10.11770044118X06296778

Mundt, M., Ross, K., & Burnett, C. M. (2018). Scaling social movements through social media: The case of Black Lives Matter. *Social Media + Society, 4*(4), 1–14, https://doi.org/10.1177/2056305118807911

Pew Research Center (2021, April 7). Social media use in 2021. https://www.pewresearch.org/internet/2021/04/07/social-media-use-in-2021/

Quintana, S. M. (1998). Children's developmental understanding of ethnicity and race. *Applied & Preventive Psychology, 7*, 27–45. https://doi.org/10.1016/S0962-1849

Racism Pandemic Task Force. (2020) *Racial trauma guide*. https://www.psychology.uga.edu/racial-trauma-guide

Russell, S. T. (2015). Human developmental science for social justice. *Research in Human Development, 12*(3–4), 274–279. https://doi.org/10.1080/15427609.2015.1068049

Scott, J. S., & Brown, N. E. (2016). Scholarship on #BlackLivesMatter and its implications on local electoral politics. *Politics, Groups, and Identities, 4*(4), 702–708. https://doi.org/10.1080/21565503.2016.1236739

Thompson, D., & Thurston, C. (2018). American political development in the era of Black Lives Matter. *Politics, Groups, and Identities, 6*(1), 116–119. https://doi.org/10.1080/21565503.2017.1420546

Tourse, R., Hamilton-Mason, J., & Wewiorski, N. J. (2018). *Systemic racism in the United States*. Springer. https://doi:10.1007/978-3-319-72233-7

Turner, E. A. (2019). *Mental health Among African Americans: Innovations in research and practice*. Rowman & Littlefield.

Turner, E. A., & Turner, T. C. (2021). The state of Black mental health: Understanding disparities through the lens of critical race psychology. In J. Chism, S. DeFreitas, V. Robertson, & D. Ryden (Eds.), *Critical race studies across disciplines: Resisting racism through scholactivism* (pp. 239–260). Lexington.

Utsey, S. O., Chae, M. H., Brown, C. F., & Kelly, D. (2002). Effect of ethnic group membership on ethnic identity, race-related stress, and quality of life. *Cultural Diversity and Ethnic Minority Psychology, 8*(4), 366–377. https://doi.org/10.1037/1099-9809.8.4.367

Utsey, S. O., & Payne, Y. (2000). Psychological impacts of racism in a clinical versus normal sample of African American men. *Journal of African American Men, 5*(3), 57–72.

Vasquez, M. J. T. (2012). Psychology and social justice: Why we do what we do. *American Psychologist, 67*(5), 337–346. https://doi.org/10.1037/a0029232

Vera, E. M., & Speight, S. L. (2003). Multicultural competence, social justice, and counseling psychology: Expanding our roles. *The Counseling Psychologist, 31*(3), 253–272. https://doi.org/10.1177/0011000003031003001

Walton, G. M., & Dweck, C. S. (2009). Solving social problems like a psychologist. *Perspectives on Psychological Science, 4*(1), 101–102.

Watson, M. F., Turner, W. L., & Hines, P. M. (2020). Black Lives Matter: We are in the same storm but we are not in the same boat. *Family Process, 59*(4), 1362–1373. https://doi.org/10.1111/famp.12613

Wilkins, D. J., Livingstone, A. G., & Levine, M. (2019). Whose tweets? The rhetorical functions of social media use in developing the Black Lives Matter movement. *British Journal of Social Psychology, 58*(4), 786–805.

Williams, M. T., Malcoun, E., Sawyer, B. A., Davis, D. M., Nouri, L. B., & Bruce, S. L. (2014). Cultural adaptations of prolonged exposure therapy for treatment and prevention of posttraumatic stress disorder in African Americans. *Behavioral Sciences, 4*(2), 102–124.

Yang, G. (2016). Narrative agency in hashtag activism: The case of #BlackLivesMatter. *Media and Communication, 4*, 13–17. https://doi.org/10.17645/mac.v4i4.692

Zuckerberg, M. (2019, January 24). Facts about Facebook. *Wall Street Journal.* https://www.wsj.com/articles/the-facts-about-facebook-11548374613

CHAPTER FOUR

#SayHerName

The Impact of Gendered Racism and Misogynoir
on the Lives of Black Women

Jioni A. Lewis

> " If Black women were free, it would mean that everyone else would have to
> be free since our freedom would necessitate the destruction of all systems
> of oppression.
>
> *(as cited in Taylor, 2017, p. 23).* "

The shooting death of Breonna Taylor, a 26-year-old emergency medical technician, who was killed by police in Louisville, Kentucky as a result of a botched raid on her apartment in March 2020 contributed to nationwide protests against police brutality in the Summer of 2020 (Oppel et al., 2021). However, despite the increased awareness about the killing of Breonna Taylor, there has still not been justice in this case. The killings of Ahmaud Arbery, George Floyd, Breonna Taylor, and many others, combined with the disproportionate negative impact of the novel coronavirus (COVID-19) pandemic on Black, Indigenous, and People of Color (BIPOC) led to a racial reckoning about systemic racism, police brutality, and racial health inequities in the United States. For example, Black people were 1.4 times more likely to die from COVID-19 compared to their white counterparts (COVID Racial Data Tracker, 2021). However, the unique experiences of Black women continue to be overlooked, marginalized, and invisible. For example, in December 2020, the Bureau of Labor Statistics monthly jobs report showed that all of the net jobs lost in that month were lost by women (National Women's Law Center, 2021). However, when the data was broken down by race and gender, Black women had the largest one-month drop in the size of their labor force with an unemployment rate 1.7 times higher than their pre-pandemic employment rate (National Women's Law Center, 2021). Consequently, Black women have been disproportionately negatively affected by the confluence of systemic racism and COVID-19. However, absent from much of the discourse about the "twin pandemics" is an intersectional analysis by race and gender to better illuminate these interlocking systems of oppression (Lewis et al., 2020; Pirtle & Wright, 2021).

Thus, the purpose of this chapter is to apply a Black feminist and intersectionality lens to elucidate Black women's experiences of intersectional oppression. This chapter provides a brief history of Black feminism and intersectionality theory. Then, this chapter outlines the role of systemic gendered racism and misogynoir on the lives of Black women and girls. In addition, this chapter highlights the impact of gendered racism on Black women's mental and physical health, the effects of police brutality on Black women, and how Black women continue to engage in resistance against systemic gendered racism in society. This chapter ends with specific strategies for Black women to cultivate radical healing as a form of resistance against intersectional oppression.

Herstory of Black Feminism and Intersectionality

There is a long *herstory* of Black women scholars and activists who have articulated the unique marginalization of Black women at the intersection of race, gender, and class oppression. This herstory dates back to the mid 19th century when Black women, such as Sojourner Truth, an abolitionist and women's rights activist, highlighted the exclusion of Black women during the women's suffrage movement (Lewis & Grzanka, 2016; May, 2015). Truth gave a speech at the 1851 Ohio Women's Rights Convention highlighting the ways that White women excluded Black women from getting the right to vote. Throughout the late 19th century and the early 20th century, there was a cadre of Black women scholars, writers, and activists who articulated the subordinated position of Black women in America, including Harriet Tubman, Maria Stewart, Anna Julia Cooper, Mary McLeod Bethune, Mary Church Terrell, Ida B. Wells Barnett, and many others (Collins, 1990/2000; Giddings, 1984; Hancock, 2016; Harris-Perry, 2011; M. S., Jones, 2020). For example, Anna Julia Cooper, born into slavery in 1858, was the fourth African American woman to earn a doctoral degree. In 1892, she wrote her first book, *A Voice From the South: By a Black Woman of the South*, which articulated the importance of self-determination for African American women and that the educational, moral, and spiritual progress of Black women could improve the African American community (Guy-Sheftall, 2009; May, 2007). Many Black women's studies scholars view Anna Julia Cooper's book as one of the earliest foundational writings in the field of Black feminist studies (Guy-Sheftall, 2009; May, 2007).

During the 1970s, several Black women scholar-activists highlighted the marginalization of Black women in the liberation movements; specifically, there was racism inherent in the second wave feminist movement as well as sexism within the Black Power movement (Collins, 1990/2000; hooks, 1981; Taylor, 2017). One of the most important contributions to Black feminist and intersectionality theorizing during this time came from the Combahee River Collective, which was a radical Black feminist collective of scholars, many of whom were Black queer women, who formed in 1974 as an outgrowth of the National Black Feminist Organization in Boston. The group was named after Harriett Tubman's raid on the Combahee River that freed hundreds of enslaved people (Taylor, 2017). In 1977, they wrote the Combahee River Collective (1995) statement, which poignantly articulated the interlocking systems of oppression experienced by Black women who are marginalized at the intersection of racism, classism, and sexism:

> We believe that sexual politics under patriarchy is as pervasive in Black women's lives as are the politics of class and race. We also find it difficult to separate race from class from sex oppression because in our lives they are most often experienced simultaneously. (p. 234)

In addition, the Combahee River Collective highlighted the necessity of Black feminist political activism and the importance of their intersectional identities as Black women to be central in their fight for liberation. Consequently, Black feminism paved the way for an intersectional analysis of systemic oppression (Collins, 1990/2000; Hancock, 2016; Lewis & Grzanka, 2016; Taylor, 2017).

During the 1980s and 1990s there was a proliferation of scholarship on Black feminism, including the work of Patricia Hill Collins, Kimberlé Crenshaw, bell hooks, Beverly Guy-Sheftall, Alice Walker, Michele Wallace, and many others (Collins, 1990/2000; Collins, 2019; Hancock, 2016). For example, sociologist Patricia Hill Collins wrote her foundational book, *Black Feminist Thought* (1990/2000), which articulated the importance of a Black woman's standpoint, lived experience, and critical consciousness to Black feminist epistemology. Collins argued that Black feminist thought centers the simultaneous experience of interlocking systems of race, gender, and class oppression. In addition, Collins highlights the importance of resistance through self-definition and the necessity to engage in political activism. Collins also critiqued the suppression of Black women's knowledge production in traditional intellectual discourse and sought to center Black feminist ways of knowing. Critical legal scholar Kimberlé Crenshaw (1989) introduced the concept of intersectionality in her critique of antidiscrimination law, which often excluded Black women at the intersection of racial and gender discrimination. Crenshaw argued that Black women could experience discrimination that looked like racism experienced by Black men, or sexism experienced by White women, or the additive effects of racial and gender discrimination, similar to "double jeopardy" (Beal, 1970). Nevertheless, Crenshaw (1989) asserted that Black women typically "experience discrimination as Black women—not the sum of race or sex discrimination, but as Black women" (p. 149). Hence, this framework critiques a single-axis analysis of discrimination and articulates a more nuanced analysis of intersectional oppression. Crenshaw (1991) also utilized an intersectional analysis of violence against women of color to illuminate interlocking systems of oppression and point toward solutions for political activism. Therefore, Black feminist scholars have a long history of centering Black women in an intersectional analysis of interlocking systems of oppression that are constructed by power to sustain inequality (Collins, 1990/2000; Collins, 2019; May, 2015).

Together, Black feminist thought is a necessary epistemological framework to situate Black women's marginalization within a historical context of White supremacy, patriarchy, and class exploitation (Collins, 1990/2000). Black feminism and intersectionality highlight the limitations of framing the injustice of Black women as either racism or sexism since this erases the intersectional effects of discrimination experienced by Black women (Crenshaw, 1989). An intersectionality lens provides an important prism to illuminate interlocking systems of oppression that negatively impact the lives of Black women and girls. Thus, applying Black feminism and intersectionality to a psychological understanding of discrimination provides a nuanced framework to elucidate the impact of intersectional oppression on the health and well-being of Black women and girls.

Intersectional Oppression Among Black Women

The intersection of racism and sexism experienced by Black women is rooted in historical gendered racial stereotypes (Collins, 2000; Combahee River Collective, 1995; Essed, 1991; Harris-Perry, 2011). Historical stereotypes depict Black women as controlling images or tropes, such as the *mammy* (i.e., asexual and self-sacrificing caretaker), *sapphire* (i.e., angry, aggressive, and combative), *jezebel* (i.e., sexually promiscuous and hypersexual), and *welfare queen* (i.e., lower class and over-reliant on public assistance) (Bailey, 2021; Collins, 2000; Harris-Perry, 2011). In addition to many of these historical stereotypes, there are also contemporary tropes, such as the video vixen (French, 2013) or the strong Black woman (Bailey, 2021; Harris-Perry, 2011). These socially constructed controlling images serve to justify and rationalize the oppression against Black women and girls. Many of these controlling images get projected onto Black women and girls through institutional, individual, and cultural mechanisms, which reinforce the structure and ideology of gendered racism.

Structure and Ideology of Gendered Racism

The term *gendered racism* was coined by sociologist Philomena Essed (1991) to refer to the simultaneous experience of both racism and sexism. According to Essed, racism and sexism "intertwine and combine under certain conditions into one hybrid phenomenon" (p. 31). Essed argued that Black women experience gendered and classed forms of racism that are based on ideologies and stereotypes of Black womanhood. Although the term *gendered racism* was developed in the context of the study of everyday racism, it is structural in nature, which refers to the intersection between structural racism and structural sexism (Lewis et al., 2020; Pirtle & Wright, 2021).

Integrating both the psychosocial model of racism (Neville et al., 2012) and the psychosocial model of sexism (Lewis, 2018), I define gendered racism as the intersection between White supremacy and patriarchy, which includes two interlocking components: (a) a structural mechanism of domination and (b) a corresponding ideological belief that justifies the oppression of women of color based on their marginalized race and gender. This definition provides a framework to place the concept of gendered racism within a systems-level analysis to locate the ideology of gendered racism within a larger context of domination and subjugation (Lewis, 2018; Neville et al., 2012). Drawing on J. M. Jones's (1997) tripartite model of racism, including individual, institutional, and cultural forms of racism, I propose three manifestations of gendered racism: *Individual gendered racism* refers to interpersonal interactions designed to denigrate women of color who are viewed as inferior in society, which can be either overt or covert (i.e., a racist and sexist slight or insult directed at a woman of color); *institutional gendered racism* includes policies, practices, and norms that perpetuate inequality by restricting opportunities for women of color (i.e., Black women only make 63 cents on the dollar compared to White men; U.S. Census Bureau, 2020); *cultural gendered racism* includes symbols and practices that are used to reinforce the notion that women of color are inferior to all men and White women (i.e., Eurocentric standards of beauty that perpetuate the notion that physical features and beauty aesthetics that deviate from Whiteness are less attractive and desirable).

For Black women, the structure of systemic gendered racism in society and the accompanying ideology that intersects White supremacy and patriarchy is held together by *misogynoir,* a term coined by Moya Bailey (2021) to refer to the "anti-Black misogyny that Black women experience, particularly in U.S. visual and digital culture" (p. 1). Misogynoir is the intersection of the simultaneous experience of racialized and sexualized violence unique to Black women's positionality in society. Misogynoir is prevalent in the media, particularly in digital popular culture, such as social media platforms, and includes stereotypical representations, hypervisibility and tokenism, or the invisibility and erasure of Black women (Bailey, 2021). Bailey highlights the harm of misogynoir to Black cisgender women as well as Black transgender, nonbinary, gender nonconforming, and gender expansive individuals.

Gendered Racial Microaggressions

Drawing on Essed's (1991) concept of gendered racism and Sue et al.'s (2007) scholarship on racial microaggressions, I coined the term *gendered racial microaggressions,* which refers to "subtle and everyday verbal, behavioral, and environmental expressions of oppression based on the intersection of one's race and gender" (Lewis et al., 2013, p. 51). Gendered racial microaggressions capture interpersonal gendered racism that includes the intersection of covert racism and sexism experienced by women of color. In the first qualitative study focused on exploring types of microaggressions based on the intersection of race and gender, my colleagues and I (Lewis et al., 2016) conducted focus group interviews with Black women college students and created a taxonomy of gendered racial microaggressions. The taxonomy included three core themes, which include two subthemes each: *projected stereotypes* (e.g., expectation of the Jezebel—being exoticized, sexualized, or objectified; expectation of the angry Black woman—being perceived as the stereotype of the angry Black woman), *silenced and marginalized* (e.g., struggle for respect—having one's power and authority questioned or undermined; invisibility—being marginalized, invisible, or silenced in academic and professional settings), and *assumptions of style and beauty* (e.g., assumptions of communication style; assumptions of aesthetics—messages about Black women's beauty and aesthetics, including body type, hair styles, and facial features) (Lewis et al., 2016). For example, a Black woman may receive negative comments when she wears her hair in a natural hairstyle, or she might be the target of sexually objectifying and denigrating comments about her curvy body type. These kinds of comments are rooted in evaluating Black women against Eurocentric standards of beauty and communicate that Black women are less attractive and desirable.

Building on previous qualitative research (Lewis et al., 2013, 2016), I developed the Gendered Racial Microaggression Scale (GRMS; Lewis & Neville, 2015), which has four subscales, *Assumptions of Beauty and Sexual Objectification* (e.g., making sexually inappropriate comments), *Silenced and Marginalized* (e.g., comments being silenced, ignored, or marginalized in workplace and professional settings), *the Strong Black Woman Stereotype* (e.g., being assumed to exhibit qualities of a "strong Black woman"), and the *Angry Black Woman Stereotype* (e.g., being assumed to be an "angry Black woman"; Lewis & Neville, 2015). Black women can respond to items on the scale based on how frequently they experience different types of gendered racial microaggressions as well as how stressful they report the experiences to be. Previous research has found gendered racial microaggressions to be positively associated with measures of subtle racism and subtle sexism; however, the GRMS has also been found to capture unique microaggressions at the intersection of race and gender for Black women (Lewis & Neville, 2015).

Research has found that Black adolescent girls also experience gendered racial microaggressions. For example, Gadson and Lewis (2021) conducted qualitative focus groups with Black adolescent girls between the ages of 13–17 and uncovered several themes that highlighted the unique ways that Black girls experience microaggressions based on the intersection of their race, gender, and social class. Specifically, Black girls reported experiencing gendered racial microaggressions that represented standards of beauty and objectification (i.e., assumptions and devaluation about beauty, aesthetics, and exoticization of hair), being silenced and marginalized (i.e., being made to feel invisible, overdisciplined, and underprotected in school settings), and projected stereotypes (i.e., stereotypes about Black adolescent girls, such as the Jezebel, angry Black girl, and ghetto Black girl). In addition, Gadson and Lewis (2021) uncovered the ways that these gendered racial microaggressions of being overdisciplined were connected to the criminalization of Black girls in the school system (Crenshaw, Ocean et al., 2015; Epstein et al., 2017; Morris, 2016). For example, Black girls in their study reported getting overdisciplined for minor infractions, such as dress code violations, whereas these same infractions often went unnoticed on White girls.

Other constructs that have been developed to contextualize the intersectional experiences of racism and sexism for women of color include *ethgender discrimination*, which refers to discrimination based on ethnicity and gender (King, 2003). In addition, *racialized sexual harassment* refers to the intersection of racial and sexual harassment experienced by women of color (Buchanan & Ormerod, 2002). Research has found that experiences of racialized sexual harassment are associated with poorer mental health and well-being for women of color (Buchanan & Ormerod, 2002).

Gendered Racism and Black Women's Health

There is a large body of theoretical and empirical research that has found racism has a negative impact on mental and physical health (Clark et al., 1999; Pascoe & Smart Richman, 2009; Pieterse et al., 2012). For example, Clark et al.'s (1999) biopsychosocial model of racism theorizes that racism is a chronic stressor that can lead to negative psychological and physical health outcomes for African Americans. In this model, coping responses are considered to buffer the negative effects of racism on psychological and physiological stress responses. Previous empirical research has found that the stress of racism can impact higher physiological responses to stress, which can impact the immune system and cardiovascular functioning, which subsequently leads to negative health outcomes (Lewis et al., 2015; Williams & Williams-Morris, 2000). However, there is a dearth of research on the impact of gendered racism on the mental and physical health of Black women.

Mental Health and Well-Being

A growing body of empirical research has found that gendered racism is associated with negative psychological and physical health of Black women (Lewis & Neville, 2015; Rosenthal & Lobel, 2018; Szymanski & Lewis, 2016; Thomas et al., 2008). For example, several studies have found that gendered racism is associated with greater psychological distress (Szymanski & Lewis, 2016; Thomas et al., 2008). In addition, research has found that greater experiences of gendered racism have also been associated with negative general health and well-being (Perry et al., 2013) as well as poor sexual and reproductive health (Rosenthal & Lobel, 2018).

There is also a burgeoning body of research on the link between gendered racial microaggressions and negative health outcomes, including greater psychological distress and depressive symptoms (Lewis & Neville, 2015; Williams & Lewis, 2019), greater traumatic stress symptoms (Dale & Safren, 2019; Moody & Lewis, 2019), greater anxiety symptoms (Wright & Lewis, 2020), and negative mental and physical health (Lewis et al., 2017). For example, Lewis et al. (2017) applied intersectionality theory to the biopsychosocial model of racism (Clark et al., 1999) to develop the biopsychosocial model of gendered racism, which conceptualizes the role of mediating and moderating variables, such as coping strategies and gendered racial identity as influencing the association between gendered racism and health outcomes among Black women. In a cross-sectional study of 231 African American women, Lewis et al. (2017) tested this model and found that experiencing a greater frequency of gendered racial microaggressions was significantly associated with poorer self-reported mental and physical health.

Physical Health and Health Inequities

The COVID-19 pandemic has highlighted the stark racial health inequities that existed in the United States prior to the pandemic. For example, Black people have a shorter life expectancy and a higher risk for cardiovascular disease, diabetes, and obesity compared to their White counterparts (National Center for Health Statistics, 2019). However, Black women experience unique stressors based on the intersections of their race and gender. Chronic stress leads to unique racial health disparities for Black women compared to their White counterparts, including increased risk of cardiovascular disease, stroke, certain types of cancer, and maternal morbidity (National Center for Health Statistics, 2019). For example, Black women are three times more likely to experience life-threatening pregnancy complications (i.e., pre-eclampsia) and nearly four times more likely to experience preventable pregnancy related deaths (Creanga et al., 2014). But often what is missing from this discourse is the role of *both* racism and sexism in these health inequities.

There has been increased attention to bias in the health care system as a potential root cause for some of these gendered racial health inequities. For example, Black women can experience gendered racism in health care settings that are rooted in some of the historical stereotypes and controlling images of Black women, which can lead to poor quality of care and treatment (Pirtle & Wright, 2021). In addition, there have been studies conducted with medical students who endorse stereotypical views that Black people can tolerate greater pain and have "thicker skin," which could lead to a minimization of Black women's pain, and in turn could be related to these gendered racial health inequities (Lewis et al., 2020).

#SayHerName: Black Women and Police Brutality

Kimberlé Crenshaw's foundational work on intersectionality reminds us that interlocking systems of racial, gender, and class oppression uniquely shape the lives of Black women. Crenshaw is the cofounder and executive director of the African American Policy Forum, which created the hashtag and digital movement #SayHerName to increase the public's awareness of police brutality and anti-Black violence directed toward Black women and girls because these stories are often made invisible in the public discourse. Crenshaw, Ritchie et al. (2015) published a report, "Say Her Name: Resisting Police Brutality Against Black Women," that outlines the gendered racial disparities in police violence against Black women and girls. Crenshaw argues that we have a framework to be able to identify police brutality against Black men. Often, these cases spark national outrage and protests; however, the police violence against Black women and girls is often marginalized, erased, or ignored in our society. Black women are also the victims of police violence, but their stories are often silenced and marginalized in the public discourse due to systemic gendered racism. Crenshaw argues that if we don't have the lens to notice police violence against Black women then we often ignore that Black women are also frequently the victims of police violence. Thus, the #SayHerName campaign centers on Black women's experiences of police violence to create a gender-inclusive approach to racial justice that centers all Black lives, which is an example of Black feminist resistance and intersectional activism. The #SayHerName campaign also highlights the impact of police violence against Black transgender, femme, nonbinary, and gender expansive individuals who are also at increased risk for police violence. For example, in a nationwide transgender discrimination survey, 38% of Black transgender people who had interactions with the police reported experiencing harassment and 20% reported experiencing physical or sexual assault (Crenshaw, Ritchie et al., 2015). Thus, it is very important to explore the intersections between race, gender, and gender identity as it relates to experiences of gendered racism and misogynoir.

Black Women and Resistance

Black women have a long herstory of actively resisting oppression from 1619 up to the present. During slavery, many Black women actively resisted domination and subjugation in a variety of ways (Davis, 1972; Taylor, 2017). Black feminist foremothers, such as Sojourner Truth, Harriet Tubman, and Ida B. Wells-Barnett exhibited a tremendous amount of strength and resistance to fight White supremacy, patriarchy, systemic racism, and systemic sexism. A fundamental component of Black women's activism is resisting interlocking systems of oppression. Collins (1990/2000) argued that Black women's activism consisted of two primary dimensions: (a) the struggle for group survival, such as creating Black women communities and networks to indirectly resist oppression, and (b) the struggle for institutional transformation to directly resist oppression. Often, Black women also engaged in subversive tactics to resist oppression. According to Collins (1990/2000), "Our strategies of everyday resistance have largely consisted of trying to create spheres of influence, authority, and power within institutions" (p. 146). Thus, resistance through education, critical consciousness, and empowerment are important components of Black feminist activism (Collins, 1990/2000). The lineage of Black feminist activists from Harriett Tubman to the Combahee River Collective, to Alicia Garza, Patrice Cullors, and Opal Tometi (the cofounders of the BLM movement) illustrates the power of resistance both for group survival and transformative change.

Black Women and Radical Healing

In the context of ongoing gendered racial trauma from living in a racist and sexist society, it is important for Black women to cultivate our strength and resistance against intersectional oppression. The psychological framework of radical healing (French et al., 2020) is a framework that can assist Black women in developing strategies for healing. Radical healing is a process of healing racial trauma that involves becoming whole in the face of identity-based wounds (French et al., 2020). This framework integrates Shawn Ginwright's (2010) concept of radical healing with several foundational theories: liberation psychology (i.e., highlights the importance of psychological liberation from oppression; Martín-Baró, 1994), Black psychology (i.e., articulates the history of racism in psychology and calls for a strengths-based and African-centered approach to mental health; White, 1970), ethnopolitical psychology (i.e., provides a model for healing from racial trauma; Comas-Diaz, 2007), and intersectionality (i.e., highlights the impact of interlocking oppressions on the lives of marginalized groups; (Crenshaw, 1989; Cole, 2009). Together, these theories are integrated to serve as the foundation of racial healing that centers BIPOC communities and promotes a multisystemic approach to healing from racial trauma (French et al., 2020).

There are five core anchors of the model, which include (a) critical consciousness (i.e., developing a critical understanding of oppression through reflection and action), (b) cultural authenticity and self-knowledge (i.e., connecting with one's cultural roots and developing one's own self-definition), (c) radical hope (i.e., fostering hope and envisioning possibilities for a better future), (d) collectivism and social support (i.e., connecting with one's cultural values and community for support) and (e) strength and resistance (i.e., relying on cultural strength and resisting oppression as a form of healing; French et al., 2020). The psychological framework of radical healing was developed to center the needs of BIPOC communities and honor the ancestral wisdom and resistance strategies that enable us to sit in the dialectic between fighting interlocking systems of oppression as well as envisioning possibilities for a socially just future (French et al., 2020).

Given that many Black women and girls have been directly impacted by the confluence of the disproportionate negative effects of COVID-19 as well as the continued intersectional invisibility and erasure of our experiences of systemic gendered racism and police brutality, this chapter ends with specific recommendations for how Black women can cultivate radical healing and work toward healing from gendered racial trauma in the current sociopolitical moment (Lewis et al., 2020).

Critical Consciousness: Recognize Gendered Racism as a Source of Stress and Trauma

It is important for Black women to recognize how intersectional oppression, such as gendered racism, negatively impacts our health and well-being. Black women can experience multiple levels of gendered racism, from institutional gendered racism to gendered racial microaggressions. In addition, experiencing a greater frequency and stress of gendered racial microaggressions in one's daily life is associated with poorer mental and physical health among Black women (Lewis et al., 2017; Moody & Lewis, 2019; Williams & Lewis, 2019; Wright & Lewis, 2020). Consequently, it is important to increase one's awareness about these interlocking systems of oppression that lead to increased stress and trauma for Black women.

Cultural Authenticity and Self-Knowledge: Practice Spirituality and Mind-Body Healing

Radical healing is about developing cultural authenticity and self-knowledge. Developing one's own self-knowledge and self-definition is also an important component of Black feminist consciousness (Collins, 1990/2000). Many BIPOC communities find that engaging in spiritual practices is an authentic way to connect with one's cultural group. Engaging in some form of daily spiritual practice, such as prayer or meditation, has been found to be beneficial for African Americans in general, and Black women in particular (Mattis &

Watson, 2009). There is also a growing body of research on the benefits of engaging in mind-body interventions, such as yoga, meditation, and mindfulness to reduce stress and trauma (Harrell, 2018; Watson-Singleton et al., 2019; Woods-Giscombé & Black, 2010). For example, Shelly P. Harrell (2018) has developed the concept of *soulfulness*, which is a contemplative practice that moves beyond individual healing and toward communal empowerment strategies, collective healing, and liberation.

Cultivate Radical Hope: Envision Possibilities for Wellness, Freedom, and Dignity

Radical hope "involves the steadfast belief in the collective capacity contained within communities of color to heal and transform oppressive forces into a better future despite the overwhelming odds" (Mosley et al., 2020, p. 3). Mosley et al. (2020) developed a psychological framework of radical hope, which involves two dimensions (a) having faith and agency (i.e., a belief that positive change for the community is possible and the capacity to actively respond to sociopolitical forces) and (b) collective memory (i.e., an understanding of the current sociopolitical reality due to ancestral and community wisdom of past racial trauma). There are also four pathways of radical hope (a) acknowledging our history of oppression and resistance, (b) gaining ancestral pride, (c) envisioning possibilities for the future, and (d) developing meaning and purpose. Given the negative toll that systemic gendered racism can take on the health and well-being of Black women, it is important to cultivate radical hope to envision a better future.

Collectivism: Lean on Support Networks

There is a large body of research on the importance of social support as a form of coping for Black women in the context of intersectional oppression (Bryant-Davis, 2013; Lewis et al., 2013; Shorter-Gooden, 2004). Although many Black women have been socialized to endorse the myth of the strong Black woman, research indicates that internalizing the strong Black woman schema can have a negative effect on Black women's mental health (Watson-Singleton et al., 2019; Woods-Giscombé et al., 2019). It is important for Black women to recognize that seeking social support is an indicator of strength. Sister circles are support groups for Black women, which have been found to be very effective in reducing stress and anxiety (Neal-Barnett et al., 2011). Having a space to give and receive support and validation about experiences of oppression can be very empowering. Cultivating a support network is also an important component of resistance (Collins, 1990/2000).

Strength and Resistance: Engage in Social Justice Activism

Black women in the United States have a long history of being leaders and taking action in the fight for equity and justice. Engaging in social justice activism has been found to promote community healing and individual healing. For example, Seaton et al. (2020) found that supporting Black Lives Matter had health benefits among Black Americans. In addition, Mosley et al. (2021) conducted interviews with Black Lives Matter activists and developed a critical consciousness model, which highlighted the importance of developing skills to engage in critical action against anti-Blackness. Engaging in social justice activism is also a part of our historical lineage of Black women's activism.

Together, it is important to increase our critical consciousness about interlocking systems of oppression and recognize that gendered racism is a source of stress and trauma. It is essential to develop cultural authenticity and self-knowledge and practice spirituality and mind-body healing. In order to have optimism about the future, it is necessary to cultivate radical hope and envision possibilities for wellness, dignity, and freedom. Building one's social support network is another important component of radical healing. Lastly, Black women need to remember the strength of our Black feminist foremothers and continue to engage in social justice activism to resist interlocking systems of oppression.

Conclusion

Historically, Black women have experienced racism within feminist movements as well as sexism within Black liberation movements (Collins, 2000; Taylor, 2017). Black women scholars, writers, and activists have a long herstory of advocating for their unique positionality at the intersection of race, gender, and class oppression. Given the historical and contemporary ways that the unique oppression of Black women continues to be overlooked, marginalized, and made invisible in the contemporary sociopolitical moment, the aim of this chapter was to apply a Black feminist and intersectionality lens to highlight Black women's experiences of intersectional oppression. This chapter also focused on the impact of gendered racism on Black women's mental health and well-being, physical health and health inequities, police brutality, and how Black women continue to engage in resistance against systemic gendered racism and misogynoir in society. One form of resistance is cultivating radical healing to be able to sit in the dialectic between interlocking systems of oppression and envisioning future possibilities for wellness, freedom, and dignity. As Audre Lorde (1988) reminds us, "Caring for myself is not self-indulgence, it is self-preservation, and that is an act of political warfare" (p. 131). Therefore, it is essential to cultivate radical healing in order to survive and thrive in the face of gendered racism as a powerful act of resistance.

References

Bailey, M. (2021). *Misogynoir transformed: Black women's digital resistance*. New York University Press.

Beal, F. (1970). Double jeopardy: To be Black and female. In T. Cade (Ed.), *The Black woman: An anthology* (pp. 90–100).: Signet.

Bryant-Davis, T. (2013) Sister friends: A reflection and analysis of the therapeutic role of sisterhood in African American women's lives. *Women & Therapy, 36*(1–2), 110–120. https://doi.org/10.1080/02703149.2012.720906

Buchanan, N. T., & Ormerod, A. J. (2002). Racialized sexual harassment in the lives of African American women. *Women & Therapy, 25*(3–4), 107–124. https://doi.org/10.1300/J015v25n03_08

Clark, R., Anderson, N. B., Clark, V. R., & Williams, D. R. (1999). Racism as a stressor for African Americans: A biopsychosocial model. *American Psychologist, 54*(10), 805–816. https://doi.org/10.1037/0003-066x.54.10.805

Cole, E. R. (2009). Intersectionality and research in psychology. *American Psychologist, 64*(3), 170–180. https://doi.org/10.1037/a0014564

Collins, P. H. (2000). *Black feminist thought: Knowledge, power and the politics of empowerment.* Routledge. (Original work published 1990)

Collins, P. H. (2019). *Intersectionality as critical social theory.* Duke University Press.

Comas-Díaz, L. (2007). Ethnopolitical psychology: Healing and transformation. In E. Aldarondo (Ed.), *Advancing social justice through clinical practice* (pp. 91– 118). Mahwah, NJ: Erlbaum.

Combahee River Collective. (1995). Combahee River Collective statement. In B. Guy-Sheftall (Ed.), *Words of fire: An anthology of African American feminist thought* (pp. 232–240). The New Press. (Original work published 1977)

The COVID Tracking project. (n.d.). *COVID racial data tracker.* (2021). *Home page.* https://covidtracking.com/race

Creanga, A. A., Bateman, B. T., Kuklina, E. V., & Callaghan, W. M. (2014). Racial and ethnic disparities in severe maternal morbidity: A multistate analysis, 2008-2010. *American Journal of Obstetrics and Gynecology, 210*(5), 435.E1–435.E8. https://doi.org/10.1016/j.ajog.2013.11.039

Crenshaw, K. (1989). Demarginalizing the intersection of race and sex: A Black feminist critique of antidiscrimination doctrines, feminist theory, and antiracist politics. *University of Chicago Legal Forum, 8*, 139–167.

Crenshaw, K. (1991). Mapping the margins: Intersectionality, identity politics, and violence against women of color. *Stanford Law Review, 43*(6), 1241–1299. https://doi.org/10.2307/1229039

Crenshaw, K., Ocean, P., & Nanda, J. (2015). Black girls matter: Pushed out, overpoliced, and under protected. *African American Policy Forum and Center for Intersectionality and Social Policy Studies.* https://www.aapf.org/blackgirlsmatter

Crenshaw, K., Ritchie, A. J., Anspach, R., Gilmer, R., & Harris, L. (2015). Say her name: Resisting police brutality against Black women. *African American Policy Forum and Center for Intersectionality and Social Policy Studies.* https://www.aapf.org/sayhername

Dale, S. K., & Safren, S. A. (2019). Gendered racial microaggressions predict posttraumatic stress disorder symptoms and cognitions among Black women living with HIV. *Psychological Trauma: Theory, Research, Practice, and Policy, 11*(7), 685–694. https://doi.org/10.1037/tra0000467

Davis, A. (1972). Reflections on the Black woman's role in the community of slaves. *The Massachusetts Review, 13*(1/2), 81–100. http://www.jstor.org/stable/25088201

Epstein, R., Blake, J. J., & Gonzalez, T. (2017). *Girlhood interrupted: The erasure of Black girls' childhood.* Georgetown Law Center.

Essed, P. (1991). *Understanding everyday racism: An interdisciplinary theory* (Vol. 2). SAGE.

French, B. H. (2013). More than Jezebels and freaks: Exploring how Black girls navigate sexual coercion and sexual scripts. *Journal of African American Studies, 17*, 35–50. https://doi.org/10.1007/s12111-012-9218-1

French, B. H., Lewis, J. A., Mosley, D., Adames, H. Y., Chavez-Dueñas, N. Y., Chen, G. A. & Neville, H. A. (2020). Toward a psychological framework of radical healing in communities of color. *The Counseling Psychologist, 48*(1), 14-46. https://doi.org/10.1177/0011000019843506

Gadson, C. A., & Lewis, J. A. (2021). Devalued, overdisciplined, and stereotyped: An exploration of gendered racial microaggressions among Black adolescent girls. *Journal of Counseling Psychology. https://doi.org/10.1037/cou0000571*

Garza, A. (2020). *The purpose of power: How we come together when we fall apart.* One World.

Giddings, P. (1984). *When and where I enter: The impact of Black women on race and sex in America.* W. Morrow.

Ginwright, S. A. (2010). *Black youth rising: Activism and radical healing in urban America*. Teachers College Press.

Guy-Sheftall, B. (2009). Black feminist studies: The case of Anna Julia Cooper. *African American Review, 43*(1), 11–15. http://www.jstor.org/stable/27802555

Hancock, A. M. (2016). *Intersectionality: An intellectual history*. Oxford University Press.

Harrell, S. P. (2018). Soulfulness as an orientation to contemplative practice: Culture, liberation, and mindful awareness. *The Journal of Contemplative Inquiry, 5*(1), 9–39.

Harris-Perry, M. V. (2011). *Sister citizen: Shame, stereotypes, and Black women in America: For colored girls who've considered politics when being strong isn't enough*. Yale University Press.

hooks, b. (1981). *Ain't I am woman? Black women and feminism*. Routledge.

Jones, J. M. (1997). *Prejudice and racism* (2nd ed.). McGraw-Hill.

Jones, M. S. (2020). *Vanguard: How Black women broke barriers, won the vote, and insisted on equality for all*. Basic Books.

King, K. R. (2003). Racism or sexism? Attributional ambiguity and simultaneous memberships in multiple oppressed groups. *Journal of Applied Social Psychology, 33*, 223–247. https://doi.org/ 10.1111/j.1559-1816.2003.tb01894.x

Lewis, J. A. (2018). From modern sexism to gender microaggressions: Understanding contemporary forms of sexism and the impact on diverse women. In C. Travis & J. White (Eds.), *APA handbook of the psychology of women: Vol 1* (pp. 381–397). American Psychological Association.

Lewis, J. A., & Grzanka, P. R. (2016). Applying intersectionality theory to research on perceived racism. In A. N. Alvarez, C. T. H. Liang, & H. A. Neville (Eds.), *The cost of racism for people of color: Contextualizing experiences of discrimination* (pp. 31–54). American Psychological Association.

Lewis, J. A., Mendenhall, R., Harwood, S. A., & Browne Huntt, M. (2013). Coping with gendered racial microaggressions among Black women college students. *Journal of African American Studies, 17*(1), 51–73. https://doi.org/10.1007/s12111-012-9219-0

Lewis, J. A., Mendenhall, R., Harwood, S. A., & Huntt, M. B. (2016). "Ain't I a woman?": Perceived gendered racial microaggressions experienced by Black women. *The Counseling Psychologist, 44*(5), 758–780. https://doi.org/10.1177/0011000016641193

Lewis, J. A., & Neville, H. A. (2015). Construction and initial validation of the Gendered Racial Microaggressions Scale for Black women. *Journal of Counseling Psychology, 62*(2), 289–302. https://doi.org/10.1037/cou0000062

Lewis, J. A., Neville, H. A., Mosley, D. V., Lewis, J. A., French, B. H., Chavez-Duenas, N. Y., Adames, H. Y., & Chen, G. A. (2020, May 16). #SayHerName: Radical healing for Black women and gender expansive folx. *Psychology Today*. https://www.psychologytoday.com/us/blog/healing-through-social-justice/202005/sayhername

Lewis, J. A., Williams, M. G., Peppers, E., & Gadson, C. A. (2017). Applying intersectionality to explore the relations between gendered racism and health among Black women. *Journal of Counseling Psychology, 64*(5), 475–486. http://dx.doi.org/10.1037/cou0000231

Lewis, T. T., Cogburn, C. D., & Williams, D. R. (2015). Self-reported experiences of discrimination and health: Scientific advances, ongoing controversies, and emerging issues. *Annual Review of Clinical Psychology, 11*, 407-440. http://dx.doi.org/10.1146/annurev-clinpsy-032814-112728.

Lorde, A. (1988). *A burst of light: Living with cancer*. Firebrand.

Martín-Baró, I. (1994). *Writings for a liberation psychology* (A. Aron & S. Corne, Eds.). Cambridge, MA: Harvard University Press.

Mattis, J. S., & Watson, C. R. (2009). Religion and spirituality. In H. A. Neville, B. M. Tynes, & S. O. Utsey (Eds.), *Handbook of African American psychology* (pp. 91–102). SAGE.

May, V. M. (2007). *Anna Julia Cooper, visionary Black feminist*. Routledge.

May, V. M. (2015). *Pursuing intersectionality, unsettling dominant imaginaries*. Routledge.

Moody, A., & Lewis, J. A. (2019). Gendered racial microaggressions and traumatic stress symptoms among Black women. *Psychology of Women Quarterly, 43*(2), 201–214. https://doi.org/10.1177/0361684319828288

Morris, M. W. (2016). *Pushout: The criminalization of Black girls in school*. The New Press.

Morris, M. (2019). *Sing a rhythm, dance a blues: Education for the liberation of Black and Brown girls*. The New Press.

Mosley, D. V., Hargons, C. N., Meiller, C., Angyal, B., Wheeler, P., Davis, C., & Stevens-Watkins, D. (2021). Critical consciousness of anti-Black racism: A practical model to prevent and resist racial trauma. *Journal of Counseling Psychology, 68*(1), 1–16. https://doi.org/10.1037/cou0000430

Mosley, D. V., Neville, H. A., Chavez-Dueñas, N. Y., Adames, H. Y., Lewis, J. A., & French, B. H. (2020). Radical hope in revolting times: Proposing a culturally-relevant psychological framework. *Social and Personality Psychology Compass, 14*(1), e12512. https://doi.org/10.1111/spc3.12512

National Center for Health Statistics. (2019). *Health, United States, 2019*. https://www.cdc.gov/nchs/data/hus/hus19-508.pdf

National Women's Law Center. (2021). *All of the jobs lost in December were women's jobs*. https://nwlc.org/resources/all-of-the-jobs-lost-in-december-were-womens-jobs/

Neal-Barnett, A., Stadulis, R., Murray, M., Payne, M. R., Thomas, A., & Salley, B. B. (2011). Sister circles as a culturally relevant intervention for anxious African American women. *Clinical Psychology: Science and Practice, 18*(3), 266–273. https://doi.org/10.1111/j.1468-2850.2011.01258.x

Neville, H. A., Spanierman, L. B., & Lewis, J. A. (2012). The expanded psychosocial model of racism: A new model for understanding and disrupting racism and white privilege. In N. A. Fouad, J. A. Carter, & L. M. Subich (Eds.), *APA handbook of counseling psychology: Vol. 2. Practice, interventions, and applications* (pp. 333–360). American Psychological Association.

Oppel, R. A., Taylor, D. B., & Bogel-Burroughs, N. (2021, April 26). What to know about Breonna Taylor's death. *The New York Times*. https://www.nytimes.com/article/breonna-taylor-police.html

Pascoe, E. A., & Smart Richman, L. (2009). Perceived discrimination and health: A meta-analytic review. *Psychological Bulletin, 135,* 531–554. http://dx.doi.org/10.1037/a0016059

Perry, B. L., Harp, K. L., & Oser, C. B. (2013). Racial and gender discrimination in the stress process: Implications for African American women's health and well-being. *Sociological Perspectives, 56*(1), 25–48. https://doi.org/10.1525/ sop.2012.56.1.25

Pieterse, A. L., Todd, N. R., Neville, H. A., & Carter, R. T. (2012). Perceived racism and mental health among Black American adults: A meta-analytic review. *Journal of Counseling Psychology, 59*, 1–9. http:// dx.doi.org/10.1037/a0026208

Pirtle, W. N. L., & Wright, T. (2021). Structural gendered racism revealed in pandemic times: Intersectional approaches to understanding race and gender health inequities in COVID-19. *Gender & Society, 35*(2), 168–179. https://doi.org/10.1177/08912432211001302

Rosenthal, L., & Lobel, M. (2018). Gendered racism and the sexual and reproductive health of Black and Latina women. *Ethnicity & Health, 23*, 1–26. https://doi.org/10.1080/13557858.2018.1439896

Seaton, E. K., Noah, A., Yoo, B., & Vargas, E. (2020). Health implications of Black Lives Matter among Black adults. *Journal of Racial and Ethnic Health Disparities, 7*, 1241–1248. https://doi.org/10.1007/s40615-020-00749-z

Shorter-Gooden, K. (2004). Multiple resistance strategies: How African American women cope with racism and sexism. *Journal of Black Psychology, 30*, 406–425. https://doi.org/10.1177/009579840 4266050

Sue, D. W., Capodilupo, C. M., Torino, G. C., Bucceri, J. M., Holder, A. M. B., Nadal, K. L., & Esquilin, M. (2007). Racial microaggressions in everyday life: Implications for clinical practice. *American Psychologist, 62*(4), 271–286. https://doi.org/10.1037/0003-066X.62.4.271

Szymanski, D. M., & Lewis, J. A. (2016). Gendered racism, coping, identity centrality, and African American college women's psychological distress. *Psychology of Women Quarterly, 40*(2), 229–243. https://doi.org/10.1177/0361684315616113

Taylor, K.-Y. (2017). *How we get free: Black feminism and the Combahee River Collective*. Haymarket.

Thomas, A. J., Speight, S. L., & Witherspoon, K. M. (2008). Gendered racism, psychological distress, and coping styles of African American women. *Cultural Diversity and Ethnic Minority Psychology*, *14*(4), 307–314. https://doi.org/10.1037/1099-9809.14.4.307

U.S. Census Bureau. (2020). *PINC-05: Work experience in 2019 – People 15 years old and over by total money earnings in 2018, age, race, Hispanic origin, sex, and disability status.* https://www.census.gov/data/tables/time-series/demo/income-poverty/cps-pinc/pinc-05.html

Watson-Singleton, N. N., Black, A. R., Spivey, B. N. (2019). Recommendations for a culturally-responsive mindfulness-based intervention for African Americans. *Complementary Therapies in Clinical Practice*, *34*, 132–138. https://doi.org/10.1016/j.ctcp.2018.11.013

White, J. L. (1970). Toward a Black psychology. *Ebony e*, *25*(11), 44–52.

Williams, M., G. & Lewis, J. A. (2019). Gendered racial microaggressions and depressive symptoms among Black women: A moderated mediation model. *Psychology of Women Quarterly*, *43*(3), 368–380. https://doi.org/10.1177/0361684319832511

Williams, D. R., & Williams-Morris, R. (2000). Racism and mental health: The African American experience. *Ethnicity & Health, 5*(3–4), 243– 268. http://dx.doi.org/10.1080/713667453

Woods-Giscombé, C. L., & Black, A. R. (2010). Mind-body interventions to reduce risk for health disparities related to stress and strength among African American women: The potential of mindfulness-based stress reduction, loving-kindness, and the NTU therapeutic framework. *Complementary Health Practice Review*, *15*(3), 115–131. https://doi.org/10.1177/1533210110386776

Woods-Giscombé, C. L., Allen, A. M., Black, A. R., Steed, T. C., Li, Y., & Lackey, C. (2019). The Giscombé Superwoman Schema Questionnaire: Psychometric properties and associations with mental health and health behaviors in African American women. *Issues in Mental Health Nursing*, *40*(8), 672–681. https://doi.org/10.1080/01612840.2019.1584654

Wright, L. N., & Lewis, J. A. (2020). Is physical activity a buffer? Gendered racial microaggressions and anxiety among African American women. *Journal of Black Psychology*, *46*(2–3), 122–143. https://doi.org/10.1177/0095798420929112

Part II

PUBLIC POLICY

CHAPTER FIVE

A Tale of Three Cities

Segregation and Anti-Black Education Policy
in Los Angeles, Chicago, and Austin

Annika Olson

I n 1903, W.E.B Du Bois famously wrote that "the problem of the twentieth century is the problem of the color line." Over 100 years later, his phrase still rings true. As such, it is crucial to understand the history of Black students in the American education system and the various policies and practices that have led to the circumstances that exist today. To illustrate historical context and the current state of education for Black students, we take a look at three cities: Los Angeles, Chicago, and Austin. And, as we dig deeper into the history of each locale, a stark picture of segregation, poverty, and school closures begins to form. The thread intertwining each of these cities and their respective issues is anti-Black racism. There were purposeful, powerful decisions made by education and city leaders to limit the equitable treatment of Black students and their families, and this theme still permeates the American education system today.

Los Angeles

It was a glaring, hot, August day in 1961 in South Gate, roughly 10 miles south of downtown Los Angeles, when Mary Ellen Crawford, a Black student, attempted to enroll at South Gate High School near her home (McGraw, 1989). South Gate was a working-class neighborhood of about 50,000 people and had experienced a boom in industry after WWII. It was an attractive city for the working class, with major factories like Firestone Tire, General Motors, and Jorgenson Steel (Creason, 2013). Mary Ellen was hoping to go to a school near her home, and was eager to hear back from the district regarding her request. It is important to note that this was nearly 5 years after the *Brown v. Board of Education* decision, which ruled that "separate but equal" had no place in the education system (U.S. Courts, n.d.).

Shortly after Mary Ellen filed the request for her school, the Los Angeles Unified School District (LAUSD) struck down the application, instead directing her to enroll at Jordan High School. The student body of Jordan was 99% Black, while South Gate High was 99% White. Her parents fought the district's decision by filing a lawsuit in Los Angeles

Superior Court, alleging that LAUSD used discriminatory attendance boundary practices (California State University, Northridge [CSUN], 2013). The ACLU took on the Crawford's case, along with Inita Watkins, another high school student, and filed a class action suit against the Los Angeles City Board of Education seeking to desegregate the two high schools (Sosa, 2013).

Nearly 5 *years* after unsuccessful negotiations, the ACLU, along with the NAACP, expanded their goal to desegregating all schools within LAUSD. In 1970, nearly a decade after Mary Ellen had attempted to enroll in South Gate High School, Judge Alfred Gitelson ruled that the Los Angeles City Board of Education and LAUSD had engaged in *de jure* segregation. This violated both the state and federal Constitutions, and Judge Gitelson ordered the board to develop a desegregation plan for the district (CSUN, 2013).

Upon appeal in June 1976, the state supreme court, while disagreeing with the conclusion that LAUSD had engaged in intentional segregation, did agree that LAUSD was obligated to take "reasonable and feasible" measures to alleviate the harms of segregation (LAUSD, n.d.). Busing was noted as just one of many methods of desegregating, with the court explaining, "local school boards should clearly have the initial and primary responsibility for choosing between these alternative methods" *(Crawford v. Board of Education of the City of Los Angeles*, 1976). In January and February of 1977, White parent boycotts ensued—one was made up of 9,000 people from nine schools and another of 65,000 from a variety of schools—all in adamant opposition to busing and integration. In 1978, the LA school board submitted a new plan for desegregating schools, but a trial court deemed the plan ineffective—it only covered grades 4 to 8 and excluded over 200,000 students in about 100 schools across the city (CSUN, 2013).

As tensions continued to flare around busing in Los Angeles, the state legislature passed Proposition 1 in 1979 that effectively ending forced busing. LA instead shifted to a voluntary busing system under court supervision and "magnet" programs were born. These special academic programs were designed to be attractive and draw White students to schools they might not otherwise attend. The program also allowed minority students from low-income South Los Angeles to take buses to schools in the Whiter and more economically advantaged San Fernando Valley, many of which needed to increase their enrollment—a daily migration called "Permits With Transportation" (Terry, 1981). The year 1979 also saw a drop in White enrollment in the district by nearly 30,000 students, or 15% over the previous year. Half of the decline was attributed to White flight due to desegregation, and the remaining White community, which made up 30% of enrollment, were even more desegregated than previous years (Terry, 1981). This White flight and increase in segregation are clear examples of anti-Blackness in action. Studies on White flight have shown that Whites were leaving increasingly integrated neighborhoods because of negative beliefs about African Americans, a simple desire not to live near African Americans, and dislike or distrust of African Americans (Krysan, 2002). Scholars highlight that students of color were perceived as low achieving, and, even worse, violent. Many White families, in an effort to maintain the Whiteness of their neighborhood, moved to the suburbs and avoided integrated schools (Schneider, 2008).

In addition to anti-Black sentiment and White flight, the early 1980s brought the devastating effects of Proposition 13, which capped funding for public schools and other services and prevented integration through forced busing. A crack-cocaine epidemic and gang violence tore through South Los Angeles, continuing to fuel racial tensions and White flight from the city (Schneider, 2008). By the 1990s, the inability to implement *Brown v. Board of Education* became evident as school segregation worsened over the ensuing years. In 1960, south LA was 53% Black and 33% White—in 1990, the White population decreased to nearly 2%, while minority communities made up over 90% of the community (Comandon & Ong, 2019).

By 2015, after nearly half a century of efforts to desegregate the district, schools in Los Angeles were still deeply segregated. Now, as it was in midcentury America, West-side schools, including Brentwood, Pacific Palisades, and Bel Air, are among the top performing schools, while those in south Los Angeles, such as Inglewood and Compton, are among the lowest. Sadly, little has changed over the past 50 years, harkening back to W.E.B Du Bois's timeless statement of the problem of "the color line" and the racist, anti-Black sentiment that permeates so many education systems.

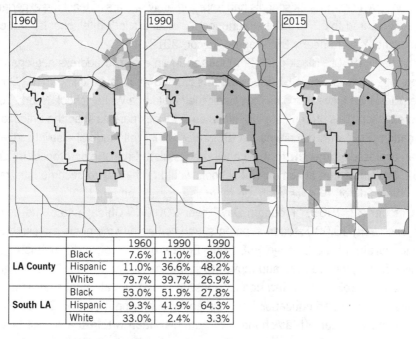

		1960	1990	1990
LA County	Black	7.6%	11.0%	8.0%
	Hispanic	11.0%	36.6%	48.2%
	White	79.7%	39.7%	26.9%
South LA	Black	53.0%	51.9%	27.8%
	Hispanic	9.3%	41.9%	64.3%
	White	33.0%	2.4%	3.3%

FIGURE 5.1   School segregation worsens across south Los Angeles.

Chicago

On a cold, harsh, winter day in 1960, a young boy walked home from school to the Robert Taylor Homes, a public housing project in Bronzeville on the South Side of Chicago. It was densely packed—28 high-rise buildings stretched from 39th to 54th street, 2 miles along the historic Black corridor. There were upward of 4,300 units and a total of 27,000 people living in the apartments, making it the largest public housing project in the world (Modica, 2009). The little boy attended class in what was known as the "Willis Wagons"—portable buildings put in place by Chicago schools Superintendent Benjamin Willis. The additional classroom space was intended to reduce overcrowding in predominantly Black schools rather than enrolling the children in larger, White schools nearby (*Chicago Reporter*, n.d.)

This story is similar to other young Black boys his age at the time. In 1960s Chicago, nearly 30% of Black families were living in poverty, compared to 7% of their White counterparts (Bogira, 2013). Additionally, 70% of the city's Black community lived in just 11 of the 76 community areas. The South and West sides became densely populated, marginalized, low-income areas (*Chicago Reporter*, n.d.). This overcrowding and marginalization was the result of a history of intentional policies meant to prevent Black residents from living throughout Chicago or earning a substantial income. There was overcrowding in many Black schools and a lack of qualified teachers, which forced students to go to school in half-day shifts. While Black students made up only 30% of the student body citywide, they were roughly 81% of the students attending school in shifts (Taylor, 2012). In addition, teachers in Black schools had approximately 4 years of teaching experience on average, compared to 12 years of experience for teachers in White schools, and classes in Black schools were nearly 25% larger (Taylor, 2012).

By the early 1960s, Black parents mobilized in an effort to address segregation and overcrowding. In August of 1961, Black parents created what became known as "Operation Transfer," in which they attempted to register their child at a White school. Nearly 160 parents were denied. This prompted a lawsuit when 22 Black parents sued the Chicago Board of Education (BoE) with discrimination (Bogira, 2013). While federal district judge Julius Hoffman expressed sympathy for the cause, he dismissed the suit on procedural grounds in 1962, explaining that at some point schools would find a way to become integrated.

Well, they did not. And, as such, de facto segregation endured.

On October 22, 1963, "Freedom Day," over 200,000 Chicago students boycotted school, and nearly 10,000 students, parents, and community members protested outside the headquarters of the Chicago BoE (Zinn Education Project, n.d.) At this point, the board was feeling the pressure and moved to settle the 2-year lawsuit. Parents agreed to settle when the BoE made a few concessions, including a statement that declared the principles of "integrated education" and a plan for achieving it (Taylor, 2012). However, integration was still far off, as changes of administration within the school board and pathetic attempts by Chicago schools Superintendent Benjamin Willis and the BoE to integrate schools continued. Two years later, in June of 1965, 100,000 Black students and their parents again took to the streets to boycott the racist, segregated Chicago public schools. In 1966 and 1968 school integration efforts saw little change—riots broke out across Black Chicago as White officials continued to keep Black schools inferior and White schools underutilized (Onion et al., 2018).

Finally, on April 12, 1980, the Department of Justice found the Chicago public schools BoE guilty of the unlawful segregation of students based on race (Stringfellow, 1991). The Department of Justice allowed the school board to enter negotiations to reach an agreement to solve the desegregation issue and, several months later, such an agreement was reached. There was ultimately a three-step process agreed on to eradicate segregation in the Chicago public school system. The parties agreed to a preliminary commitment to develop a plan, with the participation of experts and the community, which would be adopted no later than March 1981 (Jackson, 2010). The parties agreed to implement the plan beginning September 1981 (James, 2009).

Think about that—just to ensure access to equality between Black and White students, the United States had to sue the school system of Chicago. The plan would take nearly 2 years to implement.

Fast forward to the 21st century. Between 2007 and 2017, Chicago's public schools lost more than 52,000 Black students. Many leaders and academics have said that city officials make it difficult for poor Black communities to live in Chicago (Belsha, 2017). Neighborhood schools and mental health clinics closed; public housing was not rebuilt; gun violence and unemployment increased; and so on (Brownstein, 2015). There was serious disinvestment in the Black communities of Chicago, which was apparent for decades. And as Black students left Chicago, the percentage of Black students in the suburbs grew dramatically, which put a strain on already underfunded districts (Belsha, 2017).

For those families who have stayed in the city, concentrated poverty continues to be a serious barrier to education. In 2014 in Chicago, where 85% of students are Black or Latino, the concentration of poverty is overwhelming—in 77 of the 680 public schools, at least 99% of students qualify as poor or low income; in 388 schools, the share is near 90%. In only *50 out of nearly 700 schools* do less than half of students qualify as low income (Brownstein, 2015). Figure 5.2 shows the poverty rate, segregation, unemployment

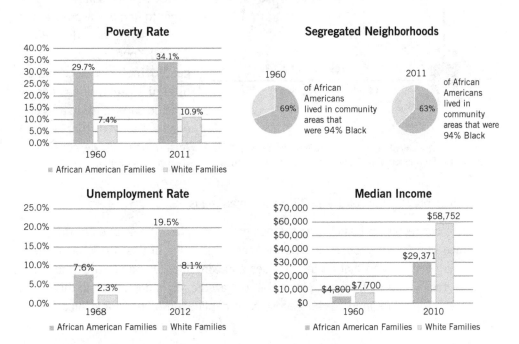

FIGURE 5.2 Disparities in 1960s Chicago still exist in the 21st century.

rate, and median income of Blacks and Whites in 1960 compared to the early 2010s. It is saddening to see that striking disparities have not changed over the course of half a century.

Austin

On another day in 1961, roughly 1,200 miles from Chicago and 1,500 miles from Los Angeles, the same story of segregation, racism, and disparities in education was unfolding in Austin, Texas. It had been nearly 6 years since the *Brown v. Board* decision, but little had changed in a deeply segregated city.

One reason Austin had become so deeply segregated by this point was the cruel and infamous 1928 plan. In 1927, the city of Austin hired the consulting firm of Koch & Fowler Consulting Engineers (1928) to overhaul the city's infrastructure, zoning, and public services. Even though the Supreme Court had already ruled that zoning neighborhoods by race was unconstitutional in 1948, engineers in Austin were eager to find a way around this ruling—and they did (Rich, 2005.) Koch and Fowler suggested that city services be offered to minorities in only specific parts of town, thus creating a "Negro district" in East Austin, on what was considered undesirable land (McInerny, 2019).

FIGURE 5.3   The city of Austin report entitled "A City Plan," which laid the foundation of racist infrastructure that pervades the city today.

The "Schools" chapter of the 1928 master plan reads,

> It is our recommendation that the nearest approach to the solution of the race segregation problem will be the recommendation of this district as a negro district; and that all the facilities and conveniences be provided the negroes in this district as an incentive to draw the negro population to this area. This will eliminate the necessity of duplication of white and black

In our studies in Austin we have found that the negroes are

present in small numbers, in practically all sections of the city,

excepting the area just east of East Avenue and south of the City

Cemetery. This area seems to be all negro population. It is our

recommendation that the nearest approach to the solution of the race

segregation problem will be the recommendation of this district as

a negro district; and that all the facilities and conveniences be pro-

vided the negroes in this district, as an incentive to draw the negro

population to this area. This will eliminate the necessity of duplication

of white and black schools, white and black parks, and other duplicate

facilities for this area. We are recommending that sufficient area be

acquired adjoining the negro high school to provide adequate space for

a complete negro play-field in connection with the negro high school.

FIGURE 5.4   A portion of the city of Austin report, "A City Plan," defining a stark, segregated, Negro district in East Austin—solidifying segregated schools across the city.

schools, white and black parks, and other duplicate facilities for this area.
(Gregor, 2010)

This racial barrier was further solidified when I-35 was constructed in the 1950s, smack dab in the middle of the city, keeping East Austin separate from West Austin.

Hence, from 1928–1954, Austin schools were segregated. And, even after the *Brown v. Board* decision, nothing changed throughout the 1950s and 1960s. In 1970, however, the federal government could no longer turn a blind eye. The Department of Health, Education and Welfare sued the Austin Independent School District (AISD) and found the district in violation of the 1964 Civil Rights Act for not complying with the *Brown* decision (Austin Public Library, n.d.)

Crazy, isn't it? Yet *another* school district is being sued—by the federal government—for limiting equal opportunity for Black students, blatant segregation, and breaking a federal law.

As a result of the 1970 court case, two all-Black schools closed on September 1, 1971, forcing students to all-White schools in other parts of the city, and one-way bussing of Black students began (Austin Public Library, n.d.).

By 1980, a judge said this didn't satisfy *Brown v. Board* and two-way bussing of both White and minority students began—fully integrating all AISD *26 years* after the momentous *Brown* decision (McInerny, 2019). Many White Austinites fought back. Because of this court-ordered desegregation, fall enrollment at Austin's private schools increased, as White families loathed the idea of placing their children in schools with Black children (*The Daily Texan*, 1980). The hatred White families felt toward sending their children to school with Black students stemmed from the deep-seeded racist beliefs that Black children and families were inferior to White children and families and the intense desire to maintain racially homogenous environments for their children (Hannah-Jones, 2019). *The Washington Post* reported that this sentiment is still alive and well today, as cities suffer from widespread segregation and the continued unwillingness of White families to share space and community with Black families (Badger, 2015).

Several years later, in 1987, the AISD board of trustees voted to end crosstown bussing for elementary students, leaving 16 schools across the district entirely minority. Despite the decades of work to integrate students, anti-Black racism and limited opportunities for minority students prevailed.

Fast forward to 2020, and the story of segregation is equally as bleak. McInerny (2020) found that schools in Travis County (which includes Austin) are the most segregated in the entire state of Texas. It is clear that Austin still has a long way to go in equalizing opportunity for all students. Figure 5.5 shows the districts in Texas with the largest gaps in school poverty between Black and White students.

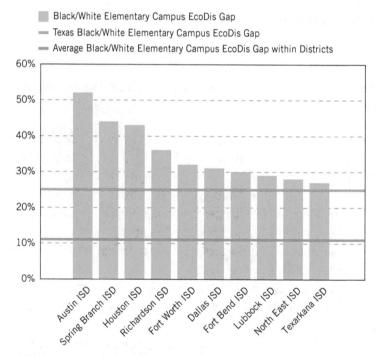

FIGURE 5.5 Districts with largest gaps in school poverty between Black and White students.

Sterne (2020) explained,

> Black and Hispanic Elementary students are tracked to elementary schools that on average have rates of Economically Disadvantaged students that are 50 percentage points greater than the elementary schools that White students attend in the same district. *There is no other district in the state that has gaps this extreme.*

In addition to the segregation, Austin faces the ongoing threat of charter schools. Charter schools—defined as public schools that have specific educational objectives and are exempt from significant state or local regulations related to operation and management—are hotly debated, to say the least (National Charter School Resource Center, n.d.). For years, promoters have pointed to the free-market concept of school choice that promotes student innovation and improves academic outcomes (Renzulli & Evans, 2005). Opponents, however, argue that these "public" schools detract resources from traditional public school districts and deepen school segregation (May, 2006; Rotberg, 2014).

From the research we, at the Institute for Urban Policy Research and Analysis, have done, it is apparent that while charter schools aggressively promote themselves as good alternatives to public schools, many are grossly discriminatory of the students they accept, rely heavily on discipline, and do not exhibit better academic performance than public schools. A 2015 study by the Center for Research on Education Outcomes (CREDO) compared the performance of charter schools to traditional public schools in Texas metro areas and found that charter school students' performance in math and reading was more likely to be significantly worse or not significantly different. Additionally, some researchers, utilizing critical race theory, explain that applying a market model to education eliminates the roles that power, race, and privilege play in upholding disparities in education (Chapman & Donner, 2015). Finally, an Institute for Urban Policy Research and Analysis report found that during the 2014–2015 and 2015–2016 school years, the

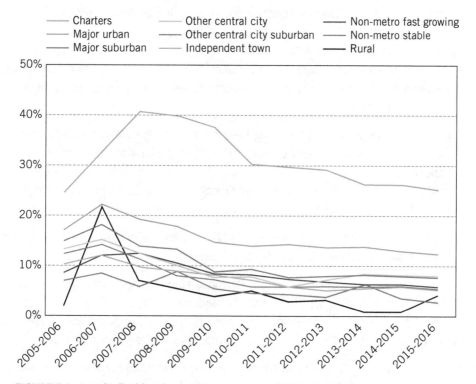

FIGURE 5.6 Longitudinal (grades 9–12) Dropout rates of Black students by district type.

dropout rate was higher and the longitudinal graduation rate lower for charter schools in Texas compared to public schools (Ross et al., 2018).

It's important, anecdotally, to note that Texas is the second largest authorizer of charter schools in the nation behind California, with over 180 charter school districts and roughly 800 campus sites (Texas Education Agency 2019; U.S. Department of Education 2017). This accounts for about 6% of the state's public school population, up from 1% in 2000. Perhaps more importantly, about 80% of charter enrollees are Black or Hispanic. Additionally, over 70% of charter schools in Texas serve economically disadvantaged students. According to Ricardo Lowe (2020), my coworker and one of the researchers in our institute, the percent change difference of charter enrollees in the city of Austin was upward of almost 800% from 2008 to 2020. Most of these schools are made up of minority students, further exacerbating the segregation in Travis county's already profoundly segregated district.

The State of Black Education Today

The historic anti-Black racism seen in the education systems in Los Angeles, Chicago, and Austin was not unlike many other cities throughout the country. It is also something that greatly impacts the state of Black education today. I've chosen a few areas—school context and achievement, poverty, and the digital divide—to provide insight into the struggles and successes Black students across the United States face today.

School Context and Achievement

Statistics from the National Center for Education Statistics (2018) demonstrate disparities between Black, Brown, and White students related to academic achievement and the school environment

- The percentage of students earning their highest math course credit in calculus: White (18%), students of two or more races (11%), Hispanic students (10%), and Black students (6%).
- In 2013–2014, roughly 2.6 million public school students (5.3%) received one or more out-of-school suspensions.

  - A higher percentage of Black students (14%) than students from any other racial/ethnic group received an out-of-school suspension.

- From 2000 to 2016, the dropout rate for Black students decreased from 13 to 6%. However, this is still higher than for White students—4.2%.
- In 2017–2018, only 7% of public school teachers and 11% of public school principals were Black. Yet more than 15% of Black students attended public schools.

Disparities like these, rampant within our education system today, are deeply rooted in racial inequities and anti-Black racism that has existed for decades. Historically segregated schools and racist policies in LA, Chicago, and Austin—and thousands of other cities throughout the country—have deeply affected the school context and achievement gaps we see today.

Poverty and Food Insecurity

In 2018, roughly one third of Black students lived in poverty compared with 10% of White students. The percentage of Black students who lived in households where the highest level of education attained by a parent was a bachelor's degree or higher was approximately 27%, compared with 70% of Asian students and 53% of White students (National Center for Education statistics, 2018).

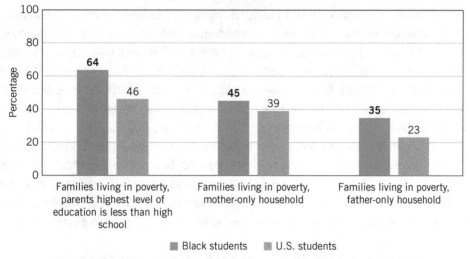

FIGURE 5.7   Percentage of Black students from families living in poverty, by parents' education level or family structure, 2018.

Striking statistics also show that a much higher percentage of Black students attend high-poverty schools. In fact, 45% of Black students attended high-poverty schools, compared with 8% of White students. This means that many Black students are in under-resourced schools—schools with fewer books, limited educational materials, crumbling infrastructure, and few (if any) specialized staff like counselors and reading specialists. Because of this, the nationwide achievement gap between minority and White students continues to grow, undermining the chance for Black students to improve their educational outcomes and be part of a pipeline of opportunity.

With regard to food insecurity, a Harvard study found that in 2018, 25% of Black households were food insecure, compared with 17% of Hispanic households. This number jumped to 40% for Black households and 37% for Hispanic households amidst the COVID-19 pandemic in 2020. The rate of food insecurity for White households with children is roughly 22% (Harvard Chan School of Public Health, 2020). Think about these numbers—nearly one in five Black families do not have enough food to eat in the year 2020. This can cause increased stress in the home, inability to concentrate due to lack of nourishment, and a myriad of other health and well-being issues. Importantly, kids who struggle with food insecurity may also struggle in school. I saw it firsthand when I worked in a Title I school in Austin—if a child came into class hungry, having not eaten at home, they were generally much more tired, unable to concentrate, and easily irritable. It affected their school work, their interactions with other students and teachers, and generally the success of their day. Food insecurity is something to worry about, especially among our most vulnerable communities.

Digital Divide

In our technologically based world today, having access to internet and computers has become a necessity, yet many school-age children are left disconnected from the digital world. Nearly 18 million young students under the age of 18 lack high-speed internet at home, and this digital divide disproportionately affects communities of color, as it has for decades (Ujifusa, 2020). While a majority of White households (80%) have broadband internet, just 66% of Black households and 61% of Hispanic households are able to log on to broadband internet at home (Anderson, M., & Perrin, A, 2018). For Black children aged 3 to 18 years, 11% had home internet access *only* through a smartphone, compared with just 2% of Asian and 3% White students (National School Board Association, 2018). For the thousands of students who only have access to internet through a smartphone, this makes homework increasingly difficult to complete. A study by Pew Research found that a quarter of Black teens say they are unable to complete their homework due to lack

Economic and Digital Divides of Children Ages 5 to 17 by Race and Ethnicity, 2018

Racial or Ethnic Group	Lacks Computer, High-Speed Internet Access, or Both	Family Income Below 100% of Poverty	Household Receives SNAP Benefits
American Indian/Alaska Native	50%	30%	35%
Black	36%	31%	39%
Hispanic or Latino	34%	25%	28%
White	20%	10%	12%
Asian/NHOPI	14%	11%	11%
Two + Races	19%	16%	23%
All Children	25%	17%	21%

Notes: Computers include desktops, laptops, or tablets. All racial groups are non-Hispanic, and Hispanics can be of any race. NHOPI is Native Hawaiian and other Pacific Islander.

FIGURE 5.8 There is a clear economic and digital divide among children, especially by race and ethnicity.

of digital access, and nearly 15% of these respondents says this happens often (Anderson & Perrin, 2018). The same year, 21% of Black teens reported using public Wi-Fi (this could be anywhere—a library, fast food parking lot, and so on) to do schoolwork because there was no internet at home, compared to 11% of White students (Auxier & Anderson, 2020). Among Black students without home internet access, nearly 40% said that it was because internet is too expensive (U.S. Department of Education, 2019).

How do we as a society expect children to complete their homework, keep up with their studies, and advance their education if they don't have access to internet or a computer at home, which are now basic necessities (utilities even) of everyday life? When barriers to technology access limit students' ability to engage with educational materials, what is known as the "homework gap" emerges, pushing marginalized students of color even further behind their peers academically (Mulverhill, 2019). Long-term negative conse-quences include limited career preparedness, as researchers find that Americans who lack broadband access are at a disadvantage to their counterparts when it comes to applying for jobs and participating in the workforce. Is this how we would like to prepare our children for the future?

Policy Implications and Conclusion

Throughout this chapter you've learned about the segregation and disparities that existed for Black students in LA, Chicago, and Austin from the 1960s until the present day. You've gained vital insight into the state of Black education today, and the numerous issues that still need to be addressed in order to ensure all children are given equal opportunity in the American education system. Hopefully, this chapter has caused you to think deeply about anti-Black attitudes polices that have pervaded the education system for decades and affected the lives of millions of students. Looking forward, what is the culmination of years of progression and regression? What are the larger policy implications? First, the Biden education plan should be implemented to address racial disparities in the education system; second, the country must focus on ridding anti-Black racism through deliberate conversations inside school classrooms; and third, it is time to address the desire of White families to not educate their children with Black children.

Biden Education Plan

One step in the right direction may come with the incoming Biden administration. The Biden education plan was recently released and details national policy reform dedicated to ensuring that "no child's future is determined by their zip code, parent's income, race, or disability" (Biden, 2021). The plan explicitly states that the federal govern-ment will invest in schools to eliminate the gap between White and non-White districts, and rich and poor districts, by tripling Title I funding. Additionally, there will be inten-tional approaches to recruiting teachers of color and collaborating with historically Black colleges and universities (HBCUs) and other minority-serving institutions (MSIs) to recruit and prepare teachers. The third pillar will "build the best, most innovative schools in the country in low-income communities and communities of color," and the fourth will reinstate the Obama-Biden administration's actions to diversify the nation's schools. The plan states that President Biden will reinstate Department of Education guidance that supported schools in legally pursuing desegregation strategies. YES. This is one of the many important systemic changes that can have a huge impact. Segregation, as explained throughout this chapter, has created enormous disparities in education and limited resource allocation to predominately Black schools. If the federal government can now legally support schools in pursuing desegregation, we may, finally, be tackling the issue at a macro, national policy level.

Confronting Anti-Blackness in Schools

A recent *Education Week* article by Dr. Tyrone Howard, UCLA professor of education and director of the Black Male Institute, highlighted several deliberate steps that should be taken to combat anti-Black racism and the irreparable harm it causes Black students, families, and teachers. Schools should be part of the solution, utilized as catalysts against racist rhetoric and behavior. He explained that anti-Black racism must be named for what it is, Black students must be believed, and we must identify and speak about Black excellence (Howard, 2020).

The first point highlights the need for educators to develop the knowledge to discuss and name the many levels of racism and anti-Blackness that have existed in the United States for hundreds of years. It must be an ongoing, intentional conversation between teachers and students, challenging prior assumptions and learning about systemic structures. This includes an African American curriculum in every public school in the United States, instead of the generally sanitized version of slavery and the civil rights movement that is taught in many schools (Yancey-Bragg, 2021). Research highlights that children's awareness of racism and racial differences begins early in life—as early as preschool—and many argue that teachers have a duty to teach and learn with children about these critical issues. (Delpit 2012; Tatum 2003). Chicago public schools (CPS) unveiled curriculum for African American studies in 2013, which allows teachers to incorporate African and African American studies into core subjects throughout the year. The *Chicago Sun Times* reported that the information these students are taught is the truest form of Black America's history:

> The one with white people having picnics to celebrate lynchings. The history of powerful Black resistance music and art. The one with dismembered body parts displayed in storefronts and Black perseverance and success through oppression. (Issa, 2020)

Secondly, Black students must be heard by teachers and the school community when they discuss their experience with racism and exclusion—from being subject to unfair discipline or feeling stereotyped in the classroom—it is crucial to *believe* students' stories, much like believing the stories of those of the #MeToo movement. There should be specific mechanisms for students to report incidents of racism to school leaders and plans in place for school leadership to proactively implement antiracist strategies (Aveling, 2007).

Lastly, Black students must be celebrated for their success and achievements, as much of anti-Black sentiment is steeped in a deep-rooted belief in the inferiority of Black people (Howard, 2020). Students need supportive teachers who can help them identify their strengths in the classroom and support sports or hobbies they enjoy, and this, in turn, can help achievement soar (Adair, 2015). Brandi Stone, head of the University of New Mexico's African American Student Services stated, "Black excellence is both a mindset and a continuous action to progress our community through various approaches, education being one of them" (King, 2020).

Confronting Anti-Blackness: White Parents

Pulitzer Prize–winning reporter Nikole Hannah-Jones, who covers civil rights and racial injustice in the United States, highlights that another essential group to consider when combating anti-Black policies in schools is parents. In a recent *Atlantic* interview she stated,

> We have a system where White people control the outcomes. And the outcome that most White Americans want is segregation. And I don't mean the type of segregation that we saw in 1955. I don't mean complete segregation. I don't think there are very many White Americans who want entirely White schools. What they do want is a limited number of black kids in their schools. (Douglas, 2017).

She goes on to say that there are some White parents who see and understand race, but they are the rare few. These more "liberal" parents will send their children to schools where they are the minority race, but these parents are an exception to the rule (Douglas, 2017). White parents have serious power and control over where they send their children to school, and as such it is time to look critically at the education policies being promoted or diminished by White parents and tackle the issues that have upheld White power in school. One way, Hannah-Jones suggests, is to outlaw private schools, which are predominantly high income and White. She explains that in the 1950s the way to subvert *Brown v. Board of Education* was to withdraw from public schools, which is what people did. If private school was not an option, White parents would be forced to look at, and thus care about, the public schools in their community and the integration of its students (Douglas, 2017).

Furthermore, a recent report from Harvard looking at parents' preferences on integration recently found that the most common reason White, high-income parents tended to pick Whiter, more affluent schools is because they value school quality more than integration. The report stated that White parents see integrated schools as "educationally inferior" and simply the presence of a significant number of Black students negatively influences White parent's assessment of school quality (Torres & Weissbuord, 2020). The researchers urged schools and parents to stop relying on school report cards, academic ratings, and levels of proficiency posted to school websites because these metrics are not always helpful when gauging quality. They stated that White, affluent parents are "insulated in information bubbles rampant with bias and rumors" and this must be dealt with. Instead, parents must physically go to their available schools—talk to principals, teachers, and so on—and figure out if it is a good fit for their child (Camera, 2020). The report ends on an optimistic note, highlighting that parenting trends have changed throughout history and that is possible with this situation we face today:

> The question is not whether [White] parenting priorities can change, it's whether we can summon the wisdom and discipline to direct that change, and how soon. (Torres & Weissbuord, 2020)

And I would say, it is about time, nearly 60 years after Mary Ellen Crawford attempted to enroll in South Gate High School and communities picketed against "Willis Wagons" in Chicago, that anti-Black racism within the U.S. education system is eliminated. The year 2021 is the dawn of a new administration and, hopefully, progress forward. It is time that Black students are fully, completely, and equitably supported in their educational pursuits, White parents take a hard look at the racism and segregation within their communities, and Black humanity is made a top priority in all schools.

References

Adair, J. K. (2015). *The impact of discrimination on the early schooling experiences of children from immigrant families*. Migration Policy Institute. http://www.migrationpolicy.org/research/impact-discrimination-early-schooling-experiences-children-immigrant-families

Anderson, M., & Perrin, A. (2018, October 26). *Nearly one-in-five teens can't always finish their homework because of the digital divide*. Pew Research Center. https://www.pewresearch.org/fact-tank/2018/10/26/nearly-one-in-five-teens-cant-always-finish-their-homework-because-of-the-digital-divide/

Austin Public Library. (n.d.). *Desegregation in Austin*. http://www.austinlibrary.com/ahc/desegregation/index.cfm?action=decade&dc=1970s

Auxier, B., & Anderson, M. (2020, March 16). *As schools close due to the coronavirus, some U.S. students face a digital "homework gap."* Pew Research Center. https://www.pewresearch.org/fact-tank/2020/03/16/as-schools-close-due-to-the-coronavirus-some-u-s-students-face-a-digital-homework-gap/

Aveling, N. (2007) Anti-racism in schools: A question of leadership? *Discourse: Studies in the Cultural Politics of Education, 28*(1), 69–85. https://doi.org/10.1080/01596300601073630

Badger, E. (2015). Obama administration to unveil major new rules targeting segregation across U.S. *The Washington Post*. https://www.washingtonpost.com/news/wonk/wp/2015/07/08/obama-administration-to-unveil-major-new-rules-targeting-segregation-across-u-s/

Belsha, K. (2017). Thousands of black students leave Chicago for other segregated districts. *Chicago Reporter*. https://www.chicagoreporter.com/black-cps-student-migration/

Biden, J. (2021). *The Biden plan for educators, students, and our future*. https://joebiden.com/education/

Bogira, S. (2013). A dream unrealized for African-Americans in Chicago. *Chicago Reader*. https://www.chicagoreader.com/chicago/african-american-percentage-poverty-unemployment-schools-segregation/Content?oid=10703562

Brownstein, R. (2015). Why poverty and segregation merge at public schools. *The Atlantic*. https://www.the-atlantic.com/politics/archive/2015/11/why-poverty-and-segregation-merge-at-public-schools/433380/

California State University, Northridge. (2013a). *School desegregation and busing in Los Angeles.* https://library.csun.edu/SCA/Peek-in-the-Stacks/DesegregationBusing

California State University, Northridge. (2013b). *The struggle to desegregate Los Angeles Schools 1940–1970.* https://www.csun.edu/sites/default/files/Lesson%203.pdf

Camera, L. (2020). *White, affluent parents like the idea of integrated schools—but not for their kids.* US News and World Report.https://www.usnews.com/news/education-news/articles/2020-02-07/white-affluent-parents-like-the-idea-of-integrated-schools-but-not-for-their-kids

Chapman, T., & Donnor, J. (2015). Equity and excellence in education critical race theory and the proliferation of U.S. charter schools. *Equity & Excellence in Education, 48*, 137–154.

The Chicago Reporter. (n.d.). *History of Chicago public schools.* https://www.chicagoreporter.com/cps-history/

Comandon, A., & Ong, P. (2019). South Los Angeles since the 1960s: race, place, and class. *The Review of Black Political Economy*, 47(1), 50–74. https://doi.org/10.1177/0034644619873105

Crawford v. Board of Education of the City of Los Angeles, 280, U.S. 130 (1976). https://casetext.com/case/crawford-v-board-of-education-2

Creason, G. (2013). CityDig: The suburban dream of south gate. *Los Angeles Magazine*. https://www.lamag.com/citythinkblog/citydig-the-suburban-dream-of-south-gate/

The Daily Texan. (1980). *Busing spurs exit to private schools.* http://www.austinlibrary.com/ahc/desegregation/index.cfm?action=year&yr=1980

Delpit, L. (2012). *"Multiplication Is for White People": Raising Expectations for Other People's Children*. New York: The New Press

Douglas, D. (2017). Are private schools immoral? *The Atlantic*. https://www.theatlantic.com/education/archive/2017/12/progressives-are-undermining-public-schools/548084/

Du Bois, W. E. B. (1903). *The souls of Black folk: Essays and sketches*. A. G. McClurg.

Gregor, K. (2010). Austin comp planning: A brief history. *Austin Chronicle*. https://www.austinchronicle.com/news/2010-02-05/953471/

Hannah-Jones, N. (2019). It was never about bussing. *The New York Times*. https://www.nytimes.com/2019/07/12/opinion/sunday/it-was-never-about-busing.html

Harvard Chan School of Public Health. (2020). *Nearly four in 10 Black, Hispanic families facing food insecurity during pandemic.* https://www.hsph.harvard.edu/news/hsph-in-the-news/nearly-four-in-10-black-hispanic-families-facing-food-insecurity-during-pandemic/

Howard, T. (2020). How to root-out anti-Black racism from your school. *Education Week*. https://www.edweek.org/leadership/opinion-how-to-root-out-anti-black-racism-from-your-school/2020/06

Issa, N. (2020). How CPS students are learning about black history and white supremacy—and how that's helping them understand George Floyd. *Chicago Sun Times*. https://chicago.suntimes.com/education/2020/6/5/21279788/1619-project-cps-chicago-public-schools-black-history-white-supremacy-george-floyd-civil-rights

Jackson, S. (2010). *An historical analysis of the Chicago public schools desegregation consent decree (1980–2006): Establishing its relationship with the* Brown v. Board *case of 1954 and the implications of its implementation on educational leadership* [Doctoral dissertation, Loyola University Chicago].

James, M. (2009). *The Chicago Board of Education desegregation policies and practices [1975-1985]: A historical examination of the administrations of superintendents Dr. Joseph P. Hannon and Dr. Ruth Love*[Doctoral dissertation, Loyola University Chicago]. https://ecommons.luc.edu/cgi/viewcontent.cgi?article=1108&context=luc_diss

King, M. (2020). *Black student excellence springs from historic inequalities*. UNM Newsroom. http://news.unm.edu/news/black-student-excellence-springs-from-historic-inequalities

Krysan, M. (2002). Whites who say they'd flee: Who are they, and why would they leave? *Demography, 39*(4), 675–696. http://www.jstor.org/stable/3180826

Koch & Fowler Consulting Engineers. (1928). *A city plan for Austin, Texas*. ftp://ftp.austintexas.gov/GIS-Data/planning/compplan/1927_Plan.pdf

LeeKeenan, L. D., & Nimmo, J. (2015). *Leading anti-Bias early childhood programs: A guide for change*. Teachers College Press.

Los Angeles Unified School District (n.d.). *LAUSD's court-ordered integration programs*. https://achieve.lausd.net/Page/6351

Lowe, R. (2020). *Examining enrollment trends between AISD and local charter schools: A demographic perspective*. Institute for Urban Policy Research and Analysis. https://utexas.app.box.com/v/enrollment-trends-charter-aisd

May, J. J. (2006). The charter school allure: Can traditional schools measure up? *Education and Urban Society, 39*(1),19–45. https://doi.org/10.1177/0013124506291786

McGraw, C. (1989). L.A. schools: Integration fight—no victor seen. *The Los Angeles Times*. https://www.latimes.com/archives/la-xpm-1989-04-06-mn-1247-story.html

McInerny, C. (2019). *Austin failed at desegregation before. That history influences today's school closure decisions*. KUT. https://www.kut.org/post/austin-failed-desegregation-history-influences-todays-school-closure-decisions

McInerny, C. (2020). Schools in Travis County are not just segregated. They're the most segregated in the state. *The Austin Monitor*. https://www.austinmonitor.com/stories/2020/07/schools-in-travis-county-are-not-just-segregated-theyre-the-most-segregated-in-the-state/

Modica, A. (2009). Robert Taylor Homes, Chicago Illinois (1959–2005). *Black Past*. https://www.blackpast.org/african-american-history/robert-taylor-homes-chicago-illinois-1959-2005/

Mulverhill, L. (2019). *Texas' digital divide*. Texas Comptroller. https://comptroller.texas.gov/economy/fiscal-notes/2019/oct/divide.php

National Center for Education Statistics. (2018). *Status and trends in the education of racial and ethnic groups 2018*. https://nces.ed.gov/pubs2019/2019038.pdf

National Charter School Resource Center. (n.d.). *What is a charter school?* https://charterschoolcenter.ed.gov/what-charter-school

National School Board Association. (2020). *Black students in the condition of education 2020*. https://www.nsba.org/Perspectives/2020/black-students-condition-education

Onion, A., Sullivan, M., & Mullen, M. (2018). *1968 Democratic Convention*. History. https://www.history.com/topics/1960s/1968-democratic-convention#section_1

Renzulli, L., & Evans, L. (2005). School choice, charter schools, and white flight. *Social Problems, 52*(3), 398–418. https://doi.org/10.1525/sp.2005.52.3.398

Rich, M. (2005). Restrictive covenants stubbornly stay on the books. *The New York Times*. https://www.nytimes.com/2005/04/21/garden/restrictive-covenants-stubbornly-stay-on-the-books.html

Ross, K., Cokley, K., Carlino, R., Phan, S., Badgett, M., & Hood, J. Schneider, J. (2018). *The state of Black lives in Texas education report*. Institute for Urban Policy Research and Analysis. https://utexas.app.box.com/v/2018-black-lives-tx-education

Rotberg, I. C. (2014). Charter schools and the risk of increased segregation. *Phi Delta Kappan, 95*(5), 26–31. https://doi.org/10.1177/003172171409500507

Schneider, J. (2008). Escape from Los Angeles: White flight from Los Angeles and its schools, 1960–1980. *Journal of Urban History, 34*(6), 995–1012. https://doi.org/10.1177/0096144208317600

Sosa, H. (2013). *Fragmented diversity: school desegregation, student activism, and busing in Los Angeles, 1963–1982* [Doctoral dissertation, University of Michigan]. https://deepblue.lib.umich.edu/bitstream/handle/2027.42/97911/hsosa_1.pdf?sequence=2

Sterne, V. (2020). *Elementary school poverty disparities in Texas*. Institute for Urban Policy Research and Analysis. https://utexas.app.box.com/file/679107860149?v=school-poverty-disparities

Stringfellow, C. (1991). *Desegregation policies and practices in Chicago during the superintendencies of James Redmond and Joseph Hannon* [Doctoral dissertation, Loyola University Chicago]. https://ecommons.luc.edu/luc_diss/3181

Tatum, B. (2003). *Why are all the Black kids sitting together in the cafeteria?: And other conversations about race* (rev. ed.). Basic Books.

Taylor, K-Y. (2012). *Challenging Jim Crow schools in Chicago*. International Sociologist Organization. https://socialistworker.org/2012/02/22/jim-crow-schools-in-chicago

Terry, S. (1981). *Los Angeles school desegregation: The 18-year-long "ride" is over*. Christian Science Monitor. https://www.csmonitor.com/1981/0410/041049.html

Texas Education Agency. (2019). *Enrollment in Texas public schools*. Austin: TEA. https://tea.texas.gov/sites/default/files/enroll_2018-19.pdf

Torres, E., & Weissbourd, R. (2020). *Do parents really want school integration?* Harvard University Graduate School of Education. https://static1.squarespace.com/static/5b7c56e255b02c683659fe43/t/5e30a6280107be3cf98d15e6/1580246577656/Do+Parents+Really+Want+School+Integration+2020+FINAL.pdf

Ujifusa, A. (2020). 1 in 3 American Indian, Black, and Latino children fall into digital divide, study says. *Education Week*. https://blogs.edweek.org/edweek/campaign-k-12/2020/07/digital-divide-1-in-3-black-latino-american-indian-children.html

U.S. Courts. (n.d.). *History:* Brown v. Board of Education *re-enactment*. https://www.uscourts.gov/educational-resources/educational-activities/history-brown-v-board-education-re-enactment

U.S. Department of Education (2016). *Public elementary and secondary charter schools and enrollment, by state: Selected years, 2000–01 through 2015–16*. https://nces.ed.gov/programs/digest/d17/tables/dt17_216.90.asp

Yancey-Bragg, N. (2021). Why is Black History Month in February? How do you celebrate? Everything you need to know. *USA Today*. https://www.usatoday.com/story/news/nation/2021/02/01/black-history-month-2021-how-celebrate-what-know/4292640001/

Zinn Education Project. (n.d.). *Oct. 22, 1963: Chicago school boycott*. https://www.zinnedproject.org/news/tdih/1963-chicago-school-boycott/

Credits

CHAPTER SIX

Policing the Black Diaspora

Colonial Histories and Global Inequities in Policing
and Carceral Punishment

Ricardo Henrique Lowe, Jr.

A ctivists have long called for societies to reimagine what a world without police and prisons would look like. The argument has been relatively consistent over the years—that carceral punishment as a presumed safeguard for democracy and public safety is ineffective because it attempts to resolve social problems by "warehousing" people rather than assessing the root causes of criminality (Davis, 2016).

This is not an untenable assertion. Clarence Thomas—who currently serves among the eight associate justices of the U.S. Supreme Court—once noted in a 1994 speech that freedom and opportunity in the United States are unattainable if "criminal law loses sight of the importance of individual responsibility." Thomas (1994) went on to emphasize that minorities and poor people are not exempt from accountability because they too are "capable of dignity as well as shame, folly as well as success."

Thomas's statements absolve the role that systems play in imposing barriers that ultimately place certain groups on the trajectory of crime and punishment. Dias (2016), for instance, says that the United States was founded on principles of apartheid and that contemporary issues in criminal law are rooted in racist polices that barred non-White groups from constitutional protections and exposed them to prolonged economic and social disadvantage. Further, Thomas's underlying presumption that institutions weigh "individual responsibility" equitably across all social groups negates decades of research that affirm that Black people in particular are significantly more likely to be arrested and receive harsher sentences than their White counterparts irrespective of their socioeconomic status (Gramlich, 2020). To be sure, disparities in criminal law persist irrespective of whether individual responsibility is prioritized.

Most discouraging about Thomas's statement is his failure to consider how racial disparities are not exclusive to the United States. It is not coincidental, for example, that Aboriginal peoples in Australia, who occupy the lowest order of that country's respective social hierarchy, are criminalized comparably to Black Americans. The Australian Law Reform Commission estimates that the Aboriginal and Torres Strait Islander population account for just 2% of the Australian population but nearly 30% of its prison population. Neither is it by chance that Black Brazilians, like Black Americans, are more likely to be killed by the police compared to their White counterparts. In Rio de Janeiro alone, almost 80% of the nearly 900 people killed by police in the first half of 2019 were Black according to the Institute of Public Security (Biller, 2020; Phillips, 2020).

Similar parallels can be made with virtually any country where racial hierarchies exist. The reason is the longstanding and relatively predictable effects of racialized and intensely violent colonial histories (Razack, 2020). Put plainly, inequities in policing and the broader veracities of crime and punishment can be interpreted as a global Black struggle rooted in White supremacy and settler colonialism. The disparities we see transpiring across the world are systemically ingrained and cannot simply be reduced to individual responsibility.

This chapter examines policing and carceral punishment through the context of global Black struggle. The purpose is to inform how Black populations in formerly colonized nations and metropoles are similarly criminalized due in large part to shared colonial histories. I begin by describing how the year 2020 serves as a momentous awakening for the Black diaspora in terms of recognizing the interrelated mechanisms of police brutality and systemic racism at scale. I relate the deaths of George Floyd and Breonna Taylor to police killings that transpired outside of the United States in countries like Brazil, France, and Nigeria. The next section historizes policing through slavery, colonialism, and postcolonialism. I show that modern-day policing can be traced to slave codes and colonial laws enforced by European imperialists. Policies were codified to uphold racial hierarchies, and systems of colonial policing were later installed to maintain institutions of exploitation in occupied territories. To this day these issues continue to inhibit Black peoples in postcolonial societies and Western metropoles where non-White peoples are increasingly growing in population share. Next, I propose solutions from all sides of the political spectrum, especially as they relate to both reform and abolition. I offer examples of strategies that have been implemented in societies across the world and examine their relative effectiveness or lack thereof in refining the institution of policing at scale. Lastly, I address public policy implications. Ultimately, I contend that global initiatives to refine policing and carcerality can only be effective if policy makers name, confront, and eliminate anti-Black racism in their policy work.

It is important to acknowledge that systems of policing and carcerality across the world are much too variable to entirely capture in this chapter. Experiences with colonial and postcolonial policing are certainly not exclusive to the Black diaspora and cannot be comprehensively understood without engaging with other colonized groups and territories. What this essay attempts to accomplish is inform how the contemporary Black struggle with policing and carcerality is situated within a shared colonial experience. The comparisons I make in this chapter exclusively pertain to the colonial legacies from which the Black diaspora collectively had to endure, and how those legacies are reflected in modern-day policing and carcerality. Examples are drawn from historical texts and scholarly works to emphasize these points but are by no means exhaustive. It is my intention to use this chapter as an opportunity to articulate how contemporary issues in policing—in relation to the Black diaspora—is predicated on a solid understanding of colonial and postcolonial legacies.

Police Brutality and Black Diasporic Solidarity in 2020

The moment footage circulated of Minneapolis police officer Derek Chauvin planting his knee into George Floyd's neck for more than 8 consecutive minutes, almost every major city in the United States engaged in immediate protest (Bogel-Burroughs, 2020). Floyd, a Black male who recently migrated from Houston, Texas, was initially apprehended for allegedly purchasing cigarettes with a counterfeit bill at a local convenience store. Chauvin, who is White, felt compelled to use excessive force due to Floyd purportedly resisting arrest. Toward the end of the footage, Floyd can be heard murmuring, "I can't breathe" and later calling for his deceased mother before dying from traumatic asphyxia induced by homicide (Banks, 2020).

Shortly afterward, news spread regarding the death of Breonna Taylor, a Black medical worker in Kentucky shot and killed by police during a no-knock drug raid gone awry (Oppel et al, 2020). Taylor's death symbolized the longstanding negation of Black women being wrongfully criminalized with impunity. She was killed 2 months before Floyd but received very little media attention—notwithstanding the fact that she served as an essential worker during one of the most unprecedented pandemics in world history and was resting in her bed the moment she was spontaneously shot to death. The fact that no evidence of illegal activity was found in her apartment only intensified rage in activist circles.

Estimates would indicate that upward of 26 million Americans rallied the streets in support of Floyd and Taylor's deaths. The demonstrations were unprecedented for several reasons. As previously noted, they transpired amidst one of the deadliest pandemics in modern history. COVID-19, the communicable respiratory illness that initially spread in Wuhan, China, and later throughout the world, immediately imposed global economic downfall and had generated millions of deaths worldwide (Higgins-Dunn, 2020). In the United States, most of these deaths disproportionately occurred among low-socioeconomic status Blacks and Latinos (Ford et al., 2020). Essentially, the fervor behind Floyd and Taylor's deaths was so intense that Black demonstrators were willing to fight a pandemic that was disproportionately killing them while also simultaneously combatting police brutality and structural racism on the streets.

Another unprecedented reality was the fact that most U.S. protests were predominantly attended by Whites, which perplexed some activists as to whether this indicated new waves of racial solidarity across the country or if White demonstrators were simply using Black rage as a catalyst for their own interests (Elnashar, 2020; Neely, 2020). For example, some White liberals found it necessary to use protests solely to express their disdain for President Trump, who mismanaged the pandemic and helped to provoke political tension throughout his presidential tenure. On the other hand, several predominantly White radical groups engaged in anarchial violence at protests with no real concern or commitment to Black struggle. President Trump claimed that one leftist radical group, Antifa (short for anti-fascist), was partly responsible for provoking full-out rebellions against riot police. He faulted the group, along with Black Lives Matter (BLM) activists, for damaging property and would later encourage state governors to activate the National Guard (Browne et al., 2020; Hamel et al., 2020; Kingson, 2020).

Perhaps the most memorable reaction to Floyd and Taylor's deaths was the overwhelming support coming from beyond U.S. borders. Weine et al. (2020) purport that BLM protests were observed across 60 different countries. In Brazil, millions marched the streets to protest the police killing of a João Pedro Matos Pinto, a Black teenager shot in the back via rifle in his neighborhood favela earlier in the year (Biller, 2020; Phillips, 2020). An article in *The New Yorker* spoke of a demonstration in France led by Black French activist Assa Traoré, who galvanized upward of 80 thousand people to highlight the similarity in outcome between George Floyd and her brother Adama, who was killed by French policemen 4 years prior and also uttered the words *Je n'arrive plus à respire* ("I can't breathe") prior to his death (Collins, 2020). Joseph-Salisbury et al. (2020) underscored events in the United Kingdom regarding the mysterious death of Simeon Francis in police custody, along with the unjustifiable tasering of Ziggy Mombeyarara and Millard Scott—all three of whom were Black men attacked weeks apart from the deaths of George Floyd and Breonna Taylor.

Later in the year, social media became inundated with hashtags addressing police brutality in Nigeria. The #ENDSARS movement pertained to Nigeria's Special Anti-Robbery Squad, which was created in 1992 with the intent to respond to violent crime and, more specifically, armed robbery (Uwazuruike, 2020). For several decades the unit has engaged in numerous human rights violations, including extrajudicial killings, shooting activists and demonstrators, police torture, prolonged detentions, and harassment. The movement to abolish the police unit gained global notoriety when a child was killed by officials without explanation, resulting in mass protests on the streets that eventually gained traction online. Local activists and celebrities took to Twitter to share countless recordings of shootings performed by SARS and managed to galvanize support from activists across the world.

Each of these events signify that the fight against injustice, state-sanctioned violence and systemic racism transcends borders and are part and parcel of ongoing racial inequities that require immediate redress on the world stage. The fact that non-U.S. Black peoples empathize with the BLM movement is not surprising given the extent to which sentiments of injustice are familiar symptoms across the world that the diaspora can identify with. The overarching logic is that these symptoms are transnational. Ellen Johnson Sirleaf, former president of Liberia, implied this when she suggested that the 2020 protests helped everyone gain "self-recognition of everyone's collective past" (Weine et al., 2020). What is this collective past, and how does it relate to contemporary issues in policing? In the following section, I attempt to historicize modern-day policing through European colonization as a means to explain why Black sentiment against policing and carceral punishment transgresses spatial boundaries.

"Everyone's Collective Past": Slave Codes and Policing Black Bodies in the Western Colonial State

Contemporary models of policing in select geographies across Africa, Asia, and the Americas are deeply entrenched within European colonial histories (Brogden, 1987). Hills (2018) says that policing emerged in Western empires from the involuntary occupation of "weaker polities," which subsequently depended on institutions of order and social control. In the New World, these institutions were largely inspired by the enactment of slave codes, prefaced by the Portuguese and Spanish empires of the 16th century.

During this period, the Portuguese and Spanish crowns were united and mutually engaged in violent conquest of the Americas. Across present-day Latin America, the Spaniards in particular had constructed a feudal-like system called *encomienda*, which not only racialized Indigenous slave labor but served as a bridge to the more economical system of chattel African slavery. Due to the rapid deterioration of the Indigene labor stock—a consequence of epidemic disease and genocide—the Crown sought to replenish their supply by importing African slaves. Initially, both empires adhered to the *Siete Partidas*, a centuries-old colonial statute borrowed almost exclusively from ancient Roman slave decrees (Saavedra, 2020). However, this statute proved inadequate in the Americas because it was too lenient in its ability to regulate slave behavior. In the Old World, for example, slave uprisings and rebellions were relatively uncommon and slavery was less predicated on the construction of race. This obviously was not the case in the New World, where Africans and Indigenes were more "unruly" and insurgences across the colonies would often result in the killing of slaveholders and their families, the setting of structures on fire, or fleeing from plantations.

Special codes were instated to deal with colonized peoples and to establish systems of law and order. These laws varied across time and space but were quite similar in outcome. For instance, the *Provisión del virrey Diego Colon*, codified in 1522, was considered the first Black code of colonial America and resulted in a colonial police force that essentially monitored slaves and prohibited them from moving freely across the colony without the permission of their slave holder (Patisso & Carbone, 2020). In Book VII of the *Recopilación de las Leyes de los Reins de las Indias,* completed in 1635, penal regulations were put in place to police Black and multiracial peoples (Duve & Pihlajamäki, 2015). Ordinances drafted in Barbarcoa (part of present-day Columbia) around 1668 made it illegal for either African or Indigene slaves to assemble with one another outside of "work" in fear that a forged alliance would result in insurrections. Free Indigenes on the fringe of society were also restricted from being "allowed to carry knives, machetes, or other arms" (Lane, 2000).

Slave codes were not exclusive to the Iberians. The French Empire occupied slave-holding territories in North America and the Caribbean and relied on their own drafts of codes to police Black bodies. Written in 1685, mostly by King Louis XIV's adviser, Jean-Baptist Colber, the *Code Noir* served to retain "order" among slaves and slaveholders by enforcing several prohibitions. Slaveholders were required to teach their slaves Catholicism and ensure that they were clothed and fed—among other things. Conversely, slaves were prohibited from engaging in numerous social and economic affairs, including gathering with other slaves who belonged to different masters, carrying weapons, selling sugar cane or other marketable goods, and running away (Arlyck, 2003). Bobin (2020) describes a vividly disturbing portrait of the latter, from which captured runaway slaves were punished by having both of their ears cropped and then branded with the French monarchy symbol, fleur de lys, on their shoulder. A second infraction would result in the slave's hamstring being slashed and being branded once again on their other shoulder. The final violation would be death. Virtually all Western empires penalized "unlawful" slaves with similarly violent measures. One account in 1612 documents how 35 Black and mulatto slaves were publicly hanged, decapitated, and openly displayed on pikes and rooftops across Mexico City in response to their plot to rebel against their Spanish slaveholders (Martínez, 2004).

Perhaps the most influential colonial empire in the New World was Great Britain, who enforced slave codes that are arguably more connected to contemporary conditions of racial inequity in postcolonial societies. By the mid-17th century, the English possessed several Caribbean islands, along with establishing 13 colonies along the eastern coast of the modern-day United States. Like other Western powers, the English sought to uphold order among slave populations by deterring insurgences. In 1661, English elites enacted the Barbadian Slave Act, which served as the first comprehensive slave code in the British Colonies and would later be adopted by nearly every other British slaveholding colony (Nicholson, 1994). Like most slave laws, these codes included numerous mandates that prohibited slaves from leaving their plantations without a pass, striking or harming any White man or woman, and resisting lawful apprehension. Some specifications of punishment included the right to whip slaves with upward of 30 lashes or the permission to kill runaways and be recompensated for loss of property by the government. However, what made these codes different than those enacted by the Iberian and French Empires were the lack of protections they had for slaves. Some historians in fact contest, disputably, that France and Spain's treatment of slaves was "less dehumanizing" compared to that of the English (Palmer, 1996). Patisso and Carbone (2020) note

> The Barbadian Code was a very rigorous slave code, which was not intended to protect slave labor. It focused, instead, on the punishment of the slaves, considered as a threat for the safety of the white population of the island. Reading the articles of the Code emerges that the British colonists considered the Africans as barbaric people … Unlike contemporaneous Spanish American and Brazilian legislation based on the medieval Siete Partidas, or the French Code Noir that would follow in 1680, the 1661 Slave Act did not attribute any positive rights to slaves whatsoever. (p. 64)

The Barbadian slave codes had a more direct and peculiar effect on the origin of public police forces in the Americas and the Caribbean. Evidence suggests that these codes were first adopted by colonists in Jamaica, where White members of the planter elite would form militias with freed Blacks and mulattos to police slave populations and ensure codes were not violated (Jaffe & Diphoorn, 2019). The Barbadian codes also directly inspired South Carolina's 1691 slave code act, which in turn became the motivation for slave patrols that served as the foundation of modern-day policing in the southern region of the contemporary United States (Rugemer, 2013). Turner et al. (2006) emphasize that slave patrols in South Carolina should be considered the forerunner of modern-day policing in the United States and that the comparisons are much too analogous to ignore. For context, the patrolling of Black slaves in British colonial America gave White southerners "peace and security" and helped to maintain racial order by reaffirming Black inferiority (Hawkins & Thomas, 1991). As in Jamaica, White southern elites could hire slave catchers to pursue and apprehend runaway slaves, prevent uprisings, and discipline slave laborers outside of legal precedent (Potter, 2013). This was fairly different than policing in the northern colonies of Boston, New York, and Philadelphia, where slave populations were much smaller and policing for the most part emerged from voluntary watch systems that served to warn the public about "impending danger."

Thousands of slave codes were imposed in the New World, some of which came from lesser renowned empires (such as the Danes and Swedes). It is not conjectural to say that almost all of them were enacted with the sole intent to police Black bodies and achieve social order. The codes also served as way of "othering" Black and Indigene peoples by ensuring that they remained incorporated into the lower ranks of the racial and social hierarchy. Ultimately, these colonial practices directly helped to inspire subsequent methods of professionalized policing in both the colonies and metropoles. This is briefly elaborated on in the next section.

The Longstanding Effect of Colonial Policing and Its Postcolonial Continuities

By the 19th century, most Western empires were forced to relinquish several of their New World territories. The British, who managed to acquire several French colonies in the Caribbean during the mid-18th century, lost the United States in the American Revolution of 1783. France had surrendered Saint Domingue (present-day Haiti) as a result of a remarkable slave revolt led by Haitian revolutionary Toussaint Louverture in 1804. This in turn forced the empire to sell their remaining territory in the Americas to the United States. Moreover, the Spaniards lost nearly all their colonies in Latin America—some to rebellions led by prominent revolutionaries like Simon Bolivar and Pancho Villa. Western empires were desperately committed to retaining their global influence by expanding their reach in other corners of the world, perhaps the most lucrative being Africa (*Gonçalves & Cachado*, 2018).

The policing of ex-slaves in the New World and Indigenous peoples in newly occupied territories relied on colonial policing to maintain social order and protect internal colonial affairs. Jaffe and Diphoorn (2019) affirm that systems of colonial policing vary substantially across European empires, but one chief similarity involved distinctions between the police and the policed. The typical marker of distinction was predicated on ethno-racial hierarchies. In most cases, the colonial police were usually White military-ranked officials extracted from the metropoles, or local non-White recruits who were perceived to be "loyal" to the colonial powers. Those who were policed of course were usually Black and Indigenous peoples who were largely defined as "problem" populations by the colonial state.

Examples of this can be seen across British colonies. As Western empires increasingly began to engage in colonial takeover of lesser developed nations across Africa and Asia, the English were very strategic in their ability to forcibly replace native languages, medicinal practices, and laws with British standards and values. Brogden (1987) classifies this process as "delegitimating." The goal was to center laws around the idea that Indigenous populations were not "sufficiently advanced to sustain [their] own judicial practices and law enforcement procedures until [they] had absorbed the colonial legal construction" (Brogden 1987). Part of this legal construction involved the installment of colonial policing units. Patrol officers and officials who moved upward in the ranks of mainland institutions, such as the Metropolitan Police and the Royal Irish Constabulary, were often recruited to Britain's colonial territories to police the areas and "protect" the empire. In some cases, local recruits were extracted from rural areas to police "strangers" in the urban centers of the colony—as in Nigeria and Ghana (Alemika, 1993). In newly emancipated societies across the British Caribbean, local White officers were hired to work beside servile Blacks to patrol the newly freed labor force (Paton, 2004). France's occupation of Algeria is also a notable example. Officers in Algeria were carefully selected among "inferior" natives who were subordinate to the empire, while French superiors were installed to monitor their duties. These tactics differed in other French colonies across sub-Saharan Africa, where the physical presence of Frenchmen was much scarcer (Kalman, 2020). Still, these strategies were integral in creating intra-racial and class-based divisions across Westernized societies.

Another prominent feature of colonial policing was paramilitarism. LaRose and Madden (2009) emphasize that colonial policing served as "a by-product of colonial occupation, paramilitary in nature, and focused more on maintaining colonial rule than protecting citizens from criminal events" (p. 335). While most Western empires can identify with this feature, the Portuguese empire serves as a peculiar example. Initially, the Portuguese underwent scrutiny for being relatively unprepared in terms of establishing public police forces to regulate ex-slaves and colonized subjects. The empire had installed a colonial police force in Rio de Janeiro as early as 1804, when nearly half of the city was enslaved, but their structures were much less sophisticated than other colonial powers (Hinton, 2005; Müller, 2016). Quelling disorder in the colonies was often the responsibility of the Portuguese army until at least the 20th century. This is evident in Mozambique and Brazil, two Portuguese colonies where the militarization of police units were in most cases less predicated on public safety as opposed to the ability to "maintain order" and "civil unrest." In former Spanish colonies across Latin America, the longstanding legacies of militarism and state-sanctioned repression intensified methods of confessional torture.

Magaloni and Rodriguez (2020) discuss the extent to which newly liberalized European codes regarding judicial torture had little effect in postcolonial Latin America:

> When Latin American countries became independent, they rejected the more liberal European codes and kept the inquisitorial system that had prevailed in the Portuguese and Spanish Americas. The main characteristics of these inquisitorial codes are that the backbone of the criminal process is a written dossier (expediente) that the police and investigating judge compile with all procedural activity; pretrial investigations remain written and secret; the verdict phase is also predominantly written and lacks a jury; and the judge investigates, prosecutes, and adjudicates. ... Because of their strong reliance on confessions and weak procedural standards, inquisitorial criminal justice systems expand opportunities for the police to torture. (p. 1015)

It is important to note that colonial policing was not exclusive to the colonies. Policing of Black populations in the metropoles was fairly similar to that of occupied territories and followed the framework of what some scholars define as *internal colonialism*. Steinmetz et al. (2016) say that theories of internal colonialism derive from Black nationalists and civil rights activists who argued that racial domination in Western nations is predicated on a colonial-type relationship where non-White people assume the role of the "colonized" while their White counterparts are designated as "settlers" by default. This of course differs substantially from classical colonialism, which refers to the exploitative and often violent occupation of territories and native peoples by *outside* forces. Internal colonialism emphasizes that invasion and domination of local populations can occur despite the fact that the settler and the colonized occupy the same geography (Blauner, 1969; Steinmetz et al., 2016). In this context, the policing of colonized peoples in Western societies aim to protect the interests of the colonizer (White peoples) by enforcing order in colonies that are predominantly occupied by colonized peoples (Blauner, 1969; Chávez, 2011). Moreover, the framework also positions the police as agents of the power structure who "do the dirty work" for the system by regulating Black criminals and ensuring their behaviors do not seep into the communities of the protected population.

An example of this can be seen in France as early as 1777 when officials enacted the Police des Noirs Act ("Police for Blacks"), which sought to police freed Blacks in Paris. The presumption was that Blacks who traveled to the French capital required policing because of their potential of bringing "the spirit of independence and indocility" back to France's external colonies, which could inspire enslaved populations to rebel (Bobin, 2020). Perhaps the most salient example of internal colonialism is the United States. Blauner (1969) states that internal colonization in the United States is particularly unique because traces of language, religion, and national loyalties were completely eradicated among the Black populace. Further, efforts to police Black populations resulted in the construction of "internal colonies" where they could better be controlled and monitored by the state. For context, the abolition of slavery in United States resulted in slave patrols transitioning over to vigilante groups who collectively worked in tandem with southern police departments to control Black freedmen and women (Potter, 2013). Stipulations in the 13th Amendment were legislated so that only nonincarcerated people were exempt from slavery, leading to overt and covert methods of criminalizing Black people for minor offenses, such as vagrancy, loitering, or soliciting, in order to uphold the legacy of bondage (Alexander, 2010; Brown, 2005). Consequently, policing in the Jim Crow South became especially gruesome because illegality was less predicated on breaking the law, as opposed to skin color. This ultimately yielded countless incidents where sheriffs and officers alike either participated in or outright ignored mob hunting of Black men, women, and children for presumed offenses (Hasset-Walker, 2019). As Black southerners fled northward to escape these issues and pursue better economic opportunities, policing across America would adapt to these demographic shifts by becoming more repressive. In cities like Detroit, Chicago, Los Angeles, and New York, Black migrants were forcibly relegated to the inner city and underwent various economic obstacles like redlining and housing segregation, which restricted Black families from acquiring home loans or pursuing homes in neighborhoods of their choice. The result was that Black families were essentially trapped in dilapidated, densely populated areas (internal colonies) that not only translated into disinvestment and impoverishment but became hotbeds for police abuse and targeted discrimination.

Today, police abuse and discrimination across former colonies and Western metropoles persist in line with colonial legacies. Jaffe and Diphoorn (2019) affirm that modern police forces in former colonies function almost indistinguishably from that of the military and still tend to prioritize "internal security over crime prevention and detection" (p. 912). Decolonization and independence from imperialist rule were supposed to allow public police forces in former colonies to reinvent themselves by "serving the needs and interests of a newly independent people rather than enforcing a colonial political and economic order" (Jaffe & Diphoorn, 2019, p. 912). This however rarely turned out to be the case. Boateng and Darko (2015) note that police illegitimacy in Ghana is directly linked to colonial practices and is reflected in the continual reliance on paramilitary policing and abuse. The divisions between the police and policed are ever present in Jamaica, where attempts to decolonize police forces have failed and features of repression continue with intent to subjugate and control populations by status (Jaffe & Diphoorn, 2019). In a comparative study on policing inequality in Brazil and South Africa, Stuurman (2020) finds that their "similar histories in colonization, race and racism" (p. 49) paved way for the adoption of militarized police tactics as a way to target urban poor populations. Even in Western societies, where policing is interpreted to be more democratic, Black populations are still considered to be treated as colonized subjects and are disparately policed and incarcerated at rates that in some cases are more alarming than those of developing nations.

Reform or Abolition?

Given the extent to which contemporary policing of Black people can be traced back to racist and prejudicial colonial practices, propositions have been made in line of reforming existing institutions or abolishing them all together. These propositions of course vary substantially across societies, with some efforts being relatively localized and others having more global implications.

Prior to engaging with the literature, it is important to note that not all propositions for reform are rooted in efforts to eliminate disparities in policing or to empathize with colonial legacies. Recent decades have been rife with media reports that speak to the impact of *global policing*, in which policing models have been transnational and strategies essentially shared between countries. The implementation of these strategies is mostly concerned with improving existing institutions of policing in ways that are in some cases more harmful to marginalized groups, especially Black people. Hönke and Müller (2016) describe how one police officer in Springfield, Massachusetts, modeled and implemented a plan to monitor local gangs after "counter-insurgency police practices" conducted by U.S. armed forces in Afghanistan and Iraq. In 2014, rumors circulated concerning collaborations between the St. Louis Police Department and Israeli military forces in relation to how predominantly Black demonstrators (who were protesting the police killing of Mike Brown) were met with overly aggressive militarized tactics (Graham & Baker, 2016). Though this particular story proved erroneous, evidence does suggest that the former St. Louis police chief did indeed work alongside Israeli militarists, and that several other agencies across the United States have engaged in such partnerships with Israel with intent to apply learned militarized tactics against protestors and other target populations. These strategies are situated within global policing and efforts to "reform" institutions without a particular focus on equity.

Other police reforms are thought be more intentional in their desire to eliminate disparities and strengthen the actual legitimacy of the public police. The general goal of such reforms is to refine the institution's ability to administer and preserve law and order in an effective and equitable way. Mani (1999) emphasizes that peace itself should be predicated on ways police carry out their assigned duties.

In Latin America and the Caribbean, violence and homicide rank the highest in the world, particularly in Honduras, El Salvador, Jamaica, and Venezuela, where at least 49 of every 100,000 people are victims of homicide (Prado et al., 2012). This violence runs counter to what might be expected from democratized nations and suggests that inequality and economic hardship remain immediate points of redress. However, evidence also suggests that policing across the region is relatively ineffective and is itself promotive of violence. Prado et al. (2012) state that Latin America has some of the most authoritarian and corrupt police agencies in the world and that the major reform needed across the region is a transition to democratic policing. Prado et al. (2012) state that policing in select countries across the region can be classified as one of the following: (a) *autocratic*, in that they work solely to protect interests of repressive regimes; (b) *criminal*, in that the police are controlled by criminal enterprises such as drug cartels; or (c) *autarkic*, with police units essentially making their own rules and executing them without the state's instruction. The authors suggest that democratic policing is particularly needed given that none of the aforementioned classifications hold policing accountable to law, whereas democratic policing—in their estimation—values "human rights, protection of civil and political rights, accountability to people outside the organization, and servicing the needs of citizens" (p. 262).

Unsurprisingly, the ability to democratize police often depends on the country's political structure. Wenner (2020) notes that police reforms in Brazil, where Black populations constitute the majority of police killings, have increasingly centered on a system of community policing—coined pacifying police units (UPPs)—which proved effective in reducing police killings between 2008 and 2013. In recent years however, police killings have escalated substantially in line with newly elected politicians whose views are characterized as right-wing extremist, making police reforms unsustainable and thus ineffective.

The fight for democratized policing as a key point of reform is also seen across Africa. As in Latin America, violence and homicide ranks extremely high across the continent, especially in the sub-Saharan region. In Nigeria, Hills (2008) affirms that reforms do less to change public policing for the better and instead help to prolong existing disparities. For instance, contemporary issues in Nigeria have not changed from the past in that they continue to involve public corruption, lack of accountability, welfare of the police officers themselves, inadequate training and resources, and public mistrust (Ojo, 2014). Ojo (2014) argues that these issues can be remedied by "the total democratization of the Nigeria police, away from the old colonial and paramilitary style" (p. 97). Similar propositions of democratization can be seen in Kenya, another former British colony, where corruption leads police officers to collect bribes and respond to political resistance with excessive force (Lynch & Crawford, 2011).

While the focus in developing nations is on democratizing the police, evidence suggests that even highly democratic nations are rife with problems in policing. In the United Kingdom, disparities in policing have always been most unfavorable for Black inhabitants. In France, policing disparately impacts Black populations and is heavily racialized among immigrants—especially those who identify as Muslim. Special emphasis, however, is given to the United States considering the country's anomaly status on the world stage. Despite the United States being the most developed and wealthiest nation in modern history, the country ranks among the worst in incarceration and police killing rates (Ralph, 2020). These rates remain dramatically high despite the fact that the United States has imposed several reform strategies in the past. That is, across the country attempts have been made to desegregate police departments, increase transparency, and ramp up de-escalation training with very little improvement toward reducing disparities.

Ralph (2020) argues that American exceptionalism has inhibited policy makers from considering quality reforms that have been affected elsewhere in the world. For instance, countries that tend to report the lowest rates in police killings (Denmark, Iceland, Japan, and Switzerland) have national oversight committees that hold officers accountable at the national level. Further, police unions in these countries tend to be less influential in protecting officers from punishment for negligible offenses. Decades of research suggest that police unions in the United States protect officers at any expense, often to an unapologetic fault. Other reforms that have worked can be seen in the Netherlands, where some roles typically performed by police officers are substituted by peace officers called *Boas*, who are mostly unarmed and are specifically trained to "help resolve noncriminal issues and to de-escalate conflict by remaining calm, inquiring about a person's well-being, and trying to reduce a person's anxiety" (Ralph, 2020 p. 199). Other strategies implemented elsewhere include the time required to become a police officer, whereas in the United States, police recruits can engage with activity in as little as 21 weeks; the requirement in Germany involves between 2 to 4 years. In contrast, Iceland, which reportedly has only ever had one police-related killing to date, necessitates at least 2 years. Lastly, suggested reforms in the United Statets have been focused on reducing accessibility to firearms, which most studies say increases the likelihood of not only police killings, but homicides as well.

As highlighted elsewhere in this essay, activists and scholars alike have persistently emphasized that reform is ineffective because it only aims to improve policing without making efforts to rectify the social conditions from which criminal behavior tends to emerge. Colonial legacies have left behind residues of inequality that ultimately work to ensure that policing and carcerality forever work unfavorably for target populations. These advocates instead propose the total abolition of police and the carceral state. As stated by Derecka Purnell (2020), human rights lawyer and community organizer, "Reforms make police polite managers of inequality. Abolition makes police and inequality obsolete."

Angela Davis is arguably the foremost critical thinker and proponent of abolition work, having dedicated her life to critiquing and challenging regimes that rely on punishment and control as a supposed safeguard for democracy. Davis's initial work centered on the abolition of prisons by utilizing the framework of abolition democracy, which Mohammed defines as "the project of building up radical community-powered institutions to sup-plant oppressive social structures inherited from the legacy of chattel slavery" (Gimbel & Muhammed, 2019, p. 1454). Davis argues that the prison industrial complex itself is oppressive in that it primarily works to warehouse people who are social problems. Contemporary activists and scholars have applied this line of thinking toward policing. The idea is that public funds should be steered away from policing budgets and instead allocated to other social institutions that directly work to eliminate adverse social con-ditions, such as housing, health care, and education. In the past year, activists have emphasized this point by explicitly calling for the police to be defunded. Not only is this call supplemented by the overspending of public dollars on policing and prisons, but by the fact that some prisons across the United States are privatized—which exemplifies the extent to which criminal law is less concerned with public safety as opposed to capital gains (Gaes, 2019). Though abolitionists do not see defunding as abolition in of itself, most argue that it serves as a steppingstone (Joseph–Salisbury et al., 2020).

Efforts to abolish policing have taken place in only a few countries across the world and are usually followed by reforms and re-creating more equitable institutions. In Estonia, for instance, where policing was initially predicated on the Soviet-colonial style *(militsiya)*, police agencies were completely disbanded and replaced by a security force that worked primarily as peace officers. Another reform in 2004 resulted in 75% of the force being reduced due to the effectiveness of the new institution. Moreover, the country of Georgia essentially abolished their police force following a violent revolution in the same year and also replaced policing units with smaller forces (Ralph, 2020). While it is difficult to compile a listing of police units that were actually defunded, it is important to note that most Scandinavian countries have among the lowest rates of crime and police killings in the world, while also having the highest commitments to social programs that work to reduce poverty.

Conclusion

Policing and the broader appendages of carcerality do not assure democratic freedoms and protections in an equitable way. This is largely due to the fact that said institutions are founded on racist and violent colonial legacies that continue to adversely impact Black well-being on the world stage. The response among Black activists in recent decades is for existing institutions to be replaced with more trauma-informed, equity-based structures. Further, many scholars and activists have called for economic restitution and the equitable distribution of wealth. As once stated by Frantz Fanon, renowned Black intellectual, and author of *The Wretched of the Earth*:

> The basic confrontation which seemed to be colonialism versus anti-colonialism, indeed capitalism versus socialism, is already losing its importance. What matters today, the issue which blocks the horizon, is the need for a redistribution of wealth. Humanity will have to address this question, no matter how devastating the consequences may be. (p. 55)

References

Alemika, E. E. (1993). Colonialism, state and policing in Nigeria. *Crime, Law and Social Change, 20*(3), 187–219. https://doi.org/10.1007/bf01308450

Alexander, M. (2020). *The new Jim Crow: Mass incarceration in the age of colorblindness.* New Press.

Arlyck, K. (2003). The Code Noir: North American slavery in comparative perspective. *OAH Magazine of History, 17*(3), 37–40. https://doi.org/10.1093/maghis/17.3.37

Banks, G. (2020, June 2). *2nd autopsy finds George Floyd died from asphyxia.* EMS 1. https://www.ems1.com/fatal-incidents/articles/2nd-autopsy-finds-george-floyd-died-from-asphyxia-j8xV3uwa82cb69jW/

Biller, D. (2020, June 18). *A teen's killing stirs Black Lives Matter protests in Brazil.* AP News. https://apnews.com/article/8bfe3a86aa1db5b9671d9d41be8617b7

Blanchard, E. (2014). French colonial police. *Encyclopedia of Criminology and Criminal Justice, 1836–1846.* https://doi.org/10.1007/978-1-4614-5690-2_465

Blauner, R. (1969). Internal colonialism and ghetto revolt. *Social Problems, 16*(4), 393–408. https://doi.org/10.1525/sp.1969.16.4.03a00010

Boateng, F. D., & Darko, I. N. (2016). Our past: The effect of colonialism on policing in Ghana. *International Journal of Police Science & Management, 18*(1), 13–20. https://doi.org/10.1177/1461355716638114

Bobin, F. (2020, July 20). How colonialism shaped policing in France. *Jacobin*. https://jacobinmag.com/2020/07/police-racism-france-africans-colonialism

Brogden, M. (1987). The emergence of the police—the colonial dimension. *The British Journal of Criminology*, *27*(1), 4–14. https://doi.org/10.1093/oxfordjournals.bjc.a047651

Browne, R., Lee, A., & Rigdon, R. (2020, June 2). *There are as many National Guard members activated in the US as there are active duty troops in Iraq, Syria and Afghanistan*. CNN. https://edition.cnn.com/2020/06/01/us/national-guard-protests-states-map-trnd/index.html

Bogel-burroughs, N. (2020, June 19). 8 minutes, 46 seconds became a symbol in George Floyd's death. The exact time is less clear. *The New York Times*. https://www.nytimes.com/2020/06/18/us/george-floyd-timing.html

Chávez, J. R. (2011). Aliens in their native lands: The persistence of internal colonial theory. *Journal of World History*, *22*(4), 785–809. https://doi.org/10.1353/jwh.2011.0123

Collins, L., Painter, N., & Lopez, R. (2020). Assa Traoré and the fight for Black lives in France. *New Yorker*. https://www.newyorker.com/news/letter-from-europe/assa-traore-and-the-fight-for-black-lives-in-france

Davis, A. (2016). *Freedom is a constant struggle*. Haymarket Books.

Dias, R. (2016). Racism creates barriers to effective community policing. *Southern Illinois University Law Journal*, *40*(3), 501–512.

Duve, T., & Pihlajamäki, H. (2015). *New horizons in Spanish colonial law: Contributions to transnational early modern legal history*. Frankfurt am Main: Max Planck Institute for European Legal History. https://www.jstor.org/stable/j.ctvqhtsd

Elnashar, A. (2020, July 29). *Researchers: White people make up large portion of protesters*. ABC 7. https://wjla.com/news/nation-world/researchers-white-people-make-up-large-portion-of-protesters

Fanon, F. (1968). *The wretched of the earth*. Grove Press.

Ford, T., Reber, S., & Reeves, R. (2020, June 17). *Race gaps in COVID-19 deaths are even bigger than they appear*. Brookings. https://www.brookings.edu/blog/up-front/2020/06/16/race-gaps-in-covid-19-deaths-are-even-bigger-than-they-appear/

Gonçalves, G., & Cachado, R. (2018). Colonial policing and the Portuguese Empire (c.1870–1961). In C. O'Reilly (Ed.), *Colonial policing and the Transnational legacy: The global dynamics of policing across the Lusophone community* (1st ed., pp. 17–32). Routledge.

Gimbel, N. & Muhammad, C. (2019). Are Police Obsolete? Breaking Cycles of Violence Through Abolition Democracy. *Cardozo Law Review*, *40*(4), 1453–1543. http://cardozolawreview.com/wp-content/uploads/2019/05/1-Gimbel.40.4.1.pdf

Graham, S., & Baker, A. (2016). Laboratories of pacification and permanent war: Israeli–US collaboration in the global making of policing In J. Hönke & M. Müller (Eds.), *The Global Making of Policing* (1st ed., pp. 40–58). Routledge.

Gramlich, J. (2020, August 6). *Black imprisonment rate in the U.S. has fallen by a third since 2006*. Pew Research Center. https://www.pewresearch.org/fact-tank/2020/05/06/share-of-black-white-hispanic-americans-in-prison-2018-vs-2006/

Hassett-Walker, C., 2021. *The racist roots of American policing: From slave patrols to traffic stops*. [online] The Conversation. Available at: https://theconversation.com/the-racist-roots-of-american-policing-from-slave-patrols-to-traffic-stops-112816 [Accessed 20 August 2021].

Hamel, L., Kearney, A., Kirzinger, A., Lopes, L., Muñana, C., & Brodie, M. (2020, August 11). *KFF health tracking poll – June 2020*. https://www.kff.org/racial-equity-and-health-policy/report/kff-health-tracking-poll-june-2020/

Higgins-Dunn, N. (2020, September 29). *The coronavirus has now killed more than 1 million people and upended the global economy in less than nine months*. CNBC. https://www.cnbc.com/2020/09/28/the-coronavirus-has-killed-more-than-1-million-people-and-upended-the-global-economy.html

Hills, A. (2008). The dialectic of police reform in Nigeria *The Journal of Modern African Studies*, *46*(2), 215–234. https://doi.org/10.1017/s0022278x08003200

Hinton, M. S. (2005). A distant reality: Democratic policing in Argentina and Brazil. *Criminal Justice*, *5*(1), 75–100. https://doi.org/10.1177/1466802505050980

Hönke, J. (2016). *The global making of policing: Postcolonial perspectives* (M. Müller, Ed.). Routledge.

Jaffe, R., & Diphoorn, T. (2019). Old boys and badmen: Private security in (post)colonial Jamaica. *Interventions*, *21*(7), 909–927. https://doi.org/10.1080/1369801x.2019.1585906

Joseph–Salisbury, R., Connelly, L., & Wangari-Jones, P. (2020). "The UK is not innocent": Black Lives Matter, policing and abolition in the UK. *Equality, Diversity and Inclusion*. https://doi.org/10.1108/edi-06-2020-0170

Kalman, S. (2020). Policing the French Empire. *Historical Reflections/Réflexions Historiques*, *46*(2), 1–8. https://doi.org/10.3167/hrrh.2020.460201

King, K. Q. (2018). Recentering U.S. empire: A structural perspective on the color line. *Sociology of Race and Ethnicity*, *5*(1), 11–25. https://doi.org/10.1177/2332649218761977

Kingson, J. (2020, September 16). *Exclusive: $1 billion-plus riot damage is most expensive in insurance history*. Axios. https://www.axios.com/riots-cost-property-damage-276c9bcc-a455-4067-b06a-66f9d-b4cea9c.html

Lane, K. (2000). The transition from Encomiendato slavery in seventeenth-century Barbacoas (Colombia). *Slavery & Abolition*, *21*(1), 73–95. https://doi.org/10.1080/01440390008575296

LaRose, A., & Maddon, S. (2009). Reforming La Policía: Looking to the future of policing in Mexico. *Policing: Toward an Unknown Future*, 61–76. https://doi.org/10.1080/15614260802586327

Lynch, G. & Crawford., C. (2011) Democratization in Africa 1990–2010: an assessment. *Democratization*, 18:2, 275-310, DOI: 10.1080/13510347.2011.554175

Magaloni, B., & Rodriguez, L. (2020). Institutionalized police brutality: Torture, the militarization of security, and the reform of inquisitorial criminal justice in Mexico. *American Political Science Review*, *114*(4), 1013–1034. https://doi.org/10.1017/s0003055420000520

Mani, R. (1999). Contextualizing police reform: Security, the rule of law and post-conflict peacebuilding. *International Peacekeeping*, *6*(4), 9–26. https://doi.org/10.1080/13533319908413796

Martínez, M. E. (2004). The Black blood of New Spain: Limpieza de Sangre, racial violence, and gendered power in early colonial Mexico. *William and Mary Quarterly*, *61*(3), 479–520. https://doi.org/10.2307/3491806

Müeller, M. (2016). Entangled pacifications: Peacekeeping, counterinsurgency and policing in Port-au-Prince and Rio de Janeiro In J. Hönke & M. Müller (Eds.), *The Global Making of Policing* (1st ed., pp. 77–95). Routledge.

Neely, C. (2020, May 31). Concerns over violence from outside groups force organizers to cancel "Justice for them All" protest at Texas Capitol; demonstrations persist downtown. *Community Impact Newpaper*. https://communityimpact.com/austin/central-austin/public-safety/2020/05/31/concerns-over-violence-from-outside-groups-force-organizers-to-cancel-justice-for-them-all-protest-at-texas-capitol-demonstrations-persist-downtown/

Nicholson, B. J. (1994). Legal borrowing and the origins of slave law in the British Colonies. *The American Journal of Legal History*, *38*(1), 38–54. https://doi.org/10.2307/845322

O'Reilly, C. (2018). *Colonial policing and the transnational legacy: The global dynamics of policing across the Lusophone community*. Routledge.

Ojo, M. O. (2014). The Nigeria police and the search for integrity in the midst of diverse challenges: An effective police management approach. *International Journal of Police Science & Management*, *16*(2), 87–100. https://doi.org/10.1350/ijps.2014.16.2.330

Oppel, R., Taylor, D., & Bogel-burroughs, N. (2020, May 30). What to know about Breonna Taylor's death. *The New York Times*. https://www.nytimes.com/article/breonna-taylor-police.html

Patisso, G., & Carbone, F. E. (2020). *Slavery and slave codes in overseas empires*. https://doi.org/10.5772/intechopen.91411

Phillips, T. (2020, June 3). Black lives shattered: Outrage as boy, 14, is Brazil police's latest victim. *The Guardian*. https://www.theguardian.com/world/2020/jun/03/brazil-black-lives-police-teenager

Potter, G. (2013). *The history of policing in the United States, part 1*. Eastern Kentucky University. https://plsonline.eku.edu/insidelook/history-policing-united-states-part-

Prado, M. M., Trebilcock, M., & Hartford, P. (2012). Police reform in violent democracies in Latin America. *Hague Journal on the Rule of Law*, *4*(2), 252–285. https://doi.org/10.1017/s1876404512000164

Purnell, D. (2020, July 24). How I became a police abolitionist. *The Atlantic*. https://www.theatlantic.com/ideas/archive/2020/07/how-i-became-police-abolitionist/613540/

Ralph, L. (2020). To protect and to serve: Global lessons in police reform. *Foreign Affairs*, *99*(5), 196–203.

Razack, S. H. (2020). Settler colonialism, policing and racial terror: The police shooting of Loreal Tsingine. *Feminist Legal Studies*, *28*(1), 1–20. https://doi.org/10.1007/s10691-020-09426-2

Rugemer, E. B. (2013). The development of mastery and race in the comprehensive slave codes of the greater Caribbean during the seventeenth century. *The William and Mary Quarterly*, 70(3), 429–458. https://doi.org/10.5309/willmaryquar.70.3.0429

Saavedra, M. B. (2020). The normativity of possession. Rethinking land relations in early-modern Spanish America, ca. 1500–1800. *Colonial Latin American Review*, *29*(2), 223–238. https://doi.org/10.1080/10609164.2020.1755938

Steinmetz, K. F., Schaefer, B. P., & Henderson, H. (2016). Wicked overseers. *Sociology of Race and Ethnicity*, *3*(1), 68–81. https://doi.org/10.1177/2332649216665639

Stuurman, Z. (2020). Policing inequality and the inequality of policing: A look at the militarisation of policing around the world, focusing on Brazil and South Africa. *South African Journal of International Affairs*, *27*(1), 43–66. https://doi.org/10.1080/10220461.2020.1748103

Tankebe, J. (2008). Colonialism, legitimation, and policing in Ghana. *International Journal of Law, Crime and Justice*, *36*(1), 67–84. https://doi.org/10.1016/j.ijlcj.2007.12.003

Thomas, C. (1994, September). *Crime and punishment—and personal responsibility*. https://h2o.law.harvard.edu/text_blocks/428

Turner, K. B., Giacopassi, D., & Vandiver, M. (2006). Ignoring the past: Coverage of slavery and slave patrols in criminal justice texts. *Journal of Criminal Justice Education*, *17*(1), 181–195. https://doi.org/10.1080/10511250500335627

Uwazuruike, R. (2020) #EndSARS: The Movement Against Police Brutality in Nigeria. *Harvard Human Rights Journal*. 5057 https://harvardhrj.com/2020/11/endsars-the-movement-against-police-brutality-in-nigeria/

Palmer, V. V., (1996). The origins and authors of the Code Noir. *Louisiana Law Review*, 56(2), 363–407. https://digitalcommons.law.lsu.edu/lalrev/vol56/iss2/5

Weine, S., Kohrt, B. A., Collins, P. Y., Cooper, J., Lewis-Fernandez, R., Okpaku, S., & Wainberg, M. L. (2020). Justice for George Floyd and a reckoning for global mental health. *Global Mental Health*, *7*. https://doi.org/10.1017/gmh.2020.17

Wenner, A. (2020, June 30). *Police reform in Brazil and Mexico: What works, what doesn't, and what the U.S. can learn*. Stanford University. https://fsi.stanford.edu/news/police-reform-brazil-and-mexico-what-works-what-doesn't-and-what-us-can-learn

Zamalin, A. (2017). Angela Davis, prison abolition, and the end of the American carceral state. In *Struggle on their minds* (pp. 119–149). https://doi.org/10.7312/zama18110-007

Building Health Equity Among Black Young People With Lived Experience of Homelessness

Norweeta G. Milburn and Dawn T. Bounds

The majority of people with lived experience of homelessness in the United States are people of color, women with children, and unaccompanied youth (Wright, 2009). Homelessness among Black people in the United States is not a new social problem. A disproportionate number of Black people are homeless in the United States at any given time. The number of Black people with lived experience of homelessness who are over-represented in U.S. homeless populations goes back to the 1980s and continues to this day (Jones, 2016). Black people are approximately 40% of the U.S. homeless population but only 12% of the U.S. general population (Jones, 2016).

While we know that there is a disproportionate number of Black homeless people in the United States, Jones (2016) notes that research has not done due diligence in examining racial/ethnic differences in understanding homelessness among Black people and has taken a "color-blind" approach that is disadvantageous in research that is needed for public policy to fully address how people move into and out of homelessness, a form of extreme poverty. Homelessness is inextricably tied to race/ethnicity in the United States given that race/ethnicity is strongly linked to poverty in general. Yet race/ethnicity has largely been overlooked in the national discourse on homelessness. More recently, greater attention is finally being given to addressing race and ethnicity in understanding homelessness for research, policy, and services. Nationally, the National Alliance to End Homelessness (NAEH) has created a Race Equity Network to better meet the needs of service providers and people with lived experience of homelessness. Locally, for example, in Los Angeles County, the Los Angeles Homeless Services Authority (LAHSA, 2018) convened the Ad Hoc Committee on Black People Experiencing Homelessness to generate policy, service, and research recommendations to reduce the disproportionate number of Black people with lived experience in the county. In part, the Black Lives Matter movement (BLM, 2015) has driven the conversation in multiple spheres for greater attention to be paid to race/ethnicity in addressing social problems and public policy. Service providers and people with lived experience of homelessness have also led the push to focus on race/ethnicity in homelessness work at all levels—research, policy, and services—given the disparity that is seen across the United States in who is most likely to experience home-lessness: racial/ethnic minority people (National Alliance to End Homelessness, 2020).

Understanding the lives and health, both physical and mental health, of Black people with lived experience is complex and challenging. This understanding is even more com-plex and challenging when we look at Black young people, ages 12 to 24 years, with lived experience of homelessness. Black young people are also overrepresented among young people with lived experience of homelessness. They are triple (40%) their number in the general population of people with lived experience (13%) (Fusaro et al., 2018). A 2018 study surveying more than 26,000 participants across the country found that Black young people between the ages of 16 and 24 years are 83% more likely to report having experienced homelessness than youth of any other race (M. H. Morton et al., 2018).

Very few studies have focused specifically on Black young people with lived experience of homelessness. As noted by Carrasco (2019), there is a significant "racial knowledge gap" in our understanding of young people with lived experience (p. 3). A systematic review of research on people with lived experience of homelessness by Jones (2016) identified four studies that have examined racial/ethnic differences among young people. Only one has looked specifically at discrimination, an important factor in the lives of Black and other people of color (Milburn et al., 2010). Overall, Jones (2016) notes that the findings of these studies are inconclusive with regard to racial/ethnic differences among young people with lived experience of homelessness in terms of outcomes related to healthy trajectories into adulthood. The findings, nonetheless, suggest that Black young people with lived experience may be more likely than their counterparts to have network members engaging in positive behaviors such as attending school (Wenzel et al., 2012) and engage in safe health practices such as using condoms (Halcón & Lifson, 2004).

Research that more fully attends to health disparities among homeless adults is emerg-ing and has not yet tapped into youth homelessness. Rhee and Rosenheck (2021) used National Epidemiological Survey on Alcohol and Related Conditions Wave III (NESARC-III) data to examine differences in individual and structural risk factors for lifetime home-lessness among Black and White adults, ages 18 years and older. They found risks for lifetime homelessness for Black adults were more likely to be structural factors such as previous incarceration, less income, and a history of trauma and less likely to be individ-ual factors (i.e., antisocial personality) than their White counterparts. More needs to be known about how structural factors such as income and educational and employment opportunities are associated with homelessness among Black young people. Research on protective factors suggests these structural factors may be important (Ferguson et al., 2018; Tyler et al., 2017).

How Youth Homelessness Is Defined and Operationalized

In addition to the lack of research that focuses on Black young people with lived experience of homelessness, understanding their homelessness and health is further complicated by the variation in how homelessness is defined for young people. This variation is based on both policy and research. The U.S. Department of Housing and Urban Development (2012) defines youth homelessness as having four categories: literal homeless, at imminent *risk of becoming homeless, homeless under various federal statues, and* "fleeing domestic violence." The U.S. Department of Health and Human Services (2016) uses the Runaway and Homeless Youth Act (RHYA) that defines homeless youth as individuals who are "not more than 21 years of age … for whom it is not possible to live in a safe environment with a relative and who have no other safe alternative living arrangement." This definition only includes unaccompanied young people who are "alone" and not with families or caregivers. The U.S. Department of Education (DoE) relies on subtitle VII-B of the McKinney–Vento Homeless Education Assistance Improvements Act of 2001 (per Title IX, part A of the Elementary and Secondary Education Act, as amended by the Every Student Succeeds Act) to define children and youth with lived experience of homelessness as not having "a fixed, regular, and adequate nighttime residence" [including] "sharing the housing of other persons due to loss of housing, economic hardship, or a similar reason; are living in motels, hotels, trailer parks, or camping grounds due to the lack of alternative adequate accommodations; are living in emergency or transitional shelters; or are abandoned in hospitals; [having] a primary nighttime residence that is a public or private place not designed for or ordinarily used as a regular sleeping accommodation for human beings"; "living in cars, parks, public spaces, abandoned buildings, substandard housing, bus or train stations, or similar settings; and "migratory children" "living in [the] circumstances described." These policy definitions drive public funding streams, national, state, and local, to meet the service needs and education of young people with lived experience of homelessness.

Research definitions also vary, but the more common definitions are inclusive of diverse young people with lived experience of homeless that encompasses street homelessness, running away, being asked to leave, and couch surfing. These broader definitions allow for researchers to examine the prevalence of homelessness. For example, over a 12-month period, a large study conducted in 12 counties across the United States estimated a household prevalence rate of homelessness experiences (including running away, being asked to leave, and couch surfing) was 5.3% for young people ages 13 to 17 and 21% for young people ages 18 to 25 (Morton et al., 2017). New research suggests that definitions of youth homelessness should not be based on a continuum that reflects the severity of housing needs as the policy ones from HUD, HHS, and DoE are. Instead, a definition of youth homeless should be based on housing instability (e.g., living with family and/or friends, ability to pay rent, being evicted, and being on the streets and/or in shelter, and number of moves in the past year) (Fowler et al., 2019).

Such definitions can be better linked to the service needs of young people with lived experience of homelessness (Fowler et al., 2019). For example, Fowler et al. (2019) applied the definition to a national sample of young people (19.5% Black), approximately aged 18 years, with child welfare involvement, and found different service needs based on their housing instability. Three groups were identified (comparisons are to their counterparts) as "stably dependent," who reported the most protective factors (i.e., family connections), more internalizing behaviors, and were the least likely to have the employment and educational skills to move into independent adulthood; "transient," who reported being the most likely to be on the streets and/or in shelters and had more externalizing behaviors; and "unstably independent," who reported the best mental and physical health but more trauma, being the most likely to have employment and educational skills, being the least likely to be evicted, and having the least protective factors. Service providers can better tailor programs to meet the needs of these different types of young people with lived experience of homelessness. Researchers can design interventions that better target the specific needs of these young people. Services and interventions would have the goal of preventing and/or reducing homelessness.

Both policy and research definitions of youth with lived experience of homelessness are based on the need to define the population for "control" to set parameters to identify who is in the population for whatever is being applied to the population; funding/legislation in the case of policy or research questions/hypotheses in the case of research. Identifying both the benefits and limitations of definitions, and being clear about the implications of a definition for young people with lived experience of homelessness, is important. The challenge is applying the seeming rigidity of a definition to a population of young people that can be fluid and evolving in response to societal factors such as the availability of housing and employment (Bassuk, 1984; Fernandes-Alcantra, 2016; Fowler et al., 2019; Wolch et al., 1988). Moreover, little is known about how well these various definitions reflect the lives of Black young people with lived experience of homelessness since race is not a lens through which they are constructed.

Subpopulations of Black Young People With Lived Experience of Homelessness

There are critical subpopulations for understanding health among Black young people with lived experience of homelessness. These subgroups are categorized by age, geography, gender, and sexual identity.

Adolescent versus Transition Age Youth

Homeless youth are typically divided into adolescents, ages 12 to 17 years, and transition age youth (TAY), ages 18 to 24 years. One reason for this division is to designate minors who are to be protected legally by the state's child welfare system. There are similarities and differences associated with these subpopulations. For instance, both adolescents and TAY may have experienced homelessness due to running away, being asked to leave their homes, or due to familial financial hardship and homelessness. Unique to TAY with lived experience of homelessness are holes in "safety nets" of services that occur when young people age out of the child welfare system or leave home after being declared an adult, which can limit access to services.

Urban versus Rural Youth

Although there are more young people experiencing homelessness in urban areas, young people in rural areas experience similar rates of homelessness at around 9% (Morton et al., 2017). Black people were 8% of the rural United States and 13% of the urban United States in 2017 (Cromartie, 2018). Poverty for Black people in rural areas has declined, but Black people in rural areas continue to experience more poverty than any other group (Cromartie, 2018). Rural young people with lived experience of homelessness reported a household prevalence rate of 4.4% for young people, ages 13 to 17 years, and 13.6% for young people, ages 18 to 25 years. Nonrural young people reported similar experiences with homelessness with a household prevalence rate of 4.2% for young people, ages 13 to 17 years, and 12.3% for young people, ages 18 to 25 years (M. Morton, et al., 2017). Rural homeless young people tend to be younger, employed prior to their homelessness experience, and reported more recently living with both parents than their urban counterparts (Morton et al., 2017).

The lived experience of Black young people may vary depending on geography. For example, homelessness is usually more visible in urban than rural areas. Unfortunately, seeing people with lived experience of homelessness is an aspect of daily life in many urban areas (Auerswald & Adams, 2018; Dworsky, 2020; M. H. Morton et al., 2018). Such visibility can have implications for access to services and housing. Urban young people with lived experience may have more access than their rural counterparts given the high prevalence of homelessness in some urban areas (Edwards et al., 2009; Gray et al., 2011; Robertson & Cousineau, 1986), but competition for services and housing can also be high.

Gender and Sexual Identity

Gender and sexual identity may also be associated with access to services and support. Men and boys make up approximately 60% of the homeless population compared to almost 40% of women and girls (Jones, 2016; Morton et al., 2017). Black young people are often "adultified," that is perceived as being older and more mature than their chronological age. Black boys are often perceived as dangerous and threatening (Dancy, 2014). Black girls are perceived as more sexually mature and more independent (Epstein et al., 2017). These misperceptions lead to the assumption that Black young people may need less protection, nurturing, and support than their counterparts, or that they do not need services for children and youth and should be placed in adult services. For example, in some locales, male young people, 18 years and older, are not allowed to stay in family shelters with their families of origin. Black sexual minority young people (lesbian, gay, bisexual, transgender, and nonbinary) are also more likely than their counterparts to be disconnected from social supports and resources, especially those that are central to Black communities such as family and church. Sexual minority young people are more than twice as likely as their peers to experience homelessness, with Black sexual minority young people being the most impacted by homelessness (M. Morton et al., 2018). Black young people cite rejection of their sexual preference and/or gender identity as reasons for being asked to leave their home as well as influencing their disconnection from other social supports (Alessi et al., 2020; Hailey et al., 2020). Despite sexual minority young people experiencing early death at rates double their peers, the unique needs of the young people most at risk (sexual minority youth of color) are overlooked by federal policies like the Runaway and Youth Homeless Act (Page, 2017). More specifically, sexual minority young people of color with lived experience of homelessness have higher rates of sexual exploitation, sexually transmitted infections, discrimination, school difficulties, maltreatment, and violence (Alessi et al., 2020; M. Morton et al., 2018; Page, 2017) than their counterparts. The high rates of family rejection reported by sexual minority young people may contribute to their disproportionate representation among homeless young people (20% to 40%) (Corliss et al., 2011; M. Morton et al., 2018; Robinson, 2018). Almost 44% of sexual minority and 12% of gender minority young people report engaging in survival sex. Additionally, exchanging sex has been associated with having recent HIV-positive sex partners (Siconolfi et al., 2020). Thus, the lived experience of Black sexual minority young people may be amplified in terms of their exposure to rejection, exploitation, and violence.

Addressing Health Disparities to Build Health Equity

Both risk and protective factors have to be taken in to account to reduce health disparities and increase health equity among Black young people with lived experience of homelessness. They experience a number of risk factors. While protective factors have not received as much attention as risk factors, protective factors are important to increase health equity.

Cascading Risk Factors

Black young people with lived experience of homelessness report a number of other risk factors that are associated with health disparities and poor health outcomes in addition to those already noted. For example, Black young people with lived experience disproportionately are more likely to be suspended, detained or incarcerated, and placed in foster care than their counterparts (M.H. Morton et al., 2018). Black young people, in particular, are over-represented in both the child welfare and juvenile justice systems and are often referred to as "crossover youth" (Kolivoski et al., 2017; Wildeman & Emanuel, 2014). Crossover youth experience high rates of recidivism, with Black young people experience disparate outcomes such as being less likely to be reunited with their families or a permanent family via adoption and are more likely to be placed in group homes and residential facilities than their counterparts (Saar et al., 2015).

All these risk factors can complicate a young person's ability to stay connected to school, one of the primary tasks of adolescence, which can undermine their academic achievement. Disconnection from school resulting in the lack of high school diploma or

GED is one of the highest risk factors for youth homelessness (M.H. Morton et al., 2018). Young people without a high school diploma or GED were found to have a 346% higher risk of experiencing homelessness than those who completed high school (M.H. Morton et al., 2018). Black youth are disproportionately suspended from school compared to their counterparts. Suspensions can create an increased sense of isolation and marginalization (Coles & Powell, 2020). Suspensions can also disrupt progress in young people earning their high school diplomas. Suspensions place Black young people at further risk of homelessness.

Homelessness is housing instability, and this instability can have a negative impact on staying connected to school, including school attendance and academic performance and achievement. The McKinney–Vento Homeless Education Assistance Improvements Act is supposed to help mitigate the negative impact of homelessness on staying connected to school. But being Black and experiencing homelessness creates unique challenges for accessing resources under the McKinney–Vento Homeless Education Assistance Improvements Act. Participants in a study by Edwards (2020) identified hostile racial climates at school as a common deterrent from disclosing their homeless status to adults at school, thereby restricting their access to federal support. Education is both a means to prevent and end youth homelessness. More attention needs to be given to the inclusion of race-conscious language in the McKinney–Vento Homeless Education Assistance Improvements Act (Edwards, 2020).

Young people with lived experience of homelessness are challenged by a diverse set of adversities that reinforces lifelong adversity such as trauma exposure and long-term homelessness. Young people experiencing poverty or living in economically under-resourced neighborhoods are more likely to experience childhood maltreatment and extreme family adversity, including caregiver substance misuse problems, than their counterparts (Coulton et al., 2007; Edidin et al., 2012; Ferguson, 2009; Hudson et al., 2008). All these adversities can exacerbate housing instability. These young people are often separated from their families and placed in the child welfare system. Separation from families, as noted, results in losing both social and financial support from their families of origin, which can further reinforce their becoming homeless (Bounds, Winiarski et al., 2020; Rice et al., 2017).

With the risk of sexual exploitation being magnified once young people are away from home for any length of time, additional exposure to trauma and violence, as well as high-risk sexual behaviors also become a concern (Saewyc & Edinburgh, 2010). Young people who have been commercially sexually exploited have the highest numbers of adverse childhood experiences (ACEs), with childhood sexual abuse being the most common (Reid & Piquero, 2016). ACEs research has connected these childhood experiences to multiple future health problems (Felitti et al., 1998). Due to the stigma associated with commercial sexual exploitation, in particular the judgment associated with violating social norms and the resultant unfair treatment in systems of care, victims of sexual exploitation are often blamed and criminalized for their involvement in commercial sex trade (Finigan-Carr et al., 2019). Black young people with lived experience of homelessness are at risk for sexual exploitation and the resultant risks and health outcomes. For instance, engaging in high-risk sexual behavior, common in commercial sex trade, is associated with elevated risk of acquiring HIV. Once HIV infection occurs, antiretroviral therapy to achieve virus suppression becomes the focus to prevent transmission and reduce viral load (Sullivan et al., 2015). Health disparities in HIV also exist wherein African Americans and Latino(a)s are the least likely to achieve viral suppression (Sullivan et al., 2015), which further exacerbates the negative health consequences if Black young people with lived experience of homelessness become infected with HIV.

Black young people with lived experience of homelessness struggle with access to health care, and greater access is necessary to prevent chronic health conditions. Improving access to health education, testing, and treatment is needed.

Young people in the United States commonly experience trauma and loss; one third to one half of young people will experience multiple traumatic events and losses during childhood to early adulthood (Layne et al., 2014). The cumulative effect of these multiple traumas has been referred to as "risk factor caravans"—risk factors that accrue and cascade over a child's development into adulthood. Social and environmental conditions are the paths to these risk factor caravans passageways that are common to underserved and under-resourced young people (Layne et al., 2014).

In addition to the cumulative and cascading impact of childhood adversity on Black young people with lived experience of homelessness, in the age of the internet and social media Black young people are not only exposed to their own negative experiences with law enforcement, but are also witnessing an unprecedented amount of police brutality. This unrelenting visual documentation of unequal treatment in the news and social media, specifically experienced as anti-Black racism to Black young people, has devastating health consequences (Silver et al., 2021; Williams et al., 2019). The lack of protection afforded to Black people by law enforcement commonly experienced in Black neighborhoods is now combined with inhumane treatment of anti-Black racism protestors, including physical attacks, the deployment of chemical irritants such as tear gas and pepper spray, and the destruction of basic supplies such as water and first-aid supplies (Boyle & Wadington, 2020; Leitch et al., 2020). Already marginalized in their experiences with homelessness, Black young people may find themselves feeling isolated amidst such national unrest. Again, little is known about how anti-Black racism affects the lives of Black young people with lived experience of homelessness because factors that are seemingly directly related to race are not examined in research and are rarely addressed in policy and services.

Protective Factors and Resources

Research on young people with lived experience of homelessness has focused primarily on risks for youth homelessness (see Giano et al., 2020 for review that focuses on risks; Cutuli et al., 2020), in part because research funding largely supports the identification of problems and pathology or illness rather than identifying solutions and wellness (Wand, 2013, 2015). Research on protective factors and resources with a prevention perspective is less developed, but this is an emerging area of importance and public health significance for research on young people with lived experience of homelessness (Sieving et al., 2017). Resilience is a protective factor that has recently gained attention in research on young people with lived experience of homelessness and has not been systematically applied in previous studies that have examined protective factors (Cronley & Evans, 2017). Resilience is defined as being able to cope with or overcome adversity. Individual, external, and environmental factors contribute to resilience (Clemens et al., 2018; Cronley & Evans, 2017; Lu et al., 2020; O'Neill & Bowers, 2020).

Resilience needs to be examined from a cultural perspective (Ungar, 2012). Protective factors that have been examined include family and peer social support and connections (Barman-Adhikari et al., 2016; Kelly, 2020; Sieving et al., 2017), resilience broadly defined (Cronley & Evans, 2017; Milburn et al., 2019), and education and/or employment (Ferguson et al., 2018).

Focusing on protective factors such as family is challenging in research on young people with lived experience of homelessness (Milburn et al., 2020). Nonetheless, family connections and positive relationships are important for young people to have a healthy trajectory into adulthood (Foster et al., 2017). Families are an overlooked resource for Black young people with lived experience of homelessness even though these young people often maintain ties to family (Milburn et al., 2009; Slesnick et al., 2009). Focusing on education and/or employment is less challenging (Ferguson et al., 2018). Historically, the service sector—service providers who work with youth with lived experience—have been reluctant to work with families. Often service providers have perceived family as the cause of youth being out of home (e.g., family abuse, family conflict). Yet research has found that social support that is associated with fewer mental health problems in young people with lived experience, ages 16 to 22 years and 26% Black, is related to having positive adult (i.e., mentors), family, and friend connections (Tyler et al., 2017). Research has also found that Black young people with lived experience of homelessness, ages 14 to 25 years, report parent communication about safe sex practices (e.g., HIV testing, condom use, and fewer sexual partners) and are more likely to engage in safer sex practices than their counterparts (Craddock et al., 2016). Family connectedness seems to be a protective factor for sexual health among young people with lived experience of homelessness (Sieving et al., 2017). Informal social support has also been identified as a significant external factor for resilience among young people with lived experience of homelessness in a systematic review using a resilience conceptual framework (Cronley & Evans, 2017). More recently, the service sector has come around to family work (Bounds et al., 2019; Bounds, Otwell et al., 2020; Chisolm-Straker et al., 2018; Slesnick & Brakenhoff, 2020), in part because family reconnection may be a way to move some young people from unstably housed to housed (Milburn et al., 2020) or retain some young people in being housed (Bounds et al., 2019; Bounds, Otwell et al., 2020).

Personal skill characteristics such as goal setting, decision-making, and self-reliance have been found to be protective factors in a sample of largely racial/ethnic minority youth with lived experience of homelessness (Lightfoot et al., 2011). These are potential malleable factors for skills building interventions and prevention of problem and risky behaviors that can increase risk for chronic homelessness.

Greater attention has to be given to how to leverage the service sector to take advantage of protective factors and build resilience and strengths to address homelessness among Black young people. More preventive services are needed. Funding streams, however, are problem and not prevention focused. Increased funding for prevention is needed.

Building Health Equity to Prevent and End Homelessness

Building health equity is linked to the prevention and ending of homelessness among Black young people. Addressing anti-Black racism and discrimination, the social and economic factors that are associated with health and healthy behaviors, and housing needs will improve health equity to prevent homelessness among Black young people, and deter chronic homelessness among those with lived experience of homelessness.

Addressing Anti-Black Racism

Anti-Black racism, like discrimination, has been under investigated in studies of youth with lived experience of homelessness. Yet anti-Black racism cannot be ignored in the prevention and ending of homelessness for young Black people with lived experience of homelessness. Many of the policy and service sector areas that are linked to the prevention and ending of homelessness are areas wherein anti-Black racism occurs, including housing, education, and employment. Anti-Black racism is a means by which White supremacy is perpetuated, specifically the perception that Black people are not human and not the same as or equal to White people. Black people are perceived as different, not human and not equal, to justify the structural racism that has maintained White supremacy. This constructed narrative about Black people leads to biases in systems that should provide services (e.g., education, housing, social services, etc.). Unfortunately, these systems are structurally complicit in perpetuating anti-Black racism, which leads to mistrust. So how can Black homeless young people trust these systems for support?

These systems have also not been supportive of Black families. Inattention to the role of family in interventions for Black youth homelessness is another example of how knowledge about what is required for healthy trajectories into adulthood, family and caring adults, are largely overlooked in interventions for youth homelessness. Little attention is given to family reconnections and building family strengths, and more attention is focused on family dysfunction, not on how to build family resilience and reconnect family and youth. The underlying role of anti-Black racism in the lack of support for Black families has not been fully acknowledged or investigated.

The disproportionate prevalence of homelessness among Black young people may lead to bias in fully addressing youth homelessness as a pressing social problem. Being young, Black, and homeless is not considered a rare event that should not be tolerated and requires immediate attention and solutions. Rather, being young, Black, and homeless seems be viewed as acceptable. How structural racism has contributed to the disproportionate prevalence of homelessness is just gaining more attention, as noted previously, and has, yet, to be fully embraced in our understanding of youth homelessness.

Defining and Building Health Equity

Young people with lived experience of homelessness dying earlier than their peers suggests that these youth have different experiences of health and well-being (Auerswald et al., 2016; Edidin et al., 2012). Therefore, addressing social determinants of health is important for improving the health of young people with lived experience of homelessness to reduce health disparities. Though health care is essential to health, it is a relatively weak health determinant. Research suggests that health behaviors, such as smoking, diet, and exercise, are the most important determinants of premature death (Banerjee et al., 2021; Carlson et al., 2018; Lariscy et al., 2018).

There is growing recognition that social and economic factors shape individuals' ability to engage in these healthy or unhealthy behaviors (Henderson et al., 2016). The complex interaction between individual, family, social, and political factors' influence on health-making theories make frameworks that only consider individual and family risks inadequate when exploring health disparities (Milburn et al., 2019). Given that a multitude of factors influence health outcomes, considering the role intersectionality plays can simultaneously inform and complicate our understanding of intervention strategies to eliminate health disparities (Bounds, Otwell et al., 2020; Bowleg, 2012; Milburn et al., 2019). Any approach to building health equity for Black young people with lived experience of homelessness should begin with the following considerations: (a) intersectionality, anti-Black racism, and discrimination's effects on health; (b) health disparities' relationships to risk behaviors; (c) holistic definitions of health and well-being that include the provision of basic needs such as housing; and (d) how protective factors can buffer the impact of adversities on Black young people.

People with lived experience of homelessness, in general, experience a large range of environmental hazards, over policing, and criminalization that is magnified by being Black (Goodling, 2020). In fact, the Centers for Disease Control and Prevention (Centers fo Disease Control and Prevention, 2020) cites racialized and minority groups being at higher risk for COVID-19 morbidity and mortality to be related to the social determinants of health such as discrimination, lack of health care access and utilization, occupation, education, income and wealth gaps, and housing conditions. The anti-Black racism experienced by Black communities results in worse health outcomes despite the measure used (e.g., life expectancy, disease prevalence, maternal mortality rates) (Leitch et al., 2020). For Black young people, there is a constellation of risk factors that homelessness predisposes them to, including poor mental health outcomes; exposure to trauma, violence, and exploitation; substance use, HIV/AIDS; and now COVID-19 (Auerswald et al., 2020; Tucker et al., 2020). The recent COVID-19 pandemic has highlighted and exacerbated these already glaring health disparities. Unfortunately, Black communities have been disproportionately impacted by COVID while simultaneously responding to escalating police brutality (Leitch et al., 2020). Potential explanations for disproportionate exposure, infections, morbidity, and mortality include being frontline workers (McClure et al., 2020), reliance on public transportation for commuting (Tan & Ma, 2020), underlying medical conditions (Fortuna et al., 2020), lack of trust in the health care system, and lack of health insurance and bias among health care workers, leading to the lack of recognition of symptoms and under treatment (Fiscella & Sanders, 2016; Fortuna et al., 2020). Ultimately, the impact of anti-Black racism must not be minimized when building health equity for Black youth who have experienced homelessness.

A discussion on health disparities, health equity, and optimal health logically leads to an exploration of definitions of health and well-being. In 2020, college leaders from across the country created the inter-association definition of well-being, defined as "an optimal and dynamic state that allows people to achieve their full potential" (NIRSA: Leaders in Collegiate Recreation, 2020). As described, Black young people have not had the opportunity to experience well-being as defined here. There are two main influences on one's well-being: individual and community well-being that integrates both one's perception of living a fulfilling life with how the quality of life for all people within one's entire community is interconnected. When considering this definition of well-being, both access to basic needs and health equity are of utmost concern.

> Objective well-being is realized when people have their basic human rights and needs met. Objective well-being includes but is not limited to: sufficient resources such as food, housing, safety, and physical/mental health care; experiences of systemic equity and diversity; experiences of liberty and freedom of participation at all levels of society; and experiences of unfettered human rights such as freedom of speech, voting access, and justice system protections." (NIRSA: Leaders in Collegiate Recreation, 2020).

The Robert Wood Johnson Foundation (RWJF, 2021) cites well-being as an expansion of health that not only includes access to basic needs but also access to one's thriving. Given these definitions focusing on sufficient resources and being able to fulfill one's full potential, which begins with building health equity, Black young people with lived experience of homelessness must have access to safe, secure environments with adequate supports in place that buffer the adversity they have already experienced.

Housing is a basic need. Maslow's (1943) hierarchy of needs is the most influential theory when discussing basic needs. It connects a child's development with the prerequisite requirement of satisfying basic needs (e.g., safety needs, love/belonging needs) (Noltemeyer et al., 2020). Poverty creates a constellation of intersecting risk factors, such as housing and food insecurity, that creates adversity (Jensen et al., 2017). The basic needs of food and shelter are not just about quantity or presence but also about quality (e.g., sufficient caloric intake, access to fruits and vegetables, and safe, consistent housing). Poverty has a multitude of consequences to childhood development. These consequences create a cascade of psychosocial and biological risk factors that may reinforce a cycle of intergenerational poverty (Jensen et al., 2017). Therefore, access to these basic human needs has a reciprocal relationship with mental wellness that is directly tied to stable employment, independence, and self-sufficiency (Winiarski et al., 2020). One complication for young people in general and marginalized young people specifically is mistrust of mental health care service providers (Bounds, Otwell et al., 2020; Winiarski et al., 2020), which creates a disparity regarding who has access to adequate quality treatment. Additionally, daily experiences of anti-Black racism encountered by Black young people can detract from getting one's basic needs related to safety, access to health care, and unfettered human rights met.

In terms of homelessness, there is a need to focus on more than being homeless or housed to truly understand the health impacts of current housing disparities, often driven by high rates of segregation by race and socioeconomic status in the United States (Rothstein, 2017). Housing and health span four key pillars that include stability, affordability, quality and safety, and neighborhood opportunity (Swope & Hernández, 2019). Patterns of these four pillars are central to understanding how social inequality contributes to the housing and health burden of certain groups and must be used when mounting practice implications for serving Black young people who have experienced homelessness.

Social prescribing programs have emerged in the health care sector that acknowledge housing stability and food security as essential to health and well-being. Although social prescribing sounds like a worthwhile endeavor, more evidence is needed to support the efficacy of this practice (Pescheny et al., 2018). While screening for social determinants of health is an increasingly common practice in U.S. health care, social prescribing research, on the other hand, seems more popular in other countries (Alderwick et al., 2018; Mulligan et al., 2020). Despite the lack of traction with social prescribing programs in the United States, housing first and rapid rehousing models have become prominent models for adults with some success in addressing homelessness among adults (Raven et al., 2020). The housing first model is not without criticism. For example, some argue that it has not been effective at ending homelessness and therefore should not be viewed as a panacea (Eide, 2020). Additionally, research is just emerging on the success of these programs for young people who will likely need additional support when compared to adults (Youngbloom et al., 2021). Housing first models that include antiracism and anti-oppression approaches showed promise in a recent randomized controlled trial in Canada (Stergiopoulos et al., 2016).

Concluding Research Implications

The research implications of race comparative models for understanding health disparities cannot be overlooked. A word of caution is necessary given the scientific community's propensity to compare outcomes between Black and White young people with White as the standard for interpretation of "normal" and/or "good." It is crucial to expand our definitions of health disparities beyond racial comparisons, particularly when White people are framed as the standard comparison for Black people to achieve healthy outcomes. The race comparative research approach has been criticized for its inherent limitations in providing a useful understanding of how to best address existing disparities (Milburn et al., 2019). One main limitation is that within group differences are missed. Underrepresented minorities and BIPOC are heterogeneous groups, and culture and experience are not exclusive to race. Additionally, deviations from the White standard can become overpathologized and misinterpreted as deviant, negative, or deficient. Finally, non-White people have been grouped into one category as underrepresented minorities, BIPOC, and so on, again to be compared against White people, missing the opportunity to compare and fully understand within-group phenomena, strengths, and opportunities.

Our approach has been to use the broad category of Black young people with lived experience of homelessness. Black, as a category, can encompass a group with considerable within group diversity, including young people who are the descendants of African enslaved people, young people whose parents are of Black African descent immigrants from African countries or the Caribbean, and young people who are Black and Latinx (e.g., Puerto Rican, Dominican, etc.). Issues of intersectionality and multiple racial/ethnic identities need to be further addressed in future research.

References

Alderwick, H. A., Gottlieb, L. M., Fichtenberg, C. M., & Adler, N. E. (2018). Social prescribing in the US and England: Emerging interventions to address patients' social needs. American Journal of Preventive Medicine, 54(5), 715–718. https://doi.org/10.1016/j.amepre.2018.01.039

Alessi, E. J., Greenfield, B., Manning, D., & Dank, M. (2020). Victimization and resilience among sexual and gender minority homeless youth engaging in survival sex. Journal of Interpersonal Violence, https://doi.org/10.1177/0886260519898434

Auerswald, C. L., & Adams, S. (2018). Counting all homeless youth today so we may no longer need to tomorrow. Journal of Adolescent Health, 62(1), 1–2. https://doi.org/10.1016/j.jadohealth.2017.10.013

Auerswald, C. L., Lin, J. S., & Parriott, A. (2016). Six-year mortality in a street-recruited cohort of homeless youth in San Francisco, California. PeerJ, 4, e1909. https://doi.org/10.7717/peerj.1909

Banerjee, S., Radak, T., Khubchandani, J., & Dunn, P. (2021). Food insecurity and mortality in American adults: Results from the NHANES-linked mortality study. Health Promotion Practice, 22(2), 204–214. https://doi.org/10.1177/1524839920945927

Barman-Adhikari, A., Bowen, E., Bender, K., Brown, S., & Rice, E. (2016). A social capital approach to identifying correlates of perceived social support among homeless youth. Child Youth Care Forum, 45, 691–708. https://doi.org/0.1007/s10566-016-9352-3

Bassuk, E. (1984). The homelessness problem. Scientific American, 251(1), 40–45. http://www.jstor.org/stable/24969410

Bounds, D. T., Edinburgh, L. D., Fogg, L. F., & Saeywc, E. M. (2019). A nurse practitioner-led intervention for runaway adolescents who have been sexually assaulted or sexually exploited: Effects on trauma symptoms, suicidality, and self-injury. Child Abuse & Neglect, 90, 99–107. https://doi.org/10.1016/j.chiabu.2019.01.023

Bounds, D. T., Otwell, C. H., Melendez, A., Karnik, N. S., & Julion, W. A. (2020). Adapting a family intervention to reduce risk factors for sexual exploitation. Child and Adolescent Psychiatry and Mental Health, 14(1), 1–12. https://doi.org/10.1186/s13034-020-00314-w

Bounds, D. T., Winiarski, D. A., Otwell, C. H., Tobin, V., Glover, A. C., Melendez, A., & Karnik, N. S. (2020). Considerations for working with youth with socially complex needs. *Journal of Child and Adolescent Psychiatric Nursing, 33*(4), 209–220. https://doi.org/10.1111/jcap.12288

Bowleg, L. (2012). The problem with the phrase women and minorities: Intersectionality—an important theoretical framework for public health. *American Journal of Public Health, 102*(7), 1267–1273. https://doi.org/10.2105/AJPH.2012.300750

Boyle, J., & Wadington, K. (2020, June 4). Fact check: Police did destroy a medic area during protests in Asheville, North Carolina. *USA Today, 3*. https://www.usatoday.com/story/news/factcheck/2020/06/03/george-floyd-protests-police-destroy-medic-station-asheville/3124847001/

Carlson, S. A., Adams, E. K., Yang, Z., & Fulton, J. E. (2018). Percentage of deaths associated with inadequate physical activity in the United States. *Preventing Chronic Disease, 15*. https://doi.org/10.5888/pcd18.170354

Carrasco, A. R. (2019). Youth homelessness and the racial knowledge gap. *Journal of Children and Poverty, 25*(1), 57–68. DOI: 10.1080/10796126.2019.1591041.

Centers for Disease Control and Prevenetion (2020, July). *CDC COVID-19 response health equity strategy: Accelerating progress towards reducing COVID-19 disparities and achieving health equity.* https://www.cdc.gov/coronavirus/2019-ncov/downloads/community/CDC-Strategy.pdf

Chisolm-Straker, M., Sze, J., Einbond, J., White, J., & Stoklosa, H. (2018). A supportive adult may be the difference in homeless youth not being trafficked. *Children and Youth Services Review, 91*, 115–120. https://doi.org/10.1016/j.childyouth.2018.06.003

Clemens, E., Hess, R. S., Strear, M. M., Rue, L., Rizzolo, S., & Henninger, J. (2018). Promoting resilience in youth experiencing homelessness through implementation of the McKinney–Vento Homeless Assistance Act. *Preventing School Failure: Alternative Education for Children and Youth, 62*(2), 105–115. https://doi.org/10.1080/1045988X.2017.1387756

Coles, J. A., & Powell, T. (2020). A BlackCrit analysis on Black urban youth and suspension disproportionality as anti-Black symbolic violence. *Race Ethnicity and Education, 23*(1), 113–133. https://doi.org/10.1080/13613324.2019.1631778

Corliss, H. L., Goodenow, C. S., Nichols, L., & Austin, S. B. (2011). High burden of homelessness among sexual-minority adolescents: findings from a representative Massachusetts high school sample. *American Journal of Public Health, 101*(9), 1683–1689. https://doi.org/10.2105/AJPH.2011.300155

Coulton, C. J., Crampton, D. S., Irwin, M., Spilsbury, J. C., & Korbin, J. E. (2007). How neighborhoods influence child maltreatment: A review of the literature and alternative pathways. *Child Abuse & Neglect, 31*(11–12), 1117–1142. https://doi.org/10.1016/j.chiabu.2007.03.023

Craddock, J. B., Rice, R., Rhoades, H., & Winetrobe, H. (2016). Are parental relationships always protective? A social network analysis of Black, Latino, and White homeless youth and sexual risk-taking behaviors. Prevention Science, 7, 914–924.

Cromartie, J. (2018, November). Rural America at a glance: 2018 edition (Economic Information Bullentin No. 200). United States Department of Agriculture, Economic Research Service. https://doi.org/10.22004/ag.econ.282512

Cronley, C., & Evans, R. (2017). Studies of resilience among youth experiencing homelessness: A systematic review. *Journal of Human Behavior in the Social Environment, 27*(4), 291–310. https://doi.org/10.1080/10911359.2017.1282912

Cutuli, J., Treglia, D., & Herbers, J. E. (2020). Adolescent homelessness and associated features: Prevalence and risk across eight states. *Child Psychiatry & Human Development, 51*(1), 48–58. https://doi.org/0.1007/s10578-019-00909-1

Dancy, T. E. (2014). The adultification of Black boys: What educational settings can learn from Trayvon Martin. In *Trayvon Martin, race, and American justice* (pp. 49–55). Brill.

Dworsky A. (2020). The prevalence of youth homelessness in the United States. In C. Warf & G. Charles (Eds.), *Clinical care for homeless, runaway and refugee youth* (pp. 1–10). Springer.

Edidin, J. P., Ganim, Z., Hunter, S. J., & Karnik, N. S. (2012). The mental and physical health of homeless youth: A literature review. *Child Psychiatry & Human Development*, *43*(3), 354–375. https://doi.org/10.1007/s10578-011-0270-1

Edwards, E. J. (2020). Young, Black, successful, and homeless: Examining the unique academic challenges of Black students who experienced homelessness. *Journal of Children and Poverty*, *26*(2), 125–149. https://doi.org/10.1080/10796126.2020.1776688

Edwards, M. E., Torgerson, M., & Sattem, J. (2009). Paradoxes of providing rural social services: The case of homeless youth. *Rural Sociology*, *74*(3), 330–355. https://doi.org/10.1526/003601109789037204

Eide, S. (2020). Housing first and homelessness: The rhetoric and the reality. https://media4.manhattan-institute.org/sites/default/files/housing-first-and-homelessness-SE.pdf

Epstein, R., Blake, J., & González, T. (2017). *Girlhood interrupted: The erasure of Black girls' childhood.* Georgetown Law Center on Poverty and Inequality. https://www.law.georgetown.edu/poverty-inequality-center/wp-content/uploads/sites/14/2017/08/girlhood-interrupted.pdf

Felitti, V. J., Anda, R. F., Nordenberg, D., Williamson, D. F., Spitz, A. M., Edwards, V., & Marks, J. S. (1998). Relationship of childhood abuse and household dysfunction to many of the leading causes of death in adults: The Adverse Childhood Experiences (ACE) Study. *American Journal of Preventive Medicine*, *14*(4), 245–258. https://doi.org/10.1016/s0749-3797(98)00017-8

Ferguson, K. M. (2009). Exploring family environment characteristics and multiple abuse experiences among homeless youth. *Journal of Interpersonal Violence*, *24*(11), 1875–1891. https://doi.org/10.1177/0886260508325490

Ferguson, K. M., Bender, K., & Thompson, S. J. (2018). Risk and resilience factors associated with formal and informal income generation among homeless young adults in three US cities. *Youth & Society*, *50*(3), 351–376. https://doi.org/10.1177/0044118X15600722

Fernandes-Alcantara, A. L. (2016). *Runaway and homeless youth: Demographics and programs.* Congressional Research Service. https://www.novapublishers.com/wp-content/uploads/2018/09/1-27-pages.pdf

Finigan-Carr, N. M., Johnson, M. H., Pullmann, M. D., Stewart, C. J., & Fromknecht, A. E. (2019). A traumagenic social ecological framework for understanding and intervening with sex trafficked children and youth. *Child and Adolescent Social Work Journal*, *36*(1), 49–63. https://doi.org/10.1007/s10560-018-0588-7

Fiscella, K., & Sanders, M. R. (2016). Racial and ethnic disparities in the quality of health care. *Annual Review of Public Health*, *37*, 375–394. https://doi.org/10.1146/annurev-publhealth-032315-021439

Fortuna, L. R., Tolou-Shams, M., Robles-Ramamurthy, B., & Porche, M. V. (2020). Inequity and the disproportionate impact of COVID-19 on communities of color in the United States: The need for a trauma-informed social justice response. *Psychological Trauma: Theory, Research, Practice, and Policy*, *12*(5), 443–445. https://doi.org/10.1037/tra0000889

Foster, C. E., Horwitz, A., Thomas, A., Opperman, K., Gipson, P., Burnside, A., Stone, D. M., King, C. A. (2017). Connectedness to family, school, peers, and community in socially vulnerable adolescents. *Children and Youth Services Review*, *81*, 321–331. htttps://doi.org/10.1016/j.childyouth.2017.08.011

Fowler, P. J., Marcal, K. E., Zhang, J., Day, O., & Landsverk, J. (2019). Defining homelessness in the transition to adulthood for policy and prevention. *Journal of Child and Family Studies*, *28*, 3051–3061. https://doi.org/10.1007/s10826-019-01480-y

Fusaro, V. A., Levy, H. G., & Shaefer, H. L. (2018). Racial and ethnic disparities in the lifetime prevalence of homelessness in the United States. Demography, 55(6), 2119-2128. DOI: 10.1007/s13524-018-0717-0.

Giano, Z., Williams, A., Hankey, C., Merrill, R., Lisnic, R., & Herring, A. (2020). Forty years of research on predictors of homelessness. *Community Mental Health Journal*, *56*(4), 692–709. https://doi.org/10.1007/s10597-019-00530-5

Goodling, E. (2020). Intersecting hazards, intersectional identities: A baseline critical environmental justice analysis of US homelessness. *Environment and Planning E: Nature and Space*, *3*(3), 833–856. https://doi.org/10.1177/2514848619892433

Gray, D., Chau, S., Huerta, T., & Frankish, J. (2011). Urban-rural migration and health and quality of life in homeless people. *Journal of Social Distress and the Homeless, 20*(1–2), 75–93. https://doi.org/10.1179/105307811805365007

Hailey, J., Burton, W., & Arscott, J. (2020). We are family: Chosen and created families as a protective factor against racialized trauma and anti-LGBTQ oppression among African American sexual and gender minority youth. *Journal of GLBT Family Studies, 16*(2), 176–191. https://doi.org/10.1080/1550428X.2020.1724133

Halcón, L. L., & Lifson, A. R. (2004). Prevalence and predictors of sexual risks among homeless youth. *Journal of Youth and Adolescence, 33*(1), 71–80.

Henderson, D. X., DeCuir-Gunby, J., & Gill, V. (2016). "It really takes a village": A socio-ecological model of resilience for prevention among economically disadvantaged ethnic minority youth. *The Journal of Primary Prevention, 37*(5), 469–485. https://doi.org/10.1007/s10935-016-0446-3

Hudson, A. L., Nyamathi, A., & Sweat, J. (2008). Homeless youths' interpersonal perspectives of health care providers. *Issues in Mental Health Nursing, 29*(12), 1277–1289. https://doi.org/10.1080/01612840802498235

Jensen, S. K., Berens, A. E., & Nelson, C. A., III. (2017). Effects of poverty on interacting biological systems underlying child development. *The Lancet Child & Adolescent Health, 1*(3), 225–239. https://doi.org/10.1016/S2352-4642(17)30024-X

Jones, M. M. (2016). Does race matter in addressing homelessness? A review of the literature. *World Medical & Health Policy, 8*(2), 139–156. https://doi.org/10.1002/wmh3.189

Kelly, P. (2020). Risk and protective factors contributing to homelessness among foster care youth: An analysis of the National Youth in Transition Database. *Children and Youth Services Review, 108*, 104589. https://doi.org/10.1016/j.childyouth.2019.104589

Kolivoski, K. M., Goodkind, S., & Shook, J. J. (2017). Social justice for crossover youth: The intersection of the child welfare and juvenile justice systems. *Social Work, 62*(4), 313–321. https://doi.org/10.1093/sw/swx034

Lariscy, J. T., Hummer, R. A., & Rogers, R. G. (2018). Cigarette smoking and all-cause and cause-specific adult mortality in the United States. *Demography, 55*(5), 1855–1885. https://doi.org/10.1007/s13524-018-0707-2

Layne, C. M., Greeson, J. K., Ostrowski, S. A., Kim, S., Reading, S., Vivrette, R. L., Briggs, E. C., Fairbank, J. A., & Pynoos, R. S. (2014). Cumulative trauma exposure and high risk behavior in adolescence: Findings from the National Child Traumatic Stress Network core data set. *Psychological Trauma: Theory, Research, Practice, and Policy, 6*(S1), S40. https://doi.org/10.1037/a0037799

Leitch, S., Corbin, J. H., Boston-Fisher, N., Ayele, C., Delobelle, P., Gwanzura Ottemöller, F., Matenga, T. F. L., Mweemba, O., Pederson, A., & Wicker, J. (2020). Black lives matter in health promotion: Moving from unspoken to outspoken. *Health Promotion International.* Advance online publication. https://doi.org/10.1093/heapro/daaa121

Library of Congress. (2015). Black Lives Matter (BLM). https://www.loc.gov/item/lcwaN0016241/

Lightfoot, M., Stein, J., Tevendale, H., & Preston, K. (2011). Protective factors associated with fewer multiple problem behaviors among homeless/runaway youth. Journal of Clinical Child and Adolescent Psychology, 40(6), 878–889. https://doi.org/10.1080/15374416.2011.614581

Los Angeles Homeless Services Authority. (2018, December). *Report and recommendations of the ad hoc committee on Black people experiencing homelessness.* https://www.lahsa.org/documents?id=2823-report-and-recommendations-of-the-ad-hoc-committee-on-black-people-experiencing-homelessness.pdf

Lu, J., Potts, C. A., & Allen, R. S. (2020). Homeless people's trait mindfulness and their resilience—a mediation test on the role of inner peace and hope. *Journal of Social Distress and Homelessness*, 1–9. https://doi.org/10.1080/10530789.2020.1774847

Maslow, A. H. (1943). A theory of human motivation. *Psychological Review, 50*(4), 370–396. https://doi.org/10.1037/h0054346

McClure, E. S., Vasudevan, P., Bailey, Z., Patel, S., & Robinson, W. R. (2020). Racial capitalism within public health—how occupational settings drive COVID-19 disparities. *American Journal of Epidemiology, 189*(11), 1244–1253. https://doi.org/10.1093/aje/kwaa126

McKinney-Vento Homeless Education Assistance Improvements Act of 2001, 42 U.S.C. § 11431-11435 (2001). https://uscode.house.gov/view.xhtml?path=/prelim@title42/chapter119&edition=prelim

Milburn, N.G., Liang, L.J., Lee, S.J., Rotheram-Borus, M.J., Rosenthal, D., Mallett, S., Lightfoot, M. & Lester, P. (2009). Who is doing well? A typology of newly homeless adolescents. *Journal of Community Psychology, 37 (2), 135 – 147.* PMCID: PMC2824440.

Milburn, N. G., Batterham, P., Ayala, G., Rice, E., Solorio, R., Desmond, K., Lord, L., Iribarren, J., & Rotheram-Borus, M. J. (2010). Discrimination and mental health problems among homeless minority young people. *Public Health Reports, 125*(1), 61–67. https://doi.org/10.1177/003335491012500109

Milburn, N. G., Beatty, L., & Lopez, S. A. (2019). Understanding, unpacking, and eliminating health disparities: A prescription for health equity promotion through behavioral and psychological research—an introduction. *Cultural Diversity and Ethnic Minority Psychology, 25*(1), 1–5. https://doi.org/10.1037/cdp0000266

Milburn, N. G., Klomhaus, A. M., Comulada, W. S., Lopez, S. A., Bath, E., Amani, B., Jackson, J., Lee, A., Rice, E., Semaan, A., & Kim, B. K. E. (2020). Reconnecting homeless adolescents and their families: Correlates of participation in a family intervention. *Prevention Science, 21*(8), 1048–1058. https://doi.org/10.1007/s11121-020-01157-9

Morton, M., Samuels, G., Dworsky, A., & Patel, S. (2018). *Missed opportunities: LGBTQ youth homelessness in America.* Chapin Hall at the University of Chicago.

Morton, M. H., Dworsky, A., Matjasko, J. L., Curry, S. R., Schlueter, D., Chávez, R., & Farrell, A. F. (2018). Prevalence and correlates of youth homelessness in the United States. *Journal of Adolescent Health, 62*(1), 14–21. https://doi.org/10.1016/j.jadohealth.2017.10.006

Morton, M. H., Dworsky, A., & Samuels, G. M. (2017). *Missed opportunities: Youth homelessness in America. National estimates.* Chapin Hall at the University of Chicago.

Mulligan, K., Bhatti, S., Rayner, J., & Hsiung, S. (2020). Social prescribing: Creating pathways towards better health and wellness. *Journal of the American Geriatrics Society, 68*(2), 426–428. https://doi.org/10.1111/jgs.16249

National Alliance to End Homelessness. (2020). *Homelessness and racial disparities.* https://endhomelessness.org/homelessness-in-america/what-causes-homelessness/inequality/

NIRSA: Leaders in Collegiate Recreation. (2020, November). *Inter-association definition of well-being.* Student Affairs Administrators in Higher Education & American College Health Association. https://nirsa.net/nirsa/wp-content/uploads/inter-assocation-well-being-definition-2011b.pdf

Noltemeyer, A., James, A. G., Bush, K., Bergen, D., Barrios, V., & Patton, J. (2020). The relationship between deficiency needs and growth needs: The continuing investigation of Maslow's theory. *Child & Youth Services, 42*(1), 24–42. https://doi.org/10.1080/0145935X.2020.1818558

O'Neill, M., & Bowers, P. H. (2020). Resilience among homeless college students: co-constructed explorations. *Journal of Social Distress and Homelessness, 29*(1), 65–70. https://doi.org/10.1080/10530789.2020.1676984

Page, M. (2017). Forgotten youth: Homeless LGBT youth of color and the Runaway and Homeless Youth Act. *Northwestern Journal of Law & Social Policy, 12*(2), 17-45.

Pescheny, J. V., Pappas, Y., & Randhawa, G. (2018). Facilitators and barriers of implementing and delivering social prescribing services: a systematic review. *BMC Health Services Research, 18*(1), 1–14. https://doi.org/10.1186/s12913-018-2893-4

Raven, M. C., Niedzwiecki, M. J., & Kushel, M. (2020). A randomized trial of permanent supportive housing for chronically homeless persons with high use of publicly funded services. *Health services research, 55,* 797–806. https://doi.org/10.1111/1475-6773.13553

Reid, J. A., & Piquero, A. R. (2016). Applying general strain theory to youth commercial sexual exploitation. *Crime & Delinquency, 62*(3), 341–367. https://doi.org/10.1177/0011128713498213

Rhee, T. G., & Rosenheck, R. A. (2021). Why are Black adults over-represented among individuals who have experienced lifetime homelessness? Oaxaca-Blinder decomposition analysis of homelessness among US male adults. *Journal of Epidemiology and Community Health, 75*, 161–170. http://doi.org/10.1136/jech-2020-214305

Rice, S., Cotton, S., Moeller-Saxone, K., Mihalopoulos, C., Magnus, A., Harvey, C., Humphreys, C., Halperin, S., Scheppokat, A., & McGorry, P. (2017). Placement instability among young people removed from their original family and the likely mental health implications. *Shanghai Archives of Psychiatry, 29*(2), 85–94. https://doi.org/10.11919/j.issn.1002-0829.216090

Robertson, M. J., & Cousineau, M. R. (1986). Health status and access to health services among the urban homeless. *American Journal of Public Health,* 76(5), 561–563.

Robert Wood Johnson Foundation. (2021). *Enhanced individual and community well-being.* https://www.rwjf.org/en/cultureofhealth/taking-action/outcome-improved-population-health--well-being--and-equity/individual-and-community-well-being.html

Robinson, B. A. (2018). Conditional families and lesbian, gay, bisexual, transgender, and queer youth homelessness: Gender, sexuality, family instability, and rejection. *Journal of Marriage and Family, 80*(2), 383–396. https://doi.org/10.1111/jomf.12466

Rothstein, R. (2017). *The color of law: A forgotten history of how our government segregated America.* Liveright.

Saar, M. S., Epstein, R., Rosenthal, L., & Vafa, Y. (2015). *The sexual abuse to prison pipeline: The girls' story.* https://rights4girls.org/wp-content/uploads/r4g/2015/02/2015_COP_sexual-abuse_layout_web-1.pdf

Saewyc, E. M., & Edinburgh, L. D. (2010). Restoring healthy developmental trajectories for sexually exploited young runaway girls: Fostering protective factors and reducing risk behaviors. *Journal of Adolescent Health, 46*(2), 180–188. https://doi.org/10.1016/j.jadohealth.2009.06.010

Siconolfi, D., Tucker, J. S., Shadel, W. G., Seelam, R., & Golinelli, D. (2020). Health, homelessness severity, and substance use among sexual minority youth experiencing homelessness: A comparison of bisexual versus gay and lesbian youth. *The Journal of Sex Research, 57*(7), 933–942. https://doi.org/10.1080/00224499.2019.1695723

Sieving, R. E., McRee, A.-L., McMorris, B. J., Shlafer, R. J., Gower, A. L., Kapa, H. M., Beckman, K. J., Doty, J. L., Plowman, S. L., & Resnick, M. D. (2017). Youth–adult connectedness: A key protective factor for adolescent health. *American Journal of Preventive Medicine, 52*(3), S275–S278. https://doi.org/10.1016/j.amepre.2016.07.037

Silver, R. C., Holman, E. A., & Garfin, D. R. (2021). Coping with cascading collective traumas in the United States. *Nature Human Behaviour, 5*(1), 4–6. https://doi.org/10.1038/s41562-020-00981-x

Slesnick, N., & Brakenhoff, B. R. (2020). Family-based treatment for runaway and homeless youth. *The Handbook of Systemic Family Therapy, 2*, 503–520.

Slesnick, N., Dashora, P., Letcher, A., Erdem, G., & Serovich, J. (2009). A review of services and interventions for runaway and homeless youth: Moving forward. *Children and Youth Services Review, 31*(7), 732–742. https://doi.org/10.1016/j.childyouth.2009.01.006

Stergiopoulos, V., Gozdzik, A., Misir, V., Skosireva, A., Sarang, A., Connelly, J., Whisler, A., & McKenzie, K. (2016). The effectiveness of a housing first adaptation for ethnic minority groups: Findings of a pragmatic randomized controlled trial. *BMC Public Health, 16*(1), 1–11. https://doi.org/10.1186/s12889-016-3768-4

Sullivan, K. A., Messer, L. C., & Quinlivan, E. B. (2015). Substance abuse, violence, and HIV/AIDS (SAVA) syndemic effects on viral suppression among HIV positive women of color. *AIDS Patient Care and STDs, 29*(S1), S42–S48. https://doi.org/10.1089/apc.2014.0278

Swope, C. B., & Hernández, D. (2019). Housing as a determinant of health equity: A conceptual model. *Social Science & Medicine, 243*, 112571. https://doi.org/10.1016/j.socscimed.2019.112571

Tan, L., & Ma, C. (2020). Choice behavior of commuters' rail transit mode during the COVID-19 pandemic based on logistic model. *Journal of Traffic and Transportation Engineering, 8*(2), 186–195. https://doi.org/10.1016/j.jtte.2020.07.002

Tyler, K. A., Schmitz, R. M., & Ray, C. M. (2017). Role of social environmental protective factors on anxiety and depressive symptoms among midwestern homeless youth. *Journal of Research on Adolescence, 28*(1), 199–210. https://doi.org/10.1111/jora.12326

Ungar, M. (Ed.). (2012). *The social ecology of resilience: A handbook of theory and practice.* Springer. https://doi.org/10.1007/978-1-4614-0586-3

U.S. Department of Health and Human Services. (2016, December 20). *Runaway and homeless youth.* https://www.govinfo.gov/content/pkg/FR-2016-12-20/pdf/2016-30241.pdf

U.S. Department of Housing and Urban Development. (2012). *Homeless definition.* https://files.hudexchange.info/resources/documents/HomelessDefinition_RecordkeepingRequirementsandCriteria.pdf

Wand, T. (2013). Positioning mental health nursing practice within a positive health paradigm. *International Journal of Mental Health Nursing, 22*(2), 116–124. https://doi.org/10.1111/j.1447-0349.2012.00848.x

Wand, T. (2015). Recovery is about a focus on resilience and wellness, not a fixation with risk and illness. *Australian and New Zealand Journal of Psychiatry, 49*(12), 1083–1084. https://doi.org/10.1177/0004867415614107

Wenzel, S. L., Hsu, H.-T., Zhou, A., & Tucker, J. S. (2012). Are social network correlates of heavy drinking similar among Black homeless youth and White homeless youth? *Journal of Studies on Alcohol and Drugs, 73*(6), 885–889. https://doi.org/10.15288/jsad.2012.73.885

Wildeman, C., & Emanuel, N. (2014). Cumulative risks of foster care placement by age 18 for US children, 2000–2011. *PloS one, 9*(3), e92785. https://doi.org/10.1371/journal.pone.0092785

Williams, D. R., Lawrence, J. A., & Davis, B. A. (2019). Racism and health: Evidence and needed research. *Annual Review of Public Health, 40*, 105–125. https://doi.org/10.1146/annurev-publhealth-040218-043750

Winiarski, D. A., Rufa, A. K., Bounds, D. T., Glover, A. C., Hill, K. A., & Karnik, N. S. (2020, February 11). Assessing and treating complex mental health needs among homeless youth in a shelter-based clinic. BMC Health Services Research, *20*(1), 109. https://doi.org/10.1186/s12913-020-4953-9

Wolch, J. R., Dear, M., & Akita, A. (1988). Explaining homelessness. *Journal of the American Planning Association, 54*(4), 443–453. https://doi.org/10.1080/01944368808976671

Wright, J. D. (2009). *Address unknown: The homeless in America.* AldineTransaction.

Youngbloom, A. J., Farnish, K. A., & Schoenfeld, E. A. (2021). Characteristics associated with housing loss among youth in a rapid rehousing program. *Child and Adolescent Social Work Journal.* Advance online publication. https://doi.org/10.1007/s10560-021-00751-2

CHAPTER EIGHT

Anti-Blackness and Housing Inequality in the United States

A History of Housing Discrimination in
Major Metropolitan Cities

Tracie A. Lowe

Anti-Blackness is a form of racism or racial prejudice damaging for only Black people (Morris, 2020). The concept emphasizes that not all racial/ethnic groups share the same lived experiences, and certain types of racism disproportionately affect Black people in America (Morris, 2020). Within the framework of anti-Blackness is the inability of non-Black persons to recognize the humanity of Black people. The "othering" of Black people is based on beliefs stemming from the transatlantic slave trade, such as our alleged inferiority (Ross, 2020). This chapter centers around the concept of anti-Blackness and its impact on the housing landscape for Black communities throughout history. Anti-Blackness consists of overt racism and covert structural and systematic racism, which predetermines the socioeconomic status of Black people in America (University of California, San Francisco, Multicultural Center, n.d.). Those in power uphold anti-Black racism through the disregard of anti-Black policies, institutions, and ideologies that, when perpetuated, create class, race, and gender privilege for non-Black individuals (University of California, San Francisco, Multicultural Center, n.d.). The examples provided in this chapter aim to illuminate how the framework of anti-Blackness formed and perpetuated the housing segregation that Black residents continue to experience today.

Chicago, Illinois (1900s–1950s)

During the late 19th and early 20th century, Black people in the North often made up less than 2% of Northern cities' population (Sander et al., 2018). The number represented a considerably smaller amount than the majority population of Black people who resided in the rural South (Massey & Denton, 1993). Sociologists have varying opinions on the level of integration experienced by Black residents within American cities at the turn of the century. For instance, early sociologists asserted Black populations in the North and South lived near Whites and were not segregated before the 1900s (Massey & Denton, 1993). However, recent scholarship examining housing segregation between Black and White populations presents a more nuanced explanation of how the two races lived.

Sociologists continue to examine data using measures that provide more detailed accounts of the segregation conditions between Black and White populations (Sander et al., 2018). The dissimilarity index is commonly used to indicate the distribution of Black and White people in a city. If the dissimilarity index is 0, the Black population in a city is uniformly distributed, and there is no segregation. Conversely, an index of 1 indicates a city is completely segregated. The dissimilarity index tool used by researchers today shows segregation levels in Chicago in the late 1800s were indeed higher between Black and White residents. This finding differs from early sociological research. Despite the small Black population in cities like Chicago, Black people were concentrated in "Black districts," or areas with many Black people. These districts would become increasingly Black due to local policies meant to concentrate the settling of Black residents migrating from the dreadful conditions of Southern living.

Although Black and White residents were segregated into distinct living areas, they were still close to White neighborhoods. In other words, Black exposure to White people and their level of interaction was high. The Black elite primarily had closer ties to White people than lower class Black residents. Transportation during this time was almost nonexistent. The required access to work and home meant the spatial distance between the races, no matter their socioeconomic status, was smaller during this period.

Racial Deed Restrictions and Restrictive Covenants

After the end of Reconstruction—a period of reintegration and enfranchisement for Black citizens—southern states established a collection of "Jim Crow" laws and statutes that legalized segregation and discrimination against Black people and positioned them as second-class citizens. As the ramifications of the Jim Crow system intensified, Black people sought refuge from the violence and economic deprivation of the South. They soon began the migration to cities beyond the southern borders. During the Great Migration (the early 1900s to the mid-1970s), over 6 million African Americans relocated from the rural South to cities in the North, Midwest, and West (History.com Editors, 2010; Tolnay, 2003). Between 1910 and 1920, Chicago's Black population had grown by 148% (History.com Editors, 2010).

The enforcement of more restrictive immigration policies during World War I further created a need for more industrial workers in northern cities. Northern employers were forced to seek new, cheap labor sources, which created new Black workers' opportunities. Black laborers were often brought in to break strikes, which spurred racism and dislike among White factory workers (Sander et al., 2018). As the migration rate to the North increased for Black people, most took up residency in the pre-established Black districts within Chicago. However, the influx of Black migrants prompted White flight among residents concerned about their neighborhoods' racial makeup.

White residents held anti-Black stereotypes and believed the integration of Black people into their neighborhoods would threaten their safety and make the area less desirable (Sander et al., 2018). Support for an increase in ethnic separation grew among White residents who wanted to end Black residents' dispersion onto their blocks. European immigrants experienced similar if not higher levels of segregation during this period, were likewise viewed as lower class citizens, and considered unsanitary and uncouth. However, these immigrant populations were later allowed to participate in processes that created a pathway to assimilation that was not accessible to Black people. As ethnic White people assimilated into mainstream White culture, their ethnicity diminished—an experience opposite to Black people. European immigrant assimilation included opportunities to access predominately White spaces—including neighborhoods—that Black residents were continually denied because of anti-Black racism. The difference in these experiences is an example of how anti-Black racism disproportionately affected Black Americans who sought better living conditions for their families.

The disdain toward and fear of Blackness in White spaces prompted cities in the North to establish several ordinances to concentrate Black residents in areas beyond proximity to White neighborhoods. In 1910, Baltimore, Maryland, became the first city to adopt a zoning law that prohibited African Americans from buying homes on predominately White blocks and vice versa (Rothstein, 2017). White residents also used racial deed restrictions and racial covenants to maintain segregation within cities. Racial restrictive covenants are described as

> Compacts entered into by a group of property owners and real estate oper-
> ators in a given neighborhood who have agreed not to sell, rent, lease, or
> otherwise convey their property to colored people for a definite period unless
> all agree to the transaction. (Weaver, 1944, p. 184)

Groups such as homeowner's associations and community organizations collaborated with property owners and real estate agents to campaign to establish and enforce these covenants (Plotkin, 2001). Chicago's first racial deed restrictions and restrictive covenants appeared during World War I (1914–1918) (Plotkin, 2001). The terms of these covenants were typically 15–20 years in length. As these covenants grew in popularity, they spread quickly throughout Chicago, further deepening the divide between Black and White areas. These racial covenants were an example of how anti-Black racism influenced White people's policies used to maintain segregation and systematically disenfranchise Black people in the housing market for nothing other than their Blackness.

Racial tensions grew in Chicago after a Black teenager drowned after being hit with a stone by White teenagers while swimming past an invisible line of segregation between White and Black people at a beach on the South Side of Chicago (Sander et al., 2018). Due to the inhumanity of the act, violence erupted. The race riots of 1919 lasted 13 days after the incident. The race problem was more evident in the North as Black residents became increasingly aware of the anti-Black sentiments that Whites shared within their city neighborhoods. White residents reconsidered living close to Black residents due to the perceived threat of increased violence and negative messaging about Black people from relators. In the aftermath of the riots, developers increased their use of racial deed restrictions in areas close to where Black populations were rising.

In 1927, the Chicago Real Estate Board also adopted codes that prevented organization members from showing homes to Black buyers on blocks that were 75% White (Sander et al., 2018). In 1927, the board established a formal standard covenant against selling or leasing African Americans' homes (Plotkin, 2001). Those who violated the code would be expulsed from the organization. Likewise, banks partook in restrictive lending practices to prevent Black buyers from purchasing homes in predominately White neighborhoods (Sander et al., 2018). Neighborhood improvement associations also used tactics to dissuade property and apartment owners from selling to Black buyers. These entities continued to adopt these policies and practices because of commonly held anti-Black and bigoted views. As a result, by 1930, nearly two thirds of Chicago's Black population lived in all-Black neighborhoods (Sander et al., 2018).

Despite the continued use of racial covenants and other segregationist housing tactics, integration continued to progress in neighborhoods on the South Side of Chicago, such as Oakland. After the Great Depression of the 1930s, the lack of legal resources among neighborhood associations made it difficult to enforce them (Plotkin, 2001). The expiration of racial covenant terms during this period also opened more opportunities for Black people to move into homes that were once off-limits. By 1939, the Chicago Housing Authority vice chairman, Robert Taylor, estimated that restrictive racial covenants covered 80% of Chicago's land area (Plotkin, 2001). The Chicago Commission on Race Relations argued against housing segregation, calling it counterproductive given the increasing Black population. This group, composed of White and Black elite members of Chicago, contended the stereotypes about Black people were untrue, and a combination of time, personal assistance, and goodwill could solve the race problem (Sander et al., 2018). The commission, however, failed to propose any meaningful measures to solve the discrimination issue.

The Fight Against Racial Covenants

In the 1940s, the Great Migration resumed in greater force as more African Americans migrated to urban areas. Black populations in the North and the South grew between 40 and 90%, significantly more than the previous migration periods (Sander et al., 2018). Most of the growth in cities occurred in the North, which created problems on the housing front. Middle-class Black households who had earnings comparable to those of Whites wanted and could afford better housing. However, the boundaries for where incoming Black populations could live were narrow. The Black ghettos of Chicago grew more overcrowded, and Black housing shortages made living conditions worse in Black neighborhoods. The neglect from city services led to the deterioration of houses and their surrounding amenities. Yet Black residents paid higher prices for the lower quality housing. Black residents grew frustrated and soon realized the root of their problems was not restrictive covenants but instead anti-Black racism.

Several prominent organizations chose sides either in favor or against the use of racial covenants in Chicago. Major institutions with a vested interest in maintaining the covenants used their monetary resources and personnel to fight cases challenging the legality of contractual agreements. The University of Chicago organized and subsidized neighborhood associations to prevent Black families from moving into subdivisions bordering university grounds (Rothstein, 2017). The university also used its financial resources to hire legal talent to ensure areas near campus, such as Washington Park, remained predominately White (Plotkin, 2001). Between 1933 and 1947, the university spent $100,000 on legal services to defend covenants and forcibly remove Black people from the university neighborhood (Rothstein, 2017).

The Chicago Committee of Racial Equity, later the Congress of Racial Equity (CORE), challenged the University of Chicago's support for covenants and exposed their involvement with organizations such as the Hyde Park Property Owner's Association who worked to preserve segregation (Plotkin, 2001). When challenged on their support of restrictive covenants, the current university president, Robert Maynard Hutchins, made a statement in 1937 that students and faculty should be content where they lived. Enforcing restrictive covenants was the university's right (Rothstein, 2017). Ultimately, White residents viewed Black residents through an anti-Black lens in which they were deemed undesirable neighbors, which White households were content to keep out.

It was also not uncommon for religious institutions to support the enforcement of restrictive covenants. In Chicago, tax-exempt religious organizations such as the Moody Bible Institute, the Louisville Presbyterian Theological Seminary, and the Board of Foreign Methodist Episcopal Church also participated in executing restrictive covenants in the 1930s (Rothstein, 2017). Priests, rabbis, and property owners engaged in efforts together, such as going door to door to obtain signatures for restrictive covenants. Churches sponsored local improvement associations and supported their plans to keep African Americans from purchasing homes in all-White neighborhoods. Although all these organizations and other nonprofits were tax-exempt, the Internal Revenue Service continued to provide funding to them despite their discriminatory practices. The IRS failed to hold them accountable for their actions and acted as an agency that helped to maintain segregation through their disregard for anti-Black racist practices among religious institutions.

Black leaders in Chicago worked with urgency to counteract racial covenants as they continued to flourish in the city. Organizations such as the Chicago branch of the National Association for the Advancement of Colored People (NAACP) were opponents of racial covenants. They worked to defend African Americans who were subjected to housing discrimination. In 1945, the organization convened a small conference on restrictive covenants to strategize on the best approach for attacking racial covenants (Sander et al., 2018). As progressive attitudes changed, judges became more critical of racial covenants and focused on their legal weaknesses. Recognizing this shift, the NAACP primarily challenged racial covenants in courts through efforts to forestall evictions or to obtain rulings that deemed the agreements unconstitutional (Plotkin, 2001). Members of the 1945 conference determined that the best route to defeating the covenants was to ultimately attain a favorable Supreme Court decision.

Carl Hansberry, a Black man and NAACP secretary, was forced to leave his home in Washington Park, a subdivision located near the University of Chicago campus, because of a restrictive covenant prohibiting Black people from buying the house (Plotkin, 2001). University of Chicago–trained lawyers worked in collaboration with the NAACP to litigate Hansberry's case. They argued in Hansberry's defense that the covenants were illegal; however, the county Court and Illinois State Supreme Court ruled in favor of enforcing the covenant. In *Hansberry v. Lee* (1940), the U.S. Supreme Court overturned the lower courts' rulings and allowed Hansberry to return to his home.

Shelley v. Kraemer (1948) would later have nationwide implications for enforcing restrictive covenants in cities like Chicago. Homeowners Louis and Fern Kraemer objected to an African American family, the Shelleys' purchase of a home in their St. Louis neighborhood explicitly because of their race (Sander et al., 2018). The Shelleys unknowingly violated a racially restrictive covenant for the community when they purchased the home. However, the block where the Shelleys lived was already integrated, and it was also unclear if the housing title appropriately included the covenant. A strong case presented by a local real estate attorney led the state court to find in their favor. However, the Missouri Supreme Court reversed the lower court's decision and enforced the restrictive covenants. They argued that the covenants did not have to comply with the Equal Protection Clause of the 14th Amendment since they were private contracts. This case demonstrates the courts' role in upholding the use of anti-Black policies that maintained segregation and prevented Black residents from enjoying the fundamental freedoms of living where they pleased.

The Shelleys' lawyer filed a petition for the case to be heard at the Supreme Court level. The NAACP, which had been uninvolved in the *Shelley* case, decided to appeal three other similar cases to strengthen the docket argument against restrictive covenants (Sander et al., 2018). The U.S. Supreme Court agreed to review all four cases together. In 1948, the Supreme Court ruled in *Shelley* that racially restrictive covenants were not illegal. But state courts could not enforce the private agreements as such discriminatory action would violate the Constitution, which prohibits states from denying any person equal protection under the laws.

Despite the ruling in *Shelley,* changes in the nation's housing arena were slow and minimal at first (Sander et al., 2018). White residents continued to bring suits against neighbors who violated the restrictive covenants to gain monetary damages (Rothstein, 2017). Racist views against Blacks continued, and both local and federal agencies sought ways to prevent Black buyers from purchasing homes on their blocks. These measures were a form of systematic anti-Black racism to exclude Black residents' from White spaces.

Although Black people were now free to make offers on any home, the likelihood of White sellers accepting the offer was minimal due to their anti-Black racism (Sander et al., 2018). White people benefited from the separation between the races in terms of their homes' financial value and appreciation and worked to maintain pure White neighborhoods void of Blackness. Therefore, Black buyers would seek housing on the "borders" of communities because of a better chance of obtaining a home (Sander et al., 2018). In 1950, over 23,000 African Americans moved into Chicago neighborhoods adjacent to the ghetto initially covered by restrictive covenants (Sander et al., 2018). Black populations would continue to expand significantly into White areas where old covenants existed for the next 2 decades (Sander et al., 2018). Simultaneously, however, White households were leaving to find a residence in the suburbs in an attempt to flee newly integrated neighborhoods (Sander et al., 2018).

Los Angeles, California (1930s–1960s)

The Great Depression of the 1930s spurred the worst economic downturn for Americans, leaving millions unemployed. The depression worsened a preexisting housing shortage that impacted middle-class White people and African Americans (Rothstein, 2017). Most families could no longer make mortgage payments or afford to purchase a new home. Without jobs, homeowners could not pay off the balloon payments required for traditional loans, and many houses fell into foreclosure. President Franklin D. Roosevelt established a series of programs and policies as part of the "New Deal" to provide relief and stimulate industrial activity. During this period, one of the acts signed into law was the Home Owners' Loan Act, which established the Home Owners' Loan Corporation (HOLC). The HOLC was created to provide relief concerning home mortgages that were subject to imminent foreclosure. The program was responsible for emergency lending and issued new mortgages with longer repayment terms up to 15 or 20 years (Greer, 2017; Rothstein, 2017).

The new loans were amortized, meaning the program set up payments such that, after the completion of low monthly payments toward principal and interest, the person owned their home (Greer, 2017). They worked with local real estate agents who made appraisals for refinancing homes. According to researchers, the HOLC expanded dramatically in a few months and processed millions of refinancing applications without regard to applicants' ethnicity or race. Though only allowed to accept applications for up to 2 years and make loans up to 3 years after the president signed the bill into law, the agency substantially changed the home financing market and rescued the housing markets.

Redlining

Though the HOLC rescued the home financing market and saved hundreds of thousands of American families' homes, the same economic factors persisted that had created the initial housing crisis (Greer, 2017). The agency, which was initially developed only to refinance homes, soon expanded its responsibilities to manage the portfolio of loans issued. In 1935, the HOLC created the City Survey Program to gather data on the extent of the nation's real estate and mortgage problems to use the information to restore or help alleviate the distress within the home financing market. To accomplish this, they conducted surveys and studies of communities where mortgage-lending institutions were failing, one of which was Los Angeles, California. The federal agency used the data collected by appraisers to create "Residential Security" maps of major American cities.

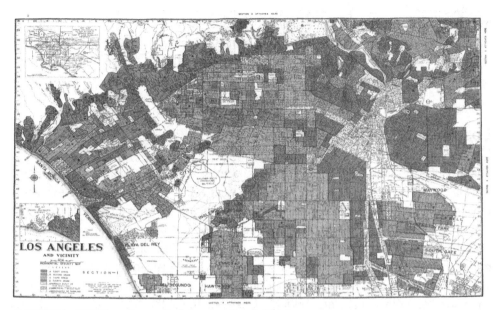

FIGURE 8.1 1939 Map of inequality in Los Angeles, California.

The color codes for each map were based on several factors, including housing quality and upkeep, amenities, the neighborhood's racial composition, and residents' occupations and income (Greer, 2017). Communities with the greatest access to lending resources for mortgage financing were given the highest grades, whereas those with limited access to conventional lending sources received lower grades (Greer, 2017). Features such as schools, shopping facilities, churches, and distance from industrial factories also affected neighborhoods' scoring (Greer, 2017). Each map was based on a code system—green for grade A or "Best," blue for grade B or "Still Desirable," yellow for grade C or "Definitely Declining," and red for grade D or "Hazardous" (Mitchell & Franco, 2018). Due to racial prejudice and the belief that Black residents brought down property values and the quality of housing, Black neighborhoods were rated as high risk or "Hazardous" and coded as red (Mitchell & Franco, 2018). The methods used for the residential security maps are a prime example of how anti-Black sentiments negatively influenced the appraisal of Black homes and spurred future conseqeuences for Black residents' access to home loans. The process, now known as "redlining," was a common practice in metropolitan cities across the United States.

The detailed maps had a lasting impact on redlined communities as lenders used the assessment tool to determine the risk of investing in certain areas (Greer, 2017). According to Dickerson (2014),

> Although the HOLC did not create the racially biased redlining rating system, it systematized and legitimized redlining by using it to create an elaborate residential mapping series that divided neighborhoods based on their desirability, stability, and security. *The color of the homeowners' skin was a*

*central factor in the rating system, and race was used to determine whether
a neighborhood was safe or desirable.* (p. 146, emphasis added)

Although seemingly objective on the surface, the criteria for receiving higher ratings
or grades placed Black neighborhoods in Los Angeles, California, at a disadvantage. City
officials also neglected utility services in Black areas. The maintenance or upkeep of
housing properties was difficult for Black residents due to low wages and discrimination in
housing lending as Black residents were more unlikely to obtain federally backed loans for
home purchases or improvements (Reft, 2017). African American redlined neighborhoods
were often zoned as industrial and located close to commercial waste treatment centers,
waste dumps, or junkyards (Rothstein, 2018). The toxic conditions compromised the
health and safety of Black residents. Zoning policies that were implemented ultimately
worked together to intensify slum conditions and overcrowding within African American
neighborhoods in Los Angeles.

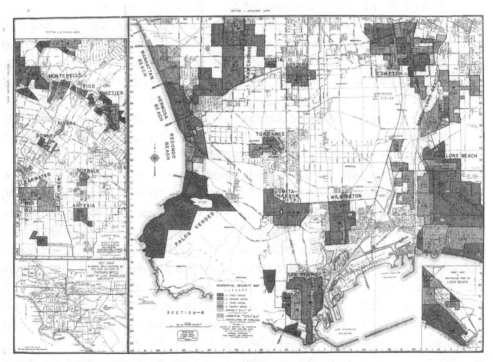

FIGURE 8.2   1939 map of inequality in Los Angeles, California.

Under the National Housing Act of 1934, President Roosevelt established the Federal
Housing Administration (FHA) a year after the HOLC. The FHA—primarily staffed by
bankers who desired to assimilate into the banking culture—was established to provide
mortgage insurance on loans made by FHA-approved lenders (Reft, 2017; Sander et al.,
2018). The insurance provided lenders with protection against any losses they might

accrue if a property owner defaulted on their mortgage. The FHA would pay the claim for any unpaid balance of interest on the loans. In 1936, the FHA produced an underwriting manual to appraise individual mortgages (Reft, 2017). When banks applied for insurance on a loan, the FHA hired an appraiser who used the manual to assess the property (Reft, 2017). The manual provided letter grades to indicate the risk of properties that were appraised. The racist views embedded in the underwriting practices of the manual discouraged banks from making loans in predominately Black urban neighborhoods and encouraged maintaining a neighborhood's racial White stability (Reft, 2017). The anti-Black redlining policies implemented in the housing industry and further sustained by anti-Black lending institutions had lasting consequences for aspiring Black homeowners. The racist references to Black neighborhoods and stereotypes used in the early 1940s and 1950s were still used by loan officers in the early 2000s as they continued to steer Black families to higher cost mortgage products (Dickerson, 2014).

Slums, Slum Clearance, and the Construction of Federal Interstate Highway Systems

Other local tactics utilized in Los Angeles further reinforced the geographic segregation between Black and White communities (Rothstein, 2017). Words such as *slum* were used as a euphemism to describe Black neighborhoods in urban areas that had significantly deteriorated due to neglect from city services and that suffered from the conditions of overcrowding. National organizations such as the Urban Land Institute supported efforts to demolish the "slums" and were critical to developing national highway legislation that would achieve this goal (Rothstein, 2017). Slum clearance involved the construction of federal highway systems designed in a manner that destroyed Black communities.

Sugar Hill, formerly West Adams Height, would experience its demise due to slum clearance practices (Meares, 2018). Once a predominately White upper-class area during the early 20th century, West Adams Heights in Los Angeles began to experience changes due to the development of a new neighborhood for the rich and famous: Beverly Hills (Meares, 2018). During the Great Depression of the 1920s, residents of the once prestigious West Adams Heights area were forced to sell their homes and were willing to sell them to anyone regardless of the racial covenants or deed restrictions that were previously established (Meares, 2018). The new possibilities of homeownership encouraged affluent African Americans to begin purchasing homes in the area (Meares, 2018). The first African American to buy property in West Adams Heights in 1938 was Norman Houston, an insurance executive who cofounded the Golden State Mutual Life Insurance Company (Meares, 2018). The neighborhood was later renamed Sugar Hill as an homage to Harlem's legendary community (Meares, 2018). Disgruntled neighborhood association leaders suggested to Houston that he move to another area and later proposed to buy his property, to which he refused both (Rothstein, 2017).

Soon, other prominent African Americans began moving into the area. The neighborhood, which became home to several actors and affluent Black celebrities, was later renamed Sugar Hill as an homage to Harlem's legendary community (Meares, 2018). White residents grew even more displeased with the influx of Black neighbors. Although these Black residents were affluent, White people still regarded them as inferior and undesirable tenants based on their race. These anti-Black beliefs prompted eight neighborhood members to use the courts (anti-Black institutions) to enforce a restrictive covenant (anti-Black policy) and have their Black neighbors evicted (Meares, 2018; Rothstein, 2017). However, Black families in Sugar Hill worked together to fight back against the suit and hired a Black attorney and NAACP activist, Loren Miller, to represent their group (Meares, 2018). The Sugar Hill case went to the Los Angeles Superior Court, and the judge ruled that the enforcement of the covenant violated the 14th Amendment, a decision that would later be reinforced in the *Shelly v. Kraemer* (1948) decision, also argued by Miller (Meares, 2018; Rothstein, 2017).

The neighborhood flourished after Miller won the Sugar Hill case. However, new developments such as Baldwin Hills in south Los Angeles drew the wealthy actors and filmmakers away from the neighborhood (Harman, 2019). Soon after, rumors that the city would build a freeway through the area emerged in the 1950s (Meares, 2018). The suspicions were correct, as the Santa Monica freeway was later routed through Sugar Hill in 1963 despite Black leaders' pleas to move it North (Meares, 2018; Rothstein, 2017). However, proponents of the freeway argued that moving it would cut through fraternity and sorority row of the University of Southern California (Meares, 2018). Dickerson (2014) argued for Congress to fund the Federal Highway Acts of 1952 and 1954 to expand highway systems and make it easier for White people to flee the inner city, which was inhabited by Blackness for all-White suburbs. Mansions in the Black community were eventually demolished because of the disregard for Black people's livelihoods in the area. The interstate highway program displaced many African Americans with no obligation to secure new housing for Black residents (Rothstein, 2017). Most families had left the area by 1964, and the new freeway destroyed a vibrant community because of the highway placement (Meares, 2018). Unfortunately, Sugar Hill was just one example of how interstate highways disproportionately destroyed Black neighborhoods in cities across the country. African Americans in other metropolitan cities faced similar challenges and lost homes due to unfavorable policies and the dismissal of their pleas to keep their communities intact.

South Los Angeles and the Rumford Act of 1963

During the mid-60s, cities across the country experienced periods of urban uprisings. The Kerner Commission (1968) was appointed by President Lyndon B. Johnson to unearth the root causes of the riots and to provide solutions. A notable finding of the report was a statement that "our nation is moving toward two societies, one black, one white—separate and unequal" (p. 1). The biased anti-Black attitudes of Whites based on race, the report claimed, resulted in discriminatory policing practices, high unemployment, and subpar education systems that contributed to the civil unrest in Black communities (George, 2018). Black populations in major cities had increased significantly in the United States. According to the report, "from 1940 to 1960, the white population rose 34.0 percent, but the Negro population rose 46.6 percent" (Kerner Commission, 1968, p. 116). In

1966, 69% of all African Americans lived in metropolitan areas compared to 64% of Whites (Kerner Commission, 1968). Inadequate housing for the growing Black population was ranked as one of the highest deeply held grievances among all the cities examined for the report (Kerner Commission, 1968).

Los Angeles was one of 12 largest central cities that collectively contained over two thirds of the Black population outside the South (Kerner Commission, 1968). South Los Angeles was 53% Black, in 1960, with a smaller White and Hispanic population (De La Cruz-Viesca et al., 2018). The 1965 uprising in Watts, Los Angeles, similarly erupted due to economic and social conditions that placed Black people at a disadvantage. Eight years later, the governor of Chicago assembled the McCone Commission to investigate the riots' causes (Dawsey, 1990). Housing was one of the primary concerns uncovered in the investigation. Before the uprisings, Black residents in Watts lived in conditions inferior to the rest of the city, despite their close location to the city's affluent areas (De La Cruz-Viesca et al., 2018). Overcrowding was an issue in South Los Angeles, as Black residents in Watts lived with an average of 4.3 persons more per household than 2.94 per household in the county (De La Cruz-Viesca et al., 2018). Segregated and inadequate housing conditions in Watts, Los Angeles, were further exacerbated by discrimination against potential Black homebuyers. The homeownership rate in 1960 for Black people was the lowest among all racial groups (36%) compared to Hispanic (40.7%) and White (45 %) rates (De La Cruz-Viesca et al., 2018). Median home values between Black ($91,000) and White homeowners ($111,000) were similar, yet home appreciation values for the two groups was greater for White residents (De La Cruz-Viesca et al., 2018). Black people gained none of the alleged benefits of homeownership due to the anti-Black structural mechanisms that were sustained for decades by government agencies such as the FHA and the HOLC (Dickerson, 2014).

William Byron Rumford, the first Black state official elected to state public office in California, was a powerful advocate for Black communities and their access to opportunities such as fair housing (Dougherty, 2019). As a legislator, Rumford was best known for the California Fair Housing Act of 1963, which sought to end racial discrimination in all public and private housing financing and the rental market (Dougherty, 2019). When passed, the law made illegal discrimination in public housing and residential properties with more than five units (Ruffin, 2011). Although Republican legislators required that most private and single-family homes be exempt, the Rumford Act's passage was still met with resistance by organizations such as the California Real Estate Association (CREA) (Ruffin, 2011).

The following year, CREA's efforts led to the Proposition 14 referendum, which nullified the Rumford Act (Ruffin, 2011). In 1966, the Rumford Act was restored when the California Supreme Court ruled that Proposition 14 was illegal (Ruffin, 2011). Two years later, the Civil Rights Act of 1968, more commonly known as the Fair Housing Act, passed (Ruffin, 2011). The law was created to decrease racial disparities in housing and homeownership and prohibited discrimination in the sale, rental, or financing of housing based on race, color, national origin, religion, sex, familial status, and disability (Ruffin,

2011). The court ruling brought a sense of presumed progress in the fight against housing discrimination in the courts (Ruffin, 2011). Yet challenges in South Los Angeles would continue, as Black homeownership rates, home values, and appreciation remain lower than those of White homeowners (De La Cruz-Viesca et al., 2018).

Segregation in the Lone Star State (1950s–Present)

Black households in Texas experienced much of the same housing segregation challenges as those in the North and West. Racial covenants, unfair housing policies, and the perpetuation of segregation through federal programs worked together to maintain the division between Black and White in cities like Dallas and Austin. After World War II, thousands of African Americans moved to Dallas from small towns or rural areas (Hazel, 1997). The number of African Americans in the city by 1950 totaled 83,352 or 13.5% of the total population (Hazel, 1997). After Jewish populations moved out of South Dallas areas such as Oak Cliff, Texas, during the 1940s and 1950s, Black people moved into the neighborhood, leaving the segregated and the crowded regions to which they were formerly bound (Kemper, 2005). The attempts at integration were met by violence, the bombing of 18 houses that decade (Lawe, 2008). However, most of the formerly White areas south of the Trinity River eventually became predominately Black neighborhoods (Kemper, 2005).

Dallas experienced significant population and employment growth during the early 1980s, which contributed to a housing boom in the city (Waddell, 1994). During the1980s, Dallas-owned banks invested a surplus of cash from oil and banking ventures (Phillips, 2006). Property values in the city soon became inflamed, eventually causing an economic downturn, a housing bust, and the plummet of banking institutions across the area (Phillips, 2006). During an unexpected recession in the mid-80s, oil prices dropped, and the real estate and agriculture industries collapsed (Waddell, 1994). Tax bases in Dallas plummeted, leading developers to obtain real estate at an extremely cheap rate (Phillips, 2006). These changes occurred to the detriment of African Americans and lower class residents, as the properties were often filled with high-priced housing and shops as a means of alluring the wealthy back to the neighborhoods (Phillips, 2006). The loss of tax revenues came when the need for social services increased in the inner city for Black residents (Waddell, 1994).

In Dallas, "White flight" progressed as White, wealthy residents looking to escape from the infiltration of Black people left the inner city and neighborhoods surrounding the urban core for the suburbs taking their tax dollars with them (Krupala, 2019; Waddell, 1994). As the elites perpetuated segregation by choosing to live in the outer suburbs, they may have increased their quality of life and their well-being. Yet their actions created social costs for everyone (Drier et al., 2004). Minority and low-income populations also moved further away from the inner city to suburban spaces due to the oversupply in housing formerly inhabited by middle-class residents (Waddell, 1994). White residents who remained in these neighborhoods became wary of the growing ethnic diversity and grew concerned about perceived public safety and a possible decline in schools' quality (Waddell, 1994). White residents feared formerly all-White educational institutions would be tainted by the inclusion of Black students who were viewed as intellectually inferior to White people. The anti-Black racist sentiments motivated White people to take their educational resources to the suburbs, which disproportionately affected the educational outcomes of Black students.

By the late 1980s, few middle- or lower class households remained in areas classified as slums due to the overbuilding and suburbanization of minorities in Dallas that decade. Unfortunately, their predictions came true as the increased presence of racial minority populations led to negative speculation about the neighborhood's future. Negligence in housing maintenance and the deterioration of schools further accelerated because of White flight and the accrued resources that accompanied them. Poor inner city neighborhoods experienced a massive exodus of middle-class Black residents, which only worsened slum conditions for those left behind.

The reverse migration of Black people living in northern cities to southern cities brought many Black households to Dallas's suburbs (Sander et al., 2018; Tolnay, 2003). The trend has changed the Dallas-Fort Worth Metroplex area, which gained 233,000 African American residents between 2000 and 2010 (Cournoyer, 2012). The southern suburbs (i.e., Desoto, Lancaster, and Cedar Hill) that experienced White flight during the 1980s are now majority Black areas (Cournoyer, 2012). The changing demographics created positive implications for the Black middle class in housing, education, and other policy areas (Cournoyer, 2012). The growing prosperity of the Black middle class in Dallas has also spurred the growth of a network of young African American professionals (Cournoyer, 2012). Middle-class residents have also been able to engage in entrepreneurial endeavors with much success (Cournoyer, 2012).

Areas such as Desoto and Lancaster hold some of the largest African American populations in 2021 (Kolmar, 2020). They have become a desirable location for Black households relocating to the Dallas area and have been cities with significant growth in the Black middle class (Cournoyer, 2010; Kolmar, 2020). The promise of better schools, less crime, and more substantial economic opportunities are all factors that attract young middle-class professionals to the suburban outskirts (Cournoyer, 2012). These trends continue today as more affluent Black people settle in areas just outside the southern portion of Dallas proper (Kolmar, 2020). Although there is the level of success that Blacks have achieved, remnants of segregation and old anti-Black practices such as the neglect of infrastructure in Black neighborhoods still pose an issue. Therefore, Black households living in these suburban areas must continue to work toward securing greater political representation within city offices to advocate and address their needs as middle-class residents.

Austin's history of anti-Blackness in housing segregation spans back nearly 100 years to the 1928 master plan. Maintaining legal segregation through zoning laws during this time was difficult, especially after the ruling in *Buchanan* v. *Warley* (1917), in which the Supreme Court found racial zoning ordinances violated the 14th Amendment's due protection clause that provided equal protection of the laws. Instead of implementing racial zoning ordinances to accomplish their segregation goals, Austin enforced a 1928 master plan that relocated schools and other public services for African Americans to the Eastside, forcing them to move (Rothstein, 2017). Soon after establishing the "negro district," the United States Housing Association funded the first public housing projects in Austin. The city chose the all-Black public housing project, Rosewood Courts, on the Eastside, with a companion project for Whites located close to the downtown area. The placement of these housing projects further perpetuated segregation within the city. Municipal services declined in the all-Black neighborhoods on the Eastside, leaving city amenities to deteriorate due to neglect.

Implications of the 1928 plan for Black residents are still evident as the city remains racially segregated. Housing segregation created by anti-Black policies (formal and informal) had enduring effects on Black populations in Austin. Living in the impoverished neighborhoods of East Austin has also limited Black residents' access to economic and educational opportunities that contribute to households' wealth and stability for generations. Recently, Black East Austin residents have faced increasing urban displacement as the city's population has expanded. The housing supply in Austin has failed to keep up with newcomers' demand, creating an unaffordability challenge for city officials today. Many Austinites' incomes are not keeping pace with the price of housing, leaving many households struggling to make rent and cover other costs of living. In 2019, the median price for homes in Austin was $404,298, and the average rent per month was $1,349 (Housing Works, 2019a). Approximately 36% of Austin residents are cost burdened, and 17% are extremely cost burdened. Both figures are higher than the state averages of 29 and 13%, respectively (Housing Works, 2019a).

The "Eastern Crescent," or East Austin, which is predominately Black, has seen the highest rise in housing costs due to the desirability of the neighborhood for those seeking to live close to downtown (Chapple & Thomas, 2020). The changing demographics east of I-35 have created varying levels of gentrification—the process in which higher income households move into a neighborhood and housing costs rise (Way et al., 2018). Neighborhoods that are most vulnerable to gentrification are typically composed of low-income households, renters, people of color, heads of households without a bachelor's degree or higher, and families with children in poverty (Way et al., 2018). District 1, an area on the east side of I-35, is where the most significant number of the Black population resides. This area's median family income is $56,954 compared to $95,900 for Austin at large (Housing Works, 2019a, 2019b). This district also has a higher poverty rate percentage of individuals living in poverty than the city (20 and 15%, respectively) (Housing Works, 2019a, 2019b). As the population further changes, low-income Black residents are no longer able to purchase or rent in Eastern Crescent neighborhoods that were once accessible to them.

The demographics of Austin are changing drastically as Black populations move to outlying suburban areas in more significant numbers in search of more affordable housing. This trend of urban displacement is one that community leaders across Austin are trying to solve urgently. It will be necessary for policy makers and city officials to reckon with the racial history of segregation and anti-Blackness that has led to the bleak outlook for Black residents in East Austin. Gaining an awareness of the discriminatory and anti-Black practices in housing and how these actions continue to perpetuate inequities should be a priority among those wishing to usher in a period of change in the housing world. Finding a solution to housing issues in America would open new possibilities for Black families, and possibly at last open the doors to their long-term wealth and prosperity.

The Enduring Effects of Housing Discrimination and Considerations for Housing Policy

Today, residential segregation remains high for African Americans more than 50 years after the Fair Housing Act of 1968 (Quick & Kahlenberg, 2019). Historical private practices of discrimination against Black people specifically and the creation of anti-Black housing policies helped maintain the division between White and Black communities. According to Richard Rothstein (2017),

> We have created a caste system in this country, with African Americans kept exploited and geographically separate by racially explicit government policies. Although most of these policies are now off the books, they have never been remedied, and their effects endure. (p. xvii)

The past consequences have equated to unequal opportunities between Black and White Americans and perpetuate disparities in wealth, homeownership, economic growth, and children's educational outcomes within Black communities. Merely 41% of Black households own their home compared to more than 73% of White households (Solomon et al., 2019).

Though more impoverished Black communities have been impacted hardest by the lack of access to affordable quality housing, the Black middle class has also suffered from thwarted ambitions to move outside the ghettos created for Black segregation (Quick & Kahlenberg, 2019). Middle-class residents remain more likely to live in lower income neighborhoods or concentrated poverty areas than lower income Whites (Sander et al., 2018). The exclusion from federal homeownership programs contributed to the loss of accumulated wealth for Black households. Government action to redress the detrimental effects of such exclusion is necessary. Providing modern-day assistance to help Black families purchase their first home, such as the first down payment tax credit proposed by the Biden-Harris administration, would be a step in the right direction (Biden, 2020). Providing funding to strengthen fair housing enforcement could also help in eliminating discrimination in the housing market that relegates Black families to segregated neighborhoods (Zonta, 2019).

Economic differences between Black and White households persists in many cities and follows the redlining patterns created 80 years ago. A report by National Community Reinvestment Coalition found there is greater economic inequality in towns today where the Home Owner's Loan Corporation (HOLC) graded areas "high risk" (Mitchell & Franco, 2018). Nationally, 74% of neighborhoods classified as "hazardous" by the City Survey Program maps created by the HOLC remain lower to moderate income areas today. Conversely, 91% of sites that were formerly given the highest grades are composed of moderate to upper income White families. Cities in the South and Midwest parts of the nation have the highest percentage of areas classified as "hazardous" that are low and moderate income, revealing how inequity has persisted over decades. Persistent residential segregation continues in cities where the HOLC gave "Hazardous" grades to neighborhoods; most are still primarily minority.

The work to undo a complicated history of residential segregation requires eliminating policies that support segregation and the creation of antisegregation policies (Quick & Kahlenberg, 2019). President Joe Biden's (2020) plan for investing in housing highlights the effects of redlining and other discriminatory and unfair practices in the housing market. The plan discusses the importance of eliminating local and state housing regulations that perpetuate discrimination. The measures taken to achieve this goal include requiring any state receiving federal dollars through community development block grants or surface transportation block grants to develop a strategy for inclusionary zoning. Biden also proposes to invest $300 million in local housing policy grants to give states and localities the support needed to eliminate exclusionary zoning policies and local regulations that contribute to sprawl.

Racial residential segregation has several consequences for Black communities and affects employment opportunities, earnings, and mortality rates. According to Sander et al. (2018) Black men, aged 25–34 living in *highly segregated* areas have higher rates of unemployment (17.4%) compared to those living in *moderately segregated* regions (10.1%). The median earnings for Black men, aged 25–34, were also lower for those in *highly segregated* areas ($20,000) compared to the same demographic population living in *moderately segregated* neighborhoods ($24,000). The point here is that higher levels of integration improve Black Americans' access to jobs and reduce Black people living in high-poverty neighborhoods.

Segregation and anti-Black beliefs have also impacted the home value appreciation in Black neighborhoods. White buyers are less likely to view Black areas as desirable, even if the area's characteristics are similar between Black and White residences. Less buyer interest means Black American homes appreciate at significantly lower rates (Quick & Kahlenberg, 2019). Homeownership provides an enormous financial asset for Americans, and Black people have been historically excluded from homeownership and the accumulation of wealth that comes with such a milestone (Quick & Kahlenberg, 2019). Lower appreciation rates place Black households at an even more significant disadvantage and hinder their ability to build equity, assisting with other major life decisions such as college payments or financial support for business ventures. Biden's housing plan for improving

American communities discusses implementing measures to tackle the racial bias, leading to lower home appraisals for communities of color (Biden, 2020). The measure includes a national standard for housing appraisals and training to reduce bias appraisers.

Lower levels of segregation also impact Black Americans' educational outcomes (Quick & Kahlenberg, 2019). Access to more robust public education programs generates more advantages and the potential for higher incomes. Yet, schools in predominately Black metropolitan areas across the nation have traditionally been provided fewer resources and less attention from city officials. Because of the residential segregation between Black and White neighborhoods, Black middle-class residents frequently reside in close proximity to lower income or poverty-stricken Black households. These neighborhoods often fall within the same districts, which determine where children attend school. Black middle-class residents who are more likely to live near concentrated areas of poverty are also more likely to send their children to high-poverty schools. Some Black students from higher income backgrounds may attend magnet programs or charter schools to circumvent attendance at lower quality schools. However, lower income students are still left at a disadvantage, as they are less likely to have the resources to attend these integrated programs.

Although education brings the promise of better life circumstances, stark differences remain between Black and White Americans with comparable or even lower education levels (Quick & Kahlenburg, 2019). African American households headed by an individual with a bachelor's degree have just two thirds the wealth of White households headed by an individual who lacks a high school degree. These outcomes are deeply intertwined with the state of housing for Black Americans. Therefore, addressing them requires acknowledging and working to correct the disparate impact of past and present housing policies that have had detrimental consequences for Black communities.

Conclusion

This chapter has highlighted pivotal moments in history that have changed the housing landscape in metropolitan cities across the nation. Anti-Black racism coupled with the use of discriminatory practices such as racial covenants in Chicago prohibited Black people from moving into White neighborhoods. The use of redlining maps in Los Angeles, California, perpetuated residential segregation and kept Black households from partaking in federal home loan lending. In Texas, a history of housing segregation has led to Black suburbanization in Dallas and Austin as Black families seek refuge in spaces that are affordable or promise more opportunity. The prevalence of anti-Black racism in housing in the form of anti-Black institutions and policies has led to consequences for Black people in areas of income and wealth, and education. Policy makers must consider the implications of past local, state, and federal practices that perpetuated the disparities caused by racial residential segregation for Black communities. Now is the time to take action and make amends for the losses experienced by generations of Black Americans.

References

Biden, J. (2020). *The Biden plan for investing in our communities through housing.* https://joebiden.com/housing/

Buchanan v. Warley, 245 U.S. 60 (1917)

Chapple, K., & Thomas, T. (2020). *Urban displacement project.* https://www.urbandisplacement.org/map/austin

Cournoyer, C. (2012). *The new Black South.* Governing: State and Local Government News and Analysis. https://www.governing.com/gov-new-black-south.html

Dawsey, D. (1990). *25 Years after the Watts riots: McCone commission's recommendations have gone unheeded.* Los Angeles Times. https://www.latimes.com/archives/la-xpm-1990-07-08-me-455-story.html

De La Cruz-Viesca, M., Ong, P., Comandon, A., Darity, W.A., Hamilton, D. (2018). Fifty years after the Kerner Commission report: Place, housing, and racial wealth inequality in Los Angeles. *Russell Sage Foundation Journal of the Social Sciences*, *4*(6), 160–184. https://doi.org/10.7758/rsf.2018.4.6.08

Dickerson, M. (2014). *Homeownership and American's financial underclass: Flawed premises, broken promises, new presrciptions.* Cambridge University Press.

Dougherty, C. (2019, August 7). Overlooked no more: William Byron Rumford, a civil rights champion in California. *The New York Times.* https://www.nytimes.com/2019/08/07/obituaries/william-byron-rumford-overlooked.html?auth=login-google

Drier, P., Mollenkopf, J., & Swanstrom, T. (2004). *Place matters: Metropolitics for the twenty-first century* (2nd ed.). University of Kansas Press.

Fair Housing Act of 1968, 42 U.S.C. 3601 et seq. (1968)

George, A. (2018, March 1). 1968 Kerner Commission got it right, but nobody listened. *Smithsonian.* https://www.smithsonianmag.com/smithsonian-institution/1968-kerner-commission-got-it-right-nobody-listened-180968318/

Greer, J. (2012). The home owner's loan corporation and the development of the residential security maps. *Journal of Urban History 39*(2), 275–296. https://doi.org/10.1177/0096144212436724

Hansberry v. Lee, 311 U.S. 32 (1940)

Harman, H. (2019, January 17). *Highways in history: Sugar Hill Los Angeles.* Medium. https://hharman.medium.com/highways-of-history-sugar-hill-los-angeles-69a0dfb57567

Hazel, M. V. (1997). *Dallas: A history of the "Big D."* Texas State Historical Association Press.

History.com Editors. (2010, January 26). *The great migration.* History.com. https://www.history.com/topics/black-history/great-migration

Home Owners Loan Act of 1933, 12 U.S.C. § 1461–1468 (1940)

Housing Works Austin. (2019a). *Austin at a Glance: Affordable housing 2019.* http://housingworksaustin.org/wp-content/uploads/2019/10/2019-Community-at-a-Glance.pdf

Housing Works Austin. (2019b). *Affordable housing district 01.* http://housingworksaustin.org/wp-content/uploads/2020/02/District01_2019_v07.pdf

Kemper, R. V. (2005). Dallas-Fort Worth: Toward new models of urbanization, community transformation, and immigration. *Urban Anthropology and Studies of Cultural Systems and World Economic Development 34*(2–3), 125–149.

Kerner Commission. (1968). *Report of the National Advisory Commission on civil disorders.* Princeton University Press.

Kolmar, C. (2020, December 21). *The 10 Texas cities with the largest Black population for 2021.* RoadSnacks. https://www.roadsnacks.net/most-african-american-cities-in-texas/

Krupala, K. (2019). The evolution of uneven development in Dallas, TX. *Human Geography*, *12*(3), 17–30. https://doi.org/10.1177/194277861901200308

Lawe, T. M. (2008). Racial politics in Dallas in the twentieth century. *East Texas Historical Journal*, *46*(2), 27–41.

Massey, D. S., & Denton, N. A. (1993). *American apartheid: Segregation and the making of an underclass.* Harvard University Press.

Meares, H. (2018, February 22). *The thrill of Sugar Hill.* Curbed Los Angeles. https://la.curbed.com/2018/2/22/16979700/west-adams-history-segregation-housing-covenants

Mitchell, B., & Franco. J. (2018). *HOLC "redlining" maps: The persistent structure of segregation and economic inequality.* National Community Reinvestment Coalition. https://ncrc.org/holc/

Morris, N. (2020, March 20). *Anti-Blackness is a form of racism that is specifically damaging for Black people.* Metro. https://metro.co.uk/2020/03/20/what-is-anti-blackness-12279678/

Phillips, M. (2006). *White metropolis: Race, ethnicity, and religion in Dallas, 1841–2001.* University of Texas Press.

Plotkin, W. (2001). "Hemmed in": The struggle against racial restrictive covenants and deed restrictions in post- WWII Chicago. *Journal of the Illinois State Historical Society, 94*(1), 39–69.

Quick, K., & Kahlenberg, R. D. (2019, June 25). *Attacking the Black-White opportunity gap that comes from residential segregation.* The Century Foundation. https://tcf.org/content/report/attacking-black-white-opportunity-gap-comes-residential-segregation/?agreed=1

Reft, T. (2017, November 14). *Segregation in the city of angels: A 1939 map of housing inequality in L.A.* KCET. https://www.kcet.org/shows/lost-la/segregation-in-the-city-of-angels-a-1939-map-of-housing-inequality-in-la

Ross, K. (2020, June 4). Call it what it is: Anti-Blackness. *The New York Times.* https://www.nytimes.com/2020/06/04/opinion/george-floyd-anti-blackness.html

Rothstein, R. (2017). *The color of law: A forgotten history of how our government segregated America.* Liveright.

Ruffin. H. G. (2011, June 5). *The California fair housing act [The Rumford act] (1963–1968).* BlackPast.Org. https://www.blackpast.org/african-american-history/california-fair-housing-act-rumford-act-1963-1968/

Sander, R., Kucheva, Y., & Zasloff, J. (2018). *Moving toward integration: The past and future of fair housing.* Harvard University Press.

Solomon D., Maxwell, C., & Castro, A. (2019, August). *Systematic inequality: Displacement, exclusion, and segregation.* Center for American Progress. https://www.americanprogress.org/issues/race/reports/2019/08/07/472617/systemic-inequality-displacement-exclusion-segregation/

Tolnay, S. E. (2003). The African American "great migration" and beyond. *Annual Review of Sociology, 29*(1), 209–232. https://doi.org/10.1146/annurev.soc.29.010202.100009

University of California, San Francisco, Multicultural Center. (n.d.). *Racial equity and anti-Black racism.* https://mrc.ucsf.edu/racial-equity-anti-black-racism

Waddell, P. (1994). Dallas: Will suburban dispersion ever cease? *Built Environment, 20*(1), 25–38.

Way, H., Mueller, E., & Wegmann, J. (2018). *Uprooted: Residential displacement in Austin's gentrifying neighborhoods and what can be done about it.* University of Texas Center for Sustainable Development in the School of Architecture and the Entrepreneurship and Community Development Clinic in the School of Law. https://www.urbandisplacement.org/sites/default/files/images/utgentrification-fullreport.pdf

Weaver, R. (1944). Race restrictive housing covenants. *The Journal of Land & Public Utility Economics, 20*(3), 183–193. https://doi.org/10.2307/3159245

Zonta, M. (2019, July 15). *Racial disparities in home appreciation.* Center for American Progress. https://www.americanprogress.org/issues/economy/reports/2019/07/15/469838/racial-disparities-home-appreciation/

Credits

Fig. 8.1: Source: https://dsl.richmond.edu/panorama/redlining/#loc=11/34.005/-118.407&city=los-angeles-ca&text=downloads.

Fig. 8.2: Source: https://dsl.richmond.edu/panorama/redlining/#loc=11/34.005/-118.407&city=los-angeles-ca&text=downloads.

Part III

COMMUNITY VOICES

CHAPTER NINE

Values-Driven, Community-Led Justice in Austin

A Project

Sukyi McMahon and Chas Moore

Austin Justice Coalition (AJC, 2019a) is a Black-led group of activists that emerged in 2015 amidst the Black Lives Matter (BLM) movement in response to a torrent of killings of Black men, women, and children by the hands of police in the United States. A long list of names were recited at local events—Mike Brown, Eric Garner, Terence Crutcher, Tamir Rice, Freddie Gray, Walter Scott, Philando Castile, Alton Sterling, Sandra Bland, and David Joseph, to name just a few lives lost during those years—and our early days were spent organizing mass protests, town halls, and vigils to combat racism and anti-Blackness.

On a summer evening in 2016, we held a large vigil for Alton Sterling and Philando Castile (Hernandez, 2016), and hundreds gathered in a park at the heart of the Black community to mourn. Our community was equally sorrowful and enraged by the constant injustices suffered by our people and demanded not just some form of systemic change in policing from the Austin Police Department, but more from *us* as organizers. We wanted more than another lit candle and another name added to protest posters. Our leadership team pinpoints that as the moment we took a radical shift in our motive and methodology.

After a year of being prominent protest leaders, we were determined to become proactive rather than reactive—to attempt to get ahead of the reasons we are being shot dead at the whim of police officers—and to base our activities on counteracting the values of domination and control that pervades the justice system, and the ways in which White supremacy is deployed by policing.

This chapter articulates our model for Black-led advocacy in the pursuit of justice in Austin that has shaped AJC over these last 5 years. Ours is a values-driven organizational model, and this chapter will detail the ways in which our values lead us, and how we model the values we want incorporated into systems designed to support the well-being of all people, push systems to operationalize those very same values, and build a community that reflects these values. Through this approach, we maintain our values as our North Star, as they are both functional and aspirational.

Organizing a Mission Around Core Values

Shortly after that notable evening in the park, AJC began a self-evaluative process to broaden our motivations and shift our goals in accord with our mission to be a stronger voice for our community. What drove this maturation was how we were living—the striking disproportionality of policing in stops, searches, arrests, and use of force (Office of Police Oversight et al., 2020)—just as much as how we were dying. The quality of life for Black Austinites became our prerogative, and we set out to impact our outcomes when it comes to interactions with local police. This came at a time when we also began to organize community-based antiracism trainings, at which facilitators presented the history of racism in the United States, guided participants through power mapping, and immersed them in deeply private and personal conversations and revelations about our shared legacy of racism. All at once, we became a Black-led antiracist racial justice group that began to intentionally organize around a set of values we could test our actions against.

Antiracism became a foundational value, and with each training we put on and attended we became more fluent and effective in coding antiracism into our DNA. Rightfully, this value holds the topmost value in our organizational and aspirational values, which in totality include the ideals presented in Table 9.1.

TABLE 9.1 AJC'S ORGANIZATIONAL AND ASPIRATIONAL VALUES

Antiracism	Truth-telling and learning from history are necessary to understand our inheritance of racism, and accountability and leadership building are needed to dismantle that legacy.
Self-determination	Our power lies in our knowledge and community, and we champion the strength of both to forge our future.
Powersharing	Decisions determining the well-being of BIPOC cannot be made without us, and we must be active in the spaces designed for that purpose as well as in developing new ones.
Inclusion	The movement must be intersectional, as White supremacy is deployed across systems and experienced (albeit differently) by all people who are racialized.
Reckoning	Undoing White supremacy requires meaningful and powerful actions to acknowledge and address harms.
Equity and dignity	Trust in people who have been oppressed, who imagine and create solutions for their own liberation and the equity and dignity that they have been deprived.

Internally, our organizational values also serve as benchmarks for our ongoing and prospective activities, operations, and expansion, allowing us to assess whether any one decision would have a result that belies our values. We therefore ask ourselves, "How do we bring up new leaders and make our tools useful to them while enabling them to be flexible and agile when facing new challenges? Are our decisions based on our own research and collective minds, while also informed by the depth of knowledge from our broad coalition? Who isn't represented at our events and why? Who has been excluded due to inaccessibility? How do our decisions and actions support a racial reckoning that our city requires to begin the process of undoing racism? Are we providing for Black people in Austin a service, resource, or tool to help us be the driving force behind our own liberation? Are we increasing economic and racial equity for Black people in Austin?"

AJC developed its outreach in civic participation; robust programs regarding Black health, art, education, employment, housing, safety, and other quality-of-life areas; and public policy focused on increasing safety and building power and opportunity for the Black community. Our goal was to embody our organization's values, embed them into our outward-facing strategy, and incorporate them into the ways our city functions.

Operationalizing Our Values Toward Community-Led Justice

Taking a page from our protest experience, we knew the power of showing up in unexpected places to claim a stake in our own futures in Austin, and that tactic would remain with us in our coming phase. We began to organize toward being present and active at city council meetings, knowing that Austin's legislative branch determines the city budget, taxes, amendment of laws, and creation of ordinances and policies (Austin City Council, n.d.) and that this was a space where we lacked representation. Austin had recently shifted from at-large elections for its city council to 10 single-member districts plus the mayor (Kanin, 2013), and our leadership was making in-roads with new progressive members and with speaking at public hearings. This was an arena ripe for our values-driven approach of engagement, and we began the process of training our volunteers to navigate city hall, including where, when, and how to engage with council members, how to develop public testimony, and how the process flows to drive inclusivity into the decision-making process at this level of government.

In the fall of 2016, we entered the city's budget meetings with an educated and activated group of advocates and issued our first major list of reforms for the Austin Police Department (APD) in response to their budget ask of $13 million for more officers. This signaled our entry into this public sphere with our strong base of values, and correspondingly, our value proposition to the city. Our Better Before More proposal demanded cultural change in our city council's decision-making process, insisting on their inclusivity and openness to hearing out young, Black advocates. Better Before More presented concrete steps to improve the police department in the course of the next year and relayed the seriousness of this need for the Black community. These included modernizing its policy manual to institute best practices that will reduce unnecessary use of force and make citizens safer; agreeing to a reasonable framework for the prompt release of body camera video; specifying how the public can be a part of the meet and confer process (the contract negotiation process with the Austin Police Association); eliminating arrests for nonjailable traffic offenses; moving mental health first response out of APD; and overhauling training for both new recruits and existing staff.

Our city council attached our proposal as a budget rider to APD's request, making the department responsible for showing progress in these areas before they were granted funds for officers the next budget season (City of Austin, 2016). This first significant public win set us on a path that would result in our achieving a number of these necessary goals, beginning with significant reforms to the labor agreement with the Austin Police Association.

The contract is where key areas of reform live that have direct implications for the treatment and outcomes for Black people who have interactions with police. Discipline, promotions, demotions, hiring, civilian oversight, and access to performance records are on the negotiation table and are only open to change every 3 to 5 years. Myriad issues plagued the contract that essentially set up a justice system exclusive to police officers that layered on protections across their range of conduct. We decided in 2016 to insert ourselves into this process.

We built a coalition to collate our reforms and to increase representation, and then prioritized and packaged our reforms into a tight set of eight improvements. This convergence unified the coalition, giving us all a horse in the race and a shared overall goal of including the voice of the community in an agreement that impacts our safety and interactions with the police. With such data as APD's own annual reports on racial profiling and use of force in hand that demonstrated, without a doubt, the overpolicing and brutality against Black bodies, we entered the negotiation process with a strong antiracist agenda that demanded we be included in this seldom-occurring opportunity to reduce the harm that the contract perpetuates.

Through our coalition's work on the police labor agreement, the city now has a drastically improved independent civilian oversight office that regularly makes public its recommendations on critical incidents, can recommend independent investigation and release reports from those investigations, and releases the chief's written explanation of disagreements with the recommendations (Office of Police Oversight, n.d.)

We celebrated a significant win for community-led justice reform when Austin's city council unanimously approved a police labor contract that was informed by the priorities of the public. This historic vote was the culmination of our 2-year effort to insert the community into a bargaining process that was once exclusive to city and police association representatives and was reportedly the first time in history (Grits for Breakfast, 2018) that a grassroots mobilization, guided by a Black-led, liberal nonprofit, had convinced a city council to reject a police contract, inserted itself as a key player in the continued bargaining, and compelled an all-in vote by city council to approve a contract that included our reforms.

In late 2016, AJC partnered with Urban Institute (n.d.) on a pilot survey in the most policed neighborhood in Austin to gain that community's perspective of policing and to lean on the voice of this neighborhood in determining future policies that would impact interchanges with police. This took place in a Black and Brown community on the east side of Austin, which decades'-old policies and city planning reserved for people of color. The basis for this project was that neighborhoods that are most likely to have interactions with police are often least likely to have a representative voice on issues of public safety, policing, and equity in the criminal justice system. In collaboration with Urban Institute,

APD, and community members, we designed a survey called *Community Voices* to field questions door-to-door on community–police relations and perceptions (AJC, 2018).

Through this survey, we were able to channel these voices into changes in citywide policies regarding policing. We did this by developing a committed policy group whose research and advocacy is based on racial justice, equity, and dignity. Our team would produce an updated use of force policy for the APD that included the department's first de-escalation policy that drew on time as a tool used to assess situations, to gather information, and to weigh more options for resolving issues (APD, 2020). We played an instrumental role in the development of a body-worn camera policy with strong privacy considerations (APD, 2020) and the body-worn camera footage release policy with a 45-day timeline for public release (KXAN, 2020). Members of the organization were involved in policies that greatly reduced arrests for ticket-eligible traffic offenses (Wilson, 2019).

In response to the uprising against racism in policing and the call of the community to reevaluate the purpose of policing and the definition of public safety that surged in 2020, AJC led a massive rally and march in Austin in partnership with Huston-Tillotson University that began and ended on the campus of our city's historically Black college and university (HBCU) (Goard, 2020). The event centered Blackness and racial justice in response to both the killings of George Floyd (Hill et al., 2020) and Breonna Taylor (Oppel et al., 2021) that were highly visible nationally, as well as the shooting of Mike Ramos in Austin (Weber, 2020). It also afforded a stage to urge for the cultural shift that could come from a new narrative of public safety that has at its core equity, dignity, self-determination, and reckoning. In his rally speech, AJC's executive director, Chas Moore, mused about White supremacy:

> We have to literally uproot this out of this evil system and think of another way to do public safety. Why do we have cops going to check on people with mental health issues? They aren't trained to do it. Why do we have cops in our schools when our kids are acting up, slamming them to the ground? They don't know what to do. It's time that we really start thinking about the "something" that has to give. ... We can't fix a police department that was designed to catch runaway slaves. The origins of policing is to catch, and police and detain Black bodies. And peep this, once we got rid of slavery, we never once had a conversation about what we do now? Maybe we need to change it. That conversation has never happened. So we still know how it operates. That's why we are not surprised when we see brothers and sisters on the street. It's operating the way it's supposed to. Which begs the question, Why do we put in the city of Austin $400 million in the police department and then come out and say we care about Black lives?

In the weeks following the march, we steered our attention to APD's budget. The lion's share of the city's public safety budget is sunk into policing, demonstrating our misguided reliance on policing to resolve most of our social issues, and with the known dispro-portionality of policing against Black bodies, also demonstrating the ways that policing deploys White supremacy. In coalition with like-minded organizations, we produced an assessment of the past year of 911 calls for service to demonstrate how our police officers are using their time and determined that very few calls are for violent crimes and that most of their activity can be handled by staff outside of the department (AJC, 2020c). We dove into the current police budget to discern where to cut or decouple $100 million from the department (AJC, 2020d). With this data, we began the process of gathering community input into the future of public safety in Austin, first by creating and fielding a poll with YouGov on the police budget that showed strong support for divesting from APD and investing in social services and alternative forms of public safety (AJC, 2020e), and then by developing a #WeFund budgeting tool that allowed respondents to reimagine our city's budget and determine new areas of investment (AJC, 2020f).

Ultimately, the Austin City Council voted to cut over $20 million from the police budget immediately and use that money to fund alternative public health and public safety services that will reduce the need for police in this fiscal year (Venkataramanan, 2020). The council identified many functions currently handled by the police that should be moved out of the department and managed independently. That process for decoupling departments has started. The council also identified a series of policing functions that should be completely reimagined over this fiscal year in partnership with community members, and AJC is one of the organizations at that table. The total package for decoupling and investing in alternatives for public safety sets aside $150 million of the police department's budget.

In addition, the council voted to raze the downtown police department building in order to "initiate a community-led effort to determine ... how the property could be leveraged to address historic economic inequities in the black community and support future black community economic success, and possibly serve as a gateway to East Austin" (Flannigan, 2020).

The $20-plus million in immediate divestment is of course less than we hoped council could cut. But it was enough to fund a big expansion of Emergency Medical Services, fully fund alternative first responders for mental health–related calls, provide a much-needed shelter for victims of family violence, increase homeless services, offer programs to support people trying to reintegrate after incarceration, add new violence prevention services, and give harm reduction a chance to help people struggling with addiction. Each of these investments signals a much-needed reckoning in our community; each delivers to the Black community services and resources either long-denied or long-required to even begin to reconcile the harms done to our community.

Broadening Our Reach and the Impact of our Values-driven Approach

Texas's legislative sessions fall on every odd year, and in the wake of the 2016 presidential election and a desire for our outcry for racial justice to have a broader reach, we launched our legislative advocacy team in 2017. We became renowned as the most visible, active, and powerful grassroots advocacy group at the capitol and came away with 26 of 41 (mostly) criminal justice bills passed (not including other accolades such as amendments and bills killed).

The AJC team showed up, had its own priorities that were grounded by racial justice, generated new and unexpected bill momentum for real police reforms like ending arrests for citation-eligible offenses, and also provided support for the entire criminal justice reform movement as well as support for certain education and housing bills. AJC volunteers elevated our local mission and messaging to the state level and became familiar faces in dozens of offices supporting Raise the Age, bail reform, school suspensions, mental health diversion, and much more. By supporting so many different bills early in the process, AJC was welcomed into offices and able to have discussions with staff, even when we opposed bills. Many offices complimented AJC on our laser-focused legislative agenda to champion racial justice for Black communities across the state, as well as our persistence and dedication. Offices started soliciting our help as the legislative session progressed.

One major victory was the Sandra Bland Act that included direction that law enforcement "shall make a good faith effort to divert" people in mental health crisis or suffering the effects of substance abuse to treatment instead of jail (Silver, 2017a). It also directed that the Commission on Jail Standards must adopt rules to implement prescription drug continuity after arrest, that jail deaths must be investigated by an independent agency not connected to the jail administration, and that racial profiling data collection include "warning" stops, whether physical force was used, the reason for the stop, and analysis of contraband hit rates (Silver, 2017a).

We also addressed fines and fees for indigent people with a bill that allows judges to make a determination upon conviction that a person can't pay fines and fees associated with a conviction and can substitute community service or waive fines and fees (Silver, 2017b). The school-to-prison pipeline was also on our legislative agenda, and we worked on a bill that limits out-of-school suspensions for kids in grades lower than third (Barajas, 2019).

In 2019, we returned to the capitol, but it was admittedly dark days for criminal justice reform advocates as Texas politics had become entrenched in the toxicity at the federal level and emboldened by the presidential administration that rebuked cultural change, especially in any effort to save Black lives. We are currently organized for the 2021 session, feeling invigorated by recent wins at the national level that signal a taste for equity, inclusion, and real change.

We gained notoriety due to our highly visible wins with police policy both locally and at the state level; however, while that was our initial entry point we recognized that it wouldn't matter if we managed to decrease overpolicing when Black Austinites are also historically and systematically impacted by gentrification, segregation, and a lack of educational and employment opportunities. In 2019 we launched into housing, mental health, and education policy with strong results.

Mental health response has always been top of mind for AJC, as Black Austinites who are in crisis often are met with a deadly response from APD. We became active in the past years' budget cycles to ask that the city prioritize funding for improvements to Austin's first-response system to make sure we address mental illness with appropriate services. The extensive community effort in which we took a strong stance paid off, and we are better able to ensure that Black Austinites experiencing a mental health issue are met with a health response. We gained ground in the 2020 budget cycle to reallocate $2.7 million from APD's budget to improve mental health first response by expanding the Integral Care-EMCOT contract for clinical staff and telehealth services, increasing community outreach to underserved communities, and adding seven new positions to the Community Health Paramedic program (Flores, 2020).

AJC has had a long-standing commitment to the youth of color in our community, and our Higher Learning program was our first yearlong offering (AJC, 2019d). Founded in 2018, Higher Learning educates and supports youth of color in owning their collective power and stepping into being the next great change makers by providing a curriculum rooted in social justice, mentorship, and community building. Our youth operate daily in a system where their voices and lives are undervalued. They are inundated with unwarranted blatant oppression, life-threatening situations, microaggressions, and racism due to the skin they were born in. Our philosophy is that youth of color need accessible, safe, nonjudgmental environments where they can support each other in discovering who they are, what they are capable of, and how they want to live in the world. We create an identity safe space by providing mentors of color who understand the societal and systemic barriers they face daily. All the Higher Learning programs are geared toward participants healing from the racism and oppression embedded in the society in which they live, play, and learn. Our youth gain critical life skills, knowledge, and strategies necessary to become the next great change makers in this world.

From this dedication to the welfare for our youth came a policy offshoot. Our education policy team's work began from AJC's convening of community members in response to the 2019 AISD school closure proposal. AISD set out to close mainly schools on the east side of Austin. We issued a list of recommendations around understanding and acknowledging our history of segregation and the Black and Brown communities that would be impacted by this decision, recommending that all AISD board of trustees and all district employees familiarize themselves with the racist history of the city of Austin and the AISD (Marut, 2019). We expressed support for and echoed the asks of the "Reframe The Game: An Equity First Rebuild of the School Changes Proposal," which states, "Major planning decisions and all district plans, programs and initiatives [should be] guided by principles of: Equity, Excellence, Balance, and Growth" (Reframe the Game, 2018). Finally, we offered a roadmap for fostering culturally proficient teaching staff, administration, and school communities and creating a culturally proficient teaching staff and administration.

We named the education arm of the policy team BASS (Building Austin School Systems), loosely based on Oakland, California's, Black Organizing Project Bettering Our School System (n.d.), or BOSS. Our vision is an Austin where all schools are actively engaging in (a) acknowledging, disrupting, and unraveling racism and oppression in their school systems, policies, and practices; (b) collaborating in relationship with staff, students, families, and community; and (c) implementing systems, policies, and practices that ensure that schools are spaces where *all* individuals are treated with the dignity they inherently deserve, are respected, nurtured, able to learn, and are guaranteed equity and justice.

A main focal area is divestment from policing. In response to the national focus on policing and its violent impact on BIPOC, AJC partnered with local and statewide organizations to demand AISD to divest from policing and instead implement policies and practices that create antiracist, policing-free, equitable, physically, emotionally, mentally, and socially safe schools. We specifically crafted our initial ask for AISD to provide more transparent and accessible information by posting the in-house Police Department budget, data, and policies online. We also linked this work to the annual budget process and asked that AISD cease from hiring any new school resource officers or filling any vacancies. We asked that this funding be diverted to restorative practices, which AISD currently funds through external grant funding.

Working in deep coalition with other groups, we organized this effort by sending our first letter (AJC, 2019b) and resolution (AJC, 2019c) to AISD and releasing a statement to the press detailing AJC's stance on divestment. Additionally, we activated the community and got more than 100 people to testify in support of the resolution at a school board meeting. Our outreach activities to increase awareness and drive inclusiveness in the decision-making process regarding our children's education have been substantial, including hosting a webinar about divesting from policing (AJC, 2020k); establishing a monthly coalition meeting with partners to work on AISD's divestment of police; joining AISD-run subgroups to advocate for divesting from police and antiracist practices and policies; engaging in ongoing capacity building by researching and studying the history of SRO's and the AISD student code of conduct; and brandishing the power of storytelling in the classroom.

In partnership with the coalition groups, we are creating a community scorecard for AISD to use as an organizing tool to hold the district leadership accountable for enacting and sustaining equitable and just practices. A community scorecard will ground us in the history and experiences of Austin's Black education community and center community-led solutions to address inequitable policies and practices. Our goals are to develop a scorecard to evaluate AISD on how they are contributing to the Black community and a report to inform the development of the scorecard. The report will include policy analysis, quantitative and qualitative data analysis, and policy and practice recommendations. Through this effort, we will foster shared knowledge of district- and school-based best policies and practices for equity and justice and foster strong relationships with Austin area community groups and individuals who prioritize just and equitable policies and practices.

BASS is in its 1st year of inception and decided to serve in a support role during the 87th legislative session with partner organizations. Our platform includes (a) divestment from policing in schools to decrease (with the goal to eventually eliminate) funding dedicated to school resource officers, (b) removing punitive discipline systems and armed adults on school campuses, (c) increasing dedicated funding for mental health services, (d) dedicating funding and enacting policies to create district-wide restorative practices, (e) eliminating systemic racism in education, (f) reducing emphasis on state-mandated standardized testing, and (g) implementing a comprehensive, inclusive, whole child sexual health education curriculum.

We are determined to have Austin schools and leadership put in place policies and practices that ensure that our schools are identity safe spaces where all children, families, and staff are respected, nurtured, able to achieve, learn, and grow and are guaranteed equity and justice. As a group we insist that our school districts acknowledge, interrupt, and unravel racism in education policies and practices, engage community voices, demand and secure equitable outcomes, and ensure that everyone thrives.

Alongside educational policy, housing and community development comprise a relatively new part of AJC's sustained community power and racial justice work. The housing and community development team has already taken on a number of major initiatives, helping to spark citywide conversations about housing equity, antidisplacement policy, and the future of mobility justice. We launched its policy work in 2019, with a detailed public statement on the city's land development code rewrite (AJC, 2019e), outlining a strategy that balanced the need for greater density and increased affordability with a recognition of the ongoing impacts of new development in neighborhoods struggling with gentrification and higher risks of displacement.

AJC's statement called on the city to take extra precautions in neighborhoods marked as vulnerable to displacement by the University of Texas' Uprooted Report (The Uprooted Project, 2018), while simultaneously encouraging a more equitable distribution of new housing density in higher opportunity areas. As a result of AJC's advocacy, in coalition with partners and allies, the city council unanimously passed the creation of an "Equity Overlay" strategy designed to protect gentrifying neighborhoods (City of Austin, 2021), following the Uprooted Report's neighborhood typologies map. The housing team showed its commitment to tracking the entire process (Reding & Oak, 2020) with two subsequent statements providing feedback on the second and final drafts of the Code (AJC, 2020a).

AJC's work on land-use policy continues to have a major impact on city zoning debates, helping to influence the city decisions on housing and community planning (Stayton, 2019). We continue to closely monitor land-use decisions and are prepared to engage with all upcoming city zoning conversations.

In 2020, COVID brought Austin to an impending eviction crisis, especially in Black and Brown communities. This set the stage for a surge of tenant mobilization, and a renewed interest in tenant rights. With other grassroots organizations, we formed the Eviction Solidarity Network (ESN, n.d.). Since its inception, ESN has successfully advocated for a citywide moratorium on evictions (Montano, 2020) and invested time and resources toward keeping tenants informed of rapidly changing city and national policies and helping them access multilingual resources about their rights. ESN works to track and review, in real time, eviction hearings to ensure tenants are supported through the eviction process and can flag abnormalities that may rise and require follow-up inquiry. Additionally, ESN has distributed thousands of door hangers and yard signs and has developed a social media campaign to help reach Austin's tenants.

The unprecedented electoral victory of Project Connect (Austin Metro, n.d.), Austin's new multibillion-dollar transit plan, promises to change the face of the city for decades to come. From early on, prior to the development of the proposition's ballot language, AJC played a key role in developing a series of equity proposals and recommendations that became embedded into the project. To do so we helped form a mobility justice coalition alongside other mobility justice and transit advocates.

Some of the major policy recommendations that became part of the project include the addition of a historic $300 million investment in displacement mitigation around new transit infrastructure (Cho, 2020), the development of a community advisory coalition, changes to specifications for ATP board membership, and the creation of an equity tool in tandem with neighborhood-level antidisplacement strategies. The equity tool is to be rolled out with a public-facing dashboard (Thornton, 2020), enabling the community to keep track of key performance indicators relating to equity and antidisplacement as the project evolves.

Over the coming years, AJC is committed to building greater transparency, accountability, and direct community participation into the process.

Another key city debate that AJC has engaged with is the future of the I-35 highway, which historically serves as the segregation line in Austin. AJC members participated in a series of conversations about the highway's future, organized by Public City and the Our Future 35 (n.d.) group. AJC has joined in calling on the Texas Department of Transportation (TxDOT) to acknowledge the legacy of racial segregation and violence that I-35 represents and demanding better alternatives that shrink the highway's footprint and that are friendlier to bike riders and pedestrians, as well as more conducive to clean air, increased quality of life, and affordable housing.

More than 700 community members shared their thoughts about the highway's future with TxDOT, in part thanks to AJC's engagement and collaboration with critical partners. We believe it is time to reimagine the highway and will continue to closely monitor TxDOT's designs, working to encourage greater community involvement and input throughout the process.

Another crucial front for AJC's efforts has been the development of a new How to House (AJC, 2019f) campaign in partnership with ECHO (Ending Community Homelessness Coalition, n.d.). This campaign is targeted to landlords, tenants, and community members at large, helping to challenge the stigma around voucher-holders and encouraging the Austin community to take pride in living in places that are inclusive and that are part of the solution to homelessness. This new campaign will have its hard launch in January 2021 and hopes to challenge dehumanizing stereotypes and "move more people experiencing homelessness into safe, stable housing and remove barriers that disproportionately affect our Black and other historically oppressed neighbors who need housing."

The campaign's slogan, "Make a choice, change a course," speaks to the way in which we hope to use proactive messaging, social media campaigns, and positive reinforcement to encourage property managers of all sizes to enter partnerships with ECHO's community housing team. Campaign results are updated weekly and tracked with a counter on the How to House website.

Aligned with our criminal justice work as an organization, the team has entered reentry work to help break down barriers for people leaving incarceration to access housing in 2019. Working with community partners, we passed the Fair Chance Housing Ordinance to reduce look-back periods and to increase housing availability for people who were formerly incarcerated (City of Austin, n.d.). Additionally, we helped revise harmful language in the state's low-income housing tax credit rules that would have blocked many people with criminal backgrounds from accessing supportive housing across the state.

During 2020, AJC also helped present, cohost, or participate in a number of key local and national conversations about housing and design justice. These conversations on housing patterns and policing, transit justice, and more helped to spark community dialogue about housing equity and structural racism, and the need to disrupt old paradigms continues to play a major part in AJC's housing work in 2021.

Facing Unprecedented Challenges that Laid Bare Anti-Blackness and Inequity in Austin

COVID-19 presented obstacles for our constant connectivity to the community, and we made quick adjustments to remain present, attentive, and responsive. We presented or collaborated on more than 50 virtual trainings, press conferences, panels, and community meetings regarding the policing, housing, educational, and mental health issues that Black and Brown people face in Austin and were laid bare by the pandemic. Of note was a tribunal of Chief Police Manley following the police killing of Mike Ramos and the violence against protestors by police (AJC, 2020g), a seven-part series on "Imagining a World Without Police" (AJC, 2020h), a "Mind Check" series focused on Black mental wellness during the pandemic (AJC, 2020i), and a COVID-19 run of panels and town halls regarding all quality of life areas.

We supported our Higher Learning families with food donations, bill assistance, and school supplies such as laptops needed for virtual learning. Community members received $85,000 in COVID relief from AJC, and those experiencing homelessness were provided snack packs, feminine care products, first-aid kits, and COVID relief packs, which included gloves, masks, and sanitizer.

Alongside the massive rally that we held in the summer that kept us highly visible in the community, we hosted our fourth annual Black Food Week and partnered in painting "Black Austin Matters" on Congress Avenue and "Black Artists Matter" on 11th Street (Oyeniyi, 2020). Our antiracist book club, which reads nonfiction and fiction books written by BIPOC authors, continued to meet monthly and discuss the racial justice implications of the literature (AJC, 2020j). We held numerous screenings in the summer that included panels and community discussions. All these events promoted the visibility, resilience, and education of communities of color in Austin and provided various ways for people to stay involved socially and politically.

One AJC piece that did suffer due to the pandemic was Project Orange, our initiative to register voters at the Travis County Correctional Complex and to strengthen the ability to vote for everyone eligible. Project Orange was launched by the Houston Justice Coalition (n.d.) at the Harris County jail in early 2018. There, inmate uniforms are orange, which is how the name came about. Travis County has one of the highest rates of pre-trial, legally innocent defendants in lock-up. According to jail population reports from the Texas Commission on Jail Standards, at any given time, Travis County Jail holds 2,100 inmates, with about 73% of them detained without conviction and eligible to vote. That means roughly 1,500 of the 2,100 inmates in the Travis County Jail on any given day haven't been convicted of a crime. An inmate with a previous felony conviction who is currently off paper (has completed their term of incarceration, probation, supervised release, or parole and has satisfied any other requirements from the court and remained conviction free) but in jail for a misdemeanor charge is eligible to register to vote. An inmate who is in jail on a felony charge but is awaiting a court date is eligible to register to vote. These inmates wouldn't be able to ride to a voting booth and vote because they're incarcerated, so AJC responded to this injustice by bringing into Travis County Correctional Complex the means for inmates to be politically active.

Through our partnership with the Travis County Sheriff's Office and the Travis County Clerk's office, we have successfully registered 1,015 people to date. We've helped inmates fill out 1191 registration forms, so we have an overall 85.23% successful registration rate since the inception of Project Orange in 2018. For context, Project Orange registered more than 300 people in 2018, and about 550 in 2019. We were unable to go into TCCC in 2020 to carry on this important project, so we spent that time planning toward expanding to Williamson County in 2021 and for our return to TCCC.

Conclusion

Anti-Black racism drew the leaders of AJC together. Survivalism, protectionism, combatting isolationism, and pushing against policies, practices, and a culture in Austin that have led to our mass outmigration brought us together. AJC is now widely regarded as one of the leading advocacy organizations in the city by community residents, civic leaders, and counterparts. Alongside our partners, who are too many to be named and to whom words cannot express our respect and solidarity, we are positioned to compel real change in Austin.

Our mission to educate and build community power for Black and Brown people who live in Austin and need support, community, and liberation in a systemically unjust society is guided by our core values, and through our work we've made headway in narrowing the scope of the criminal justice system and helping to usher in transformative justice that no longer relies on criminalization and punitive excess, but instead has human dignity as its core organizing principle and defers to community-based initiatives to improve public safety. AJC fosters racial reckoning and reconciliation in Austin by acknowledging the ties to racism across systems that are leading to the decreasing Black and Brown populations, and centering all of its programs, initiatives, and policies across quality-of-life areas on racial equity and building community power. We respond to opportunities to make changes that are in keeping with AJC priorities and the interests of its community, as they arise. Our values-driven strategy continues to create direct and indirect impact in communities of color by influencing changes in local government and advocating for policy reform. This strategy builds on AJC's experience and knowledge from its work thus far. As AJC's founder likes to say, "Our success in the past has been running through the door that is cracked and breaking it open."

References

Austin American Statesman. (2018, August 17). *Austin Police Officer Discusses Racism with Breaion King After Her Arrest.* Youtube. Retrieved 1 2, 2021, from https://www.youtube.com/watch?v=-39Xe8xvFc8

Austin City Council. (n.d.). *About Austin City Council.* https://www.austintexas.gov/department/city-council/about

Austin Justice Coalition. (2018). *Community voices: Austin pilot summary.* Austin Justice Coalition. https://austinjustice.org/wp-content/uploads/2020/07/Community-Voices-Austin-Pilot-Summary_May-24-2018.pdf

Austin Justice Coalition. (2019a). *Vision.* Austin Justice Coalition. austinjustice.org/vision/

Austin Justice Coalition. (2019b). *AJC's letter to superintendent, Austin ISD board, and community members.* https://austinjustice.org/ajcs-letter-to-superintendent-austin-isd-board-and-community-members/

Austin Justice Coalition. (2019c). *Education initiative.* https://austinjustice.org/education/

Austin Justice Coalition. (2019d). *Higher learning.* Austin Justice Coalition. https://austinjustice.org/higher-learning/

Austin Justice Coalition. (2019e, October 24). Complete communities: AJC's response to the land development code revision. *Medium.* https://medium.com/impact-hub-austin-impact-accelerator/ajcs-response-to-the-new-land-development-code-revision-ef1cd92932e2?sk=935fea7baa5bf1e45d-1e9649d877e1fc

Austin Justice Coalition. (2019f). *How to house.* Austin Justice Coalition. https://austinjustice.org/howtohouse/

Austin Justice Coalition. (2020a, February 13). AJC's letter in response to the 2nd reading of the new land development code. *Medium.* https://medium.com/@austinjusticecoalition/ajcs-letter-in-response-to-the-2nd-reading-of-the-new-land-development-code-efe56361d07f

Austin Justice Coalition. (2020b, September 2). *Imagine a world without police: Ep.6—Policing & schools* [Video]. https://youtu.be/ITOeSakP57s

Austin Justice Coalition. (2020c, June). *Assessment of Austin Police Department Calls for Service.* Austin Justice Coalition. https://austinjustice.org/assessment-of-apd-calls-for-service/

Austin Justice Coalition. (2020d). *Proposed First $100 Million in Cuts and Reorganization.* Austin Justice Coalition. https://mailchi.mp/austinjustice/how-we-cut-100-million-now?e=5a37d5af66

Austin Justice Coalition. (2020e). *YouGov poll results.* https://austinjustice.org/yougov-poll-results/

Austin Justice Coalition. (2020f). *#WeFund budgeting tool for the people of Austin.* https://austinjustice.org/wefund-community-budgeting-tool-results/

Austin Justice Coalition. (2020g). *Chief Manley virtual "tribunal."* Facebook. https://fb.me/e/9w6wGcPyo

Austin Justice Coalition. (2020h). *Imagining a world without police.* Facebook. https://fb.me/e/En50hOhZ

Austin Justice Coalition. (2020i). *Mind check: Black mental wellness during 'Rona*. Facebook. https://fb.me/e/ J5Miud9v

Austin Justice Coalition. (2020j). *Austin Justice Coalition book club*. Facebook. https://www.facebook.com/ groups/376612339419025

Austin Justice Coalition. (2020k) https://www.facebook.com/events/3216961991725644

Austin Metro. (n.d.). *Project Connect*. https://www.capmetro.org/project-connect

Austin Police Department. (2017). *Austin Police Department response to resistance report: 2017*. Response to Resistance Reports. https://www.austintexas.gov/sites/default/files/files/Police/2017_response_to_resistance_report.pdf

Austin Police Department. (2020). Body worn camera systems. *Austin Police Department General Orders*. https://www.austintexas.gov/sites/default/files/files/Police/General_Orders.pdf

Austin Young Chamber. (n.d.). *Civics 201: Issues and policy in Central Texas*. https://austinyc.org/civics-201/

Barajas, M. (2019, August 18). Texas schools suspended students between pre-K and second grade more than 70,000 times in a year. *Texas Observer*. https://www.texasobserver.org/texas-schools-suspended-students-between-pre-k-and-second-grade-more-than-70000-times-in-a-year/

Black Organizing Project Bettering Our School System. (n.d.). *Home*. http://blackorganizingproject.org/bettering-our-school-system/

Cho, Y. (2020, July 28). *Proposed project connect funding plan includes $300 million for anti-displacement efforts*. KXAN. https://www.kxan.com/news/local/austin/proposed-project-connect-funding-plan-includes-300-million-for-anti-displacement-efforts/

City of Austin. (n.d.). *Resolution No. 20200611-094*. https://www.austintexas.gov/edims/document.cfm?id=342168

City of Austin. (2016, September 6). *City council regular meeting transcript*. https://www.austintexas.gov/edims/document.cfm?id=262329

City of Austin. (2021, November 22). *Direction for potential equity overlay*. https://austincouncilforum.org/viewtopic.php?t=1204

Colloqate. (n.d.). *Home*. Colloqate. https://colloqate.org/about-cq

ECHO. (n.d.). *Home*. ECHO. https://www.austinecho.org/

Eviction Solidarity Network. (n.d.). *Home*. https://evictionisnotacure.com/

Flannigan, J. (2020, July 27). *Police budget proposal to reconstruct and deconstruct*. Austin Council Forum. https://austincouncilforum.org/viewtopic.php?t=1307

Flores, C. (2020, July 13). *Proposed city budget slashes $11.3M in funding from Austin Police Department*. Fox29. https://foxsanantonio.com/news/local/austin-city-manager-to-present-proposed-budget-monday-afternoon

Goard, A. (2020, June 7). *Austin rally focuses on Black Lives and Black voices*. KXAN. https://www.kxan.com/austin-george-floyd-mike-ramos-protests/austin-rally-sunday-aims-to-focus-on-black-lives-and-black-voices/

Grits for Breakfast. (2018, November 28). *Union contract fight gave Austin advocates leverage to improve police oversight*. https://gritsforbreakfast.blogspot.com/2018/11/union-contract-fight-gave-austin.html

Hernandez, N. (2016, July 15). No justice. No peace. Picking up the pieces after a week of terror. *Austin Chronicle*. https://www.austinchronicle.com/news/2016-07-15/no-justice-no-peace/

Hill, E., Tiefenthäler, A., Triebert, C., Drew Jordan, Willis, H., & Stein, R. (2020, May 31). How George Floyd was killed in police custody. *The New York Times*. https://www.nytimes.com/2020/05/31/us/george-floyd-investigation.html

Houston Justice Coalition. (n.d.). *Project Orange*. https://www.houstonjustice.org/inmatejustice

Jankowski, P. (2016, September 4). Austin police: Teen killed by officer identified as David Joseph, 17. *Austin American Statesman*. https://www.statesman.com/news/20160904/austin-police-teen-killed-by-officer-identified-as-david-joseph-17

Kanin, M. (2013, December 2). What's left? *Texas Observer*. https://www.texasobserver.org/whats-left/

KXAN. (2020, May). *APD policy 117 critical incident: Public release.* https://www.kxan.com/wp-content/uploads/sites/40/2020/05/APD-Policy-117-Critical-Incident-Public-Release.pdf

Marut, M. (2019, December 15). *Austin Justice Coalition calling to continue equity conversation After AISD school closure vote.* KVUE. https://www.kvue.com/article/news/education/schools/austin-isd-justice-coalition-equity-vote-discussion/269-08f49e7d-e530-403c-a239-93c7c786bb1flling to continue equity conversation after AISD school closure vote

McBride, J. (2016, July 24). *Breaion King: 5 fast facts you need to know.* Heavy. https://heavy.com/news/2016/07/breaion-king-arrest-video-teacher-texas-austin-police-you-tube-officer-bryan-richter-patrick-spradlin-watch-art-acevedo/

McMahon, S., & Moore, C. (2019, April 8). To reform the police, target their union contract. We did this in Austin and won. *The New York Times.* https://www.nytimes.com/2019/04/08/opinion/austin-police-union-contract.html

Montano, J. B. (2020, August 14). As eviction crisis looms, local leaders ramp up relief. *Austin Chronicle.* https://www.austinchronicle.com/news/2020-08-14/as-eviction-crisis-looms-local-leaders-ramp-up-relief/

Office of Police Oversight. (n.d.). *Home.* https://alpha.austin.gov/en/police-oversight/

Equity Office, Office of Innovation, and Office of Police Oversight. (2020, November 16). *2019 joint report: Analysis of APD racial profiling data.* https://alpha.austin.gov/police-oversight/2019-joint-report-analysis-of-apd-racial-profiling-data/

Oppel, R., Jr., Bryson Taylor, D., & Bogel-Burroughs, N. (2021, January 6). What to know About Breonna Taylor's death. *The New York Times.* https://www.nytimes.com/article/breonna-taylor-police.html

Our Future 35. (n.d.). *Home.* https://www.ourfuture35.org/

Oyeniyi, D. (2020, July 16). "Black Austin Matters" Is an artistic challenge to the city. *Texas Monthly.* https://www.texasmonthly.com/news/black-austin-matters-artistic-challenge-city/

Reding, S., & Oak, M. (2020, February 11). *Dozens of community members voice opinions on Austin's controversial land development code.* KVUE. https://www.kvue.com/article/money/economy/boomtown-2040/austin-land-development-code-rewrite-second-vote/269-0d9d6839-749b-400a-88b5-19a2fea2400e

Reframe the Game. (2018, November). *Reframe the Game: An equity-first rebuild of the school changes proposal.* https://drive.google.com/file/d/1-zgu8znXkvyUilm4I2G681cMU-FLVcl4/view

Silver, J. (2017a, June 15). Texas Gov. Abbott signs "Sandra Bland Act" into law. *Texas Tribune.* https://www.texastribune.org/2017/06/15/texas-gov-greg-abbott-signs-sandra-bland-act-law/#:~:text=The%20Sandra%20Bland%20Act%20mandates,enforcement%20agencies%20investigate%20jail%20deaths

Silver, J. (2017b, May 23). House votes to end jail time for being too poor to pay fines. *Texas Tribune.* https://www.texastribune.org/2017/05/23/texas-house-clears-bill-eliminating-jail-time-being-too-poor-pay-traff/#:~:text=Senate%20Bill%201913%2C%20by%20state,only%20offenses%20or%20court%20costs

Stayton, J. (2019, December 10). *Activist urges Austin to look At land development code through lens Of equity.* KUT 90.5. https://www.kut.org/austin/2019-12-10/activist-urges-austin-to-look-at-land-development-code-through-lens-of-equity

Texas Association of Community Development Corporations. (n.d.). *Texas community economic development.* https://www.tacdc.org/sessions

Thornton, R. (2020, September 9). City unveils affordable housing and transit dashboard ahead of Project Connect. *Austin Monitor.* https://www.austinmonitor.com/stories/2020/09/city-unveils-affordable-housing-and-transit-dashboard-ahead-of-project-connect/

The Uprooted Project. (2018). *Austin Uprooted report & maps.* https://sites.utexas.edu/gentrificationproject/austin-uprooted-report-maps/

Urban Institute. (n.d.). *Home.* https://www.urban.org/

Venkataramanan, M. (2020, August 13). Austin city council cuts police department budget by one-third, mainly through reorganizing some duties out from law enforcement oversight. *Texas Tribune.* https://www.texastribune.org/2020/08/13/austin-city-council-cut-police-budget-defund/

Weber, A. (2020, October 14). Mother asks Austin police chief whether he'll fire officer who killed her son. *KUT*. https://www.kut.org/austin/2020-10-14/mike-ramos-mother-asks-austin-police-chief-whether-hell-fire-officer-who-killed-her-son

Wilson, M. (2019, August 16). *Austin police's cite-and-release effort taking hold, arrest data show*. Austin American Statesman. https://www.statesman.com/news/20190816/austin-polices-cite-and-release-effort-taking-hold-arrest-data-show

World Population Review. (2020). *Austin, Texas population 2020*. https://worldpopulationreview.com/us-cities/austin-tx-population

CHAPTER TEN

Leveraging the Power of Education to Confront Anti-Black Racism

David W. Nowlin, Robert Muhammad, and Llyas Salahud-din

*E*ver since its humble beginnings in 1998, Texas Empowerment Academy, a charter school in East Austin, Texas, has demanded excellence from its students—all of whom live in vulnerable populations, and 95% of whom are African American. It's a story of stunning success, an ongoing movement whose impact on the community confronts anti-Black racism every day. Here is the story, including the academy's origins, in the words of three people who continue to be instrumental in that success: Mr. David Nowlin, cofounder and superintendent; Mr. Robert Muhammad, assistant superintendent, and Mr. Llyas Salahud-din, chief development officer.

David Nowlin

Every day, Texas Empowerment Academy (TxEA) equips its students from underrepresented populations in East Austin, Texas, to pursue excellence—the most powerful weapon we have for confronting stereotypes and racism in education, in particular.

As just one example of racism in education, people of color comprise 37% of the U.S. population, but only 10% of published children's books include multicultural content—a gap that has existed since 1994 (Jalissa, 2018). Addressing racism in education is a large part of why TxEA and our programs exist.

Here's how the institution came about:

Soon after I returned from serving in Operation Desert Storm in Iraq, I was awarded custody of my 2-year-old son. While I dabbled at a series of day jobs, my seriousness about my main job as a father led me to join the Board of Child Inc., a Head Start program. My mentors and activities during my 10 years on that board—along with my experience as a corporal in the Marine Corps—taught me a lot about how to run organizations, formulate and implement ideas, and overcome challenges.

I never expected to go to college, but after losing my last day job, I decided to take a shot at it. (I also had the GI bill and didn't want to give that $300 a month away!) After selling everything I owned, I enrolled in the University of Texas. During my first semester,

I took a course in African American history whose professor, Roland Hayes, took me under his wing. African American studies became my major, and 3 years later, I graduated, the first of five children in my family to do so.

My studies got me thinking about where I came from: a middle-class neighborhood in Abilene, Texas. Everyone I knew lived with their mom and dad, nobody went hungry, and everyone had a roof over their head and clothes on their back. But when I looked back on the African American boys I went to school with, only four of the 17 of us were doing decently in life. The rest were on drugs, in and out of the prison system, or even dead—the victims of violence in our little town. I tried to figure out what the hell had gone so wrong.

The answer soon became clear: Inadequate education was harming African Americans as a people. We were the first real generation to go to desegregated schools, and we came out holding the short end of the stick. What the schools taught and how they taught it were destructive to everyone, but no one more than African Americans. Most of the kids who weren't involved in athletics dropped out in the ninth grade. They didn't have a clue about how to get a job or job training, let alone any thoughts about going to college.

Our predominantly White Abilene public schools had taught us nothing about our culture or about how to be outstanding Black men. If we showed up at all in our history books, it was only as slaves, and our teachers didn't know our history well enough to teach it. Then my parents moved us to Houston, and I had African American teachers for the first time, which was an eye-opening experience. They showed us we had value and made sure we learned.

Of course, I wanted the same for my son, but when I sat in on his history class one day, I found that African American teachers alone were not the cure. I actually heard his teacher telling the students that George Washington—a former *slave master*—stood for freedom! I yanked my son out of that room and into a language class. It wouldn't be long before I could do much better for him.

Charters Held Promise

The stars aligned because around this time the first charter schools were being established in Texas. I taught in one of the first ones, and then joined a team that received a charter and started TxEA. But the team didn't have much of a plan, and charter schools in general were so new that no one really knew what they were doing. Before long, the school started running out of money, and someone had to step up and try to lead it.

Although I didn't have a background in education, I knew I could give the children of East Austin an experience that would help them claim their rightful status in the world. We would write a curriculum that speaks to the needs and aspirations of our students, teaches their real history, and changes their direction in life. I raised my hand.

Early Challenges

When I took over the school, education was not the only gap in my background. What really got in my way was not knowing how a school operates, the ins and outs of special education or food programs, or even how the money came in and how to budget it. For the first 3 years, I spent late nights and every weekend reading manuals and asking questions until I acquired the knowledge I needed.

My other big issue was overcoming the community's belief that I could not be successful without the White man's help. (Well, I had my surrogate father and mentor, Richard Strickland, but I needed him because of his *knowledge*, not because he's White.) Everyone thought I would fail in the 1st year or two, and here we are 21 years and hundreds of students later. Despite our success, we still have to fight the misconception that, because we're Black, we can't be doing the things we're doing.

Overwhelming Success

We started slowly, with only seven students—whom other public schools had rejected; we were their last resort—and five grades: fifth through ninth. By the 2nd year, we grew to 27 students, and a remarkable thing happened: *Our test scores were the best in the area, even compared with those in the predominantly White schools.*

Those results got us noticed, and our student population almost doubled by the following year. We found a bigger space and were able to expand again, this time to 120 students. About 8 years into the program, we bought our own building to serve a hundred more. Today, we span kindergarten through 12th grade on two campuses—elementary (K–7) and secondary (8–12)—serving 377 children.

In 2021, we had our first graduating class: 16 students; all but two were with us since kindergarten. We're especially proud that all 16 were accepted to three or more colleges or universities.

We plan further growth because the more students who come through our doors, the more will go on to live productive lives. We've had so many children come to us with diagnoses such as mildly mentally retarded, ADD, ADHD, oppositional defiant disorder, and learning disabilities—so many parents who were told their child couldn't learn. Maybe it's because I didn't have educational training, but none of those labels convinced me that I could not teach the child.

So many parents have been told their child couldn't behave or learn. I can get them to learn, and I can remove behavioral issues. I'm thinking of one child who was getting into fights every day at her previous school. Extensive psychological testing showed that everything in the world was wrong with her, but we took her in and worked with her. Six years later, she's one of our 16 graduates, and she has earned early college admission.

There's not one child who has spent time with this institution that we haven't been able to teach. The students who need tutoring receive it for 1 or 2 hours a day. We're indefatigable in our efforts. What's more, TxEA has never turned a student away, including those with a police record. That doesn't mean every child will stay. I'm a Marine through and through, and we run a tight ship. But every kid knows we love them.

In standardized tests, we've outperformed the schools around us year after year after year. We've also led our state groups. One hundred percent of our students who took the U.S. history, English, and biology high school exit test, passed them; 98% passed the algebra I test. We provide a better form of learning. The scores aren't always what we want them to be for every class and every situation, but remember, we're achieving these results with a student population that includes some children nobody else could teach.

Our goal was not just to create a school for Black kids (and in fact, 5% of our students are not Black), but to create something of *quality* for Black kids. As I tell them, "Don't worry about being equal. What's wrong with being better?"

We're known in the community for being able to take away all the excuses a parent comes in with for why their child can't learn. "Her teacher didn't care." Well, *my* teachers care. "Nobody can teach my child how to act." *We* can. "He can't learn." No, we'll *show* you he can learn!

We also remove society's excuses. When people talk about the historical failure of African Americans in public schools, they often say, "The community's no good," "The parents aren't educated," or "The parents don't care." Education is the only industry that blames the *client* for the *industry's* failure. (Imagine a surgeon removing the wrong organ and then blaming it on the patient for lying down the wrong way!)

We don't expect our parents to be perfect. Most of them love their children and try to do the best they can to raise them. But in addition to a lack of resources, they've rarely had partners in traditional schools. With us, they find a partner. I take full responsibility for each child's success, and all I ask of parents is to send their children to class every day. If I have them for 8 to 10 hours a day, we're going to perform, and we'll be successful at least 90% of the time.

Teaching Black History and Culture

Part of our full curriculum includes a focus on teaching our students the complete story of their history. The Black Lives Matter movement may have found its name in 2013, but it really started long before, and having that historical reference is essential to understanding how to change things. African Americans no longer drink from separate water fountains, but you only have to look at economic disparities, education levels, and the rates of home ownership to know that nothing has really changed.

Yet if you ask the people on the streets with BLM banners what they'll build to replace the current situation, they have no idea. That's because if you don't know where you've been, you don't know where you are, and you sure don't know where you're going. Marching isn't changing economic, social, and political disparities, the same ones behind more African American, Latin American, and poor White folks getting COVID-19, but fewer of us are getting testing and vaccines.

At TxEA, we provide historical reference in our efforts to remove these disparities. We teach our children about great leaders like Martin Robison Delaney and other African Americans with important accomplishments. We teach them to ask questions and confront falsehoods. We give them the knowledge to be able to say, "We're not going to do it this way anymore. The world can be a better place, and because of what my people have been through, I know better than to do what you did."

We also provide a traditional curriculum, including literature. Our teachers and I love to read, and we share that love with our students, immersing them in books like *The Alchemist*, *Lord of the Flies*, and *Cat's Cradle*. We expose the children to fantastic minds of all races, like Copernicus and Galileo. We give them a well-rounded education with the students at the center.

When you can educate someone and help them make sense of their world—when you can get a child to pick up a book on their own—you've done a wonderful thing. You've given them a spirit that can never be taken away. You've given them a desire to do well in life. That's what education is supposed to be. It's not about passing a STAR test; that's only training. Education is not about putting things *into* students; it's *bringing out* their innate gifts.

How We're Changing People's Lives

Our students are different people when they come out of TxEA. They walk with a sense of pride, they talk with a sense of confidence, and they understand how to take their position in the world. Because they've learned about Black history and culture, every student understands what it means to be African American. Their knowledge, success, and ability to express themselves confronts stereotypes and racism.

It's easy to see the difference we make when you look at families with only some of their kids at TxEA. The ones who couldn't attend (because we didn't yet offer their grade) are not doing well in life. The parent of one of our students told me, "She's the only one I've got left—she's *got* to be successful!" Well, this year, she's graduating and heading to Texas A&M in the fall. I have no doubt she'll continue to be successful.

How Else We're Specifically Fighting Anti-Black Racism

In addition to our emphasis on a well-rounded education, along with unflagging love, hope, and inspiration for every student who comes to TxEA, we're working to change statistics like these: 51% of public school students in the United States are of color, but less than 20% of their teachers are. Worse still, *40% of public schools lack a single teacher of color.* By contrast, every teacher at TxEA is African American. That's not by intention; all ethnicities are welcome. The numbers just worked out that way. But there's an undeniable benefit to having so many role models of color to interact with the students every day.

How Else We Impact the Community

We give families hope and pride. I often hear, "My baby's doing this; my baby's doing that," and they might not have been able to brag about their babies who weren't able to come to TxEA. Our students are often able to help bring their families out of poverty.

We affect parents in other ways as well. We invite them to sit in on the children's classes, and some have even attended a whole semester. We've also done classes just for parents. Many would love to go back to school for a diploma, and a few have, but the reality is that, with two or three children at home, they're working 60 hours a week just to get food on the table. At the very least, though, the children are influencing their parents by talking at home about what they're learning.

And we support our staff members: We have 57 of them, and every one of them has health insurance and a retirement. Many have bought a house. They're optimistic about the future. Even having a business of our size is bringing money into the community. The lion's share of our $5 million budget—$4.5 million—is going right back into the community.

When the pandemic hit, our focus was on keeping our children learning and our staff employed. We responded quickly because we knew we had to. If you bring people into a school environment and you can't keep them safe, you shouldn't have the job. Every one of our teachers was trained in Google Classroom, and by the fall, every student had a Chromebook with internet service or a hotspot in their home and access to our learning portal.

To prepare for a return to the classroom, we set up air purifiers and desks with shields around them, placed 6 feet apart, and sanitized the school on an hourly basis. Where other schools lost 30% of their students, we were unable to engage only 10 students during the pandemic.

We also fed students who learned from home, providing 5 days of breakfast, lunch, and snacks for each child—delivered if the parents could not pick them up. We also used grants to help families that the pandemic put in financial trouble. We try to cover every base when it comes to our parents and our staffs and their families. We care about each other, and we make decisions together.

Sharing Our Methods

Other schools have expressed interest in learning how we do what we do, and we're happy to cooperate. But so far, we haven't seen it duplicated. It may be because it's really hard work. As kind of an exchange program, I sent 10 of our students to a neighboring school. All 10 of them graduated in the top 20, and six of them were in the top 10.

The superintendent was flabbergasted, so he and the assistant superintendent visited us to find out what the hell we were doing to get these African American students to perform at that level. When I looked at their school's other scores, it was easy to see the problem. His White students' scores in reading, math, and science were 98% or above, while those of his Black students were only at 30%. "Before we get started," I said, "I just have to ask you this: How can two African American men do such a great job of educating White students and such a horrible job of educating Black students?" As you can imagine, the response was crickets.

Then I showed them our curriculum and the books we were using in sixth through eighth grade. The superintendent took a couple of African American history books with them, and he said he would present them to the board and see if they were serious about educating all their students. We never heard back from them. (I didn't mind that they didn't return the books. As I've often said, you can steal *some* things from me, and I'll tear your head off, but if you steal one of my books, I'll congratulate you.)

My Calling

If you ask me what I was put on this earth to do, this is it. I'm living my dream. Some days, I'm tired as hell, but I can honestly say that there's not a single day that I'm not as excited to come to school as I was when we began. I eat, breathe, and live the school, but it's never "work." The school is a community, it's a family, and we're changing lives, families, communities, and the world. It's a wonderful feeling.

Robert Muhammad

When I met David Nowlin in 1993, he was already talking about the failure of traditional public schools to educate and connect with African American, Latino, and students from low-income families. The data said it all, no matter what standardized test results you looked at: The scores of African Americans were always at the bottom of the range, with those of Latinos only slightly higher.

Why could Black children sit in the same classroom as White children year after year and continue to get much lower scores? Either African Americans and Latinos were pre-disposed to learning problems, or there was something very wrong with the curriculum and the environment in which it was being delivered. The curriculum and environment had to be to blame, and we needed to do something about them.

We tossed around ideas for meaningful change and concluded that the solution was not painting picket signs, and it was not going down to the school board and speaking out. Instead of focusing on what traditional public schools were *not* doing, we needed to show what *to* do. We needed to put a clean glass up next to the dirty one.

David had a dream to ensure that vulnerable populations, particularly African Americans, would have access to an education that would make them more productive citizens of the world. Five years later, he had the opportunity to begin to realize that dream, in a humble little house on Rosewood in East Austin. In those early days, we would have to keep checking our bank account for the arrival of Texas Education Agency allotment and our ability to make our ends meet.

I wouldn't become an employee of Texas Empowerment Academy (TxEA) for another 4 years. But I shared in those opening discussions. I also joined David as he went door to door in the local housing project, trying to persuade parents that TxEA could do for their children what traditional public schools had not done for them.

One of the many benefits that TxEA brings to students is a limited class size. Our maximum number of students in any class is 22, but our average is 16, compared with 30 to 40 students in a traditional public school class. With smaller classes, teachers are able to form relationships not only with the students, but also with the parents.

It's easier to be effective with a student when you have the support of their parents, but as David wrote, we don't ask more than that they get the child to school. Because we have the kids for up to 10 hours a day, 188 days a year plus our summer program, we're responsible for their success. One of our slogans is, "We make it hard to fail," and we mean it.

More Ways We Measure Our Success

The scores of African American and Latino students and students in general have increased by 20 to30% or more in their 1st year at TxEA. We've also seen that if a student stayed with us for at least 2 years, not only would they pass the test that they had been failing for so many years, but they would score above 80%.

We figured that if we could get students at a younger age, we could have a greater level of success with them, so we sought and received approval from the Texas Education Agency to add grades K through 4. With further expansion through the 12th grade, we've seen our first students graduated—some of them 2 to 4 years early and many about to become first-generation college students.

There's no scarcity of success stories around here. Here's one of my favorites:

A student came to us from a special education program in the Austin Independent School District. For the meeting with the diagnosticians in our special-ed department, the parents brought paperwork from doctors saying the student would never be able to read above a fifth-grade level—and he was coming to us *in* the fifth grade! They were telling us, the administrators in his new school, that there was *nothing* we could do with this child that could advance him!

David wasn't listening. Being the optimistic person he is, he said, "Well, I'm not a doctor; I don't have all of these degrees. The only thing I can tell you is to leave him with us, and we'll do our best to move him forward." We purchased resources, including software, that would help that young man increase his reading level. For 2 years, we would literally have to go find him after school to make him spend 40 minutes working on his lessons.

But after those 2 years, for the final 2 years he was with us, we no longer needed to go looking for him. He finally understood the value of what we were doing for him and could sense the scope of his progress. He learned how to work with his disability, and when he left us to go to Pflugerville High School (TxEA stopped at the ninth grade at the time), the school took him out of special education because he was in the top 20% of his class there. They had seen the paperwork we had received 4 years before, and they wanted to know what we had done to get the young man at his current reading level.

As we told them, there are no magic tricks to this thing called education. We simply pinpointed where he was having difficulty, showed him how to work with and around it, and encouraged him every step of the way. That young man went on to graduate from both high school and college. He's now back at TxEA teaching math. That's the power of what we do for our students.

I can also testify to what TxEA can do for them with a story about my own family: My children graduated from high school at 14 or 15 years old, with enough college hours to skip the first 2 years of college. They went on to graduate from college as teens. As we often say around here, "At TxEA, your age does not determine your altitude." What actually determines altitude and achievement is a student's ability to grasp the content. We put all our resources into supporting that ability.

We've had students who have gone on to become educators, entrepreneurs, politicians, and in one case, a nuclear engineer. But we also had one who went on to prison. He wrote us that he would not be in his current position if he had applied what we taught him and heeded our warnings. He also wrote that he intended to use all we taught him to ensure that, after his release, he would never go back behind bars.

Safety, Not Fear

People have visited us who want to tap into our expertise on anything from how to be a band director to how to put together a good STEM or STEAM program. But so far, we've heard from only a handful of administrators with a goal of cloning our overall successes. One planned to start a charter school in the Austin–Pflugerville area. She brought along someone from a national management company that had been charged with turning around some public schools in Gary, Indiana.

David and I also accepted their invitation to tour one of the Indiana high schools.

To enter the school, we had to walk through metal detectors and past security guards. When we were in the hallway and the bell rang for students to change classes, our hosts urged us to step back against the walls—to protect ourselves from the students! That advice spoke volumes about why the schools were in trouble. Of course, David and I refused to back off; we intended to get to know the students, and we did. We could have done a lot for them.

After attending TxEA, my daughter attended a local public high school and experienced a huge difference between the two environments. She referred to the high school setting as "relaxed" (and not in a good way) and "wild"—from kids making out in public to using illegal drugs to fighting and other things that she and every other TxEA student has never seen on our campuses.

Loving Our Students

For TxEA educators, the school bell doesn't inspire fear, and it doesn't tell them when to go home. Our bell signals an opportunity for them to tutor students for 2 or 3 more hours. Even though our pay is competitive with the surrounding districts, our teachers work for much more than the money. To be successful and to remain at TxEA, they're *required* to love what they do and the students for whom they do it. That's why you'll see teachers working with students here in the morning before classes start, in the afternoon and evening after they end, and even on Saturdays, depending on where we are in the year and what we need to prepare for.

You'll see them not only teaching but also leading extracurricular activities. With some students who are harder to reach, we push the arts—visual arts, music and band, dance, theater, and martial arts. (We're serious about getting the academic work done, but we also allow time for kids to be kids, to express themselves, and to have fun. Also, every other week or so we suspend academic classes and focus on the human side of our students.

We choose a subject that may range from career choice and time management to hygiene or life skills in general, and staff members or sometimes outside experts develop and present the curriculum.)

It's not as though it's easy to find such educators. A person can do everything right on the way in—submit a glowing resume and nail the interview and the background check. But it's not until we see people start working with the children or handle a difficulty with a parent that we know if they'll measure up. It's not until a child shuts down, and the teacher is either capable of turning the lightbulb back on in that child's head or not that we know whether that teacher is going to work out. We train our teachers, but we've never seen a higher education institution that can instill what makes a teacher successful at TxEA. They have to be born with it.

One opportunity to observe whether they're born with it is our summer program. It allows teachers—college interns and veterans alike—to hone their abilities, and it allows us to assess them.

I didn't know I would love working at TxEA. When David began the school, I was the first person he tried to bring on board, but I told him no. My own four children needed my attention, and I was finishing college. But I volunteered at TxEA for a while, and I enjoyed it, so when I needed a job, I knew where to go. In my 19 years here, I've done just about everything: I help out with administration, including recruiting and conflict resolution, I've run the after-school program, and I've worked as a janitor. Recently, when the art teacher left, I used my art education background to take her place.

At some point, after working with the children, parents, and school board, I realized this is where I'm supposed to be and what I'm supposed to be doing. The place can certainly be stressful, but it's not just a job for me. It feeds my *soul*. (It also feeds my children's souls. All four of them have matriculated through TxEA, and they all have a bright future.)

Every person here loves our students and what we do, but no one more than David Nowlin. He has dedicated his life to doing everything he can for the students and the families who come through here.

More About Our Impact on the Community

We always wanted to ensure that TxEA would be even more than a first-rate educational institution. It would also be a community resource. Due in large part to the fundraising of our colleague, Llyas Salahud-din, we were able to provide rent money to families that fell on hard times during the pandemic. Over the years, we've also offered free classes that include GED courses and parenting. The classes are open to anyone, even people who don't have students at TxEA.

Our relationship with the Black community is strong, and we support others who do in their fields what we're doing in ours. For example, we place all our advertising with a local community-based radio station (KAZI 88.7FM) and two African American newspapers (*NOKOA* and *The Villager*) in the Austin area. We want to support others who do in their fields what we're doing in ours.

We're in discussions with our collaborators at Huston-Tillotson University, our local HBCU (historically Black college and university), to create a high school in their name using our model. We would train their students to teach and open a successful institution, while giving us both a greater footprint in the community.

Our 10-year vision also includes expanding our reach beyond Austin in our quest to provide an exceptional education to every student. We plan to duplicate our program in every major city in Texas and possibly even many in other states, producing many more students who are equipped to confront anti-Black racism.

Llyas Salahud-din

You might say that my background destined me to work at TxEA. I spent 15 years in the foster care system—one of 53 boys raised by my foster mother, Miss Anita Flores. Watching her care for us inspired me, as I got older, to want to pay those gifts forward in my community.

Giving back became part of my DNA, so even as an undergraduate, I did volunteer work. I didn't know then that I would become a professional fundraiser, but my eventual career was undoubtedly influenced by the supporters of the well-run foster organization who donated their time, money, and resources to my foster brothers and me.

What also influenced my career choice was unexpected opportunities, starting with this one. My class needed to raise money to go on a leadership trip. Our professor gave us a list of people to ask, but no one else in the group was willing to do it. I told my classmates, "You set up the meetings. I'll do the asking."

I saw I had a knack for the job when I raised the $12,000 that we needed for the trip.

Later, fate intervened again, during an internship with an Indigenous culture who live near the Colombia–Panama border. When I wondered aloud where the money came from for our projects, my director said, "We have to raise it." She gave me a book about fundraising. When you're living with an Indigenous culture, time goes by very slowly with little to fill it. By the third time I read the book, I realized that I could make a profession out of my "knack."

Back in the States, on my second internship, I started to see how. That was the year the United Way opened its fundraising campaign to college students, and I was fortunate enough to be one of them. Working with retired executives was my introduction to corporate fundraising. I got to soak up all the resources, expertise, and encouragement of these experts. Not only did we raise $44 million for United Way, but these relationships also guided me to my first jobs.

Before I found my way to TxEA, I had always worked for White-led philanthropic organizations. There are few African American philanthropic organizations. And although I lived in Austin, I didn't know about TxEA until I visited a friend there who was on staff. I saw all these Black kids walking around (in the church the school rented at the time) and became interested in the institution's mission.

My friend introduced me to David Nowlin, and I told him what I do and asked if I could help. He said, almost jokingly, "Yeah, we could use some extra funds around here." That brief conversation began my relationship with TxEA, which had never had a fundraiser before. They had relied on federal and state money and doing more with less. I raised more than $160,000 as a hybrid volunteer/consultant. I loved the mission so much that I decided to go all in for TxEA. When I went full time, I raised more than $1 million in 1 year. Now they could do more with more. As David often says, "The stars aligned."

A Win-Win Situation

They aligned for me, too. I'm fulfilling my wish to use my professional expertise to give back to the community and address the financial issues that face a lot of Black-led organizations—having access to funding, being able to scale, and spanning the digital divide.

For example, take that digital divide: The average Black kid doesn't have the technological resources in their home that the average White kid does. But our students aren't average: Our extra funding ensured that the children and families in the TxEA community had the technological resources they needed to stay connected to the school and their education throughout the pandemic.

The stars also aligned for me in another way: As a foster kid, I did not have much exposure to the Black community, and I always yearned to connect with it. Now I'm learning a lot about the history and culture right along with the students. I've had to start small because I'm playing catch-up, there's so much to learn, and it's so rich and beautiful. This learning stimulates my mind and emotions to such an extent that I have to wonder how it would have affected me if I had been exposed to it in my early years. Even now, though, it has been life-changing for me.

Where We Came From

TxEA has been teaching Black history and culture throughout its more than 20 years. We know that Black history is American history. There's a psychological and emotional benefit—a deep sense of self-confidence and self-worth—when Black people can see themselves in their country's story and draw inspiration from the many examples of excellence and achievement. And there's motivating power to be drawn from learning about destructive issues of policy that have been passed down over generations.

The greatest challenges in our community stem from racial misunderstanding. It's horrifying that it took a modern-day lynching to awaken America to the importance of equity and the historical mistreatment of Black America. But since the murder of George Floyd, which reinvigorated the Black Lives Matter movement, more people understand the value of learning about them. When people put in the time to learn the facts, they're able to have a conversation with less bias and stereotyping creeping in. They're better able to *empathize*.

Yet in most schools, this teaching has been left out of the classroom. (In fact, it was not until 2020 that the Texas Board of Education approved an African American studies course as an elective in high schools. At TxEA, it's mandatory.)

Our students are trained to be ambassadors of understanding about Black history. Both by their words and their example, they're capable of changing the mind-set of anyone who believes in any form of stereotype or has an implicit bias about Black youth and education. Not only does the school itself prove what you can accomplish when you place students in the right environment for learning, but it also proves the value of teaching Black history to all students.

I'm not saying that studying Black history and culture is a silver bullet, but it is undeniably powerful. This knowledge benefits students socially and emotionally, not only academically. Students who understand the truth about their history from a young age are better equipped to make their own decisions as they get older. Even in the brief time I've been at TxEA, I've witnessed that our youth know who they are, where they come from, and what they can achieve are more likely to succeed. If we all learned about all of history, including Black history, in a more comprehensive way, we would all have better communities and a better nation.

More Awareness Equals More Support

By bringing national attention to racial disparities, George Floyd and the Black Lives Matter movement have helped TxEA to attract resources, and we needed the help. When I worked for White-led organizations, it was so much easier to raise money. We've done well, but we can do better, and we've begun to since the summer of 2020.

Because there are so few Black-led philanthropic organizations, the majority of our private support has come from White-led foundations. Notable exceptions include our partnerships with three organizations:

- The Austin Area Urban League provides various engagement opportunities for our students and their families.
- Austin Community College works with us on the Dual Enrollment Program, which gives our students the opportunity to earn free college credit—and a savings of $28,000 on average—before they graduate from high school.
- 100 Black Men of Austin, the local chapter of a national initiative that mentors the health, wellness, and academics of Black youth, participates in community activities, including the Stock Market Game, which, every Saturday, engages 22 kids about this valuable financial skill.

What excites all our supporters is that we're addressing a need. Locally and nationally, Black youth are behind academically; they have the highest dropout and expulsion rates, and the lowest rate of graduation. This negative narrative reinforces negative stereotypes.

But when these organizations look at our school, they see instead a narrative of achievement—our positive outcomes show that if a child receives appropriate stimulation, they can be successful.

Making Our Own History

To my knowledge, TxEA will be the first Black-led organization to construct its own building to better serve Black youth and education. That type of investment has not been made in the Black community for more than 140 years, when Huston-Tillotson University was built. My role is to help raise enough funding to bring the new campus to fruition and allow us to serve more students in East Austin.

We're also making history with all we're doing both inside and outside of the class-rooms. As you've seen in this chapter, those contributions far exceed academics. TxEA stimulates their hearts, not only their minds. We make sure they feel supported and loved.

The students, the leadership, and every staff member wear a uniform. Looking in sync with everyone else on campus is both discipline for the kids, and it communicates our sense of community. At the same time, those uniforms save families a lot of money over the years. Although students dress the same, they're definitely not required to sound the same. As you've seen elsewhere in this chapter, we encourage them to be themselves, express themselves, and think for themselves.

As David wrote, we welcome diversity and serve any student who comes through our doors. This include Latino kids, White kids, as well as Arabs and Native Americans. Every one of our students—of any demographic—has a unique and beautiful story. Some of them have faced challenges in their lives, but they've learned by example the value of sticking together, working hard, and taking advantage of the opportunities TxEA provides. The students work hard because they see everyone working hard around them, from the staff to the administrators.

They also work hard because they know we care about them. Having people who push, love, and praise them every day fuels their drive to personal excellence.

Now they're reaping the benefits of going to college and looking forward to a meaningful future. We've given them a clear pathway to get there.

A Well-Rounded Education

We supplement our academic curriculum (math, science, history, language arts), and "Career in Tech" and arts programs with social engagement. For example, we provide the kids with opportunities to get together and talk about what's going on in their life, in the community, or at home. We also make mentors available. (I'm one of them.) And we get off campus for activities—rope climbing, canoeing, science fairs, robotics, cooking and etiquette classes, competitive outdoor games, and more—that help students build relationships among themselves and with their teachers as they learn skills.

"Hidden jewel in Austin" is how I describe TxEA: "hidden" because I found it by chance, and "jewel" because if you ever tour the campus, you walk away with an emotional high. You see kids smiling and laughing because they feel comfortable and safe. They quickly learn that safety is inherent in looking after each other, and it's mandatory: No matter what, if a child does not feel safe, if they don't feel that they're in a welcoming environment, they can't learn. Here, they feel safe, they *are* safe, and they *learn*.

Nowhere will students receive a better academic education than at TxEA, but it's really the relationship aspect of what we do that's our secret sauce. We nurture students as soon as they step foot on campus. Anytime we bring in a student from a high school, until they absorb our ways, we see a night-and-day difference in how they carry themselves. As you've read, at TxEA, there has not been one fight on campus in its entire history. If one even began to brew, it couldn't go anywhere because the kids are empowered to intervene before the teachers can. They monitor *themselves* and understand the importance of communicating and holding themselves and each other accountable.

I stay visible in the community, leveraging my relationships and working hard to bring our jewel out of hiding. My goal is to raise the school's profile, along with money, bringing more awareness to the good work we're doing. Everything I do is to ensure that students will have access to resources that will benefit them in the short and long term. It feels no less than divine that this work touches all 377 students, and in the next 2 years, more than twice that number as we scale. I'm grateful that I have an opportunity and the ability to leave a legacy for others, as Miss Flores did for me.

As we write this chapter, TxEA's first graduation is 4 months away, but I already can tell you this: It will be an extremely proud and emotional experience for the whole school. I don't know how David will be able to get a word out during his speech.

That pride could not be more justified because of what TxEA has proven throughout its history: If you provide the proper environment, resources, and people to educate students—and if you help them understand who they are and where they came from—you can level the playing field.

Reference

Jalissa. (2018, May 10). The diversity gap in children's book publishing, 2018. *The Open Book Blog*. https://blog.leeandlow.com/2018/05/10/the-diversity-gap-in-childrens-book-publishing-2018/

CHAPTER ELEVEN

Let the Òrìṣà Speak

Traditional Healing for Contemporary Times

Ifetayo I. Ojelade

Arguably one of the biggest artists of our times, Beyoncé makes a bold move in her song *Black Parade* by invoking the names of Yorùbá goddesses. She describes herself as possessing Ọ̀ṣun energy and her sister that of Yemọja. The 2020 hit HBO series *LoveCraft Country* also offers a bold proclamation by situating a god-like image ("I am") as a woman of African descent (Green et al., 2020). In Beyoncé's invocation, she communicates to a global audience that her reference point for aspects of the divine to emulate are embodied by an African woman. Such an assertion for an artist with a global audience is bold and courageous. Admittedly, Beyoncé is not the first artist to praise African divinities. Fictional character Ricky Ricardo of the *I Love Lucy* series belted out praises to the Òrìṣà (divinity) Babalúaiyé in his famous song *Babalù*. Other groups such as *Ibeyi*, *Orishas A Lo Cubano*, and a host of Latin American– and U.S.-based artists sing about the Òrìṣà. In fact, the Black arts movement of the 1960s was a breeding ground for artists to explore connections between their work and an aesthetic informed by African spirituality (Bracey et al., 2014).

Current times challenge us to expand beyond the artistic realm in order to examine how the Yorùbá-based system of Ifá is utilized for healing. Used either in conjunction with or independent of Western psychology, Ifá provides people of African ancestry with healing strategies to address race-related stress associated with living in a global system rooted in anti-Black racism and fueled by White supremacy. Grounded in a womanist worldview, this chapter uses Yorùbá ontology (metaphysical ways of being), to impart lessons for women as they navigate intersectional labyrinths of oppression to build psychological well-being. Consistent with the definition of womanism offered by Layli Maparyan (2006) in her foundational work, the *Womanist Reader*, this chapter is grounded in the every-day experiences and problem-solving methods used by women of African ancestry. The following stories highlight how Ifá can be used to address all forms of oppression while demonstrating our ongoing connection to nature. These stories are used as a metaphor for psychological concepts and are not like the rituals conducted by trained priests. Readers who need spiritual services should consult with a trustworthy priest who is initiated and trained. It is best to seek such services via a personal referral. Readers are cautioned against using services of individuals who advertise online or personally reach out to solicit you as a client. It is taboo in Ifá to proselytize, and most sacred ceremonies are in-person and private. Thus, online offerings are generally scams.

Yorùbá Ontology

As the largest African-based spiritual system practiced outside of its country of origin, Ifá and its Diasporic manifestations boast large constituencies throughout the Americas and the Caribbean (Abímbọ́lá, 2006; Fálolá & Childs, 2004; Olupona & Rey, 2008; Ọ̀jẹ̀làdé, et al., 2014). Given its global reach, the name of the spiritual practice changes in differing regions of the world to include Lucumi in Cuba, Santeria in Puerto Rico, Candomblé in Brazil, Umbanda in Uruguay, and Yorùbá in the United States. Devotees of the traditional aspects of Ifá use the term ìṣẹ̀ṣe to describe their practice. However, devotees of each manifestation of Ifá live in different countries. Thus, how one labels their practice, the characteristics attributed to the Òrìṣà, days of worship, and even the gender of some deities are specific to a particular group of practitioners. From a Western worldview, these differences may be dismissed as evidence of the primitive nature of the healing system. Instead, the dynamic nature of Ifá speaks to the fact that the people known today as the Yorùbá comprise several subgroups with differing dialects (K. Abimbola, 2006; Fálolá & Childs, 2004).

Ifá is an oral tradition passed down through meticulous study beginning in early childhood. In more recent years, information about the healing system has become available through written translations due to its popularity in the African diaspora. The scripture is referred to as the *Sacred Literary Corpus* and is comprised of 256 chapters called *odù*. Each odù has many verses known as ẹsẹ. Yorùbá ontology describes the odù as possessing all knowledge of the past, present, and future. Through a process of divination (spiritual contact with the divine), a priest accesses all 256 odù when conducting a reading with Ọ̀pẹ̀lẹ̀ or ikin and 17 odù during *Eérìndínlógún*, which uses cowrie shells. It is believed that the Òrìṣà speak, provide guidance, and instructions for healing through the odù.

Centering the focus of this chapter on female Òrìṣà provides women of African ancestry a resource for navigating intersectional patterns of oppression while also seeing themselves as a reflection of the divine. Differing from Western concepts of womanhood, in Ifá, the female Òrìṣà are described as possessing knowledge of all aspects of life. In addition, these divinities are described as business owners, mothers, warriors, leaders, wives, and the creators of banking and finance. Well known Òrìṣà include Ọ̀ṣun, Yemọja, Ọya, Ọbà, Odù, Ewa, and Ajé (Edward & Mason, 1998; Fálolá & Genova, 2005;; Olupona & Rey, 2008). Òrìṣà who are not as well known in the African diaspora include Aja, Ijamido, Idanre, Yemoó, Olosa, Ọ̀ṣunle, Otin, Òwò, and Òrònsèn (Badejo, 1996; Olajubu, 2004). This chapter presents two conceptual aspects of Ifá (*ìwà* and *orí*) in addition to stories of Ọ̀ṣun, Yemọja, Ọya, and Ọbà. While the author is a Western-trained psychologist and initiate in African American and ìṣẹ̀ṣe aspects of Ifá, this work is not designed to privilege one version of the system over the other. Instead, readers are encouraged to enjoy this work as an example of the dynamic flexibility inherent in the healing system and its global influence. It speaks to a strongly held belief of many practitioners that the Òrìṣà will never die. Instead, they are a source of guidance, healing, and protection.

Ìwà

Character is like smoke; it cannot be hidden for long. This African proverb reminds us that the true nature of one's character is always revealed to others. In the Yorùbá worldview, character is a foundational principle for ethical living (Afọlayán, 2013). It is seen as a determining factor as to whether a person has a successful or trouble-filled life. In this worldview, having wealth, status, or fame without good character is worthless. In fact, the progenitor of the Yorùbá people, Odùduwà is believed to be the creator of character. Thus, good character is foundational in Yorùbá ethical teachings and is considered indicative of being a worthwhile adult. Individuals who fail to demonstrate good character are seen as rejecting Olódùmarè (god) in both the living and ancestral realms. Thus, bad character follows you to the grave and has implications for whether you will be remembered as an ancestor.

Translated into English, *ìwà* is described as the essence of being, while *pèlè* means gentle. *Ìwà pèlè* is then translated to gentle or good character, while *ìwà burúkú* is bad character. In fact, good character is so important to the Yorùbá that it is equated to a female divinity whose close companion is Orí (inner spirit guide), whose father is Sùúrù (patience), and whose husband is Òrúnmìlà, the witness to your destiny (Ẹlẹ́rìí ìpín). Examining the concept of ìwà pèlè is useful for African-descended people globally. It allows us to reimagine a system of ethics that dismantles anti-Blackness in our relationships and centers authentic engagement built on mutual trust and accountability.

The odù Ogbè alara (i.e., Ogbè túrá) describes Ìwà as the beloved wife of Òrúnmìlà (Abímbọ́lá, 1975; Badejo, 2008; Ẹlẹ́bùibọn, 1994). The specifics of their relationship vary depending on the version of the odù read and the author's interpretation. However, it is generally believed that Ìwà agreed to marry Òrúnmìlà if he respected her boundaries. He is told that he cannot use Ìwà carelessly, force her to leave their home, or abuse her. Initially things go well but trouble soon occurs. Both Ìwà and Òrúnmìlà do inconsiderate things to each other. Òrúnmìlà responds to the conflict by being argumentative and abusive, so Ìwà decides to leave (some versions suggest that Òrúnmìlà kicked her out). Once she leaves, Òrúnmìlà immediately regrets his behavior. His life becomes miserable, his clients abandon him, and his finances are in ruin because he no longer has Ìwà in his life. He then travels to 16 different towns disguised in the ceremonial dress of the Egúngún (ancestral) masquerade, searching for his wife but never finds her. Òrúnmìlà finally discovers that Ìwà has returned to heaven and is living with her father Sùúrù. He attempts to convince her to return home, but she refuses. Ìwà decides that she will reside with Òrúnmìlà in spirit but will no longer be physically present. She warns him that if he wants happiness in the future, he must have good character and take care of his wife and children. Ìwà tells Ọ̀rúnmìlà that whatever he does to her will determine the quality of his life in the future.

Scholars often focus on Ọ̀rúnmìlà in the analysis of this story and the lesson he learns by mistreating, losing, and then going through difficulties finding Ìwà (Abímbọ́lá, 1975; Badejo, 2008; Ẹlẹ́bùibọn, 1994). It is also important for us to consider Ìwà herself as an example of ethical conduct. Prior to entering the marriage, Ìwà clearly outlined her boundaries for consenting to the relationship. In the marriage she was not perfect. However, Ìwà was unwilling to allow Ọ̀rúnmìlà to be abusive and violate her boundaries just because she had shortcomings. This story teaches us that good character includes setting boundaries and taking decisive action when an agreement is violated. Ìwà reminds women that all of us have a right to set boundaries despite our imperfections. Her actions show us that even in our relationships with powerful men, it is important to advocate for our position and leave when the situation becomes abusive.

This story is important because possessing ìwà pèlè is often limited to the idea of not harming others. However, good character also requires us to take decisive action when we are mistreated. Rather than forgiving the person and moving on as if the abuse never occurred, Ìwà teaches us to hold the person accountable, demand acknowledgement of the harm done, and require restitution and long-term behavioral change. Her actions do not promote forgiveness without justice and restitution. Ìwà's teachings can be applied when responding to the pattern of anti-Blackness, racist violence, and misogynoir that African-descended women experience globally. In the United States, this has recently manifested via legislation attacking voting rights, critical race theory, and other educational initiatives addressing systemic racism. Ìwà demonstrates that psychologically healthy responses to these and other racist and sexist attacks include proactively addressing the situation, not allowing the agenda of your oppressor to be a distraction, refraining from tolerating further abuse, demanding reparative justice, and lasting institutional change. The following activities are designed to assist you in creating a personal model of ethics.

ACTIVITIES

1. Create a collage that is a physical representation of the aspects of ìwà pèlè you are striving to uphold.

2. Journal prompts:

   a. How comfortable are you with setting boundaries with others?

   b. Make a list of people you need to set boundaries with.

   c. What were the first ethical lessons you received? How are those lessons relevant/irrelevant in your life today?

   d. What sources do you draw from to guide your personal system of ethics?

      i. *If none, which sources can you use for support? (e.g., religious and/or spiritual texts, 42 admonitions of Ma'at, the teachings of Ptah Hotep).*

  b. List the relationships you need to end because the other person does not respect your boundaries, has pushed you away, or is abusive.

3. Spend at least 5 minutes each day meditating on an aspect of good character you would like to cultivate.

Orí

Many authors have written about the importance of the head among the Yorùbá for humans, animals, and inanimate objects such as thunder (Abímbọ́lá, 1997; Abiodun, 1994; Afọlayán, 2013; Lawal, 1985; Òjẹ́làdé et al., 2011). Yorùbá ontology describes two types of heads. The physical head, *orí odé* and the spiritual one, *orí inú*. The Òrìṣà Ọbàtálá is believed to be the creator of the orí odé, while the spiritual being Àjàlà creates the orí inú. Similar to picking a destiny, each person chooses an orí inú (Orí for short), which becomes a personal divinity. The Yorùbá describe Orí as the most powerful divinity as it is personal and never abandons its owner (Abímbọ́lá, 1997). In turn, one's Orí chooses its ìwà (character), whether good or bad. Ultimately this combination represents your personality, character, and destiny (fate). Those who choose a good Orí are believed to be capable of making a bad destiny more tolerable. However, someone who chooses a bad Orí can destroy even the most advantageous destiny. There is no way to tell the type of Orí someone has chosen outside the process of divination. However, Yorùbá ontology teaches us that we can improve the outcome of our destiny by demonstrating ìwà pèlè. Thus, while your choice of Orí is fixed, ìwà is not. At each moment, we all have an opportunity to engage in ìwà pèlè and therefore improve our life experiences.

This verse in Ògúndá Méjí describes how Orí's commitment outweighs all other Òrìṣà. One day Ọ̀rúnmìlà gathered all the Òrìṣà and asked which of them would be able to travel overseas with their devotee and not abandon the person. Ṣàngó was the first to suggest that he could easily accomplish the task. The other Òrìṣà asked Ṣàngó what would happen if he passed his father's hometown during the journey. Ṣàngó responded by stating that he would stop and visit his father. The Òrìṣà pointed out that his actions would cause him to abandon his devotee. Thus, they decided that Ṣàngó was not up to the task. Ọya spoke up next, believing that she could accompany her devotee with success. However, when asked about arriving at the town of her father, Ọya provided a similar response as Ṣàngó. One by one, the Òrìṣà's Ọbàtálá, Èṣù, Ògún, Ọ̀ṣun, and Ọ̀rúnmìlà bragged of their ability to complete the task. In turn, each acknowledged a willingness to abandon their devotee when arriving at their father's hometown. In the end, Ọ̀rúnmìlà remined the Òrìṣà that only Orí could accomplish this task without abandoning the devotee. Wándé Abímbọ́lá (1997) provides the following translation from an excerpt of an ẹsẹ (verse) of Ògúndá Méjí:

It is Orí alone who can accompany a devotee to any place without turning back.

If I have money,

It is my Orí I will praise.

My Orí, it is you.

If I have children on earth,

It is my Orí to whom I will give the praise.

My Orí, it is you.

All good things I have on earth,

It is Orí I will praise

My Orí, it is you.

The sociopolitical importance of the head and the inappropriateness of touching a woman's hair is well documented throughout the African diaspora (Brown, 2018; Mbil-ishaka, 2018, 2020;; Prince, 2009). While the head may not be perceived universally as a divinity, sayings within the African American community such as "Common sense ain't common" and "A hard head makes a soft behind," suggest that there is value placed on using the metaphorical head appropriately. Readers in other countries are likely to identify similar sayings, pointing to the importance of using one's head wisely. These sayings suggest that the head has a utility beyond the physical structure and can improve your life circumstances if used correctly.

Let us further consider the Orí inú by examining the way in which the Yorùbá make offerings to it. While there are rituals that take place with a separate Orí icon, the naval of the devotee is also ritualistically fed, suggesting that Orí is also a metaphor for intu-ition. This connection of Orí inú through the naval also symbolizes an ancestral bond to our foremothers via the umbilical cord. In other words, you were connected to your mother, as she was connected to hers, and so on. Thus, caring for your Orí also means cultivating your intuition, learning to trust yourself, and strengthening the bonds with your ancestral guides. Trusting your intuition and remaining connected to your ancestors is critical for navigating anti-Blackness. These are also the areas of your life that are most under attack and devalued.

Women of African ancestry learn early in life to doubt their intuition, question their judgment, and nurture self-doubt. While you may receive affirming messages at home, the external world suggests that you are not valued and your lived experiences are not real. Anti-Blackness nurtures toxic levels of insecurity in women, teaching you to doubt your intuition and deny any connection to your ancestral mothers. However, the concept of Orí offers a starting point for healing as you begin to embrace the fact that your intu-ition is real, tangible, and providing you guidance throughout your life. It also serves as a reminder that you have a physical (via the umbilical cord) and spiritual connection to your ancestors. The activities that follow are designed to help you strengthen your connections with your intuition and ancestors.

ACTIVITIES

1. Cultivating intuition. Spend at least 5 minutes each day journaling about times when you followed/ignored your intuition and the outcome.

2. Ancestral connections. Write down the names of your personal ancestors and their characteristics that you desire to have in your life.

   a. Spend time learning the stories of these ancestors, including their success and failures.

   b. Identify specific activities of remembrance for these ancestors. This can include hanging pictures, cooking a favorite meal, sharing stories with family members, pouring libation, and/or creating a sacred meditation space using pictures, names, and other memorabilia for these ancestors.

3. Journal prompts:

   a. How can I tell the difference between my intuition and thoughts?

   b. How can I tell the difference between my fear/insecurities and my intuition?

   c. Are there times when I am blaming intuition for not moving forward on something when it is really my self-doubt?

   d. How does knowing about your family benefit you psychologically?

   e. What strengths have been passed down in your family?

   f. What keeps you from researching your family history (if applicable)?

   g. What spiritual role do the ancestors play in your life?

4. Fast from sugar, alcohol, caffeine, drugs, and other addictive substances for 1 week. Notice whether there are any changes to your ability to discern your intuition from fear and/or thoughts.

Òṣun

Perhaps the most well-known of all female Òrìṣà is the Goddess Òṣun. Known as the only female to be among the 17 Ìrúnmọlẹ̀ (heavenly sent Òrìṣà) charged with creating the earth, Òṣun is often written about in scholarly and commercial literature. This Òrìṣà's full title is Òṣun Ṣẹ̀ẹ̀gẹ̀sí Olóòyà-iyùn, meaning Òṣun *the owner of the flawless, perfectly carved, beaded comb*. Badejo (1996) suggests that Òṣun's role within the Òrìṣà pantheon is equivalent to that of the Asante Queenmother. In this vein, Òṣun is hailed for her political, literary, historical, and social prowess (Badejo, 1996, 2008). Known as the goddess of love, fertility, wealth, and beauty, Òṣun is the giver of children, to whom many women pray. Among Ifá devotees, Òṣun's image is praised as symbolic of leadership, entrepreneurship, healing, and the warrior female spirit. Òṣun is the ultimate symbol of womanism, modeling both the independence and interdependence of women.

The odù Ọṣẹ Túrá describes Ọṣun's role in relationship to the other male Òrìṣà. The only woman among a group of male deities charged with creating the earth, Ọṣun was initially excluded from the creation process by her fellow male Òrìṣà. Without engaging in direct conflict, Ọṣun withheld her womanly powers, preventing the prosperity of the male Òrìṣà's creation (Badejo, 1996, 2008). Fallow crops and barren women prompted the male Òrìṣà to ask Olódùmarè (the owner of heaven, e.g., god) for assistance. Olódùmarè informed them that their exclusion of Ọṣun was the source of their troubles. The male Òrìṣà started to pay homage to Ọṣun, who later provided the power they needed for the earth to prosper. From that point forward, the male Òrìṣà understood that they required Ọṣun's support to begin any new project. This story is significant since it highlights the role of women in the planning, execution, and success of any project. Although there were 16 male Òrìṣà present, the project did not flourish without the assistance of the one female deity.

This story outlines the importance of women in Yorùbá ontology, describing them as foundational in the creation of human existence. It is in sharp contrast to a Western worldview that privileges White, male, Judeo-Christian thinking in all aspects of human existence. Ọṣun reminds women to withhold their talents when disrespected or ignored in the spaces they occupy with others. Women of African ancestry are often surrounded by people who are dismissive of their gifts, ignore their existence, attempt to diminish their power, or steal their work. In Ọṣẹ Túrá, Ọṣun does not struggle with the male Òrìṣà for power or acknowledgment. Instead, she does not provide her aṣẹ (power), thus bringing the project to a halt until they respect her gifts. Women of African ancestry can follow Ọṣun's example when faced with similar situations of disrespect. We are often expected to overlook such situations for the good of the team. However, Ọṣun teaches us that no matter how significant the project, we should never use our talents for the benefit of those who do not respect us.

In the Eérìndínlógún divination system that is comprised of 17 chapters, the odù Ọṣẹ describes Ọṣun as a warrior for the king (Badejo, 1996; Bascom, 1993). The women of a town go into seclusion after growing tired of the men and their problematic behaviors. Facing extinction due to their refusal to return, the king calls on the Òrìṣà for assistance. The male Òrìṣàs Ṣàngó, Ṣọpọnná, Egúngún, and Ògún try to conquer the women and fail. They initially dismiss the idea of sending female Òrìṣà to attack the town but later agree, seeing no other option. Ọya volunteers first but is quickly defeated by the women. Ọṣun volunteers to try next. Prior to departing, she seeks divination and is told to make an offering to ensure her success. She is also advised to play a calabash and sing while heading to town. Ọṣun heeds the advice and sings a song letting the women know that she has not come to fight but is inviting them to a party. The women are initially skeptical but eventually join Ọṣun as she leads them back to the men singing and dancing. As a result of Ọṣun's victory, the women became the confidants and wives of the king, holding more power than their male counterparts.

Ọṣun is providing an example for women regarding how to display strength and leadership without being destructive. The male Òrìṣàs Ṣàngó, Ṣọpọnná, Egúngún, and Ògún, are symbolic of fire, disease, death, and war, which are all possibilities when conflict arises.

Here, Ọ̀ṣun represents firm leadership, nurturing, and the joy that can occur even during a conflict. The concept of finding Black joy despite oppressive circumstances is critical for the emotional well-being of African-descended women. Historically we see this theme in the narratives of enslaved African women who discuss their ability to find love, maintain family bonds, nurture friendships, and foster hope without being destructive (Keckley, 1865; Jacobs, 1861). Whether it be through reading these narratives or the example of Ọ̀sun, use the stories as a reminder to find joy even in the midst of a battle. Dealing with the pervasiveness of anti-Black racism is exhausting. The system of White supremacy is designed to ensure that you are fatigued, ignore your own health, and have little time for joy. Thus, neglecting your well-being and relationships becomes a tool in service of White supremacy. By contrast, intentionally engaging Black joy and self-care is an act of political resistance. The following activities will help you remember the things in life that bring you joy.

ACTIVITIES

1. Make a physical or electronic memory book of all the things that bring you joy. A social media image-sharing site is ideal for this activity.

2. Journal prompts:

   a. Describe how you handle conflict.

      i. *What is the best part of how you respond to conflict?*

      ii. *What are the things you want to change about how you respond to others?*

   c. How do you respond when other people underestimate your abilities?

   d. Are there areas of your life that you use strength as an unhealthy coping mechanism to manage race-related stress?

   e. What does Black joy mean to you?

   f. What causes you to feel inspired?

   g. What are your hobbies?

3. A cleansing bath

   a. Run a bath and add essential oils or herbs that are sacred to Osun such as chamomile, lotus, myrrh, or Echinacea (Awojoodu & Baran, 2009).

   b. Sit in the bath and meditate.

   c. Visualize Ọ̀sun bringing you the characteristics you need as you wash.

   d. Journal when you are done.

Yemọja

Water has no enemies and makes no friends, although it settles all disputes. This adaptation of a Yorùbá proverb helps us understand the power of water in all aspects of our lives and the aṣẹ of Yemọja. Many suggest that she, rather than Ọ̀ṣun, is the most well-known Òrìṣà in the world. Settling such a dispute can be left to the devotees of these river goddesses. Yemọja, meaning the mother of children who are fish, derives her name by combining the Yorùbá words *yeye* (mother) ọmọ (children), and *eja* (fish). She originates from Abeokuta, Nigeria, and is associated with the Ògún river, which flows south into the Lagos Lagoon and finally spills out into the Atlantic Ocean (Otero & Fálolá, 2013). Her diasporic exportation resulted in Yemọja being associated with the top layer of the ocean in most of the Western world. Yemọja is known by many names, including Yemayá, Yemanjá, and Imanjá, to name a few.

The characteristics of Yemọja vary by region. However, she is considered to have a close connection to the descendants of those who endured the transatlantic trade in human beings. Yemọja is symbolic of motherhood, protection, and our emotional depths. Her historic iconography is that of an African mermaid with two long breasts that nurture both pregnant women and children. Water is a metaphor for her power to give life, be mysterious, provide healing, and have depth. This is all while being the ideal role model for resistance, resilience, and strength.

Many countries hold annual festivals in honor of this Òrìṣà. Cubans celebrate the Our Lady of Regla Festival as a syncretized blend of this Òrìṣà and Catholicism. People also flock to the *Festa de Yemanjá* in Salvador, Brazil, to celebrate this water goddess. Devotees in Uruguay also hold an annual *Yemanjá* Day. In fact, a quick Google search yields hotels, jewelry, statues, and other merchandise bearing diasporic versions of this Òrìṣà's name and likeness. There is only one problem: Given the cultural and commercial popularity of Yemọja, many of these images feature a woman with distinct European features and skin tone. While some merchants like a hotel in Nicaragua bearing the Òrìṣà's name acknowledge her African origins, others simply ignore this fact. Even a Wikipedia entry outlining the African origins of the goddess displays a sculpture from the Nigerian National Art Gallery with distinctly European features. Overall, diasporic depictions of Yemọja are a metaphor for the ways in which the contributions of Black women are often ignored, co-opted, or flat out stolen for the benefit, comfort, and profit of the White gaze. This is particularly significant since Yemọja is a symbol of the divine. Thus, any action to alter her features is tantamount to the anti-Black violence that seeks to erase women of African descent as global contributors to history, culture, and theology.

The psychological implications of this anti-Black cultural theft are clear. If we are unable to see ourselves in the image of god, we will elevate others as sacred while denigrating ourselves as profane. However, like the water she represents, Yemọja teaches us to resist attempts at diminishing our power or place in global history. This includes unapologetically reclaiming the image of Yemọja as a mermaid with distinctly African features in every space that she is worshiped. To accomplish this, we must engage in a mental shift to see ourselves as an embodiment of the divine. Yemọja provides us this opportunity as an ancient reminder of when god was an African woman.

ACTIVITIES

1. Draw a picture or create a sculpture, painting, or other artwork that symbolizes your image of god and include gender, skin color, body type, and hair.

2. Journal prompts:

   a. What feelings come up for you when thinking about god being a woman?

   b. What feelings are invoked for you by seeing god written in lower-case letters?

   c. How is your image of god the same or different from what you were taught growing up?

   d. Are there aspects of anti-Blackness that influence your perception of what god can look like?

3. Visit the ocean (if you are in Nigeria, go to the Ògún river).

   a. Take time to walk on the beach and get in the water.

   b. Sit and meditate.

   c. Visualize Yemọja bringing you the characteristics you need as the waves draw near. Consciously release any negative thoughts and limitations that do not serve your highest good. Allow those things to be swept away by the ocean.

   d. Journal when you are done.

Ọya

Known as a warrior goddess, Ọya is the embodiment of wind, storms, and thunder. She is a market woman, giver of wealth, protection, and children to her devotees. Indigenous to the Yorùbá town of Ira, this Òrìṣà's full name is Ọya Akanbi (Olajubu, 2004). Today, the river Niger bears her name. As the wife of Ṣàngó, scholars debate whether she was more favored by him than Òṣun (Barber, 1990; Gleason, 2000). Regardless, Ọya is known as Ṣàngó's loyal wife, using her thunder to announce the arrival of her husband's lightening. The sacred *Odù Ifá Literary Corpus* also points to Ọya as being married to Ògún and connects her intimately to the society comprised of ancestral priests (Gleason, 2000). Yorùbá ontology indicates that the origins of Ọya begin in the animal kingdom (Olusola, 2005). Known as the mother to all buffalo, the following story illustrates the connection between this sacred animal and the beginnings of Ọya worship.

One day while hunting, Ògún watched a buffalo approach a termite's nest. He was astonished to see that the buffalo removed its skin and turned into a beautiful woman. The buffalo then put the skin into the nest and walked away. Ògún decided to take the skin and wait until the woman returned. As expected, Ọya could not find her skin since it was now in Ogun's possession. The hunter appeared and offered to show Ọya the hiding place of the skin if she agreed to be his wife. After much persuasion, Ọya agreed to the marriage if Ògún promised to keep her secret from others. The couple had three children and lived together for many years. Throughout this time, Ògún's senior wife became more curious about Ọya's true identity. She frequently asked her husband for information but was always disappointed by his response. Finally, the senior wife was able to manipulate Ògún into revealing Ọya's secret. Realizing his betrayal of Ọya, Ògún swore this wife to secrecy.

One day, Ògún and his son went to the family farm and a quarrel broke out between the two wives at home. The senior wife responded by revealing her knowledge of Ọya's secret and disclosing the hiding place of the magical buffalo skin. Ọya immediately retrieved it, transforming herself and her two remaining children into buffalos. The three left the family compound and went to confront Ògún. Initially, he prepared to defend himself and their son but recognized Ọya as the attacker. Ògún realized that his betrayal had been revealed and a great battle ensued. The buffalo was victorious over Ògún, but Ọya's son was spared from her wrath. This son was unable to turn into a buffalo because his father had used special medicine on him. However, Ọya told her son that he and his descendants must worship her from that point forward. To this day, Ọya worshippers use the buffalo horn as a symbolic representation of this deity (Olusola, 2005).

The story of Ọya demonstrates a womanist worldview that highlights the connections between spirituality, the environment, and women of African descent. Ọya's experience of being forced into a sexual relationship by a male using coercion to assert his privilege is familiar for women of African ancestry. Global systems of misogynoir devalue the beauty, manipulate the reproduction, and attempt to control our intimate relationships. Historically, our foremothers endured this through the indignities of enslavement and forced reproduction and marriage. Currently, this is enacted via reproductive injustice, unsolicited commentary on how we construct our families, and domestic and sexual violence.

In this story, Ọya reminds us to continue fighting injustice no matter who is the opponent. As the Òrìṣà of war and symbol of justice, male privilege, and dominance, Ògún appears unbeatable. However, Ọya takes him on in battle and wins. She represents the ability to use our aṣẹ (power) to stand up against powerful systems of injustice and win. As we seek to dismantle and reconstruct criminal justice, education, policing, health care, housing, and other institutional systems rooted in White supremacy, Ọya provides us a reminder that we already possess the psychological tools for our success.

Ọya is also symbolic of our power to transform ourselves and larger institutional systems when we remain connected to the environment. As a buffalo who transforms into a woman, she highlights this bond. In this story, Ọya is liberated and transformed by her connection to the earth. For women of African ancestry, she is symbolic of our ability to engage in personal transformation, go to battle when needed, and garner the respect of others through fostering a connection with the environment.

ACTIVITIES

1. Create a three-dimensional representation of the transformation you want to occur in your life.

2. Journal prompts:

   a. In what areas of your life do you feel stuck?

   b. How can you harness the change that Ọya brings to your life?

   c. Ògún coerces Ọya to marry him by hiding her buffalo skin. Are there areas in your life that you have felt coerced to do things by men?

   d. Ọya 's relationship with her cowife is contentious. How do you manage contentious relationships with other women?

3. Either sitting outside when the wind is not too strong or observing from indoors, take a moment to observe the aṣẹ of Ọya as represented by the wind.

   a. What do you notice about the wind? What moves? What remains the same?

   b. What are the qualities of the things that move and those that remain in place? How are you similar or different from those items?

   c. If you are standing outside, where do you feel the wind on your body?

   d. Visualize the force of the wind bringing change to your life. Create a vivid picture of the change you want to experience and how you will feel once it occurs.

   e. Journal when you are done.

Ọbà

Ọbà (or Obba) is a warrior Òrìṣà of domesticity and wifely devotion. In some areas, she is also associated with the ancestors and lives in the cemetery (Seilier, 2015). Originating in Igbon, this Òrìṣà is now predominately worshipped in the town of Ogbomoṣo, Nigeria, and is associated with the Ọbà River. Stories of this Òrìṣà are also found in Brazil, Cuba, and the United States. The most popular story is her rivalry with her two cowives, Ọ̀ṣun and Ọya, for the affections of their husband Ṣàngó. While the details of the story change, the outcome generally remains the same. The following version of the story was recorded in Òṣogbo, Nigeria (Bascom, 1976).

Ọbà, Ọya, and Ọ̀ṣun were in a constant rivalry for the affections of their husband Ṣàngó. Ọ̀ṣun was an excellent cook and Ṣàngó constantly showered her with affection and praise. Ọbà wanted to please her husband and asked Ọ̀ṣun for cooking advice to ensure Ṣàngó's love. Ọ̀ṣun made a pot of stew and added a large mushroom to the top. When Ṣàngó ate the stew, he raved about it while showering Ọ̀ṣun with further praise. Ọbà went to Ọ̀ṣun and asked how she prepared the stew to elicit such as response. In anticipation of Ọbà's request, Ọ̀ṣun had covered her head with a *gele* (decorative head tie) and said that she had cut off her ears and added it to the stew. Eager to please her husband, Ọbà did the same.

When Ṣàngó ate the stew and discovered the ear, he became enraged and rejected Ọbà. Ọṣun then removed her *gele*, revealing that she had not cut off her ears after all. Ọbà flew into a rage and attacked Ọṣun, who became one river and Ọbà another. People say that to this day, the site where these two rivers meet is always tumultuous. It is also the reason that a child of Ọbà cannot be initiated to the secrets of Ọṣun.

This story highlights several important lessons. First, the Òrìṣà are not viewed as infallible or above suffering the consequences of their actions. We see that even Ọṣun can have *ìwà burúkú* or bad character. Ọṣun ultimately pays the price for her bad character by sparking an ongoing battle with Ọbà. She also loses her place as the favorite wife of Ṣàngó after turning into a river, thus reminding us that short-term victory fueled by bad character has long-term consequences. For Ọbà and all women of African descent, it is a reminder not to take advice from people who do not have your best interest at heart. In addition, the story warns women not to sacrifice their physical health even for people they love. As Ọbà learned, the person is unlikely to appreciate the sacrifice despite its lasting consequences.

Ọbà is also a model for women with a limb, mental health, or other disabilities. Despite her being known as the Òrìṣà with a missing ear, this does not relegate Ọbà to the status of an outcast. Instead, she continues to function in a central role as an Òrìṣà, providing healing and standing up for herself when she is dishonored by Ọṣun. Ọbà's story is a reminder to the disability community of African descent to expect and demand respect from everyone. It also highlights the fact that in Yorùbá ontology, the nondisabled are not automatically privileged. It speaks to a larger worldview ensuring that all women are perceived as divine, capable of serving others, and engaging in full lives whether they are part of the disability community or not.

ACTIVITIES

1. Write a list of 50 things that you love about yourself.

2. Journal prompts:

   a. Do you have a disability?

      i. *If so, describe it.*

      ii. *Do you hide it? Why or why not?*

   c. How can you use Ọbà's story to reframe your disability?

   d. How can you use Ọbà's story to address conflict with other women?

   e. Are there times in your life when you sacrifice for others and it is not appreciated?

      i. *What is the reason behind your sacrifice?*

   b. Are there times in your life when your behavior toward other women is similar to Ọṣun's?

   c. Make a list of people who have betrayed you and vice versa.

3. Sit by a body of fresh water with the list of names of the people who have betrayed you.

    a. Read each name on the list and visualize yourself releasing the emotional attachment to the situation.

    b. Journal when you are done.

4. For the people on the list you have betrayed, one by one, work through your list and come up with a plan to acknowledge what you have done and make restitution to the person that was harmed.

Conclusion

As we consider the current global tensions associated with the political push toward fascism, a nurturance of White supremacy and elevation of White Christian nationalism, women of African ancestry must be diligent about their psychological well-being. As Meghan Markle quickly learned, even joining the ranks of a powerful monarchy via marriage will not protect you from racism rooted in misogynoir. The critiques of Meghan Markle, the Duchess of Sussex, follow the classic sapphire trope of the pushy, scheming, money-hungry woman with no morals. This is in sharp contrast to those one would expect to be conjured up for a woman raised by a make-up artist turned travel agent, then yoga instructor. It suggests that as women we must protect ourselves, our image and community, since no one else will. If we remember the call of Yaa Asantewaa when fighting the British Crown, she provided the Ashanti with a charge. She said, "If you, the men of Asante will not go forward, then we will. We, the women will. I shall call upon my fellow women. We will fight! We will fight till the last of us falls in the battlefields." This battle cry for women to stand up against anti-Black racism is still relevant today. Through invoking the Abosum (Akan divinities) and the ancestors, Yaa Asantewaa called on women to save the Ashanti kingdom. We can do the same in our own push for global justice by calling on the Òrìṣà, our ancestors, and other female divinities of the African diaspora to support our psychological well-being as we stand against all forms of oppression.

References

Abímbọ́lá, K. (2006). *Yorùbá culture: A philosophical account*. Iroko.

Abímbọ́lá, M. (2016). The role of women in Ifá priesthood. In J. Olupona & R. Abiodun (Eds.), *Ifá divination, knowledge, power, and performance* (pp. 246–259). Indiana University Press.

Abímbọ́lá, W. (1975). Ìwà pèlè: The concept of good character in Ifá literary corpus. In W. Abímbọ́lá (Ed.), *Yorùbá oral tradition* (pp. 389–420). Department of African Languages and Literature. *University of Ifẹ̀*, Ilé-Ifẹ̀, Nigeria.

Abímbọ́lá, W. (1997). *Ifá: An exposition of Ifá literary corpus*. Athelia Henrietta Press.

Abiodun, R. (1994). Understanding Yorùbá art and aesthetics. *African Arts*, 27(3), 68–78.

Afọláyán, M. O. (2013). Èṣù má ṣe mí ọmọ ẹlòmíì ni o ṣe: A religious principle for ethical living. In T. Fálolá (Ed.), *Èṣù: Yorùbá god, power, and the imaginative frontiers* (pp. 301–314). Carolina Academic Press.

Awojoodu, O., & Baran, D. (2009). Traditional Yorùbá medicine in Nigeria: a comparative approach. *Bulletin of the Transilvania University of Brasov. Medical Sciences. Series VI, 6,* 129.

Badejo, D. (1996). Ọ̀ṣun Ṣ̀ẹ̀ẹ̀gẹ̀sí: The elegant deity of wealth, power and femininity. Africa World Press.

Badejo, D. L. (2008). The pathways of Ọ̀ṣun as cultural synergy. In J. Olupona and T. Rey (Eds.), *Òrìṣà Devotion as World Religion: The Globalization of Yorùbá Religious Culture* (pp. 191–201). The University of Wisconsin Press.

Barber, K. (1990). Oriki women and the proliferation and merging of Òrìṣà. *Africa, 60,* 313–337.

Bascom, W. (1976). Ọba's ear: A Yorùbá myth in Cuba and Brazil. *Research in African Literatures, 7,* 149–165.

Bascom, W. R. (1993). *Sixteen cowries: Yorùbá divination from Africa to the New World.* Indiana University Press.

Bracey, J. H., Jr., Sanchez, S., & Smethurst, J. (2014). *SOS—calling all Black people: A Black arts movement reader.* University of Massachusetts Press.

Brown, S. (2018). "Don't touch my hair": Problematizing representations of Black women in Canada. *Journal of Pan African Studies, 12*(8), 64–86.

Cuoco, A. (2014). *African narratives of orishas, spirits and other deities: Stories from West Africa and the African diaspora: A journey into the realm of deities, spirits, mysticism, spiritual roots and ancestral wisdom.* Outskirts Press.

DeLoach, C. D., & Petersen, M. N. (2010). African spiritual methods of healing: The use of candomblé in traumatic response. *Journal of Pan African Studies, 3*(8), 40–65.

Edward, G., & Mason, J. (1998). *Black gods: Òrìṣà studies in the New World.* Pitman, Yoruba Theological Archministry.

Ẹlẹ́bùibọn, I. (1994). *Apetebii, the wife of Ọ̀rúnmìlà.* Athelia Henrietta Press.

Fálolá, T., & Childs, M. (Eds.). (2004). *The Yoruba diaspora in the Atlantic world.* Indiana University Press.

Gleason, J. (2000). Ọya in the company of saints. *Journal of the American Academy of Religion, 68,* 265–292.

Green, M. (Writer), Houston, S. (Writer), & Sieling, C. (Director). (2020). *I am* [Season, 1, episode 7, HBO series]. Afemme, Monkeypaw Productions, Bad Robot Productions, & Warner Bros. Television Studios.

Jacobs, H. A. (1861). *Incidents in the life of a slave girl: Written by herself.*

Keckley, E. (1868). *Behind the scenes: Formerly a slave, but more recently modiste, and rriend to Mrs. Lincoln or, thirty years a slave and four years in the White House.*

Lawal, B. (1985). Ori: The significance of the head in Yorùbá sculpture. *Journal of Anthropological Research, 41*(1), 91–103.

Maparyan, L. (2012). *The womanist idea.* Routledge.

Mbilishaka, A. (2018). Psychohairapy: Using hair as an entry point into bBack women's spiritual and mental health. *Meridians, 16*(2), 382–392.

Mbilishaka, A., Ray, M., Hall, J., & Wilson, I. P. (2020). "No toques mi pelo" (don't touch my hair): Decoding Afro-Cuban identity politics through hair. *African and Black Diaspora: An International Journal, 13*(1), 114–126.

Ọ̀jẹ́làdé, I., McCray, K, Ashby, J. Meyers, J. (2011). Use of Ifá as a means of addressing mental health concerns among African-American Clients. *Journal of Counseling and Development, 89,* 406–412.

Ọ̀jẹ́làdé, I. I., McCray, K., Meyers, J., & Ashby, J. (2014). Use of Indigenous African healing practices as a mental health intervention. *Journal of Black Psychology, 40*(6), 491–519.

Olajubu, O. (2004). Seeing through a woman's eye: Yorùbá religious tradition and gender relations. *Journal of Feminist Studies in Religion, 20,* 41–60.

Olupona, J., & Abiodun, R. (2016). *Ifá divination, knowledge, power, and performance.* Indiana University Press.

Olupona, J. K., & Rey, T. (2010). *Òrìṣà devotion as world religion: The globalization of Yorùbá religious culture.* University of Wisconsin Press.

Olusola, A. G. (2005). Animals in the traditional worldview of the Yoruba. *Folklore: Journal of Folklore,* (30), 155–172.

Otero, S., & Fálolá, T. (Eds.). (2013). *Yemoja: Gender, sexuality, and creativity in the Latina/o and Afro-Atlantic diasporas.* SUNY Press.

Prince, A. (2009). *The politics of Black women's hair.* Insomniac Press.

Selier, Y. F. (2015). Ayabbas: Memory, sacred performance and the restoration of afro cuban women's subjectivity to the cuban trans/nation. *Black Diaspora Review, 5*(2), 55–80.

CHAPTER TWELVE

The Victorious Mind

Addressing the Black Male in a Time of Turmoil

Rico Mosby

O ne of my very first clinical cases was a male who entered the community clinic in a very irate state, very loud, boisterous, and clearly demonstrating a psychotic episode. The person who previously screened this individual informed me that this patient had been diagnosed as schizophrenic and was actively experiencing both auditory and visual hallucinations. The screener, as well as a colleague, stated that this male patient "seemed to be a pretty big and scary guy" and asked if I was comfortable with working with this individual. After reading over his clinical paperwork, I felt that I needed to be ready to engage in whatever may have come out of this encounter.

As I entered the waiting area to greet this individual for his scheduled appointment, he appeared very emotional, brimming with energy, and speaking out loud but conversing with himself. We made eye contact and stayed engaged as he continued with heavy breathing and loud talking while moving toward the therapy room. After making it into the therapy room, I allowed him to continue to express himself. As he sat, he openly engaged with the voices he was hearing, speaking both to the voices and to me. With eyes trained on his movements and body language, I actively listened to ensure I was attuned to what he was trying to communicate both verbally and nonverbally. He proceeded to tell me about the various people he needed to, and was going to, kill. To demonstrate both my attentiveness and command of the situation, I leaned forward and asked, "Am I one of those people that you need to kill?" He said, "No, not you." After acquiring this confirmation, diffusing the situation, and assuring him the safe space to express himself, I asked him to continue speaking. He was then able to express a notable amount of pain, hurt, and a great deal of distress. By the end of the session, it was unquestionable that he needed to be committed. He agreed with this assessment, expressed that he was ready to be committed, and knew it was best for him to be hospitalized. He looked at me with locked in eyes and said, "But can you please come with me?" Even though it was not clinic protocol, I made an attempt to meet him at the hospital. He was evaluated and stayed for 3 to 4 days. Upon discharge he returned to the clinic, and we continued with a long-term very meaningful, powerful, and successful therapeutic relationship.

What stood out about this encounter was how several colleagues who previously encountered this gentleman reduced him to the "big, scary, and threatening schizophrenic." I, however, saw and treated him as a man—a person with so much to say, with so much that he needed to emotionally unpack, who was so in need of being truly heard and understood. It was at this point, early in the start of my professional development, that I realized the calming mechanism of connectedness, the true art of listening, and the healing power of the therapeutic relationship. These in-the-moment encounters and communicative skill usage increased my desire to be a true helper and characterized my approach.

Now as a licensed psychologist with more than 20 years of experience in the mental health field, I am eclectic in my approach while still relying on true connectedness, masterful listening, and real relating. Over several years of practice, I have worked in a variety of treatment venues, including but not limited to community-based mental health clinics, hospitals, and universities. Moreover, I have worked extensively in brief and long-term therapy addressing the needs of individuals, couples, and families. In the early years of my career, I found myself attending to the needs of those referred to the community clinic as part of a psychiatric treatment discharge, or the patients in hospitals who were already undergoing medical care in addition to their psychological treatment. I was also able to provide care to college students utilizing campus access to counseling or mental health centers. Although these experiences were rewarding, I became highly disappointed in being unable to effectively reach those "clients from other points of reference." I also had limited exposure to other significant populations who were in need of mental health services.

Just as I have always felt it my duty to be the true helper for those in times of need, I realized it was also my duty to ensure beneficial and needed mental health treatment was accessible to the larger community. In creating The Victorious Mind, PLLC, a mental health and empowerment services clinic, I sought to effectively address the mental health issues of the community abroad, with a particular focus on those who have struggled to find or who mistrust the notion of real mental health assistance. My focus was, and continues to be, those who feel beat up by life and have been fighting the perceived battle with a defeated mind. Although these individuals might feel overwhelmed, they are quite capable of developing and housing the strength and personal will to effectively fight and persevere—in other words, those who are in much need of and ready to acquire their victorious mind. Acquiring a victorious mind starts by going through the therapeutic process with a mental health professional to allow one to truly relieve and manage the carried stress and uncover, process and deal with the personal issues of their life. It is important to be able to safely and openly get to the root cause of the personal struggles and implement healthy ways to process deep feelings of distress.

Effective Management of the Deep Levels of Black Males' Distress

As a result of the pain and heightened stress associated with the social climate and clear racial division, issues such as aggression and control, cultural alienation and disconnection, self-esteem, vocational and work stress, interpersonal conflict, dependency issues, help-seeking attitudes and behaviors, racial identity issues, and invisibility have manifested themselves in daily lives of the Black male. Some of the common stressors experienced by Black men at a higher rate than other groups are racism, discrimination, crime, and poverty (Ellis et al., 2015). These real experiences are a chronic source of a significant amount of stress that conducted clinical studies have proven is one of the leading causes of poor health conditions experienced by Black men (Ellis et al., 2015). In comparison to White men, improper stress management has led to Black men having shorter life spans and higher rates of illnesses such as type 2 diabetes, hypertension, and various forms of cancer (Ellis et al., 2015). In working with our Black male clients, one of the most common stressors our clients experience is the pressure to be perfect in the workplace. They feel the need to outperform their coworkers just to keep their jobs. Dealing with the pressures to overperform, microaggressions and discrimination in the workplace have caused many Black men to feel burned out. When this stress is expressed to managers or colleagues, or these individuals leave their jobs to find relief, they are prejudicially labeled as angry Black men. Likewise, having to work twice as hard as others in the workplace is an unspoken rule that many Black professionals follow, understanding that appearing ungrateful for their jobs or being unproductive can cause them to lose their jobs. These pressures coupled with the everyday stress of providing for their families has led some Black men to feel emotionally exhausted, losing sight of their hopes and dreams or even abusing alcohol and/or other substances. Some even experience physical symptoms such as chronic headaches, ulcers, and high blood pressure when this stress is not managed in an effective manner (Cohen et al., 1998).

Another stressor often expressed by our clients is the sense of inferiority and invisibility they experience because they feel as though they are not seen, heard, or valued. Having a safe place to express their feelings with others who not only understand them but also have shared life experiences is not only crucial in helping men manage stress but also critical in improving their self-worth. Connecting with and talking to others who have shared cultural experiences and values, and who can empathize with their pain, helps process frustrations, avoiding explosive episodes that can lead to negative consequences. As a result, we encourage our clients to connect with supportive networks and groups in addition to and outside of therapy where they can feel a sense of belonging, connecting with like-minded people and communities where they are seen and heard.

Given the awareness of the notable amount of potential unaddressed trauma buried within the chronic stress of many clients when they first enter the practice, our treatment utilizes strength-based and culturally appropriate interventions. These approaches highlight and implement emotional awareness and active coping mechanisms associated with desired positive growth and change. Simply put, our stress management involves making sure the client feels the connection of the therapeutic relationship, the sense of being truly heard and understood, and guidance on becoming more self-aware of potential stressors so that clients are emotionally equipped to handle any and all feelings of distress.

So much of the absorbed distress of the Black man has an extended range of impact not only on the individual, but also on connected relational and social ties. Therefore, proper management of the stress involves inquiring about all the dynamics that make up the client's support community. Given the awareness of the cultural influence of religion and spirituality in the Black community, stress management with our Black males also involves the incorporation of religion and spirituality when appropriate. It is important to also understand the associated power of religion and/or spiritual support in times of turmoil, even when an individual is not a member of a particular church or any form of organized religion. With an adequate understanding of the social structure, support mechanisms, and role of spirituality for the Black male client, as providers we can better plan and apply the most tailored approach. Assisting our clients to effectively manage stress involves utilization of four effective stress-management treatment approaches: cognitive behavioral therapy, mindfulness-based stress reduction, health and wellness emphasizing a self-care approach, and Black male empowerment.

An effective and common stress management technique (one that is considered by some as the gold standard), is cognitive behavioral therapy (CBT). CBT is a psychological treatment and therapeutic approach proven effective at mitigating a full range of problems of distress. Various challenges with anxiety, depression, relational and marital discord, vocational stress, eating disorders, alcohol and drug use issues, and severe mental illness are treated by way of CBT. CBT is suggested to lead to significant improvement in functioning and quality of life (American Psychological Association [APA], 2020). Ample scientific evidence has shown CBT methods actually produce change (APA, 2020). CBT is a treatment approach that encompasses assessment strategies and cognitive and behavioral treatment techniques and relies on collaboration between clinician and client, who has the responsibility to complete homework assignments.

It is crucial that we at The Victorious Mind provide culturally appropriate stress-management techniques to effectively address the mental health needs of Black men. The utility of CBT centers on tailoring therapy to the needs of the client, so utilizing this form of therapy to address the treatment needs of Black males has produced positive results (Kelly, 2019). "This might include gathering information by: (a) looking for common themes, (b) direct questioning, (c) suggesting hypothesized rules, attitudes, or assumptions the client might ascribe to, and (d) using the downward arrow technique, wherein the counselor asks clients the meaning they would ascribe to themselves were an automatic thought true" (Steele, 2020, p. 219). CBT can effectively help Black men faced with a number of environmental stressors reframe negative thought processes and release internalization in order to cultivate a positive life outlook. In addition, the fringe benefits of applying effective CBT as a treatment measure can result in improved interpersonal relationships, emotional regulation, addiction prevention, changing from maladaptive to adaptive behaviors, and improved quality of life. Black males' experience with structural racism can be counterworked by CBT.

Another stress-management approach we implement to help combat the daily stressors Black men may face is mindfulness-based stress reduction (MBSR)—a group program developed by Jon Kabat-Zinn (2013) in the 1970s to treat patients struggling with life's difficulties and physical and/or mental illness. There are different ways for the Black male client to employ mindfulness techniques into daily practice as a way to alleviate mental and physical distress and constitute a safe and effective approach for reducing stress. The method is universal in that it can be implemented in a number of settings and across disciplines and client demographics; therefore, it can be readily integrated into clinical settings. Mind-body practices include meditation, yoga, acupuncture, breathing exercises, relaxation training, qigong, and tai chi. Such practices involve interactions of the mind and body and play an important role in disease and healing (Mayden, 2012). There is heightened interest in mind-body interventions as effective use of the mind can notably influence one's behavioral functioning, health, and wellness. Research findings by Woods-Giscome and Gaylord (2014), showed that

> Participants felt that mindfulness meditation helped them with enhanced stress management, direct health improvement, and enhanced self-awareness and purposefulness. They felt that they would recommend it and that other African Americans would be open to the practice but suggested that its presentation may need to be adapted. They suggested emphasizing the health benefits, connecting it to familiar spiritual ideology and cultural practices, supplementing the reading material with African American writers, increasing communication (education, instructor availability, "buddy system," etc.), and including African Americans as instructors and participants. By implementing minor adaptations that enhance cultural relevance, mindfulness meditation can be a beneficial therapeutic intervention for this population. (p. 1)

In light of accumulating empirical evidence for stress-reducing outcomes of mindfulness meditation in the general population, this therapy may be a viable option for stress management with Black males. Findings suggest that mindfulness is a central component of the treatment effectiveness and that the mindfulness of participants and of therapists is a strong predictor of effective mindfulness-based treatment (MBT) (Khoury et al., 2013). As current research studies concerning the use of mindfulness techniques targeting Black men specifically are limited, it affords the opportunity to explore the impacts of it through research design studies coupled with empirical evidence of its benefits. According to Watson-Singleton et al. (2019), mindfulness-based interventions can be culturally tailored to address the unique health needs of Black Americans. Culturally responsive modifications, like use of Black facilitators and inclusion of cultural values, are recommended. Additionally, culturally relevant mindfulness-based interventions may be especially effective in reducing Black Americans' health disparities. In addition to it being an effective treatment modality, MBSR has proven very useful with the Black millennial and Gen Zs in particular, who face an increasing group of newfound stressors and are at even higher risk of mental and physical decline. MBSR enables the client to deal more effectively with stressors associated with daily living. As a good percentage of the client population at our practice includes millennials, and MSBR techniques have been employed with that group, participants have expressed their ability to deal more effectively with the stresses of illness, pain, and daily life.

At The Victorious Mind, we use mindfulness appropriately adapted and tailored for Black men who face challenges in the form of racial aggression and racial isolation. For example, with the social climate and state of unrest, Black males have entered the clinic with patterns of emotional reactivity to police interactions. Through mindfulness work, they have been able to and have learned how to reflect on and come in full contact with their feelings of irritation, anger, or painful memories versus running away from the feelings or holding in or overanalyzing feelings that they have yet to come truly aware of first. In managing and/or preventing heightened distress, when in a difficult or challenging situation, we emphasize how it is best to be mindful and fully aware of their total being (physical and emotional) in the moment versus being unaware and overly reactive. Mindfulness techniques utilized include an inclusive space where the Black male can feel he is a part of a harmonious collective that supports, engages, encourages, and most importantly looks like him. Due to the challenges of a racially divided society, the mindfulness movement should be further explored by people of color.

There is increasing attention focused on the benefits and implementation of preventative measures to mitigate stress-related symptoms that can lead to poor health outcomes. Health and wellness with the emphasis on wholesome nutrition, physical activities, and good sleep hygiene has had significant positive impacts on stress management. These preventive measures are very useful and important tools that Black men can apply to their life to lessen the harmful effects of increased stress and are important in holistic health. The brain contains a network of neural connections, and when an individual is under stress the mind is affected, but other areas of the body also feel the impact (Uptmor,,n.d.). Hence, we find importance in encouraging our clients to engage in some form of physical activity, preferably one that is derived from pleasure. Among the many benefits of engaging in exercise, the brain releases endorphins, which are our "feel good" neurotransmitters that counteract stress. Promotion of health and well-being and health teaching has empowered our clients to turn to positive and adaptive coping practices to reduce stressors. Numerous studies have shown that physical activity is a mood booster, improves health, and lowers the risk of being diagnosed with chronic conditions, including diabetes, heart disease, and stroke.

The University of Minnesota (n.d.) Earl E. Bakken Center for Spirituality & Healing discusses steps to take that combat and prevent stress, as well as promote self-care practices to effectively manage stressors. Clients need to be self-aware and sometimes intentional of the foods they are consuming as a part of their health and wellness journey. With the daily and sometimes heavy stressors of life, how we nourish and how our bodies process certain foods can have a negative or positive effect on mental health and stress.

Detoxifying foods such as colorful fruits and vegetables and antioxidant-rich edibles, which include berries, nuts, and fruits are some examples of healthy food options. Through development of healthy eating habits, maintaining a steady sleep routine, centering around a self-directed sense of purpose, and maintaining interconnectedness to one's community, an increased level of optimism is developed that effectively counters stress and induces positive response to stress triggers.

The Victorious Mind has implemented a model of health and well-being into our clinical practice that has yielded notable benefits. Utilizing it to complement existing therapeutic techniques has enhanced and maximized stress reduction in Black male clients. With a well-being model implemented in the practice environment, our Black male clients have expressed the positive effects of engaging in health-promoting activities. This is an area we will continue to explore and expand, with the eventual goal of creating a mindfulness space that incorporates shared experiences and health practices that a cohort of Black men have found to be very beneficial ways to cope with stressors and in empowering them to be the best versions of themselves.

We recognize the power and significance of mitigating the deep layers of stress we often carry. However, due to the clear manner in which stress manifests physically by way of body tension, strain, and pain, we understand that having a victorious mind does not fully occur when the body feels beat up and diminished by the stress it is and has been carrying. Therefore, part of The Victorious Mind's treatment paradigm is a collaborative care model that involves a strong partnership with in-community local chiropractic, acupuncture, and massage therapy clinics that are tied to and connected to the successful development and maintenance of true wellness of the mind and body of those treated at The Victorious Mind. When there are notable stress and associated pain triggers that may be interfering with the Black male client's sense of feeling truly victorious, they are often scheduled for the proper consultation and start of treatment with the appropriate therapist within the collaborative care team.

As mentioned earlier, proper stress management approaches and techniques are beneficial for the clients and equally effective and needed for the providers. Therapists and providers are sometimes both an agent of facilitated growth/change and an experiencer of the same current emotionally weighted distress. In these cases, as it is at our practice, it is important for our providers to not only guide and facilitate proper stress management of the patient, but also stay properly emotionally fit and energized for the fight. It is valuable to note that it is the Black male empowerment work that actually energizes both the clients and providers.

The Black male is constantly portrayed as violent, angry, and hostile; criminally minded; lazy; lacking intelligence; hypersexual; and even hopeless. They often find that they must work extra hard for others to perceive them in a positive light. This constant, uphill battle focused on changing other people's perceptions of the Black male can cause them to feel tired, exhausted, and fatigued. It is through the Black male empowerment approach to treatment that we address the deep distress of Black men through helping them cope by acquiring their personal power. It is the invisibility syndrome and conceptual model

(Franklin, 2006) that is part of the framework of our Black male empowerment work. Invisibility is often times manifested by a totality of an individual's experiences. Frequent interactions with implicit biases, microaggressions, lack of emotional intelligence, and so on often foster this feeling of invisibility. It is through the Black male empowerment work and assisting Black men in disengaging from the societal norms of racism and instead embracing culture and racial socialization that ethnic visibility is obtained. In other words, Black men are able to acquire the feelings of being recognized and satisfied, having a sense of legitimacy, being validated, having dignity, and being comfortable with their identity and the truth of who they are.

These Black Lives Matter

It is an understood reality that no one was able to escape the pandemic-related distress associated with the COVID-19 pandemic, which amplified the stress experienced by the Black male. Intensified exposure to the senseless killings of Black men and the proliferation of the Black Lives Matter movement added to the unavoidable chronic stress and prevalence of exposure to trauma.

A key challenge for Black males is the need and expectation to be resilient and strong, regardless of the extent and nature of pain, turmoil, and heightened distress that is ever present in their lives. National data reveals that Black males are greatly impacted by immeasurable levels of distress associated with racism, coupled with historical trauma, and are in dire need for mental health assistance. They are, however, less likely to utilize mental health treatment because of barriers such as the stigma of being perceived as weak, mistrust of the health care system, and/or the difficulty with locating and accessing Black mental health providers. Hence, these Black lives matter!

With the unique challenges experienced by Black males coupled with the barriers to mental health assistance experienced by that population, The Victorious Mind was developed. With 13% of the country being Black, and a mere 8% in Austin, Texas (U.S. Census Bureau, n.d.), The Victorious Mind was formed in Pflugerville, Texas. Pflugerville, where the highest percentage of Black population in the Austin Metro (16%) resides, was chosen in an effort to be accessible to the majority of the Black audience.

For the past decade The Victorious Mind has provided mental health assistance in the Pflugerville area. A review of patient data for the last 5 years indicates 37% of the patient population is adult Black males (ages 18–68). This percentage, however, does not reflect the number of Black male adolescents who have and/or also sought care and are committed to their therapeutic process of change and personal growth at The Victorious Mind.

Although the current caseload at our practice includes Black men at a rate of 40%, most mental health providers will acknowledge that Black males represent a usually small percentage of their caseloads. The small number of Black men engaged in mental health care services is not a reflection of provider care or the practices themselves, but a result of stigmas associated with mental health care and societal factors. A number of additional considerations about the meager number of Black men actively engaged in mental health care services include perceived stigmas; few referrals; lack of health insurance or inadequate health insurance; primary care providers' inability to recognize the signs of mental health decline; the lack of screening tools in practice to identify the needs; or the distrust of the medical community.

With all these factors taken into consideration, we utilize the connectedness approach to reach Black male clients in particular. From the first point of contact with our providers, the "in-need client" will experience an immediate presence of warmth, sincerity of care, value, and artful listening. Providers at The Victorious Mind are expected to be fully aware of all the complex and crucial factors at play behind the potential client's appeal for assistance and hone in on the potential clients' need to be heard and understood. Subsequently, an instantaneous connection forms. This accession debunks distrust and apprehension and heightens the client's motivation, readiness, and excitement to begin their journey toward obtaining a victorious mind.

At The Victorious Mind, we have served and continue to serve the treatment needs of a full spectrum of Black men that includes fathers, husbands, high school and college students, businessmen, entrepreneurs, corporate professionals, stay-at-home dads, veterans, first responders, and athletes (high school, college, professional and Olympic). Our practice has been committed to and inspired by the process of building the mental strength of many overwhelmed, emotionally worn, and mind-deflated adult Black males. Representing five different generations, previous and current clients of The Victorious Mind are significant extensions of and contributors to larger family systems, church communities, and/or neighborhoods. Building their mental strength and developing a triumphant attitude and drive toward conquering real and perceived obstacles, The Victorious Mind is of utmost importance to not only those men, but also the families, churches, neighborhoods and communities they are tied to. It is this systemic awareness of "the whole Black man" that provides the framework of how such clients present issues, how they are identified, and how they are ultimately addressed at The Victorious Mind.

It is worth noting that in recent years there has been an effort within the United States to normalize mental health; however, for most Black men, a lingering stigma and negative connotation surrounds therapy. Within the Black community, going to therapy is still somewhat a taboo topic, and for most Black men, usually not even a consideration. In the minds of many Black men, they are still very much concerned with being labeled "crazy." Although aware of treatment options and potentially even having access to mental health assistance, for many Black men, awareness and availability often does not evolve into actually entering a clinic as a client in need of services. In the midst of these challenges, the Black community has found ways to process anger and frustration in both healthy and unhealthy ways.

It is both with personal knowledge and what is suggested in the treatment-seeking literature that we know negative perceptions about mental health and historical skepticism about seeking help has caused many in the Black community to seek assistance from nonclinical sources such as the church, family, friends, neighbors, and so on. as opposed to mental health professionals. One of the most prevalent sources of therapy used in the Black community is the church. From slavery to today, the church has provided comfort and peace to the Black community as it has endured the pain of systematic racism, the ongoing fight for racial equality, dealing with the discrimination, hate crimes, and deliberate injustices inflicted on Black people (Blank et al., 2002). The church has also been used to help cope with the financial struggles of daily survival in a society built to subjugate the Black male. Through the church Black men are encouraged to "Take it to Jesus," "pray about it," and "let go and let God" to deal with the hardship and pain they perpetually experience. Although these mantras serve to strengthen spiritual fortitude, many Black men still struggle with their mental health issues and effectively processing painful events that occur in their life. Bereft of systems to help them deal with mental "demons" and distress, this void leaves them still feeling hopeless and defeated.

The barbershop has been identified as another source for mental self-care for the Black male (Dennis, 2018). Many men go to not only be groomed, but also to discuss their thoughts on politics, issues in the community, injustice toward Black people within law enforcement, and sports, celebrities, and personal issues they may be dealing with. Although many may not admit it, a trip to the barbershop becomes an exercise at expressing shared thoughts and common experiences. This "outing" provides a sense of belonging, a safe place to be heard and understood, which, in turn, helps release negative emotions and feelings. Although many men may be experiencing similar issues, they may not know how to properly express them.

There are also a number of unconventional, and often detrimental means Black men utilize to cope with their loss, trauma, and/or mental health issues. For some, joining a gang, overindulging in activities (such as sports, video games, sex, and pornography) or selling and/or using illicit drugs are methods Black men have used to manage their pain (Ellis et al., 2015). Although these may not be healthy, productive forms of therapy, engaging in these activities provides some Black men with an outlet and a community where they feel supported, heard, understood, or accepted while also providing affirmation of their egos and a semblance of relief.

The numerous barriers that inhibit Black men's motivation to seek mental health care coupled with the avenues of community care, contributes to the pervasiveness of many Black men struggling with mental health issues and disorders that often go undiagnosed. Lack of formal diagnosis and treatment can have disparaging results not only in their lives but also in the lives of their loved ones and community. The increase in, or rather increased witness of, negative encounters of Black men with police over the past few years is a prime example. Collectively we have seen this issue play out right before our eyes as the police have inaccurately deemed Black men a threat, while they're experiencing a mental health crisis. Police often overreact and end up killing them. Witnessing these acts has further traumatized Black men and boys who wonder if the same miscalculations will be made toward them, resulting in their lives ending as well.

The racial tension and killings of Black men and women at the hands of the police was painful and heartbreaking to process as a community as 2020 came to a close. Watching men like George Floyd and Ahmad Mabry deliberately and unwaveringly killed before our eyes was, for some, reminiscent of an all too painful past of racial injustice inflicted toward Black people. With the feelings of rage and anger that Black people have tried to express to those outside of the Black community deemed as an overreaction, having a safe place to express these emotions in a healthy, effective, manner is vital to the emotional and physical well-being of Black men today. Although many will continue to engage in the unconventional and traditional sources of therapy used within the Black community, most men will still deal with unmet psychological issues and trauma that will play out in unhealthy behaviors and lifestyles.

Consistently, in the face of intense social reckoning, many Black males have presented concerns such as depression, lack of motivation, pain management, anxiety, stress, marital issues, communication problems, grief, and/or loss. Although common issues, this list is by no means exhaustive. For detailed evaluation, let's consider the following brief case example of a Black adult male client who entered our practice in the late fall of 2020, herein referred to as Joe. Although a strong connection with Joe had already been made over the phone during his consultation and clinical screening, when he entered the clinic for his initial session he openly stated how glad he was about being able to get in and "talk through a few things." At the same time, he also emphasized how he was "usually not much of a talker or into all that emotional crap." Joe was a man of large stature and disclosed that he was usually referred to as 'Big Joe." As we explored what was at the core of his concerns and what sparked his need for help, he expressed that he was "struggling with this pandemic and trying to manage a little stress about being furloughed and a close friend is in the hospital with COVID, that's basically it."

Although Joe minimized what was a notable amount of distress by continuing to refer to himself as a "little stress[ed]," the therapist engaged Joe by inquiring details of Joe's job experience and the extent of his relationship to the close friend that was on a ventilator struggling to survive COVID-19. The therapist expressed interest in Joe pricked his participation, and he became more emotionally present as he answered questions. At a point of unlocking some deeply buried pain, Joe expressed that his last statement "is probably the best way [he] can put it." The therapist then interjected, "It is not that easy to explain words that I'm waiting to hear ... but it's the words that are lurking and crawling right behind your face eager to be released that I'm waiting on. It is the unspoken words that have caused your eyes to become all of a sudden so glossy and watery, that I'm waiting to hear. ... It's those deeply internalized words of pain that are causing your legs to buckle slightly right now, that I'm waiting to hear." Big Joe then belted out a loud moan and verbalized the weariness of so much pent-up and never-before-touched despair and anguish that he had for some time needed lifted off of him. After having the emotional release and unload, Joe even disclosed, "[I] so needed that. I don't feel as heavy and I've never felt so light before. I don't even feel like a Big Joe." The therapist affirmed that he was "still Big Joe, but Big not because of weight, as [he was] light as a feather [then]. But Big because of the strength [he] showed to emotionally go to a place(s) [he] had never ventured before, and it is now that [he is] truly ready to engage in the work toward your process of growth and positive change."

The therapeutic relationship with Joe started with the therapist's ability to ask probing questions while concurrently conveying a style that balances professionalism and warmth coupled with a sympathetic attitude. It was also the therapeutic art of listening that validated Joe's' need to be heard, understood, and not judged. Through the one-on-one, open dialogue the discussion focused on Joe's current life and relationships within his family, social, and work environments. This approach, coupled with communicative exchanges, revealed that Joe was not just "a little stressed," but had unresolved family-of-origin issues, traumatic experiences, interpersonal distress, and was currently experiencing grief and loss. All these embedded emotional weights manifested in clearly endorsed depressive and anxiety symptomology. Joe has continued his treatment by way of weekly intensive individual psychotherapy.

One might ask why Joe would choose individual therapeutic assistance from a licensed clinician over engaging his pastor or a respected friend or family member with his concerns. Pastoral counselors offer an integrated religious and spiritual approach to treatment. Their work is seen as redemptive/supportive and restorative in character, which is an important part of healing. By the same token, people can talk with trusted family or friends who can provide the same restorative advice as their pastors. However, the care of a qualified mental health professional adds depth to the needed processing, and at times is simply what is warranted. Oftentimes, those needing mental health assistance don't divulge everything that's going on in their head or in their lives to their pastors or family and friends—not out of lack of trust but because they fear being judged. In Joe's case, just as it is for many who seek professional help, there was a strong motivating force. Although Joe passively sought help by coming to the clinic, he strongly felt help was unavailable to him. He had previously sought help needed through other means and expressed not knowing who, where, or how to be assisted. His conviction at our first meeting was that there was not anyone to truly help him. The Victorious Mind was able to facilitate Joe's, and many others, process of desired positive change by being the respite and place of emotional refuge and needed help. By giving way to honest communication that allows open and frank discussion without reservation, we addressed mental illness and traumatic historic underpinnings. In turn, that freed him of the burden of mental anguish carried by so many of our Black men trying to be as strong as they look. Once a client such as Joe garners that unexpected but much desired therapeutic assistance, the power of the community is naturally amplified. A contagion effect is created as many of the Black male clients seen at our practice inform their friends and family of the benefit of their efforts to seek help in the midst of their emotional storms.

Utilizing the proper modality of treatment is a highly emphasized point at The Victorious Mind as well. In Joe's case individual therapy was ideal. Individual therapy is a powerful therapeutic relationship within a trusting, safe, nonjudgmental space in which there is genuine respect, warmth, honesty, and care about clients reaching their desired change and personal growth. However, in other cases, it can be better to utilize couples therapy, family therapy, and/or group therapy to effectively address the needs of the Black male.

Having a partner who has been notably impacted by all the racial, social, and economic unrest experienced by the Black male can further connectivity through the couples therapy experience. In couple's therapy, the Black male can acknowledge how his distress has been a source of personal unrest that has notably impacted his mate. Addressing the deep channels of pain and distress the Black experience can put on a relationship can be monumental for improving the relationship dynamic. Couple's therapy is a meaningful way for the pair to learn how to better communicate with their mate and know, understand, love, and support each other during a time of notable turmoil. It can also reveal how being the partner of the Black male does not always mean that mate truly understands or has the ability to grasp the heartache, pain, and fears of the Black man.

Potential clients might also find themselves struggling with family dynamics as a whole. This strain could be a result of couples sorting through the challenges that surface from varying parenting styles. There could also be a lack of knowledge or agreement on how to address the emotional or behavioral problems of a child or multiple children. There could also be contentious in-law or extended family member dynamics. Although every family struggles with issues from time to time, unwanted disruption or dissolution in the family system can be a tough reality to endure. In this case family therapy would be the proper treatment modality. Although Joe's presenting concerns never resulted in the need for family therapy, another case comes to mind. Herein we will refer to that client as Jack. Jack entered the clinic after realizing that his behaviors on the job had not only prevented him from maintaining his job but also adversely impacted his wife and child. Although Jack entered the clinic seeking individual psychotherapy, during the first few sessions of individual work he would repeatedly express how his wife and child were the actual source of some of his distress and how they understood the problem better than he did. When asked if he felt having his family in the room with him would be helpful, he expressed that it "was worth a try."

It was during our work as an entire family that we were able to clearly identify the source(s) of Jack's reported "nearly life-long experience" with anxiety and stress. Through the open discussion and processing of emotions with his wife and child, it was revealed that Jack had some unresolved pain and insecurities associated with his upbringing in a single-parent home. Although he had been comfortable with his role as husband, he expressed that he never had a model, desire, or assurance to be "anybody's dad." His internalized sense of incompetence played out in his negative communication, poor con- nection, and uneasiness with his preteen son. This sour relationship with his child was a point of contention that Jack's wife had with him and something she regularly expressed to Jack. The distress he was carrying was impacting his focus and efficiency with his job duties. Through the course of shared time as part of the family therapy experience, Jack was able to address his need for an improved sense of self-worth. He became aware of his character strengths as a man, (even though he did not have an actual model example of how to be a "good dad" from his biological father) and acquired the skills to better communicate and connect with his son.

By way of his therapeutic work in family therapy this Black male worked at alleviating his anxiety symptomology and becoming an empowered husband, dad, and team lead at his job. As the systemic therapist, it is believed that an individual's obtained desired systemic affiliations and interactions, such as those of this Black male client and his wife and child, have more power in the person's life than a single therapist could ever hope to have, so it is important to be attentive to more than just the individual in the room, but everything that makes them who they are.

Group therapy, on the other hand, might be the proper modality for the strong but emotionally wounded Black man. Via shared experience, Black men in group therapy can achieve power, growth, and hope together as a unit. Unlike what is garnered during a valuable barbershop visit, additional support from the group leader(s) enables the members (Black men) to resolve issues while strengthening interpersonal relationships. An example of the therapist-led group therapy sessions is our Black male empowerment group. This group was designed to provide the space for Black men to feel less isolated, less dependent on self-reliance for validation of their worth, and liberated from internalized fears. Sometimes Black men may have difficulty saying, "I need help," "I am sorry," and particularly, "I need love." We also recognize that Black men search for and might create an "alternate family" to compensate for the "disconnects" in their immediate biological families. In the Black male empowerment group men find a supportive and nurturing environment in which issues germane to the Black male experience are explored. Topics discussed include personal power, relationships, self-esteem, racial identity, academics, careers, family, sexuality, spirituality, future goals, and other member-decided topics. Built on the understanding that Black men experience a sense of powerlessness and isolation relative to the mainstream, the Black male empowerment group's interpersonal structure is intentional at providing the opportunity to feel a sense of connection, similarity, and validation. In addition to the open dialogue and processing of raw feelings, these group experiences involve rituals, song, music, poetry, creative expression, and quotes that all give members a sense of ownership to both their group and individual experience at moving toward acquiring and/or maintaining their victorious mind. Participant feedback in this particular group has indicated that after only the first few sessions, attendees' feelings of isolation are vastly reduced. They have stated they became more comfortable talking to other men in the group and were more likely to develop friendships that carried outside of the group. They appeared to achieve more trust, support, and openness and even seemed to learn more about themselves. In the group support and connections with other Black males are made; mentoring and guidance permeates throughout each session; and the Black male's uniqueness is recognized and celebrated. The group aggrandizes the male bonding experience in the presence of committed and dedicated facilitators. Consequently, the Black male empowerment group at The Victorious Mind has become the manifestation of Marianne Williamson's (1992) musings

Our deepest fear is not that we are inadequate. Our deepest fear is that we are powerful beyond measure. It is our light, not our darkness that most frightens us. We ask ourselves, Who am I to be brilliant, gorgeous, talented, fabulous? Actually, Who are you not to be? Your playing small does not serve the world. There is nothing enlightened about shrinking so that **other people won't feel insecure around you**. We are all meant to shine. ... As we are liberated from our own fear, our presence automatically liberates others. (pp. 190–191)

Given the reality and awareness of the still urgent need for Black men to engage in proper mental health treatment, The Victorious Mind has a developed outreach program that seeks to connect with Black men in places that they comfortably frequent—churches, places of employment, schools and various social organizations. These off-site and community meetings are usually in the form of workshops and trainings about various mental health topics that are presented in large enough settings that the Black men in attendance would not feel singled out. The workshops and trainings are designed so that attendants feel open to express their deeper unspoken thoughts in a forum where they are valued and heard. Through such moments of interpersonal connection and a provided avenue for expression of the usually untapped, deeply buried feelings of hurt, pain, and various distress, Black men are and have been able to find their voice and demystify the negative "going to therapy to talk through what I need," viewpoint.

A regular workshop and training series that we provide is one geared toward young Black men who are seniors in high school and freshman college students. The format of the workshop is driven by the desire to help young Black men develop the personal awareness and skills necessary to overcome problems. An additional objective is to facilitate participants' growth and development in ways that will allow them to take advantage of the educational opportunities at their various colleges and/or universities. These goals are pursued while at the same time encouraging youth to become physically, emotionally, and spiritually equipped to obtain their sought-after career and personal aspirations. With these young men feeling both excited about and full of questions, doubt, and fears associated with this major point of transition to college life and adulthood, the workshop allows for a safe space for them to openly express their feelings to a presenter who is passionate about everyone in attendance being truly heard and helped with their concerns. Through an interpersonal and engaged workshop approach, young Black men often express their feelings of doubt, insecurities, foreseeable alienation, and stress and worry about familial matters, school, career aspirations, and relationships. In other words, the physical, emotional, and relational symptoms of stress and depression are discussed, and proper coping practices, communication skills, and empowerment components are relayed and favorably responded to.

What is so rewarding about these workshop experiences is to hear the young Black men relay how much better they feel after realizing they are not alone in how they feel and that there are ways to properly manage, cope with, reduce, and/or change some of those shared concerns and worries. Many express being "now comfortable with doing the counseling thing," "now know[ing] the importance of [their] mental health," or "[realizing] acquiring good communication skills can clearly decrease some of [their] stress." As a result of their workshop experience, a good number of young Black men have participated in counseling services either through The Victorious Mind or at their respective colleges/ or universities. They have felt comfortable with disclosing to our practice staff that their counseling work has provided them with an increased sense of self-worth and coping and communication skills, lessened conflict with their family of origin, a better ability to clarify academic and professional goals, a deeper understanding of relational issues among self and others, and a deeper self-awareness of their own attitudes toward their culture-of-origin shared concerns and worries.

This outreach has been a powerful and successful way to connect with Black males who were able to get preliminary contact with counseling services without having to search for and/or initiate any face-to-face in-clinic treatment. However, COVID-19 and the long-standing impact of this pandemic and need for social distancing stimulated the notion of expanding the outreach program to the internet and using virtual workshops (just as our telehealth psychotherapy platform) in situations in which the powerful and suggested in-person and interpersonal approach is not feasible.

Although primary care physicians and/or insurance providers have referred a number of male clients for service at The Victorious Mind, many Black male clients have indicated that a family member or friend referred them. Likewise, a number of clients have been referred by a coach, athletic trainer, minister, or school guidance counselor, or self-referred after previously attending a The Victorious Mind workshop or training. Regardless of how the Black men arrive at The Victorious Mind, once present they have been involved in individual, couples, family, and/or group therapy as they address their various levels of needed therapeutic assistance.

A Sense of Calm, Power, and Balance

In contemporary American society, Black men face major challenges to their development and well-being. Social and economic indicators of Black male development provide a profile of an individual whose quality of life is in serious jeopardy. From an early age, it has become increasingly apparent that Black males are confronted with a series of obstacles in their attempts to attain academic, personal, and career success. According to some Black men, being a Black man in America is often a roll of the dice and always a challenge. Despite the history of oppression, racism, suppression, and discrimination that stemmed from slavery, through Jim Crow, police brutality, and workplace discrimination, and what it means to be a man, Black people have historically demonstrated strength, resilience, hope, and endurance. It is these strengths and positive attributes that therapists need to tap into, complementing them with research-based, effective therapeutic approaches. This focus on the positives and personal power of the Black male is the key to achieving mental health equity. Recognizing the historical and traumatic consequences of racism that has impacted Black men and the underutilization of mental health treatment is a first step and start to regaining ground in the quest for mental health equity.

Our treatment efforts and collaborative, connected experiences with stress management have assisted both Black teens and adults feel relevant. Through therapy, clients have developed an attitude of greatness in who they are; they have become connected, relational, and effective communicators; capable and able; not easily deterred; ambitious, driven conquerors, with a vision for their futures that is victorious. It has been fascinating to see the Black teens and adults who, after becoming emotionally aware of their own deep-rooted pain and need for professional help, get the desired help and then encourage their sons, daughters, relational partners, spouses, family, and friends: "Please go do what I did to get to where I am now, and how good I feel about myself." Black men and teens are the models and examples of healthy help-seeking behaviors that is reducing the mental health stigma at a time in which it is so crucial and so needed. With granted permission, I end with a current client's mid-June 2020 journal entry:

Why 2020? I think most humans are experiencing new shocks of fear, pain, tension, and confusion, with fluctuating emotions unfolding daily. It's hard to absorb and process the amount of bad news we hear before its time for the next news cycle. My treatment has given me the tools to acknowledge there are many things outside of my control, yet there are also many ways I can manage the ups and downs of whatever life throws at me. I am still scared, and angry, and exhausted by the events of this year. But because of my therapeutic work, I'm also grateful to be finally satisfied in my career. I have a partnership that now enriches me. I now take the mini pauses I need, take photographs, and play music. I breathe and stretch, and I struggle and scream. I walk near the lake, and pray, and write.

I put myself first, and I am Victorious.

References

American Psychological Association. (2017). *What is cognitive behavioral therapy?* https://www.apa.org/ptsd-guideline/patients-and-families/cognitive-behavioral

Blank, M. B., Mahmood, M., Fox, J. C., & Guterbock, T. (2002). Alternative mental health services: The role of the Black church in the South. *American Journal of Public Health*, *92*(10), 1668–1672. https://www.ncbi.nlm.nih.gov/pmc/articles/PMC1447305/

Cohen, S., Kessler, R., & Gordon, L. (1998). *Measuring stress: A guide for health and social scientists.* Oxford University Press.

Dennis, C. H. (2018, August 24). What is barbershop therapy? *Yes!*. https://www.yesmagazine.org/issue/mental-health/2018/08/24/what-is-barbershop-therapy/

Ellis, K. R., Griffith, D. M., Allen, J. O., Thorpe, R. J., Jr, & Bruce, M. A. (2015). "If you do nothing about stress, the next thing you know, you're shattered": Perspectives on African American men's stress, coping and health from African American men and key women in their lives. *Social Science & Medicine*, *139*, 107–114. https://doi.org/10.1016/j.socscimed.2015.06.036

Franklin, J. A. (2006). *From brotherhood to manhood: How Black men rescue their relationships and dreams from the invisibility syndrome*. Wiley.

Kabat-Zinn, J. (2013). *Full catastrophe living: Using the wisdom of your body and mind to face stress, pain, and illness*. Bantam.

Kelly, S. (2019). Cognitive behavior therapy with African Americans. In G. Y. Iwamasa & P. A. Hays (Eds.), *Culturally responsive cognitive behavior therapy: Practice and supervision* (pp. 105–128). American Psychological Association.

Khoury, B., Lecomte, T., Fotin, G., Masse, M., Therien, P., Bouchard, V., Chapleau, M-A., Paquin, K., & Hofmann, S. G. (2013). Mindfulness-based therapy: A comprehensive meta-analysis. *Clinical Psychology Review*, *33*(6), 763–771. https://doi.org/10.1016/j.cpr.2013.05.005

Mayden K. D. (2012). Mind-body therapies: Evidence and implications in advanced oncology practice. *Journal of the Advanced Practitioner in Oncology*, *3*(6), 357–373.

Steele, J. M. (2020). A CBT approach to internalized racism among African Americans. *International Journal for the Advancement of Counseling*, *42*, 217–233. https://doi.org/10.1007/s10447-020-09402-0

Uptmor, A. (n.d.). *Use the wellbeing model to reduce stress*. https://www.takingcharge.csh.umn.edu/use-wellbeing-model-reduce-stress

U.S.Census Bureau (n.d.).*U.S. Census quick facts,* https://www.census.govhttps://www.census.gov/quickfacts/fact/table/pflugervillecitytexas/PST040219#PST040219

Watson-Singleton, N., Black, A. R., & Spivey, B. N. (2019). Recommendations for a culturally-responsive mindfulness-based intervention for African Americans. *Complimentary Therapies in Clinical Practice*, *34*, 132–138. https://doi.org/10.1016/j.ctcp.2018.11.013

Williamson, M. (1992). Our deepest fear. In M. Williamson (Ed.), *A return to love: Reflections on the principles of a course in miracles* (pp. 190–191). HarperCollins.

Winters, M. F. (2020). *Black fatigue: How racism erodes the mind, body, and spirit*. Berrett-Koehler.

Woods-Giscombé, C. L., & Gaylord, S. A. (2014). The cultural relevance of mindfulness meditation as a health intervention for African Americans: Implications for reducing stress-related health disparities. *Journal of Holistic Nursing: Official Journal of the American Holistic Nurses' Association*, *32*(3), 147–160. https://doi.org/10.1177/0898010113519010

Part IV

STUDENT VOICES

CHAPTER THIRTEEN

Unsung, Underpaid, and Unafraid

Black Graduate Students' Response To
Academic and Social Anti-Blackness

Marlon Bailey, Shaina Hall, Carly Coleman, and Nolan Krueger

B lack graduate students face unique challenges that often go unaddressed by their institutions. Undeterred, Black graduate students have had to assess and voice those problems even when they have been ignored. Ultimately, Black graduate students have had to be their own support system while they simultaneously demand others see their value. This chapter describes some of the ways the Black graduate experience is different from other campus populations. It delineates some of the specific nuances of anti-Blackness in academic and social contexts and explains some of the ways Black students have responded to those problems to shine a light on the immeasurable worth of Black lives.

Underrepresentation as an Individual

It can be challenging to feel productive in a setting in which a student does not feel comfortable (Walton & Cohen, 2007). The campus environment plays a paramount role in students' experiences in their programs (Ellis, 2001; Hurtado, 1994). When campuses become environments that exemplify anti-Blackness many Black graduate students feel like they are being denied the opportunity for a "rich social experience" (Johnson-Bailey et al., 2009). Golde (2000) found that graduate students may leave their programs due to a lack of connection with classmates. The lack of representation in a program can stifle opportunities for pleasant social experiences (Pryor et al., 2012). Students may feel invisible in the classroom and larger campus contexts (Haskins et al., 2013). Therefore, not only are students challenged by the strenuous level of graduate coursework, but they also contend with navigating social relationships in this setting.

In the United States, it is not uncommon for Black graduate students to feel isolated and unwelcomed at times. Black graduate students experience feelings of loneliness and exclusion as they find themselves in environments with few other students or faculty of color at academic institutions (Milner, 2004). Being the only Black student in a class has become so customary that students may not attend to the lack of representation. In some cases, a numbness to limited diversity has developed over time. However, for others, there are times sitting in class when a Black student might imagine a situation where all the White people in their classroom suddenly decided to violently express anti-Blackness toward them because of the color of their skin. What chance would they have at survival when they are the only person of color in the room? If there is more than one person of color, the two or three individuals would have limited options to defend themselves against the rest of the class. In this situation, even turning to the authority figure in the class may not be safe. Even if you consider this hypothetical situation unlikely, numerous experiences of White group violence toward Black people make this a possibility (Anderson, 2019). Consequently, students can be distracted by thinking about race and how uncomfortable or volatile a situation could become rather than the course material.

The experience of being a Black graduate student at a predominantly White institution (PWI) can be overwhelming, especially when Black students and students of color are blatantly outnumbered by White students (Daniel, 2007; Haskins et al., 2013). It requires special attention to find peers who can relate closely to their experience. It often involves combing through organizations and clubs trying to find a safe place to belong. Students are frequently forced to look outside of their departments to find those connections (Ellis, 2001; Gasman et al., 2008). Even at a large public institution, it can be difficult to find students who share the same identity. At times it can be so arduous that students stop trying and settle into alternative groups that do not entirely satisfy their longing for community. Classmates, academic club members, coworkers, and lab mates may become the only community a Black graduate student has. If given a choice, students would choose a diverse peer group. However, predominantly White peer groups may be their only option for a support system.

Attending a university with a diverse demographic is important to the college experience for all students. College provides more than just academic instruction for students. For Black graduate students, a scarcity of people of color can create an atmosphere that feels suffocating, like there is no space that feels comfortable. Even though a student may not be the target of overt racial remarks, subtle comments may be more prominent or even pervasive. These subtle comments are known as microaggressions (Pierce et al., 1977). Microaggressions, clear examples of anti-Blackness, are often dismissed as innocuous or unintentional and therefore unworthy of attention like more blatant forms of anti-Blackness. Large public institutions usually contain multiple White students who have limited experience with other students of color (Hu & Kuh, 2003). This inexperience may result in ignorant and insensitive comments or questions. Hearing these insensitive remarks can be draining and create a reluctance to be around members of the educational institution. Students may feel the burden to educate people who make callous remarks; however, that burden can become weighty and tiresome (Haskins et al., 2013).

Impostor Phenomenon

Black students, especially at PWIs, often report experiencing the impostor phenomenon (McClain et al., 2016). Students find themselves doubting their intelligence and even seeking validation from White peers (Stone et al., 2018). Some consider the impostor phenomenon a symptom of underrepresentation at a PWI. The impostor phenomenon is described as the traits and behaviors of high-achieving students who struggle to internalize their success (Clance & Imes, 1978). These students feel as though they are intellectual frauds and do not belong where they are based on their merit (Clance & Imes, 1978). It is easy to attribute the success achieved to some external source. Specifically, Black students can struggle with the idea that their acceptance to a prestigious university is a derivative of the university's need to diversify instead of the value Black students bring.

Imposter feelings make it nearly impossible to be proud of the hard work that has been accomplished. One result is that students may exhaust themselves so that they can reach "the same level" as their peers (Gasman et al., 2004). Fear of failure and inadequacy are the most salient feelings for students experiencing the impostor phenomenon (Ross et al., 2001). As a result, students become consumed in academic work, continually attempting to prove they belong in programs they have already been admitted to. Intense feelings of impostorism create a self-imposed prodigious workload that can negatively affect well-being (Henning et al., 1998). The extensive pressure that manifests itself in hyper-exertion on academic tasks takes its toll on other areas such as interpersonal relationships and mental stability (Cokley et al., 2013; Stone et al., 2018). Navigating the rigors of higher education is challenging enough; coupling that with feelings of the impostor phenomenon makes it even more challenging to succeed.

When a student is one of the very few Black graduate students or possibly even alone in their college, department, or cohort, it is common for these feelings to persist, but difficult to find someone who may understand or relate. Students often bury these feelings because there is no outlet for them (Okahana & Zhou, 2019). Others may challenge, "Why not just find the other minority students at the institution?". The reality is, the options are limited when looking for people who not only look like you, but have similar values, work ethic, and interests (Okahana & Zhou, 2019).

The experience of a Black graduate student at a PWI is not unique, yet each student may feel like they are enduring the experience alone. The environment is often unwelcoming, leaving Black graduate students feeling excluded (Haskins et al., 2013; Smith et al., 2007). Consequently, many public universities increasingly report the attrition of ethnic minority students (Heisserer & Parette, 2002). When a student feels like they are a part of a university in an integrated way, it plays a contributing role in the success of minority students (Freeman et al., 2007). In response, universities need to confront anti-Blackness within their campuses and be more inclusive. For some Black graduate students, the campus environment feels toxic and nonconducive to their learning (Felder & Barker, 2013). Black students face many difficulties regarding race, and coupling that with the laborious academic struggles of a graduate student yields an unpleasant experience that is threatening to their well-being.

Underrepresentation as a Group

Being a Black graduate student presents unexpected challenges and hard-fought triumphs. The Black community is limited at most universities, and the Black graduate community is even more scarce. Black students have had to struggle for value and equity in addition to dealing with underrepresentation and under-resourcing.

Black students who serve in positions of leadership on campus often find themselves isolated and advocating alone, even when meetings are expressly scheduled to discuss policy, resources, and change for Black graduate students. Student testimony and even attempts to present policy reports are often disregarded, leaving students struggling to find an inlet to administrations to seek assistance. Black graduate students are asked by administration, alumni, and faculty to be content with progress and allocations distributed to other Black campus populations. They are told that a win for one Black organization is a win for all of them. However, this mentally leaves the needs of Black graduate students overshadowed by the larger Black undergraduate population and as a result, graduate student needs are left unmet. There must be equitable and inclusive resources for Black graduate students, separate from the undergraduate resources, but equitable to predominantly White graduate organizations.

Black graduate students often advocate for the abolition of prior systems of unjust and inequitable resource distribution. Proposed actionable steps to address the current unjust systems are eliminating merit-based scholarships to increase admission of qualified, need-based, minority students (Farrell, 2004); eliminating culturally biased standardized testing (Sealy et al., 2019); investing in the equity and accessibility of the admissions process; and increasing minority-based fellowships and grants to vitiate the financial inequities that prevent Black students from matriculating into and successfully completing their graduate programs (Johnson-Bailey, 2004). This advocacy is essential to the sustainability and recruitment of Black students to higher education. The administration of the university must value Black student advocacy because the student perspective is the cornerstone of institutional change. Black graduate students take time away from their rigorous studies to push for their needs and the needs of other students to university administration with great resistance. They are often met with veiled opposition and told their efforts are "too long to digest" and "do not seem feasible." These attempts at gaining more resources are weakened by the short supply of Black graduate student voices.

Black graduate students' underrepresentation is widespread, as evidenced in a 2020 report by the Council of Graduate Schools. In the fall of 2019, 4,955 of the 518,721 graduate students who enrolled were Black or African American and 244,312 were White enrollees (Okahana et al., 2020). Furthermore, Black students only account for 6.1% of incoming doctoral students enrolled at universities with "Very High Research Activities"

(p. 9). These numbers have had a small increase over the past 10 years. In the fall of 2009 Black graduate students made up 5.3% of incoming graduate students for doctoral universities with competitive research activities (Okahana et al., 2020). This data shows us that more Black students want to continue their education, so universities should equip themselves to serve this growing population.

While there has been substantial progress in Black higher education recruitment numbers, there is a new generation on the rise within the institution. It is easy to imagine the progress that could be accomplished to retain these Black students with equitable academic, financial, and personal investment. Recruiting Black graduate students works in tandem with retaining the Black graduate students currently attending the university. Dedicating resources to the sustainability of the Black community starts by allocating resources to initiatives and programming for and by Black graduate students, focusing on updating the graduate-level curriculum to represent people of color, and creating spaces specifically for Black graduate students (McClain & Perry, 2017). Investing in spaces for Black graduate students to socially integrate into the new university may prove to have lasting effects. The disproportionately low number of Black graduate students prevents a large network of Black professionals and connections, personal and professional.

The shortage of social capital along with scarce community resources can have a detrimental impact on the sense of belonging, academic engagement, retention, and subsequent intention to persist (Beasley, 2020; Cokley et al., 2004; Golde, 2005; Hausmann et al., 2009; Hurtado & Alvarado, 2015; Museus et al., 2017). The low Black enrollment at PWIs and lack of resources means that there is a narrow avenue for Black graduate students to connect with each other or understand the full scope of the institutional barriers experienced by those who came before them and those suffering with them. The decentralization of communication among Black graduate students is a product of underrepresentation and aids the under-resourcing of Black graduate students departmentally and institutionally.

Undersourced as a Community

The under-resourcing of Black graduate students is a likely culprit of insufficient recruitment, mental health difficulties, strained community building, and attrition (Dyrbye et al., 2007; Okahana, et al., 2020; Sowell et al., 2015). When faced with high levels of stress, there can be ugly consequences for a student's mental health and everyday functioning (Lazarus & Folkman, 1984). Graduate students must often relocate and leave full-time jobs to enter their programs and take on a substantial academic and professional workload. Students pursue positions as teaching assistants, research assistants, mentors, and campus leaders, not to mention navigating the new professional expectations and politics within academic departments. Institutional support is necessary for students to handle the pressure and responsibility generally put on by the institution itself. It is unhealthy to increase the amount of stress Black graduate students take on and internalize but maintain the current set of insufficient resources. Black graduate students at universities in large cities often work at rates below the cost of living and take on multiple roles to survive, without the proper mental and physical health considerations to thrive.

The result of the high-stress lifestyle graduate students endure can also take a toll on their level of motivation. This stress over time, without adequate coping resources, can take the form of burnout, or disengagement, feelings of fatigue, cynicism, and inefficacy (Allen et al., 2020; Koeske & Koeske, 1991; Maslach & Jackson, 1981). Burnout is incredibly prominent among doctoral students, with about 40% of students not persisting through to the end of their program (Golde, 2005). Lovitts (2001) posits that "graduate student attrition is a function of the distribution of structures and opportunities for integration and cognitive map development. The causes of attrition are deeply embedded in the organizational culture of graduate school and the structure and process of graduate education" (p. 2). Without the direct intervention of university administration, Black graduate attrition will stay on the rise (Sowell et al., 2015), and recruitment may ultimately decrease due to the lack of representation.

Black graduate students need a unique investment into resources such as mental health care. Black graduate students often find that the resources are not catered to the graduate experience, or too small to hold enough Black students. When looking for mental health care, Black graduate students are told to find care in the community or start their own group. There is not an emphasis on inclusive care for Black graduate students, and they are left to fend for themselves. Shortages of Black mental health specialists and lack of funding for needed care leave most universities insufficiently prepared to serve their Black graduate students. Black graduate students' gross undersourcing is pervasive and generational, leaving no recompense to address the traumas they endure.

The low enrollment of Black graduate students means that successfully advocating for more institutional support is increasingly difficult. The lack of resources, in turn, works against the recruitment and retention of Black graduate students as many Black students are not able to surmount the deep-rooted barriers put in place by the institution. It is the institution's responsibility to remedy these barriers and eliminate inequitable financial, social, academic, and professional inequities. This task is not as easy as the Black graduate students' underrepresentation works cyclically with the under-resourcing of this community. University administration must focus simultaneously on eliminating the barriers at admission to graduate school and holistically supporting the current Black graduate students. The long-overdue informed and concerted investment into the Black graduate community will ensure an institutional foundation for any Black student who wants to pursue higher education.

Sociopolitical Systemic

Stretched deadlines and empty pages characterized most of the year 2020, where initial ambitions of production collided with an unexpected pandemic, elevated and broadcasted racism and anti-blackness, and a contentious political election. For many students, no amount of positive self-talk, uplift from friends, or soul-stirring viral podcasts were sufficient to produce enough motivation to meet expectations during the time. Who possessed the focus to drown out the cacophony of sirens or the cries of George Floyd? In a world marked by staying inside and social distancing to avoid spreading COVID-19, so many questioned why the relatively few interactions people seem to have with one another ended up as viral videos about refusals to wear masks, political arguments, or unarmed Black people killed while jogging, shopping, or any number of innocuous activities. Understanding the importance of being kind and understanding toward themselves and others does not assuage the guilt that follows unproductive days. Students are expected to navigate academic, occupational, and social expectations regardless of their environment's debilitating fluctuations. While the year 2020 specifically seemed overwhelming, any year can be overwhelming in several sociopolitical contexts. This chapter so far has relayed numerous individual and systemic academic barriers for Black graduate students; however, several socio-political barriers also impede their success.

Graduate students are often tasked with creating new academic scholarship or presenting the most recent scholarship from their discipline. There is pressure to publish in academic journals, complete personal research, learn the most updated methodological advances, or summarize the state of the literature in their topic of interest, regardless of the postgraduate degree they are pursuing. These challenges often distinguish postgraduate degrees from undergraduate accomplishments.

Unfortunately, racism does not pause to allow a reprieve to meet these graduate school challenges, and Black graduate students face specific threats to self and academic progress. Black graduate students often face the danger of direct racism and harm, such as when a White student called the police on a Black graduate student who slept in a common room of her dorm in Connecticut (Dill, 2020). Black graduate students are also privy to the gamut of stress from the experiences of racism. These effects are known as race-related stress (Utsey & Ponterotto, 1996). It is important to note that race-related stress is the stress from suffering direct racism and recognizing racism in cultural and institutional contexts. For example, Black people have been denied occupational opportunities because they wear a natural hairstyle. In court cases, Black defendants have been convicted of severe crimes based on rap lyrics while other genre's lyrics are rarely, if ever, accepted as admissible evidence.

Race-related stress can be experienced via vicarious means. As racist incidents are shared and circulated through news distributors, social media, and conversations within student cohorts, family, and social circles, it becomes difficult to avoid knowledge or often even graphic video of racial violence incidents. For example, when a Minneapolis, Minnesota, police officer murdered Black resident George Floyd, the violent footage pervaded news station coverage as well as online news and social media feeds. Attempting to avoid the footage or description of the killing required exceptional skill or isolation from social places when many needed the comfort of their social groups.

Race-related stress is likely compounded by news fatigue or the feeling of being worn out or exhausted by overwhelming news (Song et al., 2017). While remembering George Floyd in isolation might conjure painful memories and emotions, it must be understood in the context of a pattern of killings of unarmed Black men, women, and children all over the United States. Names and stories like those of Trayvon Martin, Tamir Rice, Atatiana Jefferson, and Breonna Taylor have become seared in people's minds not only because of their killings but because justice for their killings has truly been denied to their families.

This kind of news and news fatigue affects more than just Black graduate students but may specifically affect Black graduate students because they often share many characteristics with victims of unjust killings, including race, age, and location. If they do not, they may have family members or deep connections with others who do. Black graduate students, however, also are often tasked with writing, researching, counseling, or teaching about the painful experiences they are enduring. Imagine needing to write about news fatigue for Black students while suffering news fatigue. Consider how it might feel for Black graduate students to teach a class where students show the video of the murder of George Floyd in a presentation. Consider that Black graduate students may need to counsel other students through the same pain they may not have navigated themselves. Now assume that Black graduate students are often given little support or told to use the painful experiences to improve their creativity or productivity. Students are inconceivably told that they should not be concerned because they will somehow be deemed immune by their status as a graduate student.

In addition to the under-resourcing of mental health services for Black graduate students at many universities, Black graduate students are left wanting services that do not exist. And, if deadlines are not extended to account for the time students need to heal, they are forced to stretch them or miss them. Many Black graduate students find it impossible to complete manuscripts, papers, or grading when anxiety about their safety, the safety of their families, and their longing for justice weigh heavy on their minds.

Racism is going to take more than small-scale interventions at the individual and campus level to solve. In 2020, at least two pandemics affected the world. History inspires hope that the world and the United States will respond successfully to a viral pandemic but conjures strong doubts that it will respond successfully to racism. The universal vulnerability to sickness like COVID-19 often inspires cooperation among the medical and research community to address the global problem as quickly as possible. The United States in particular has seen efficient responses to H1N1, the flu, Ebola, SARS, and Zika during the past 100 years. The United States has not historically experienced efficient responses to racial profiling, systemic racial oppression, or lynching. One difference is a pandemic targets everyone. Being Black or a person of color increases vulnerability to a pandemic, but White people are also at risk. Racism, in contrast, excludes a lot of the United States population as a target. As a result, racism does not get the same emergency response. Black graduate students often feel that they have to respond where others do not. Racist events have inspired them to leave their homes, even in a pandemic, to stand publicly against the violent oppression toward Black people.

For many Black graduate students, activism is a strategy to respond to the sociopolitical turmoil and academic systemic barriers against Black graduate students. It is an external strategy in that students join or even lead the massive movements or local displays to address injustices. There are also internal strategies to address many of the stressors Black graduate students deal with individually and collectively.

External Response

Bent on one knee; faces covered; masks, shirts, and signs declaring "Black Lives Matter," "Defund the Police," "White Silence is Violence," they protested. Through written demands to university leadership and Zoom boycotts; on Twitter, Instagram, TikTok, and Facebook, they protested. Through the summer and fall of 2020, against the backdrop of a global pandemic, Black graduate students joined and often led multiracial coalitions of collegians to fight White supremacy and police violence. In the last 4 years alone, police have shot and killed 1,387 Black Americans—more than twice the rate of White Americans (*The Washington Post*, 2021). And while racial persecution dates to America's colonial days, citizen journalism and social media have exposed the world, directly, to the ubiquitous scope and breadth of police brutality (Hurst et al., 2018). Now, in the wake of numerous, highly publicized incidents of anti-Black violence (e.g., the murders of George Floyd, Breonna Taylor, and Ahmaud Arbury), Black collegians have mobilized and organized to demand bold, evidence-based action against racial injustice. This current period of college student activism is unique in certain key respects (e.g., interracial coalitions, increased convergence of class- and race-based protest; Sugrue, 2020). However, student-led activism for Black lives both in and beyond higher education is rooted in a rich tradition (Kendi, 2012; Rhoads, 2016).

The Black campus movement (BCM) of the late 1960s has received considerably less scholarly and mainstream attention than its counterpart civil rights and Black Power movements. Yet, the BCM profoundly reshaped the landscape of American higher education. Among other signal achievements, college student activism during this period cemented Black studies into the curricular offerings at many American institutions of higher education (Rooks, 2006). In the 1980s and 1990s, college students fervently protested South Africa's racist system of racial apartheid (Favors, 2017). Students at the University of California (UC), Berkeley staged daily sit-ins and class boycotts that lasted over a year from 1985–1986, forcing the UC Regents to divest more than $3 billion from companies with business in South Africa (One Bold Idea, 2018). More recently, in the 2000s and 2010s, college student activism has played a pivotal role in influencing major judicial decisions to uphold race-based affirmative action (Jean-Jaques & Lopez, 2016). In 2003, student organizers at the University of Michigan coordinated a 50,000-person march on Washington, DC in support of affirmative action (Rhoads, 2016). In the last decade, students are increasing pressure on university administrators and officials—demanding they address racially hostile campus environments that exclude Black students (Carlton, 2020). In 2015, University of Missouri Black graduate student activists alongside the school's football team went on strike to protest racial bigotry, ultimately forcing the university system's president and campus chancellor to resign (Hartocollis, 2017). Most recently, Black-led student coalitions are protesting publicly as well as seeking ways to leverage the financial resources and networks of their universities to fight institutional racism (e.g., urging colleges to cut ties with the police, diversify campuses, and closing the educational opportunity gap) (Dennon, 2020).

As students, staff, and university funding sources, Black graduate students occupy a unique position in higher education. They maintain relationships with undergraduates, staff, faculty, and administration. Thus, these students are well-suited to liaison between campus communities and galvanize coordinated activist efforts (Grant, 2020). Black graduate students are often tacitly expected to lead institutional activist efforts as, for example, members on diversity committees or mentors to undergraduate students of color (Boyd, 2020). Graduate students already contend with demanding professional and academic obligations. Black graduate students shoulder this additional responsibility and have called for increased funding to support their efforts and mental health, among other needs. University administrations, however, tend to prioritize undergraduate concerns, failing to adequately respond to the unique challenges Black graduate students face. Campus administrators and student affairs educators are ultimately responsible for performing the emotional, physical, mental, and social labor needed to address racial injustice and anti-Blackness in university systems (Linder et al., 2019). However, it is often Black graduate students who are spearheading campus movements to demand higher education be reenvisioned through the lens of racial and social justice. Nevertheless, through traditional and nontraditional activism, graduate students are making Black lives matter. This multiracial, intersectional coalition of student activists standing together in the fight for racial justice is vital, not only to ensure the safety, health, and well-being of Black Americans but also to ameliorate America's racial divide and better position our citizenry to combat phenomena that directly threaten us all.

Internal Response

Black graduate students have historically been a part of numerous movements where they have exercised an external response to many academic and societal grievances. Simultaneously, while they spend time and resources to tear down oppression, they spend additional time and resources attempting to build up other Black graduate students at the local and national levels.

Impostorism for Black graduate students may present its script that students are lucky to be admitted or their acceptance results from a school's attempt to look diverse. Further, students are just one mistake or low grade away from being told that their acceptance was a regrettable decision and being outed for the ill-prepared student they feel they embody. Intervention could be solicited from advisors, counselors, professors, or friends. However, the best intervention is often from other Black graduate students who informally share their struggles with impostorism or give insight into what Black graduate students should reasonably expect. Often, even the phrase "I don't understand that either" can be sufficient to introduce doubt in the accusatory thoughts of impostorism. Impostorism attempts to convince a student that they alone are confused while everyone else has expert-level knowledge that they missed. "I don't understand that either," "That took me a long time," or even just "I hated that class" can mitigate impostor anxieties that create the feeling of isolated ineptitude. These kinds of shared experiences motivate the creation of peer relationships and formal and informal mentoring relationships that Black graduate students often rely on (Apugo, 2017, 2019; Defour & Hirsch, 1990; Johnson-Bailey, 2018; Jones, 2018).

When schools attempt to increase their diversity while failing to provide sufficient support to students of color upon their arrival, it is rarely a change in policy or provision of institutional support that intervenes. Instead, it is other Black graduate students who find a way to support their peers even when they are outside departments or even schools. Even during interview periods, Black graduate students will reach out to prospective students about helpful interview strategies, where to eat and stay during campus visits and interviews, and what faculty are safe to speak and interact with and who should be avoided if possible (Apugo, 2019).

Instead of competition, which often defines academic spaces, Black graduate students are known to share and pass down to incoming students the solutions to common barriers that they have surmounted. Common advice like where to find funding sources and what large expenditures like internships or tests should be planned and budgeted for, are often shared eagerly. Older students are likely to share how they survived particular courses or how to avoid classes with professors who microaggress or do not intervene when microaggressions occur (Apugo, 2019; Jones, 2018).

Communal intervention has also been employed to address academic systemic barriers. Universities must allocate more funding and resources to Black graduate students if they hope to increase their recruitment, retention, and intellectual capital. Black graduate students contribute a great deal to the university's intellectual reputation, mentorship, undergraduate teaching, student leadership and advocacy on campus, cultural training, and education that universities need to operate each semester. These tangible contributions, along with cultural and social influence, make up the fabric of academic excellence among all Black students and are invaluable to universities' future growth and tenacity. The cyclical nature of the issue of low admission of Black graduate students has resulted in under-resourcing, yet under-resourcing undergirds Black graduate students' limited admissions and makes breaking the cycle incredibly daunting.

The lack of resources has made Black graduate students vulnerable to financial, academic, and mental health difficulties with no hope of intervention. In response to universities failing to properly break the cycle, students have taken it upon themselves to attempt to fill the gaps with mentorship, helping to find funding sources and providing social support for students. Through graduate organizations such as the Black Graduate Student Association (BGSA), students are able to make connections with faculty, give back to the community, and connect with other Black graduate students (Guiffrida, 2000). Furthermore, the hard-fought battle for equitable investment into Black graduate students impacts both current students and alumni. Increased alumni mean more mentorship opportunities, which aids retention and academic success and more funding opportunities because successful alumni are more likely to donate monetarily.

Though the mental health consequences like impostorism and news fatigue and the academic consequences like lack of funding can make Black graduate students feel isolated and alone, students have found a sense of community together. When they leave their homes to protest they find they are not alone in projecting their voices. Alongside them, other Black graduate students and Black graduate student alumni walk the steps to demand change at every level (Hurst et al., 2018; Stone et al., 2018).

Conclusion

Black lives matter should never be a controversial statement, yet it is often met with resistance or caveats. Black graduate students are many times told they are not at risk for the violence that befalls other Black people because they will be bestowed respect because of their academic accomplishments. However, Black graduate students are often ignored and devalued even in academic contexts by university administrations. When the world seemingly struggles with making Black lives matter, Black graduate students invest in ensuring that their peers never struggle to believe they matter. Black graduate students belong both in the academic community and everywhere.

References

Allen, H. K., Lilly, F., Green, K. M., Zanjani, F., Vincent, K. B., & Arria, A. M. (2020). Graduate student burnout: Substance use, mental health, and the moderating role of advisor satisfaction. *International Journal of Mental Health and Addiction*, 1–17. https://doi.org/10.1007/s11469-020-00431-9-

Anderson, G. (2019, September 17). *A racist attack at Arizona*. Inside Higher Ed. https://www.insidehighered.com/news/2019/09/17/arizona-students-criticize-university-police-response-alleged-assault

Anderson, G. (2020, June 9). *Organizing for change: Students at Rice University and colleges across the U.S. are seeking ways to leverage the wealth and connections of their universities to combat racial injustice*. Inside Higher Ed. https://www.insidehighered.com/news/2020/06/09/students-organize-racial-justice-campus-and

Apugo, D. (2017). "We all we got": Considering peer relationships as multi-purpose sustainability outlets among millennial Black women graduate students attending majority White urban universities. *The Urban Review, 49*(2), 347–367. https://doi.org/10.1007/s11256-017-0404-2

Apugo, D. (2019). All power to the peers: Black women graduate students' peer relationship typologies in PWIs. *Journal of Women and Gender in Higher Education, 12*(2), 224–244. https://doi.org/10.1080/19407882.2019.1573690

Beasley, S. T. (2020). Student-faculty interactions and psychosociocultural influences as predictors of engagement among Black college students. *Journal of Diversity in Higher Education*. https://doi.org/10.1037/dhe0000169

Boyd, C. (2020, June 11). *Being a Black Ph.D. Student Following George Floyd's Murder*. Inside Higher ED. https://www.insidehighered.com/advice/2020/06/11/black-phd-student-describes-having-balance-his-career-prospects-responding-racial

Carlton, G. (2020, May 18). *Student activism in college: A history of campus protests*. Best Colleges. https://www.bestcolleges.com/blog/history-student-activism-in-college/

Clance, P. R., & Imes, S. A. (1978). The impostor phenomenon in high achieving women: Dynamics and therapeutic interventions. *Psychotherapy: Theory, Research, and Practice, 15*(3), 241–247.

Cokley, K., Komarraju, M., Patel, N., Castillon, J., Rosales, R., Pickett, R., Piedrahita, S., Ravitch, J., & Pang, L. S. (2004). Construction and initial validation of the student-professor interaction scale. *College Student Affairs Journal, 24*(1), 32–50.

Cokley, K., McClain, S., Enciso, A., & Martinez, M. (2013). An examination of the impact of minority status stress and impostor feelings on the mental health of diverse ethnic minority college students. *Journal of Multicultural Counseling & Development, 41*(2), 82–95. https://doi.org/10.1002/j.2161-1912.2013.00029.x

Daniel, C. (2007). Outsiders-within: Critical race theory, graduate education, and barriers to professionalization. *Journal of Sociology & Social Welfare, 34*(1), 25. https://link.gale.com/apps/doc/A160228606/OVIC?u=txshracd2598&sid=OVIC&xid=b5ced7fe

DeFour, D., & Hirsch, C. (1990). The adaptation of Black graduate students: A social network approach. *American Journal of Community Psychology, 18*(3), 487–503. https://doi.org/10.1007/BF00938119

Dennon, A. (2020, June 17). *Students demand racial justice and equity on campus*. Best Colleges. https://www.bestcolleges.com/blog/college-student-activists-black-lives-matter/

Dill, E. (2020, January 17). Student at center of "napping while Black" furor lashes out at Yale officials and "woke intersectional feminists". *The Chronicle of Higher Education, 66*(17) https://www-chronicle-com.ezproxy.lib.utexas.edu/article/student-at-center-of-napping-while-black-furor-lashes-out-at-yale-officials-and-woke-intersectional-feminists/

Dyrbye, L. N., Thomas, M. R., Eacker, A., Harper, W., Massie, F. S., Power, D. V., Mashele H., Novotny, P. J., Sloan, P. A., & Shanafelt, T. D. (2007). Race, ethnicity, and medical student well-being in the United States. *Archives of Internal Medicine, 167*(19), 2103–2109. https://doi.org/10.1001/archinte.167.19.2103

Ellis, E. M. (2001). The Impact of Race and Gender on Graduate School Socialization, Satisfaction with Doctoral Study, and COmmitment to Degree Completion. *Western Journal of Black Studies, 25*(1), 30. SocINDEX with Full Text.

Farrell, P. (2004). Who are the students receiving merit scholarships? In D. E. Heller & P. Marin (Eds.), *State merit scholarship programs and racial inequality* (pp. 47–77). The Civil Rights Project at Harvard University.

Favors, J. (2017, March 29). *It's a different world: Black student activism from the civil rights movement through the Trump era*. Process. https://www.processhistory.org/favors-black-student-activism/

Felder, P. P., & Barker, M. J. (2013). Extending Bell's concept of interest convergence: A framework for understanding the African American doctoral student experience. *International Journal of Doctoral Studies, 8*, 1–20. https://doi.org/10.28945/1754

Freeman, T. M., Anderman, L. H., & Jensen, J. M. (2007). Sense of belonging in college freshmen at the classroom and campus levels. *The Journal of Experimental Education, 75*(3), 203–220. http://www.jstor.org/stable/20157456

Gasman, M., Gerstl-Pepin, C., Anderson-Thompkins, S., Rasheed, L., & Hathaway, K. (2004). Negotiating power, developing trust: Transgressing race and status in the academy. *Teachers College Record, 106*(4), 689–715. https://doi.org/10.1111/j.1467-9620.2004.00355.x

Gasman, M., Hirschfeld, A., & Vultaggio, J. (2008). "Difficult yet rewarding": The experiences of African American graduate students in education at an Ivy League institution. *Journal of Diversity in Higher Education, 1*(2), 126–138. https://doi.org/10.1037/1938-8926.1.2.126

Golde, C. (2000). Should I stay or should I go? Student descriptions of the doctoral attrition process. *Review of Higher Education, 23*(2), 199–227. https://doi.org/10.1353/rhe.2000.0004

Golde, C. M. (2005). The role of the department and discipline in doctoral student attrition: Lessons from four departments. *The Journal of Higher Education, 76*(6), 669–700. https://doi.org/10.1353/jhe.2005.0039

Grant, A. (2020). Interview with Alexis Grant, founding president of Black Graduate Student Association. *The University of Illinois at Chicago's Women's Leadership and Resource Center*. https://wlrc.uic.edu/bgsa-an-interview-with-wlrc/

Guiffrida, D. A. (2003). African American student organizations as agents of social integration. *Journal of College Student Development, 44*(3), 304–319. https://doi.org/10.1353/csd.2003.0024

Hartocollis, A. (2017, July 9). Long after protests, students shun the University of Missouri. *The New York Times*. https://www.nytimes.com/2017/07/09/us/university-of-missouri-enrollment-protests-fallout.html

Haskins, N., Whitfeld-Williams, M., Shillingford, M. A., Singh, A., Moxley, R., & Ofauni, C. (2013). The experiences of Black master's counseling students: A phenomenological inquiry. *Counselor Education & Supervision, 52*, 162–178. https://doi.org/10.1002/j.1556-6978.2013.00035.x

Hausman, L. R. M., Feifei, Y., Schofield, J. W., & Woods, R. L. (2009). Sense of belonging and persistence in White and African American first-year students. *Research in Higher Education, 50*, 649–669. https://doi.org/10.1007/s11162-009-9137-8

Heisserer, D., & Parette, P. (2002). Advising at-risk students in college and university settings. *College Student Journal*, 36(1), 1–12.

Henning, K., Ey, S., & Shaw, D. (1998). Perfectionism, the imposter phenomenon and psychological adjustment in medical, dental, nursing, and pharmacy students. *Medical Education, 32*(5), 456–464.

Hu, S., & Kuh, G. D. (2003). Diversity experiences and college student learning and personal development. *Journal of College Student Development, 44*(3), 320–334. https://doi.org/10.1353/csd.2003.0026

Hurst, A., Bailey, M. L., Krueger, N., Garba, R., & Cokley, K. (2018). The psychological impact of policing on African American students. In S. Weissinger & D. Mack (Eds.), *Law enforcement in the age of Black Lives Matter* (pp. 53–74). Lexington.

Hurtado, S. (1994). Graduate School Racial Climates and Academic Self-Concept among Minority Graduate Students in the 1970s. *American Journal of Education, 102*(3), 330–351. JSTOR.

Hurtado, S., & Alvarado, A. R. (2015). *Discrimination and bias, underrepresentation, and sense of belonging on campus.* Los Angeles CA: Higher Education Research Institute at UCLA

Jean-Jaques, W., & Lopez, D. (2016, July 6). *Student activists turning up the heat on affirmative action.* The Century Foundation. https://tcf.org/content/commentary/student-activists-turning-heat-affirmative-action/?agreed=1

Johnson-Bailey, J. (2004). Hitting and climbing the proverbial wall: Participation and retention issues for Black graduate women. *Race Ethnicity and Education, 7*(4), 331–349.

Johnson-Bailey, J., Valentine, T., Cervero, R. M., & Bowles, T. A. (2009). Rooted in the soil: The social experiences of Black graduate students at a southern research university. *The Journal of Higher Education, 80*(2), 178–203. https://doi.org/10.1080/00221546.2009.11772138

Jones, P. (2018). Black psychology graduate students' lives matter: Using informal mentoring to create an inclusive climate amidst national race-related events. *Professional Psychology, Research, and Practice, 49*(1), 75–82. https://doi.org/10.1037/pro0000169

Kendi, I. X. (2012). *The Black campus movement: Black students and the racial reconstitution of higher education, 1965–1972.* Springer.

Koeske, G. F., & Koeske, R. D. (1991). Student "burnout" as a mediator of the stress-outcome relationship. *Research in Higher Education, 32*, 415–431. https://doi.org/10.1007/BF00992184

Lazarus, R. S., & Folkman, S. (1984). *Stress, appraisal, and coping.* Springer.

Linder, C., Quaye, S. J., Lange, A. C., Roberts, R. E., Lacy, M. C., & Okello, W. K. (2019). "A student should have the privilege of just being a student": Student activism as labor. *The Review of Higher Education, 42*(5), 37–62.

Lovitts, B. E. (2002). *Leaving the ivory tower: The causes and consequences of departure from doctoral study.* Rowman & Littlefield.

Maslach, C., & Jackson, S. E. (1981). The measurement of experienced burnout. *Journal of Organizational Behavior, 2*(2), 99–113. https://doi.org/10.1002/job.4030020205.

McClain, K. S., & Perry, A. (2017). Where did they go?: Retention rates for students of color at predominantly White institutions. *College Student Affairs Leadership, 4*(1). https://scholarworks.gvsu.edu/csal/vol4/iss1/3

McClain, S., Beasley, S. T., Jones, B., Awosogba, O., Jackson, S., & Cokley, K. (2016). An examination of the impact of racial and ethnic identity, impostor feelings, and minority status stress on the mental health of Black college students. *Journal of Multicultural Counseling & Development*, *44*(2), 101–117. https://doi-org/10.1002/jmcd.12040

Milner, H. R. (2004). African American graduate students' experiences: A critical analysis of recent research. In D. Cleveland (Ed.), *A long way to go: Conversations about race by African American faculty and graduate students* (pp. 19–31). Peter Lang.

Museus, S. D., Yi, V., & Saelua, N. (2017). The impact of culturally engaging campus environments on sense of belonging. *The Review of Higher Education*, *40*(2), 187–215. https://doi.org/10.1353/rhe.2017.0001

Okahana, H., Zhou, E., & Gao, J. (2020). Graduate enrollment and degrees: 2009 to 2019. Washington, DC: Council of Graduate Schools. One Bold Idea. (2018, May 2). *How students helped end apartheid: The UC Berkeley protest that changed the world*. University of California. https://cgsnet.org/ckfinder/userfiles/files/CGS_GED19_Report_final2.pdf

Pierce, C. M., Carew, J. V., Pierce-Gonzalez, D., & Wills, D. (1977). An experiment in racism: TV commercials. *Education and Urban Society*, *10*(1), 61–87. https://doi.org/10.1177%2F001312457701000105

Pryor, J. H., Eagan, K., Palucki-Blake, L., Hurtado, S., Berdan, J., & Case, M. H. (2012). *The American freshman: National norms fall 2012*. Higher Education Research Institute, UCLA.

Rhoads, R. A. (2016). Student activism, diversity, and the struggle for a just society. *Journal of Diversity in Higher Education*, *9*(3), 189202. https://doi.org/10.1037/dhe0000039

Rooks, N. (2006). *White money/Black power: The surprising history of African American studies and the crisis of race in higher education*. Beacon.

Ross, S. R., Stewart, J., Mugge, M., & Fultz, B. (2001). The imposter phenomenon, achievement dispositions, and the five-factor model. *Personality and Individual Differences*, *31*(8), 1347–1355. https://doi.org/10.1016/S0191-8869(00)00228-2

Sealy, L., Saunders, C. T., Blume, J., & Chalkley, R. (2019). The GRE over the entire range of scores lacks predictive ability for Ph.D. outcomes in the biomedical sciences. *PLoS ONE*, *14*(3), e0201634. https://doi.org/10.1371/journal.pone.0201634

Smith, W. A., Allen, W. R., & Danley, L. L. (2007). "Assume the position . . . you fit the description": Psychosocial experiences and racial battle fatigue among African American male college students. *American Behavioral Scientist*, *51*(4), 551–578.

Song, H., Jung, J., & Kim, Y. (2017). Perceived news overload and its cognitive and attitudinal consequences for news usage in South Korea. *Journalism & Mass Communication Quarterly*, *94*(4), 1172–1190. https://doi.org/10.1177%2F1077699016679975

Sowell, R., Allum, J., & Okahana, H. (2015). *Doctoral initiative on minority attrition & completion*. Council of Graduate Schools.

Stone, S., Saucer, C., Bailey, M., Garba, R., Hurst, A., Jackson, S. M., Krueger, N., & Cokley, K. (2018). Learning While Black: A Culturally Informed Model of the Impostor Phenomenon for Black Graduate Students. *Journal of Black Psychology*, *44*(6), 491 531. https://doi.org/10.1177/0095798418786648

Sugrue, T. J. (2020, June 11). 2020 is not 1968: To understand today's protests, you must look further back. *National Geographic*. https://www.nationalgeographic.com/history/2020/06/2020-not-1968/

Tinto, V. (1993). *Leaving college: Rethinking the causes and cures of student attrition* (2nd ed.). University of Chicago Press.

The Washington Post (2021, January 2). *Fatal force*. https://www.washingtonpost.com/graphics/investigations/police-shootings-database/

Utsey, S. O., & Ponterotto, J. G. (1996). Development and validation of the index of race-related stress (IRRS). *Journal of Counseling Psychology*, 43(4), 490-501. DOI:10.1037/0022-0167.43.4.490

Walton, G. M., & Cohen, G. L. (2007). A question of belonging: Race, social fit, and achievement. *Journal of Personality and Social Psychology*, *92*(1), 82–96. https://doi.org/10.1037/0022-3514.92.1.82

CHAPTER FOURTEEN

To Be Young, Gifted, and Black

Marlie Harris, Mercedes Holmes, Kuukuwa Koomson, and Brianna McBride

To be a Black student in the United States is to be under pressure. As soon as some Black students enter K–12, they are hit with the expectations to attend college, possibly get an advanced degree, and find a way to live the American dream in the throes of racial oppression. To prepare students for these impending academic rigors, teachers remind them of the importance of good attendance, academic integrity, and work ethic. However, the current education system leaves students of color woefully unprepared for the realities of a predominately White institution's undergraduate experience. Black students are forced to encounter situations entirely independent from traditional academic expectations. Instead, they face challenges dictated and controlled by their Blackness and the perceptions of it.

Those are the life lessons that the K–12 system fails to include in their visible curriculum. Throughout this chapter, you will hear the unique experiences of four Black undergraduate students in an academic system that was not designed for them. Despite this, they tell stories of self-love against anti-Blackness, overcoming imposter syndrome, leadership development in the midst of adversity, and the healing power of solidarity. These stories are unique to themselves, but each share a thread of commonality through the collective Black experience. Combined they tell a larger story of the true struggles of going to a White college while Black—the stories that they don't include in our textbooks, the stories we don't learn until after we win the right to attend.

Marlie Harris: Redefining Internalized Racism With a Sense of Purpose

Growing up much like other young students, I had Harvard and the Ivy Leagues burned into my mind as the necessary steps toward greatness. When my teachers encouraged me to consider historically Black colleges and universities (HBCU)s, I shied away from them. I thought about how I wouldn't fit in there. I thought about how I was shamed by my own family for my lack of "Blackness." The melanin that was meant to bring me a sense of belonging and connection to people from my own community had left me feeling isolated and afraid of my own identity. I had experienced so much rejection from my own community that I had lost hope for any future with the only people who could relate to my experiences.

I was in a sense of identity limbo because I knew my Blackness would never allow me to truly be accepted by any other group of people. I always stood out as the outlier. From White girls pulling my microtwists and patting my puffs with glee in middle school, to my White male best friend reminding me how he would never date Black women because he just didn't perceive them as attractive, I was constantly reminded how I was different.

However, this commentary runs completely contrary to the constant messaging reminding me of my lack of Blackness such as constantly being called an "Oreo", not acting Black, or talking Black. It leaves a young girl lost and confused and searching for worth in all the wrong places. But while I was struggling to find value in other areas of my life, I thrived through my academic successes. I tried to put all of myself into my education and grades. I tried to define myself with intelligence, good grades, and academia, but I failed to recognize that all my previous racial trauma shaped the way I viewed myself. The constant mixed messaging I got about my own identity caused me to internalize the toxic racial messaging thrown all around me.

I thought I could escape my own demons by focusing on academia, but I had to learn that attending a predominantly White institution (PWI) exacerbated my own internalized racism because my Blackness became the only thing people around me saw and on which they based their interactions.

But I had accepted the problematic anti-Black messaging to such a vast extent that I thought attending a "good" university would amplify the worth that I drastically felt I was lacking. My first mistake was believing the ideology that a better school was actually based on its proximity to Whiteness. I told my high school mentors that I was seeking a university with diversity and academic rigor. Before long, I found myself won over by the University of Texas's aggressive marketing toward diversity even though they only had a 4% Black population. And while I would never admit it at the time, I didn't see a problem with it because I was too busy trying to run away from my own skin. However, my time during my undergraduate years made me recognize how inescapable my melanin was.

Attending a PWI as a STEM major had a way of making you feel like a statistic. If you fell behind it was expected. I distinctly remember sitting in my introductory chemistry course as one of the few Black people in the room and remember my chemistry professor proudly announcing how many of the students would be out before the semester ended. I took this statement as a challenge and had a drive to succeed. I spent hours at the library grinding for good grades, which had become a form of positive reinforcement I had grown dependent on. But in my first few semesters I didn't get those results at all. I got my professor's laughter during office hours when I told him how I was struggling after failing a test. I found myself crying in office hours with professors who did not care. I didn't make a single "A" until my sophomore year of college, and it beat me down because I had placed so much value on my grades. And I found myself failing some classes and just getting by with C's in other classes. I had never experienced anything like that in my life. And to put it frankly, I felt like a failure. Grades were all I had left, because I had so many other insecurities shaped by mixed messaging in my upbringing. And if you know anything about mental health, this is 100% a precursor to a mental health crisis. I started to struggle with overwhelming anxiety and depression that I tried to cover up by giving back to my community; however, regular microaggressions made it difficult to pull myself out of my funk.

I had just started my locs before coming into college and in a bout of young exuberance decided to dye them purple. In college White men would regularly tell me how I looked like the prominent rapper Lil Uzi, and while they saw no flaws in their logic it was a clear example of society's propensity to masculinize Black women. They had no problems comparing me to a man because they saw us as one in the same and it brought me back to my own trauma with my father regarding my own femininity. Despite not being around for a large period of my life due to familial conflict, when I was a child he would often express discomfort about my looks and hair. He even questioned my sexuality when I said I would go to prom with a female friend and laughed saying, "What are you going to wear, a suit?" When I brought up insecurities with my mom, she would try to cure them by pushing me to wear makeup. But this does little when there is regular commentary in my household about how unattractive dark skin was because it made you look "African." Even if I tried to pretend this messaging didn't sit with me, the emotions it invoked and insecurities it created haunted me. Then suddenly to be surrounded by White people who lacked empathy in the damaging nature of their words was overwhelming. However, comments about my looks were not the only microaggressions I faced. Sometimes I struggled with outright aggression.

I tried to get involved in the PWI party culture and quickly came to understand the segregated nature of fraternity culture. After party hopping a variety of fraternity houses on campus, I attended a White fraternity party with a group of Black students that was literally a sea of White people dressed in all White. I immediately knew we were somewhere we didn't need to be, but we were quickly dragged away and asked to teach them how to dance. (Full disclosure: I cannot dance). This was an uncomfortable experience that was based purely off of my Blackness, but after being there for a few minutes members of the fraternity started to throw beer cans at us as a clear sign that we had overstayed our welcome. While this blatant racism seems it would be limited to ignorant students, I often encountered racial microaggressions directly in my classes.

In one of my psychology classes we discussed in detail how Black women were per-ceived to be the least attractive group of people. This was followed by a test question to rank which demographic would be perceived the most attractive, Black women or Asian women. And if I felt ugly before, I definitely felt some type of way hearing that scientif-ically Black women were considered the ugliest group. It is absolute ridiculousness that professors are so removed from the perceived negative group that they fail to recognize how it could be psychologically damaging to have a lecture telling the 3 Black girls in the class they're ugly. But it doesn't end there. One of my biology classes used slides from the 1960s and had a true or false question asking if Whites and Blacks typically "back-crossed," or had kids together. But I think the worst offender was a German professor teaching intercultural communication while talking about Black people as if they were creatures to be studied. He attempted to break down "doing the dozens" as a cultural phenomena and asked students in the class if their culture does something similar. Then he talked about how Black women have a habit of talking bad about other people to their faces as if this was a characteristic specific to Black culture. It was a bizarre semester and was completed entirely over Zoom, so there were multiple instances where students had to explain how racism occurred in the United States.

I know I just listed a bunch of wild experiences from my undergraduate years, and it easily could have broken me, but in my sophomore year things changed because I met people who actually believed in me. They suddenly told me rhetoric that was completely contradictory to my negative experiences up until that point. It took three semesters before someone told me that I was smart on that campus and it came from Black men I am forever grateful for. They told me how this school wasn't designed for people of color to succeed. They had faith in me, and they wanted me to succeed. They encouraged me to do independent research. And after being turned away from some professors because I wanted to specifically focus on psychology as it relates to Black people, I randomly asked a Black speaker advocating for mental health for help with my project, and he opened my world to the McNair scholar's program. He continued telling me this new messaging about my potential and intelligence and I felt myself beginning to recover.

Over time, I found myself with newfound confidence and understanding that the only place to get the social support I needed was my own community. That brought me to the Association of Black Psychologists (ABPsi), which I went on to lead and grow on campus. I wanted to create a space to reaffirm students in ways that the campus failed me. It was the first place I heard the history behind my experiences on campus. While trying to create an independent project that analyzed mental health in the Black community, I went to psychology professors for help and was promptly turned away. I heard comments like "That is not psychology. Psychology doesn't really consider race in that way and that wouldn't be a proper project here. You should go try the sociology department instead." I thought I had finally found a field that really spoke to me, but I was confused and discouraged. That is until I heard Dr. Kevin Cokley talk about the racial divide and politics built within academia of our own school. Classes called "Psychology of the Black Experience" or "Psychology of Race and Racism" could not give you psychology credit at school even though they were taught by renowned psychologists and professors. Some students were even advised away from these classes because they would be unable to get credit. I was livid. Not only were I and other students being turned away in our academic pursuits, but this was an endemic problem to the culture of the university. It sent a larger message that the University of Texas at Austin did not prioritize multicultural psychology or even consider it "real" psychology. It motivated me to use my positionality in the ABPsi to bring awareness to issues Black students were facing in their classes and take them straight to the current chair of the psychology department. He was shocked to hear about the experiences undergraduate students were having. How students felt unheard, hypervisible, and uncomfortable in their classes. Although they had regular meetings with graduate students, undergraduate students largely went unheard in their experiences. Our ABPsi student organization meetings were where we discussed a general sense of dissatisfaction of our classes and experiences. This was the most our academic leaders heard from their undergraduate student body, which is a problem itself. Academia has such a prioritization around research and the ways students will come back and contribute to the university's research prowess that they forget and deprioritize the students furthest removed from this research. When compared to graduate students who are mainly attending classes for research purposes, there is no guarantee that an individual undergraduate student will take a liking to research or even come back to contribute to the university's legacy in any beneficial way, so it feels as though they are deprioritized as a result.

Considering the undergraduate demographic has the highest number of Black students compared to graduate students, a lot of Black students go unheard and unprioritized. My academic experiences will not be unique as long as diverse student experiences from the lowest to the highest levels continue going unheard. From my meeting with the chair of the psychology department and the events following Black Lives Matter, the chair made a vow to make changes and create a section within the academic catalogue toward classes that cover diversity and race in psychology.

In my time studying psychology as it relates to race, I came to understand the magnitude of the effects of the negative racial messaging I received. I would not be able to bring myself healing and conquer my own personal insecurities without recognizing how I internalized those messages and how these messages are not unique to myself. I have spent my time outlining experiences and messaging Black students face on a daily basis. The psychological turmoil I had to face and attempt to overcome is a collective experience. While we have a history of prioritizing strength and resilience in the Black community against adversity, I would like to implore any reader to be honest with their own pain and trauma and sit with it. Take some time to get to the heart of it, because there is a common need to keep pushing forward and covering up pain. It feels as if there is no time for it when there are so many tragedies taking place around us, but we all need time to heal. My time and journey so far has taught me about personal accountability toward my mental health. Our surroundings may try to tear us down, but we need to be our own pillar of strength and surround ourselves with people who can strengthen us against the waves of racial oppression.

Mercedes Holmes: Combating Isolation and Finding Solidarity

“

Mixed kid, this Whiteness around us has made us sick.

(Poetry Slam, Inc., 2016, 1:37).

”

At my predominantly White elementary school, located in the heart of my predominantly White hometown, we had a tradition. Every year, the third graders would embark on a history-art project: to choose a culture from our heritage, investigate, and turn a blonde-wood clothespin into a person to represent our culture. When I told my red, White, and blue teacher that I was going to study Mexico, I was the only student implored to find something "more interesting," as my teacher was sure I had a "richer" lineage to be proud of and learn about than "just" Mexican. I did not have the materials to recognize the suggestion as code for finding something more White and European. My mother read between the lines on my behalf and confronted my third grade teacher over it in a spectacular, public fashion—much to my horror at the time. Though well-intentioned, and I no longer regret her confrontation—it painted an easy target on my Black, Brown, adultified back for another clearly out-of-touch, overpowered White woman.

That teacher pulled an 8-year-old me aside the next day, alone, while everyone else in the pod was at lunch, to whisper-spit at me, among other sentiments, that she did not need her time wasted, nor character offended, with disrespectful people accusing her of being a racist! And since I was mixed, I should *want* to present something more "unique" than all the other kids of color in class, who "only have one option." There was a disturbing ease she took in purposefully isolating and reciprocally ambushing an 8-year-old, brown-skinned little girl over an encounter I had not even been present for and an assignment I had no part in designing.

Though I did not think much of the actual clothespin offense, the subsequent demeaning made it abundantly clear whose ego, self-worth, feelings, heritage, and side of the story actually mattered. Properly put in my place, she felt better having reminded me that a Black mixed girl ought never feel *too* comfortable and never veer off-script.

It was from this tokenizing, selectively hostile environment that I was emerging when I entered UT. Though I found these characteristics to thoroughly permeate the faux progressive, White, liberal atmosphere of Austin as well, this time there was a visible and available Black community to be in solidarity with. Finding and becoming a part of said Black community helped me cope with the intense, cumulative exhaustion that came with anti-Black surroundings.

> Tell the world you're Black … do not stutter with shame. Tell them they can never truly love us until they see all of us. That to love us radically is to see the magic in our Blackness. (Poetry Slam, Inc., 2016, 2:41)

In my first semester, I took the famous Black Power Movement course with Dr. Leonard Moore. Race was a consistent focus in the course, and while I objected to more than a few perspectives throughout the semester, I rarely left the classroom without feeling energetic. What was left to be desired in class discussion, in terms of ignorance and anti-Blackness from classmates, did not weigh on me as much as very similar conversations often did and do. The mental exhaustion was partially alleviated because I was learning more about my history, for once, in that classroom. I identified, for once, with the beliefs and frustrations of the figures and movements we were studying. And what I have come to understand is vital: I was doing so *with* other Black people.

Even in a course titled Black Power Movement, White and other non-Black students, opinions, and ideologies significantly populated the class and discussion, so it was an important power to have Black folks in the room and in command; we set a tone of Black solidarity for the course—I felt a bond to, and support from, my Black peers that allowed me a different kind of academic and social confidence. There was a new freedom to speak critiques and lived experiences out loud, which opened a door to intellectual development I did not know existed. Collaborating with other Black minds gave me the opportunity to consider, accept, and reject more ideas more freely, without being slowed down by constant re-justification and fragility management. I do not know if it was conscious, but we protected each other in class; we checked who needed to be checked, we listened when each other spoke, we gave credit to our peers for inspiring our thoughts, and we responded directly to each other with intelligence.

Under that protection, the beautiful diversity of Black thought in the community was highlighted. For the first time in my life, a group of Black students were allowed to help direct academic conversation. With our thoughts finally being centered, we had the chance to utilize our common ground beyond the way it is used to academically tokenize us. Instead of repeating the same few universal truths of Black lives for the benefit of our non-Black counterparts, we got to use our common ground to improve our own conversations. Our common ground does not just unite us in purpose, but it also gives us useful context to recognize nuances in each other's positions, making room for our distinct and unique contributions. My Black peers followed lines of thought and made inquiries that I resonated with, that felt important, interesting, and relevant to me. This level of community allowed for, in so many ways, the best possible work we could do in that classroom.

It was rejuvenating.

> You cannot escape your magic.
>
> *(Poetry Slam, Inc., 2016, 2:53).*

I feel that community bond in action every time I work with other Black students at my PWI. There simply are not enough Black students in most UT classrooms to have or feel such a community everywhere on campus, but I have benefitted and grown tremendously working in and with Black student organizations.

I attended meetings for different Black student organization meetings nearly every day after class during my 1st year at UT; Black preprofessional organizations, Black student alliances, Black women's groups, Black faith-based organizations—I attended them all. I was intentional about making time and spaces to work, play, and just exist with other Black people because it inspires me and validates me. As a 1st year, it was a vital dose of empowerment to go to these meetings and be Black out from under the White gaze that followed me, quite literally, everywhere else I went (even my dorm bedroom was shared with a proudly racist White student).

As a 3rd-year undergraduate student, having served on seven different executive boards for Black student organizations over two executive terms, these organizations have come to define my experience at UT. Through these organizations I have invested in our community's taking up of space; I have coordinated protest demonstrations, scholarships, guest lecturing events, community gatherings, performance showcases, support groups, volunteer events and philanthropy initiatives, and other efforts to serve the diverse needs of the Black community.

One need close to my heart is the Rodney Reed case. Rodney Reed was falsely convicted of the 1996 murder of Stacey Stites in Bastrop, Texas, only about 30 miles from Austin. His conviction was based on recanted evidence and testimonies and relied on the racist myth that Black men are inherently a sexual predator to White women. Reed and others have maintained that he and Stacey were having an affair, which accounted for the sole physical evidence of the trial. During the trial, important evidence of Reed's innocence was not presented. This included hidden eyewitness testimony, misleading expert witness testimony, and the failure of the defense to call either an alibi witness or the multiple witnesses who could have testified to the affair between Stacey and Rodney.

In September 2019, just months before his then scheduled execution for a murder he did not commit, the Reed Justice Initiative shared Rodney's story at a general meeting of the Black Student Alliance, which I was serving as political action chair for at the time. As Reed's family member laid out the overwhelming evidence of a cover-up and all the incredible advocacy they had done for decades on his behalf, I knew Reed had to be a priority of Black UT's activism and support. Utilizing my political action chair position with the Black Student Alliance and our membership of the Big XII Council on Black Student Government, I tried to do my small part by organizing support efforts for Reed from the Black student community in and beyond UT. I helped coordinate clemency letter campaigns, call campaigns, social media campaigns, support rallies, watch parties, and awareness meetings across universities. Yet, the Black turnout at these events demonstrated the challenges we were facing at uniting Black students behind this cause. I knew the community cared because awareness was spreading, yet we failed repeatedly to really mobilize or make an asset out of our community for Reed in such a crucial and time-sensitive moment.

Thanks to the tireless work so many have put in for decades to free Reed, his life was saved and his execution is indefinitely stayed while he is awaiting a retrial. Yet, the fight is not over to ensure this is a fair retrial and that justice is dealt. I still had to ask myself what had gone awry in my community organizing. Admittedly, I felt I had let Reed's family down after committing the Black Student Alliance as his ally and proponent. I felt like I was the reason we delivered a less impactful moment in the movement than I hoped. I lost some confidence in my ability to meaningfully contribute to our community and our needs and doubted my ability to read and understand what our community wants from our student activists.

Even in doubt of my place in the community and our politics, my fellow Black student leaders never ceased to amaze and inspire me. That same year, I watched the Black women on campus step up and lead one of the biggest student movements on campus ever, leading to concrete change in sexual assault policy at UT. I have seen our beautiful and strong community unite to tangibly better our own lives and position. We have started mutual aid collectives, we have rallied, we have written and passed legislation. Through protests, insurrections, and natural disasters we are not just there for each other, but we are there *with* each other. Even when I felt I had failed the Black community, the Black community showed me how powerful our activism really is and can be.

Kuukuwa Koomson: Growing to Hate the System While Falling in Love With My Blackness

Black Lives Matter is *not* a trend. It's not an aesthetic. It's not something fun for you and your best buds to participate in. Black Lives Matter was not a month-long event to help oppressors walk in the shoes of the oppressed as a fun after-school activity. It's definitely not a bandwagon you can hop on while it's a hashtag on social media. Most importantly, it won't achieve its goal if all you did and continue to do is post "We see you. We hear you. We stand with you. #BLM" on your social media. Finally, it's not an opportunity for you and your business to profit on.

On May 25, 2020, George Floyd was unjustly executed, sparking outrage throughout several communities. For a lot of people this was the first time they realized that racism is still a thing, and many people, especially people within the Black community, have been suffering at the hands of police for years. However, for Black people, this was just another day in our life—a gut-wrenching and emotionally taxing day, yes, but not something we weren't accustomed to. The Black Lives Matter movement began in 2013 as a direct response to the murder of Trayvon Martin in 2012. I remember exactly how I felt when I heard about his death, Flashback to 2012: Trayvon had just been murdered and I was having a rough time wrapping my head around the situation. As the reporter walked us through the events it felt as if each word uttered flew across the room and laid like a weight on my chest, pressing down on me and making it harder and harder to breathe. In the midst of me fighting back my tears and trying to not let my anxiety get the best of me, several thoughts raced through my mind until it finally clicked: Being Black in America was a death sentence. The darker and bigger you are, the more of a threat you appear to be. The only reason Trayvon was killed was because he was Black. He didn't have a weapon on him, he wasn't escaping crime, nor was he a wanted criminal. Unfortunately, the only mistake he made that night was being in the wrong place at the wrong time. As sad as I was about the situation, I was even more so terrified and traumatized. The anxiety attack I was trying to prevent hit its peak as panic and confusion filled my mind. How do I know that when I leave the house to walk to school tomorrow I'll make it back home to my family? How do I know that if I reach my hand into my packet to grab my phone, a cop won't pull out a gun on me because he thinks I have a weapon? How do I know that couldn't happen to me next?

What is beyond me is that there is a large population of people who don't have these same fears. Since 2012 I've felt ridiculously uncomfortable leaving stores empty handed because I don't want anyone to think that I've stolen something. I pray to God that I never get pulled over, because if I do the first thing on my mind will be that I'm not making it back home to my friends and family. If I'm walking on the sidewalk and see a White man walking toward me, I'm quickly crossing the street. Having a casual morning run through a predominantly White neighborhood? Absolutely not. A lot of people don't understand the kind of privilege they have to just be able to live their lives without the fear of racism, discrimination, and prejudice watching their every move. One wrong mistake and you're taking your last breath.

Now 8 years later we are in 2021. Ask yourself if anything has changed. Eric Garner (2014), Micheal Brown (2014), Tamir Rice (2014), Sandra Bland (2016), Alton Sterling (2016), Stephon Clark (2018), Breonna Taylor (2020), and George Floyd (2020). Please tell me what has changed. If anything, White supremacists, police, and other racists feel more comfortable acting the way they do because their president, Donald Trump, is one of them. They are left to run rampant like a bunch of rabid animals committing terrorist acts but have somehow convinced themselves that what they are doing is right. I believe that's called delusion and mental illness, but what do I know?

Anyone paying attention can tell you that America is a divided nation, and for lack of better words, in the middle of what some would refer to as a race war. On one side we have the Black community and our allies screaming Black Lives Matter, marching, protesting, begging. and pleading to be treated like human beings with basic human rights, asking the people who are put in place to protect us to stop killing us, fighting nonstop to make sure that our kids and future generations don't ever have to experience something like this. In the other corner we have White Lives Matter, Blue Lives Matter, White supremacists, terrorists, and the president of the United States telling us we need to stop complaining and instead make America great again. It's enough learning about slavery, segregation, prejudice, and racism in school but living in the 21st century and still experiencing it? It just goes to show that America will always revert to the foundation on which it was built. Instead of trying to fix the system we need to abolish the whole thing and start over with a completely new foundation, one that is accepting of everyone regardless of color, race, sex, gender, income, job, nationality, and so on, a foundation that acknowledges that all human beings should be treated equally and with basic human rights.

I'm going to backtrack a little bit. It is important to explain my personal growth experience and how going to a PWI helped me find pride in my Blackness and myself. Like most students, my journey of self-discovery began in college. Something important to note is that I came from a majority-minority high school. Coming into college I didn't realize how detached I was from my Blackness, but it's very hard to love being Black when society constantly tells you that being Black isn't something to be proud of. Everywhere I turned it was, "Oh wow you're really dark!" "Is that your real hair?" "Do you know your dad?" "Can you play basketball?" "Do you speak African?" What made it worse was that it wasn't just White people, but also people of color. I did everything to not be too Black so I could avoid being "one of those Black girls." Throughout high school, middle school, and even elementary school I tried to blend in. I didn't talk too loud or express strong emotions because I didn't want people to call me aggressive. I purposely avoided getting braids and any hairstyles that were "too Black," settling instead for jet black straight bundles. I wouldn't say that I disliked my skin or my Black features, but they weren't my favorite traits because at the time it was all tied to something negative.

I harbored all these feelings within me as I stepped on campus freshman year. That year was probably my hardest year on campus, but I survived. I came to this big PWI with no friends, as a first-generation student, no pride in my race, and completely lost. It didn't help that college classes were a lot more difficult than high school classes and my GPA was suffering. My whole life I've been told that I was smart and school was never too hard for me, but I couldn't understand why college was so difficult. I was not finishing the year; the year was actually finishing me. It got to the point where I didn't think I belonged at UT. I didn't see anyone who looked like me, I still hadn't made any friends, I was struggling in my classes, and my mental health was suffering. It was so bad I even thought about transferring to College Station since I had a few friends down there, but I thank God every day that I didn't do that because my college experience did a 180 at the beginning of sophomore year.

After that awful first attempt at college I told myself that I needed to make some changes, starting with the way I viewed classes and grades. I hated and still hate that grades, GPA, and numerical achievements are the bases in which students are judged. It adds so much pressure on students and makes learning unenjoyable. In the midst of me trying to save my GPA and convince myself that UT didn't accidentally accept me, my mental health was deteriorating severely. It got to the point where I had to realize "I can't come and kill myself for this school." Not getting a 4.0 is okay. Having a bad semester is okay. Taking breaks is okay. Not doing homework because you need to self-care is okay. Grades and homework will be here tomorrow, but if you push yourself too far you may not be here tomorrow. Once I adopted this mind-set I started working on myself, and that ended up helping my grades. Occasionally imposter syndrome sneaks up on me, but I do my best to keep moving forward.

The second change I needed to make that year was finding the Black people on campus and making some friends. At the beginning of each year one of the Black organizations on campus (Black Student Alliance) has an event called Black Student Orientation. The purpose of this event is to showcase Black organizations on campus so incoming students know what clubs they can join. That year I told myself that by fire or by force I was going to go and would leave with a new friend, and I did exactly that. I didn't just leave with one friend but two, and now they are my best friends. The whole year we made sure to go to everything, and when I say everything, I mean everything! We joined The Association of

Black Psychologists (ABPsi), African Student Organization (ASO), Black Student Alliance (BSA), African American Culture Committee (AACC), Black Business Students Association (BBSA), the ASO dance team, Texas Black homecoming planning committee (TBHC), and so much more. If there was a Black event going on, we were there. I met more people in the first semester of sophomore year than I did all of freshman year.

This was my defining year because I got introduced to Black UT and they pushed me to want better for myself. There were countless shades of beautiful Black and Brown skin all around me, talented and creative individuals all in one space—I absolutely loved it. I fed off their energy just as they fed off mine. My favorite part about Black UT was the women, strong, beautiful, courageous, and amazing women. They wore their kinky curls so gracefully, strutting down Speedway, braids swaying side to side, and looking unapologetically Black. These women were not afraid to be loud about their Blackness nor loud about their beliefs. They were outspoken, leaders, women with plans and means to execute them. I wanted nothing more than to be in love with my Blackness and powerful like they were. I started experimenting with my hair, my clothes, and speaking what's on my mind without fear of being called "aggressive." I started paying attention to racial matters and getting involved. I became more involved in organizations and even ended up being in a handful of leadership roles. Ideally, I was doing whatever I could to meet new people, boost my resume, and discover who I was, all while fully supporting the Black community. By the end of the year I was absolutely in love with being Black. I loved my dark skin, my big lips, my 4c hair, my African name, and my people. I wanted nothing but the best for us.

Being a part of the Black community on campus opened my eyes and allowed me to see a new perspective on not only how I viewed myself but also how I viewed social and political issues. Am I still scared for my life, absolutely, but now I'm more angry than scared. I'm angry that we are still forced to have a conversation about race in 2021. I'm angry that White hate groups are not held to the same standard as other terrorists. I'm angry that innocent Black people had their lives prematurely ended as a result of a broken system. I'm angry about law enforcement thinking that it's their job to be judge, jury, and executioner. I'm angry that Breonna Taylor and so many more people haven't gotten justice. I'm angry that a group of terrorists were able to storm the Capitol protesting God knows what but we can't have peaceful protest in support of Black Lives Matter.

However, I am beyond thankful for the Black community on campus, because without them I would still be the same lost, scared, and insecure Black girl from high school. Today I can look in the mirror as a proud Black woman with 4c curls, big lips, and dark skin who is unapologetically Black and happy to have found myself in the midst of chaos.

Brianna McBride: Drawing Power From Community Development and Collectivism

As an incoming freshman, moving into your first college dorm is usually an emotional process. You're leaving home for the first time, getting ready to embark on a new journey. My entire immediate family came to move me into my new home. While most freshman's stomachs would be turning, mine was filled with adrenaline. I texted my friends, "I'll be there as soon as I wrap up here" as my older sister and mother finalized my dorm decor. "You're officially moved into your dorm; how do you feel?" my sister asked. "I'm happy. Thank y'all so much; big hugs because you have to go now right?" I responded quickly. "I hope you're not trying to get rid of us" my mother added. "Oh nooooo, never that!" I said with a smile. They didn't know that during the entire move in process, I was thinking about the Block Party. Block Party was the first event of New Black Student Weekend where I could *finally* meet the Black community on campus. As soon as my family drove off, I ran back to my dorm, threw on my best "first impression" outfit, and jolted down to the event. Walking into the large room with my friends, I was met with controlled chaos. There was music blaring, multiple conversations happening at once, and most importantly Black students everywhere. Upperclassmen walked up, welcoming me to the event and rushed me toward other incoming freshmen. In this moment, I let out a breath of relief and thought, *I am exactly where I need to be to survive.*

I attend one of the largest predominantly White state institutions in the South with a low percentage of Black students on campus, so feeling lost in the sea of students was common. However, after attending New Black Student Weekend, a welcome program for incoming Black students created and executed by the Black undergraduate community, I was instantly immersed in a home away from home. The weekend included team-building exercises with my fellow incoming students, workshops on how to navigate college, and testimonies from current Black students and faculty. Overall, it was a vital introduction to all the resources I would need on campus to not only survive, but thrive. Not only were there Black student organizations, but we had spaces on campus dedicated to Black students as well. Hanging out in lounges with direct access to upperclassmen for mentorship and guidance helped me realize that I wasn't in this experience alone.

As a person who longs for and thrives within a supportive community, I saw the value in being a part of Black student organizations and found myself gaining leadership roles very early my freshman year. Understanding that leadership development was a big deal, as it made it easy for me to want to be a part of it. I saw all the hard work that upperclassmen students did to create family and admired that. Small things such as loaning old textbooks, giving advice on good professors, or providing a list of places to get my hair done, made all the difference. It inspired me to grow, flourish in, and fight for this community I was becoming a part of.

Ultimately, my personal identity was being shaped by the roles I took on, and I began to grow as a leader and integral member of the community on campus. This helped me learn more about my role and how I could always find my place on campus. It also became apparent that Black events were the one place where, as an entire community, we could see each other. The mere sight of Black people on campus put myself at ease throughout my time at UT Austin. However, when I stepped out of my safe haven, my identity was challenged at each turn.

A unique challenge presented itself in one of my favorite organizations. Campus Events and Entertainment (E+E) was an umbrella organization that housed student-led committees that had the opportunity to organize university-funded events on campus. I joined African American Culture Committee my freshman year because of my simple interest in event planning. I had experience in high school coordinating fundraisers as well as events for Black History Month, so this organization was truly perfect for me. I was able to lead the planning of the largest showcase of Black culture on the 40 acres, which in turn fueled my love for my community building. I joined the leadership team of this organization and found that being connected directly to the university came with many issues. As a committee, we often found ourselves having to explain the importance of our type of events that would be centered around food, music, and fellowship. A recurring problem we faced was getting allocated funds for food for events.

We were told, "food is not an event," suggesting that we were not focused on creating a quality event, but wanted to spend unreasonable amounts of funds toward food. This experience was frustrating because of the historical importance that traditional Black food had within the community. "Breaking bread," as we like to call it, is more than just a meal; it's a way of fellowship and a standard within Black households. The fact that E+E leadership would question our choices to include food in all events was insulting. To come to a compromise, we had to agree to always insert some form of education within the events.

Another issue we faced was balancing inclusivity and Black empowerment. It was mandatory that all E+E events had to be inclusive to the entire UT community. This meant that for the African American Culture Committee we were not allowed to market events as "Black" specifically. For example, "Black Thanksgiving" was not a permitted name of an event, and our Black History Month events could not be exclusive to Black students. For me, being inclusive on a campus that was not designed for me creates this sense of pressure that I cannot be my authentic self, especially at an event that is meant for me. Our events were the only place we could find solace from the microaggressions of classes, workspaces, and more. Unfortunately, this rule made us feel like we had to create a palatable version of ourselves for campus.

I learned quickly what it meant to be Black in the eyes of E+E and what expectations were. Once I became president of the organization, it didn't take long to see that I was the only Black person at the table in cabinet meetings. None of the other eight communities had more than two or three Black members, so I found it unfair that my organization was the only one constantly ridiculed about inclusion when it was obvious Black people didn't feel safe in other E+E spaces. In order to combat this, as president it was my goal to feed my members by focusing on the needs of the Black community and what we wanted out of AACC events regardless of the requests from top leadership.

These issues pushed me to work even harder to support my community because no one was able to advocate for us but us.

Once I came to the conclusion that the best course of action for dealing with micro-aggressions, antiracist practices, and ignorance was through intentional community empowerment, I was able to balance working with E+E and in other organizations created and sustained by Black students. Being an integral leader, having been involved in almost every organization by the end of my junior year, I quickly recognized an issue: Our Black organizational events clashed. This led to much turmoil and a competitive nature between the organizations. I explored potential solutions because I saw the value of every Black organization on campus. Attempting to make change, I presented proposals and even applied for the codirector position of the Black President's Leadership Council (BPLC), a council composed of all Black undergraduate student organization presidents. Although I was initially denied, the unprecedented global pandemic and horrific events of George Floyd and Breonna Taylor led to me filling in the codirector position. Over the summer of 2020, while Black student organizations were making public statements calling for action, the UT administration was looking to Black student leadership on campus. Regrettably, BPLC was not yet a functioning organization. When I filled the role, I maintained my mission: to make BPLC a more cohesive organization and lead a complete revitalization of the council.

In 4 days, we decided to write a constitution and refocus our purpose. Next, I called on all the Black presidents, notifying them of our goal: to provide a united front among the Black undergraduate community and present our collective demands to the university. After informing UT administration of this change, we had a single month until our meeting with our interim president and dean of students. Four weeks and countless meetings later, we had our Black community united demands. Little did I know that our administration meeting would lead to a letter from President Hartzell outlining "A More Diverse & Welcoming Community." Community members told us that "we've never seen change happen like this," and I was proud because I had a part in this change. My ambition started with a simple goal, to recreate a space where Black student leaders could come together and think, collaborate, and avoid clashing events. Two years later, my resilience and determination lead to a creation of a council that we, as a Black community, can be proud of.

An essential piece to much of this effort to balance collective empowerment and combating racism is getting a grasp of my mental health. Mental wellness is discussed very often throughout the Black community at UT, yet the conversation usually focuses on self-care, not the integral parts of actively maintaining wellness. Honestly, it wasn't a concept that I took seriously until my senior year of college. I had dealt with mental health crises as a witness within my friend group as I wasn't able to acknowledge and pinpoint my own anxiety until things took a turn for the worse. The hardest issue about dealing with my anxiety is suffering from imposter syndrome. The lingering feeling that "I am not doing enough," "I am not as important as people believe me to be," and "if I don't succeed, I am a failure" haunted me throughout my work as a leader on campus.

It is difficult because I find satisfaction in the work that I do, so slowing down or even prioritizing myself isn't in the cards for me. Also, most people believe that low confidence and self-esteem equates with low achievement, but because all my mental health issues are disguised with my achievements, it's extremely difficult to conceptualize how I feel. I find myself sitting in my room wondering, "Am I really the person to take on this job?" "Will I even achieve everything I set out to do?" and "Can I even do this?" As I write this, I am exploring the best practices for my mental health, and it has been a journey filled with trials and errors. First, surrounding myself with an encouraging support system is vital. Currently, the best strategies I've found are as follows: identifying triggers and reducing exposure to them, speaking encouraging words and affirmations daily, and prioritizing time for self-care throughout the day. I believe that moving forward with intentional work toward my anxiety will continue to help me, and as a result, I can help my brothers and sisters as well.

Being a Black leader means constantly having and executing multiple roles. One day you may just be an event planner, another day you could be an activist, and you may even stand to represent your entire community at an event. You find yourself being overly involved because you are needed everywhere. But at the end of the day, we are students. We are here to get our education and learn who we want to be in the world. In order to do that, we must be in an environment that propels us to excel, and that is what the Black community at the University of Texas at Austin does for me. The mere existence of a thriving and supportive community has made a world of difference in my life. They created a foundation for me to soar from. The love and security I felt from this Black UT family gives me the energy to go to bat for them any day against anti-Black racism on and off campus. And I will continue to do so because who better to do it than us?

Reference

Poetry Slam, Inc. (2016, December 4). *Nps 2016 Finals - House Slam - Ashley Davis & Marshall Gillson "Mixed Kids."* https://www.youtube.com/watch?v=gkAaj1XH84I

CHAPTER FIFTEEN

From Segregation to Disinclusion

The Anti-Black Experience of Graduate School

Keoshia Harris and TaShara Williams

Black students being perceived as unworthy of attaining a quality education, particularly at a historically White institution, is unfortunately not a novel idea. This perception dates to slavery when our ancestors would be severely beaten because of their desire for knowledge (Anderson, 2016). Even the most basic skills of being able to read, write, and spell could cost them their life. Through the use of severe punishments, Black individuals quickly learned that education was a privilege for White individuals only. Furthermore, this was the beginning of Black individuals being intentionally excluded from the educational sphere, which reiterated that Black and White individuals were not to be seen as equals (Anderson, 2016). The Declaration of Independence states that we all have unalienable rights: life, liberty, and the pursuit of happiness. However, this statement would be better suited with an asterisk next to it to exemplify that these rights are conditional upon who is being referred to.

The enslaved Black folks were deprived of their right to educate themselves so they could have access to a better quality of life for themselves and their families, including having better paying jobs, understanding voting schemes, deciphering political messages, and living in a nice neighborhood that is zoned to a quality school for their children (Anderson, 2016). There appears to be a domino effect present. Ironically, at the core of many of the inequalities that are present in our current society is education. All these factors are not coincidentally connected. There is a purposeful action and plan to prevent us from achieving Black excellence, which began with removing our ancestors' opportunity to learn (Anderson, 2016).

People like to counter this perception with the argument that since Black people are no longer enslaved, they should "pull themselves up by their bootstraps" to capitalize on opportunities to achieve a higher status (Bonilla-Silva, 2006). This argument is not only invalidating but also ignorant of the systemic woes Black people must overcome. Although we may not be physically enslaved and physically beaten, which is also conditional given the uprising of police brutality against Black people, we are not truly free to exercise our free will.

This plan has transcended and transformed from a physical beating to a psychological beating meant to deter Black students from pursuing education, particularly advanced degrees. The stereotypes that Black students do not value their education and are not intelligent is constantly perpetuated in arguments supporting the Black-White student achievement gap (Cokley, 2006). Unfortunately, the gravity of these stereotypes seems to grow as Black students progress in their educational careers (Felder, 2010; Stone et al., 2018).

We cannot recount the many times we introduced ourselves as doctoral graduate students and others automatically assumed we were master's students or were taken aback by us being enrolled in graduate programs at all. After receiving this reaction one too many times, it caused us to reflect on why this was the reaction of others when a Black female indicated being in a doctoral program and engaging in the traditional tasks of research, presenting, and networking. For us, it implied that a doctorate degree was just far too difficult for Black students and a farfetched, unattainable goal. The eagerness and twinkle in our eyes that we had for pursuing a doctorate degree slowly diminished as we learned that being accepted into a doctoral program was the beginning of our uphill battle.

Pro-White or Anti-Black Graduate School Process?

Being a Black person in America comes with a different set of experiences and standards than being a White person in America (Stone et al., 2018). In the admissions process the varying standards become apparent, when viewing the lower percentage, 6% to be exact, of Black individuals successfully attaining a doctoral degree (Posselt, 2016). Some would justify this percentage demonstrating that programs are using effective "gatekeeping" to uphold the prestige of the doctoral degree and only admitting the "desirable" few into an elite circle. Posselt (2016) argues that this is a problematic perspective because it encourages programs to remain complacent with the lack of diversity within their doctoral programs. Posselt (2016) continues by noting that prioritizing Graduate Record Examination (GRE) scores and the previous institution continuously disadvantages certain groups, further demonstrating the inequities that exist in higher education.

After investigating the admission process at a few graduate programs, their approach seemed to align with a color-blind approach (Posselt, 2016). This can be dangerous as it tends to minimize how impactful discrimination can be for people of color (Bonilla-Silva, 2006). Even for faculty members who believe themselves to be nonbiased and antiracist, implicit bias cannot be escaped (Posselt, 2016). This demonstrates the difficulties of merely being considered for an interview at a graduate program for Black applicants. Furthermore, it showcases that education cannot be viewed in isolation of the larger sociopolitical environment (Smith et al., 2011).

In the event that a Black student is chosen for an interview, it is likely that the applicants interviewing with them will be from a different demographic. The reduced number of Black faculty and students (Beasley et al., 2016; Felder, 2010; Stone et al., 2018) would suggest that there appears to be a movement to deescalate efforts to racially desegregate graduate programs. Thus, programs who enact "faux-multiculturalism," meaning selectively attend to the needs of groups based on what is "trendy," should not be applauded. Instead, programs should be exercising *true* multiculturalism, which encourages simultaneously uplifting multiple marginalized communities. Numbers going into programs should not be the only numbers monitored, as these numbers are only used to make entrance demographics look good. How much effort is being made toward retention and graduation should be the priority. Sadly, right now, even retention numbers are abysmal when you look at Black students' entrance numbers (Johnson-Bailey et al., 2008).

Anti-Black Graduate Environment

Black academics have to continually undergo being deprived of the necessary support to excel in an environment that has far too often closed doors and blocked Black individuals from working toward success (Felder, 2010; Johnson-Bailey et al., 2008; Pizzaro & Kohli, 2020). These obstacles being cemented in place do not just affect that one individual but also the entire community. Granted the argument could be made that we are in a place of educational privilege that was not afforded to our ancestors; however, our ancestors endured emotional and physical pain and sacrificed their lives for us to not just be allowed into school to survive. Our ancestors envisioned Black students finally being given an equitable opportunity to thrive in educational settings. Unfortunately, this vision has not been our experience as we have had to endure and navigate the treacherous waters of graduate school as Black students.

From the outset, we were treated differently than our White peers, especially related to research. In this program, students were required to complete a major research project. This project was significant in that it determined if students could remain in the program and was a prerequisite to begin comprehensive exams. Failure to complete this project in a timely fashion could delay achieving other requirements necessary for graduation, or in the worst case, dismissal from the program.

In the first term of school, it was required that the foundation of this major research project be completed. This included finding a topic, completing a thorough literature review, creating a data analysis plan, and presenting these sections to the class. Given that this was a major requirement within the 1st weeks of school, the project required a lot of collaboration between us and a chosen faculty member, particularly related to the research plan. Other students, who were not Black, were given weekly individualized time and continuously communicated with the faculty member about their project. We were not given weekly time, if any, and communication was brief between us and the faculty member. Worse yet, when having meetings with the faculty member, we were made to feel belittled and given no direction. How helpful is a faculty member if all they say is, "This is a good start, but do more." Initially, we did just that, but oftentimes at the detriment of our own health.

Unlike our colleagues, we were not given credit for our contributions to publications, yet we were each tasked with the most work and with the more difficult tasks on every project. Rather than publication status being awarded based on contribution, authorship was arbitrarily decided by the faculty member depending on their level of like for you and years in their lab. According to the American Psychological Association (APA) (2017), "Principal authorship and other publication credits accurately reflect the relative scientific or professional contributions of the individuals involved, regardless of their relative status. Mere possession of an institutional position, such as department chair, does not justify authorship credit. Minor contributions to the research or to the writing for publications are acknowledged appropriately, such as in footnotes or in an introductory statement" (Standard 8.12b). Hence this practice was unethical yet continued to be practiced even after informing the program administrators. The administrators simply assumed that our recount of the situation must have been flawed and we "misinterpreted" what the faculty member really said. From there, we learned that any issue or concern (e.g., disparate treatment) that plagued Black students was in direct opposition to what was perceived as important.

Professional and personal development is traditionally encouraged. With Black students, this encouragement tended to be dependent on the nature of the event. Prior to attending the Association of Black Psychologist Conference, we were met with much resistance. It was implied that we were being "unprofessional" for missing a day of class to attend "some Black event." Funding was not provided, and we were given new deadlines on research that was due shortly after we returned. As a result, we had limited time to truly and happily engage in fellowship with other like-minded scholars because of this arbitrarily and newly imposed deadline. In comparison to the APA conference preparation, the program provided funding, moved class assignment deadlines, and discussed at length the benefits of attending the conference. Everything that could possibly prevent a student from attending APA was addressed, and the program was willing to be flexible to ensure no obstacles were present.

Black students were used as pawns for departmental, and even inter departmental arguments and battles. Even after the issue is resolved, the Black student who holds no power is still left to bear the brunt and scars of the battle. It was common for there to be a difference in opinions related to research between faculty and the institutional review board (IRB) board, which delayed the students in meeting deadlines for program milestones, including the major research project noted. Rather than contextualizing the situation and reprimanding the person with the power, these delays were seen as the fault of the Black student. Now, one of the authors has been labeled "lazy" and "irresponsible" for not attending to her student duties, which were later noted on her yearly evaluation.

As a Black student, this was a stress-inducing experience where she now had a negative and false portrayal of her character documented in writing, forever! The program continued to use this as ammunition to create a blanket false narrative of Black students being "unfit" for the doctoral program, and for some, being threatened with academic probation for the selfish actions of someone else trying to prove a point that had nothing to do with them. Of course, the projects of our White peers never underwent this level of drama with the IRB, nor did they have to worry about being given haphazard labels as a result of a faculty member's actions. Faculty did not use their "favorite" students to take a stance against administration; they always used students who they felt added no value to the program and could be easily sacrificed without any reason. In each case it was a Black student.

As Cokley (2006) notes, it is difficult to ascribe racism as the reasoning for such behavior when there could be a multitude of contributing factors. We initially excused the behaviors of the program and operated from a place of denial that their actions were indeed racist. This quickly changed when the pattern continuously emerged that Black students were always on the oust. These malicious behaviors continued during our entirety of attending the program and continued to increase in the level of aggression. The tactics used became so severe, pungent, and unethical that we sought the assistance of a university leader to hopefully create a more tolerable experience. During the meeting they were inattentive, checking messages on their phone, refusing to review the evidence we had shared about the abuse we experienced in the program, and ended by saying, "Maybe you should just take a break. Don't focus on racism. When you're ready and rested, then return to the program to finish." Again, we were dismissed, belittled, and made to feel as though we created a false narrative.

It was solidified that we had no allies, and no one would believe two Black women, or to them, two "little Black girls" that, according to a professor, "should only be seen and not heard." As Black women, this was an experience that was all too familiar in our daily lives. Historically, society has placed constraints on what we can achieve, our level of worth, and our truth. This was the same feeling we felt every day we entered the school building to attain an advanced degree. This culture of "disinclusion" was purposeful, isolating, and surprising given the level of emphasis on multiculturalism within this psychology graduate program and the standards set by APA accreditation. Taking the rose-colored glasses off and finally acknowledging to ourselves that they did not intend for us to feel included or to graduate was a painful realization.

Racial Battle Fatigue

Related to support, crafting a welcoming environment is crucial for Black students to be successful in spaces that have historically and continue to be predominately White (Beasley et al., 2016; Ragland-Woods et al., 2021; Smith et al., 2007, 2011). Professors that exclude the commentary of their Black students in the classroom (Beasley et al., 2016), endorse lower expectations (Cokley, 2006), or fail to create conversations surrounding race-related topics in the classroom (Stone et al., 2018) can be easily viewed as oppressive practices. These all may seem like small grievances that are miniscule in comparison to their overall experience; however, it is these small microaggressive acts that, cumulatively, can have a negative impact on the student's academic performance and mental health (Ragland-Woods et al., 2021; Smith, 2004; Smith et al., 2007, 2011).

Microaggressions are defined as "subtle, stunning, often automatic, and non-verbal exchanges which are putdowns" (Pierce et al., 1977, p. 66). Further demonstrating how detrimental these acts are, Pierce (1970) discussed how these micro instances extend beyond interpersonal encounters and are woven into the fabric of society's perception resulting in racial minorities constantly being "ignored, tyrannized, terrorized . . . and minimized" (p. 267). It is important to note that these messages may be communicated unintentionally or through unconscious behavior (Pierce, 1970). Regardless of the intent or level of awareness of the perpetrator, the consequences remain the same for the target (Pierce, 1970, 1975; Smith, 2004; Smith et al., 2006; Sue et al., 2007).

Using the biopsychosocial model as a framework, it is clear why there is a relationship between experiencing events that are perceived negatively and stress responses. Clark et al. (1999) suggest that racism is related to many of the inequities that Black people experience (e.g., housing, wage gap). Furthermore, environments that have instances of racism, acute and chronic, can be perceived as stressful by the individual and result in varied psychological and physiological stress responses. In the educational environment, it is not uncommon for Black students to encounter racism-related instances in their environment and engage in passive coping, such as being in denial that a transgression has occurred, which further contributes to their overall stress levels (Clark et al., 1999).

These instances, that initially may seem isolated, all contribute to creating a racially hostile environment for Black students (Smith et al., 2007) which further complicates their graduate experience. Support has been shown to be an important factor for the successful completion of a graduate program; however, Black students are less likely to receive significant support from their White peers and faculty (Beasley et al., 2016; Johnson-Bailey et al., 2008). Some Black graduate students are fortunate to seek and successfully obtain outside support to strengthen areas where their program is lacking (Gasman et al., 2008). With this approach, we would encourage students to use discretion and caution. We found ourselves in an exploitative situation that, over time, revealed a relationship that entailed some of the same aspects we had experienced with our program faculty. Our determination and willingness to succeed became a double-edged sword as we were eager to collaborate with other professionals who, on the surface, appeared genuine, kind, and posed as mentors to help us navigate our discriminatory program and university. Nevertheless, it seemed like we had nowhere to go, no one to ask for help, nowhere we belonged. This is when racial battle fatigue began to become a normal feeling for us.

Racial battle fatigue (RBF) asserts that Black students who are subjugated to an unwelcoming environment that continues to other and isolate them will result in elevated stress levels (Smith et al., 2006, 2011). These stress responses could include a psychological ("e.g., frustration, shock, anger, hopeless"), physiological ("e.g., headache, backache, insomnia"), or behavioral response ("e.g., stereotype threat, John Henryism, social withdrawal") (Smith et al., 2011, p. 67). RBF is based on the work of Pierce (1970,

1975), who posits that these hostile environments are the product of systemic oppression that serves to maintain a racial hierarchy. Pierce (1970, 1975) and Carroll (1998) noted that negative racial encounters can be considered *mundane* because they are a part of our daily activities and interpersonal interactions; *extreme* in that the impact is so large that it negatively impacts multiple areas; *environmental* because they can be difficult to navigate, or even escape, such encounters because they are ingrained into the systems; and *stress*, the cumulative nature of the encounters can be draining and detract energy to complete necessary tasks.

Unfortunately, Black graduate students have to navigate these unfriendly terrains with limited support, if any, to obtain an advanced degree, placing them at a heightened risk for negative health outcomes (Franklin, 2016; Smith, 2004; Smith et al., 2011). We were generally healthy people before entering graduate school. It started with getting the common cold every academic year. Each time, it progressively got worse and more expensive as the doctor visits began to accumulate. Rather than taking these as moments to reflect and reconsider how the stress of our program was contributing to our illnesses, we continued to do more until our bodies were near shut down.

We thought our coping mechanisms and the unconditional support we provided for one another was enough to overcome the obstacles we were experiencing. We failed ourselves and each other by underestimating the power of continuously being disincluded and the emotional, psychological, and physical toll everything cumulatively had on us. As we learned and literature has shown, regardless of the coping mechanism implemented, symptoms associated with racial battle fatigue can still be present (Smith et al., 2007). Specifically, the "memories" from the negative encounter are not forgotten but are integrated into a "person's life history" (Smith et al., 2007, p. 555). Even symptoms being expressed at minimal levels should still be of concern and monitored closely as it could easily spiral into race-based trauma (Pizzaro & Kohli, 2020).

Race-Based Trauma

The infamous example of the Little Rock Nine that stood for change is a historical reminder of how we have always had to fight to receive quality education. Despite being referred to as a racial slur or other derogatory insults, these students continued to show up each day to receive their education. Imagine going to school in such a hostile environment that you have to be escorted by marshals every day. Given the significance of their actions, a documentary was created to display how the actions of the nine students have impacted the present experience at the same school, Central High School.

In the opening scene, Minnijean Brown Trickey is seen having a strong reaction to being back at the school where she was one of the nine Black students to attend and desegregate an all-White school (Renaud & Renaud, 2007). Her surprise that she was having a reaction, after 50 years, was a powerful and disheartening scene to witness. She stated in a quivering voice, "You're supposed to be over it" (Renaud & Renaud, 2007).

She had a vision of seeing herself obtaining a quality education, excelling beyond the expectations of the naysayers, which paved the path for us to attend any school of our choice; however, this vision came with a heavy price tag and sacrifice. She was experiencing what we would now term race-based trauma.

The current conceptualization of trauma, which is supported by the reigning diagnostic manual in psychology, is not inclusive. The criteria to warrant a diagnosis of posttraumatic stress disorder (PTSD) requires a physical stressor that is life threatening (APA, 2013). Experiences with racism sometimes do not include a physical stressor. Research has shown that while there is some overlap between PTSD and race-based traumatic stress (Pieterse et al., 2010), there are also some unique characteristics of race-based traumatic stress (Carter, 2007; Carter et al., 2020; Kirkinis et al., 2018). There may be others who have not been discovered yet, which is plausible since this area of study is fairly new (Carter, 2007; Carter et al., 2020). There is a vicarious component related to race-based traumatic stress that is not acknowledged in PTSD such as having access to disturbing images and videos of people who share the same racial or ethnic background being treated poorly, and unfortunately murdered. The DSM criteria limits the experience to direct exposure or learning details about a close family member. This small difference may seem irrelevant; however, when your safety is in danger on a daily basis because of the color of your skin, that is not a "minute" detail to be overlooked.

The criteria for race-based trauma are not as black-and-white as the DSM may present PTSD. Given that race-based trauma can present in various and complex ways, it is important to properly educate graduate students to ensure they are operating from a place of cultural competence. Contrary to this belief, Hemmings and Evans (2018) found that a large number of their clinician sample had not received training on how to identify or treat race-based trauma. This is alarming and underscores that more work needs to be done to acknowledge race-based trauma in the mental health field. Otherwise, clinicians may engage in microaggressions, misdiagnose clients, and implications of racism will be minimized, resulting in a misunderstanding of the Black experience, further deepening the disconnect between the Black community and mental health providers (Williams et al., 2017).

Carter (2007) noted that racism is a form of violence. Over time these violent acts, small and large, that are sudden, negative, and uncontrollable may transpire into trauma (Carlson, 1997). Even when compared with other people of color, Black students tend to endorse trauma-related symptoms at a higher rate (Pieterse et al., 2010). The severity of the race-based traumatic stress depends on the reaction of the target after assessing the cumulation of negative encounters. Reactions could be (a) *intrusion* or reexperiencing, (b) *arousal* or hyperactivity, and (c) *avoidance* or psychic numbing (Carter, 2007). This could range from withdrawing in a relationship to having more frequent physical ailments to an overall increase in fear (Carter, 2007). The reaction categories overlap with symptoms described in the racial battle fatigue framework, which suggests that the two phenomena may indeed be related.

Carter (2007) has encouraged the expansion of the term *trauma* to include race-based traumatic stress injury. He proposed that conceptualizing the responses to racism as injuries is nonpathological; acknowledges that the stress is situational, meaning that the responses of the target are the result of hostilities individuals may encounter in their environment; and confirms that the target of the racist actions rights has been violated in some way. Continuing with this line of thinking, we conceptualized a *continuum of race-based injury* to demonstrate how racial battle fatigue and race-based trauma are connected. At the lowest level of injury are stress responses associated with everyday stressors. Given that society views Black individuals as inferior (Carter, 2007; Pierce, 1970), it could be reasonable to assume that Black people sustain some level of race-based injury. As Black individuals continue to experience more severe and frequent stressors, they begin to enter the middle level of race-based injury, which is associated with features of racial battle fatigue. Operating from a place of heightened stress could lead to the body responding with more severe ailments and worsening of symptoms (Carter, 2007; Hall & Fields, 2015). This is when Black individuals enter a high level of race-based injury when they develop symptoms associated with race-based trauma. We were intentional about using the term *injury* to imply that recovery is possible regardless of the level of race-based injury endured by the individual. As an individual progresses further along the continuum, enacting more coping mechanisms may be necessary to return to a less heightened state.

Trauma is complex and manifests differently in people. For one person, one major event could be one big encounter, while for another person small incidents occur and slowly erode your resiliency, your confidence, and your identity. Unfortunately, for individuals who have multiple identities (e.g., socioeconomic, gender, disability status) that are considered inferior by those in power, their level of suffering is multiplied (Carter, 2007). Related to our experience, there wasn't much of anything micro about the aggression that we continuously were the targets of even when trying to demonstrate how we were discriminated against to people in high and prestigious places of power. After each encounter, our reactions continued to worsen. Triggering news and hostility being transmitted through email was not unusual. One of the authors remembers avoiding (avoidance) her email to prevent the pit in the stomach (arousal) feeling she would get with every email from the program given that they had historically contained upsetting material. Recounting the details of these scenarios for this chapter, we are reexperiencing the thoughts and emotions that we had when we first experienced these events (intrusive). More than 60 years after schools were segregated, there is still a strong presence that we are not welcomed (Pizzaro & Kohli, 2020). Unlike Minnijean, we were not required to be escorted to school by marshals; yet we still encountered the same toxic culture.

Collectively, we had experienced so many transgressions that our tunnel of hope began to darken. Each person in power we spoke to about our situation did not believe us, even with witnesses present. We followed the chain of command to discuss our grievance and sometimes scheduled multiple meetings with individuals in hopes that one of the meetings would result in our concerns finally being taken seriously. With every conversation, it seemed the responses became more bold and less ethical as the higher up administrators openly disclosed troubling information without even flinching. In one meeting, an administrator noted that they had denied students access to the program solely due to their disability status because they believed it was improbable they could be a psychologist. Traditionally, this information is not privy to a student and should not be disclosed in a matter-of-fact manner as if it's not problematic. For us, we began to think that if they can just casually discuss biases, then what do they think about us and our concerns? That question was answered daily by their actions, or lack thereof, to remedy some of the concerns we had presented.

Later we realized that these meetings only made the situation worse by creating a larger target on the Black students who were already suffering relentlessly and provided an outlet for administrators to *really* show how they felt about accusations related to discrimination. Their lack of fear and nonchalant attitude toward Black students really demonstrated that we were not in a position of power and that we had just begun to run the gauntlet to graduation.

Despite everything we encountered, the most painful memory is our pregraduate school selves. It was a tough realization and recognition that our tortuous grad school experience had changed us. We can fondly remember those little things we appreciated; how bubbly our personalities were among many other things that we will never be able to get back. What some fail to realize is that trauma changes you forever!

The Myth of Vulnerability for Black Students

Before delving into this section, we wanted to acknowledge the irony of having a section dedicated to what some people would believe to be our trivial experiences of being vulnerable as Black women yet having composed a chapter filled with our experiences to be read by many readers. Writing about experiences is surreal, but necessary. How we reconcile this juxtaposition is easy: We refuse to be silenced and allow others to control our narrative any further. In doing so, we are sure that a similar experience will occur as when we have read the writings of the many other authors, that aha moment of commonality, empathy, or maybe even anger. Either way, a depth of understanding through experiences and delving past the superficial truth will occur. In the words of Brené Brown (2012), vulnerability makes you open to "attack." We do not know who the readers will be, their experiences, their educational journey, and their comfort with vulnerability. All we can do is hope that the readers engage with an open heart to hear our perspective.

Brown (2012) defined vulnerability "as uncertainty, risk, and emotional exposure" (p. 34). In the same breath, she noted that vulnerability should be shared with people who have "earned the right to hear them" and that a "mutuality [related to] ... boundaries and trust" are crucial components with sharing any information (p. 45). This was an assigned reading in our program, yet there was selective attention to the sections that encouraged students to share information without any consideration for boundaries and trust. The program failed to do the one thing that they were training us to do—be multiculturally sensitive and meet the student where they were. What Brown fails to do in her book, *Daring Greatly*, is acknowledge the dangers of vulnerability for marginalized groups who do not share the same identities as her. She mentioned very briefly oppression, trauma, and culture but did not expand on how these unique combinations of factors can create a different experience with vulnerability than indicated in her book. Even though Brown may not be sure how her audience will perceive her body of work, a disclaimer reiterating that this was *her* lived experience would have portrayed a tone of suggestion rather than a definite tone regarding vulnerability. It is not uncommon for authors to provide a disclaimer within their bodies of work to prevent people from taking their research out of context, particularly when race is involved (Carter, 2007; Pieterse et al., 2010). From a young age, the socialization process is much different for racial and ethnic group members such that expecting threat is necessary to survive (Carroll, 1998; Pierce, 1975). Thus, being vulnerable as a Black woman can be a risky gamble, particularly given the systemic pressures and intersectional oppressions that operate outside our control to maintain an inferior position.

With *Daring Greatly* being used as supporting evidence, the faculty became quite savvy with ruling from a stance of intimidation and weaponizing the personal information shared by students. After seeing the consequence of sharing information, we and other students began to become selective about oversharing, especially if it had nothing to do with professional development. Faculty did not take well to this adjustment in vulnerability and vocalized their dismay for students under sharing on yearly evaluations. Black students were labeled as "defensive" and being "unwilling to engage in process." The faculty's standard of vulnerability even began to dictate what would need to be shared in class assignments. In a course, a paper assignment required students to discuss information about their personal sex journey (e.g., occurrences of STDs, discovery of sexual orientation, number of partners, satisfaction with sex, first sexual experience). When brought to the attention of the administrators, they did not find the request to be inappropriate and threatened that failure to enroll in this class would prevent students from going to internship.

One of the authors was in need of an extensive orthopedic surgery prior to the start of the term. Although she was extremely fearful of repercussions already, she was proactive about communicating crucial details related to the surgery, recovery time, and accommodations that would be needed to facilitate a healthy recovery due to written departmental policies. Initially, the faculty agreed and ensured they would be flexible, allow her to attend class through alternative methods (e.g., Skype), and cooperate with any medically related mandates. The faculty contacted her nearly immediately, not related to her well-being or convalescence, but to inform her that she was to return to school promptly or she could be facing dismissal or other punitive consequences for falling behind although her absence had only taken an approximation of 1 week's class time. Due to fear of reprisal, she had scheduled the bulk of her convalescence over the longest school break, as discussed with the faculty and department chair.

After 3 weeks, she was forced to return prematurely which caused complications with her healing process. The physicians overseeing her care immediately notified her and sent another letter to the Psychology Department and Office of Disabilities noting the danger of her driving more than an hour for class each direction, to which the faculty originally agreed yet did not adhere to. The Veterans Affairs Hospital, where she was working as an intern at that time, sent her home on numerous occasions because her supervisors there determined that it was risky for her healing process, not to mention the pain was excruciating to be at the practicum site. Yet as a Black student with a lack of power, she persisted with what she felt was her required responsibility as a graduate student even though she knew it was not ethical due to her physical pain causing an inability for her to perform at her highest levels as a clinician. As a Black graduate student, her school had left her with no options. She had to go and she still worried that she would be penalized for being sent home!

This was the first time she openly admitted to the faculty that she had some limitations due to the major surgery she had just undergone. She was left vulnerable and forced to disclose personal health information per the written policies in hopes that faculty would, for the first time, adhere to policies and claims that were created to benefit students in unconventional circumstances and hardships. Instead, she was met with hostility and threats.

This was not the case for her White counterparts. Even minor surgeries, aches and pains, and extended periods of absences were permitted. In the event of a hospitalization, home convalescent extending weeks past the hospitalization until the student was feeling "well" were not unheard of. Sometimes there was dismissal of course work or final exams to lessen stress loads. This flexibility even applied to comprehensive examinations or when the illness was not that of the student's but that of a spouse or a beloved pet, yet a Black student was not permitted to attend to their own child's surgery without their priorities being called into question.

The Psychology of Black Women

In the words of Malcolm X, "The most disrespected person in America is the Black woman. The most unprotected person in America is the Black woman. The most neglected person in America is the Black woman." These words spoken in 1962 still ring true today. We are constantly undergoing intense scrutiny and having our identities defined by outsiders to continue to oppress Black women. The negative and controlling images that are frequently depicted in media (angry Black woman, jezebel, mammy, strong Black woman) are two-fold: as a reminder of a painful period of enslavement and to signify that as a society we have not advanced much since that time (Jacobs, 2017; Jones et al., 2021; Stanton et al. 2017).

For years, Black women have struggled with being recognized and acknowledged (McNair-Barnett, 1993). In the work environment, Black women are often overlooked for promotions (Buchanan, 2020). White colleagues have also been found to recount incorrect details about Black colleagues, and when corrected, White colleagues assert that the Black woman is incorrect (Robinson, 2018). With regard to education, there is a lack of representation of Black female professors (Buchanan, 2020) and Black peers in the classroom (Felder, 2010; Johnson-Bailey et al., 2008), which creates an isolating experience. When seeking health care, Black women have alluded to the need to establish a relationship with the health care provider to be seen as a person and not as "chopped liver" (Sacks, 2018, p. 65). The numerous hurdles that Black women have to surmount on a daily basis is not the experience of their White female counterparts, and even Black males who share the same racial group membership.

Kimberlé Crenshaw (1989) was the first to coin a term, *intersectionality,* to distinguish how Black women were not given the racialized privilege that White women received or even the slight gender privilege afforded to Black men. In this paper, she details court cases that dismissed the thought of Black women being discriminated against regarding their race and their sex. To the courts, this felt like a foreign proposition, and the courts did not rule in favor of the Black women. After these unfavorable rulings, Crenshaw (1989) created a paper to discuss how Black women were essentially invisible and at this difficult intersection where no help had been afforded them. Although this argument was lost in court, the facts are no less true. Yet after the term gained popularity, the case for intersectionality was taken up by nearly every group, including the very groups who already were in places of privilege. Again, Black women were relegated to being minimized and invisible.

With everyone standing proudly in the intersection, there is no one on the side of the road, which gives a false sense of inclusivity, multiculturalism, and a postracism utopia. This creates a color-blind society, a dangerous "Me Too" culture of a different sort, that maintains a racist system by promoting equality when the emphasis should be on equity to truly foster a multiculturally sensitive environment. The world we live in does not give everyone a cookie. Some people live in a world where they are harassed, disincluded, stereotyped, and a call to the police for help could easily end in them being shot. However, how often in the psychological community do you see Crenshaw given her proper citations and references? Crenshaw—attorney, scholar, advocate, developer of the term and theory of intersectionality, and Black woman—is rarely cited or referenced. This disrespectful practice would not happen to a White man or even likely to a White woman of such renowned success. Still across the social sciences, the term *intersectionality,* is thrown around without hesitation or acknowledgement for how the term was originally intended to protect Black women from obscurity. Frequently, this is not even taught. Unless you are interested specifically in the study of critical race theory, the theory of intersectionality or specific Black race-related social, legal, or psychological sciences, you may never be exposed to this area of research.

These sorts of double standards and questions of humanity about suffering as related to Black personhood are common. Frequently, Black mothers are not admitted to programs due to questions of their commitment or ability to prioritize graduate programs (Adams,

2009; Tucker, 2016). In reality, Black mothers are completely committed to their families as well as completely committed to elevating themselves and their families to statuses unachievable to generations before themselves. However, from our experience, no one dares ask this insulting question of White mothers or White fathers.

The culmination of our experiences is the result of our intersectional identity as Black and women. The number of painful names that we have been called are too graphic to even be placed in this chapter. Similar to the court cases mentioned, we lost many battles because of the failure of others to really see and listen to our experiences from an intersectional perspective. It is disappointing to know that even with stature and an elevated status, the world will still not see us. Achieving prestige with degrees and promotion means nothing when race is the factor that holds the most weight.

Conclusion

The journey to attaining an advanced degree is an arduous process. When you add in racial and ethnic considerations, the process becomes even more complicated. All PhDs are not created equally. Black students have to work and endure so much more stress for the same three letters: P-H-D. Those who are fortunate enough to make it to the end of their program and graduate may find themselves questioning, Was it even worth it?

Some readers may assume that we, and other students with similar narratives, are prime examples of victimology, which implies that racism is overly and unjustifiably used as an explanation for why Black students are unable to achieve academically (McWhorter, 2000). Not only does projecting this perspective on our experiences invalidate everything, but this perspective could be perceived as a color-blind approach to a serious issue. This *could* be a fair argument if the death of Black unarmed men and women was not a common occurrence. This *could* be a fair argument if we did not witness Barack Obama being publicly challenged by a U.S. representative during an address. We have not seen previous egregious actions done to past presidents by U.S. representatives. President Barack Obama encountered many obstacles, his character was assassinated on multiple occasions, and people questioned if he had the ability to fulfill his role. The blatant disrespect for this position and vocalizing their dismay for a Black person filling this position was clearly articulated on numerous occasions. This *could* be a fair argument if Black faculty were not being physically attacked by students and then blamed as if they incited the violent incident (Buchanan, 2020).

These varied contexts show that in multiple areas, the color of your skin takes precedence over everything. Even when you are in a high official position, people still only see you as the N-word who is only good to pick cotton. Defying the stereotypes by striving for and attaining excellence has not shown to be an effective strategy to receive equal treatment (Hall & Fields, 2015). From our experience, it appears to incite non-Black folks to use more aggressive tactics to relegate Black students to a lower position of power.

We challenge programs to evaluate their implicit biases and provide support to their Black students so they can graduate. Furthermore, we encourage programs to include more instances of diversity besides the traditional classes such as multicultural counseling (Beasley et al., 2016). Research Black scholars in your area and include their bodies of work in classroom material. If there are none in your area, acknowledge this and note how this could be an area of growth for your specific area of study. Ignoring the invisible elephant in the room, race, does nothing for Black students and deepens the feeling of being othered (Stone et al., 2018).

The disheartening aspect about everything we shared is that we are not the only students who have endured such pain while in graduate school. We are constantly hearing anecdotes from other Black students detailing their horrific experiences, which shows this is a never-ending cycle, if nothing is done to hold programs accountable. For programs and administrators who have read this chapter, we challenge you to really reflect on your program to determine your areas of growth. If there are significantly more Black students on probation, even though they encompass a small portion of your program, there is an issue there. If there are grievances that are predominately being expressed by Black students, there is an issue there as well. Perhaps, Black students are not the problem, and the program needs to undergo some changes to create a more welcoming environment.

Harnessing the title of being a psychology program does not exempt graduate programs from falling victim to the very topics they research—oppression, racial inequity, microaggressions, multicultural incompetency, and insensitivity. If anything, it should encourage the program to use the research and create a better experience for their Black students. Doing nothing is not an option because it only continues the cycle of oppression for Black students. Punishing the whistleblower who draws attention to areas that could be improved is a common (Pyke, 2018) yet unproductive solution that also perpetuates this cycle. Based on our experiences, we believe that the blame should not be placed on the student.

It is our hope that students will use this chapter as a source of strength and to know that they are not alone in their graduate school experience. Your feelings are valid. Your experiences are real. You matter! We really empathize with your experience. More importantly, we want to emphasize that healing from a traumatic experience requires time. Regardless of how unaffected you may feel, there is still a process to healing. Even if you find yourself physically distanced from the program, there still might be small triggers that result in an emotional reaction. A strong network of people who will uplift you during these times is so crucial (Pizzaro & Kohli, 2020). Additionally, seeking individual therapy if it is available and feels safe to do so could be pursued to facilitate the healing process. Rechanneling that negative energy (Stone et al., 2018), such as helping Black undergraduate students gain admittance into a program that will value them, could also help renew your spirit. Above all else, just give yourself a moment to breathe and take care of your well-being.

With America's longstanding history with racism, over time, it has infiltrated and became ingrained into our system, resulting in the oppression of Black people in various avenues (Beasley et al., 2016; Harrell, 2000; Pierce, 1975; Sue, 2010). Thus, understanding how this line of thinking will affect the future generation of Black scholars is of the utmost importance. Hopefully, our experiences have caused you to pause and reflect on your contribution to the trauma that some Black students undergo. The only question that remains is "Are you the perpetrator of these microaggressive acts? Or are you the survivor of these constant attacks?"

We encourage programs and non-Black professors who are educating Black graduate students to be diligent about fostering an inclusive, healthy learning environment (Beasley et al., 2016; Ragland-Woods et al., 2021; Smith et al., 2011). Unfortunately, our experience was riddled with anti-Black sentiments, but with the future generation you have the opportunity to change the narrative and create a better experience for them. The suggestions we provided are starting points, and it will take much more to change the system to prevent other students from encountering another anti-Black experience.

References

Adams, U. (2009). *The impact of academic climate on black women's experiences in higher education* (Publication No. 3362713) [Doctoral dissertation, University of Illinois at Urbana-Champaign]. ProQuest Dissertations & Theses Global.

American Psychiatric Association. (2013). *Diagnostic and statistical manual of mental disorders* (5th ed.). Author. https:// doi.org/10.1176/appi.books.9780890425596

American Psychological Association. (2017). *Ethical principles of psychologists and code of conduct.* https:// www.apa.org/ethics/code/index.aspx

Anderson, C. (2016). *White rage: The unspoken truth of our racial divide* (P. Gibson, Narr.) [Audiobook]. Audible Audio.

Beasley, S. T., Chapman-Hilliard, C., & McClain, S. (2016). Linking the emancipatory pedagogy of Africana/Black studies with academic identity outcomes among Black students attending PWIs. *Africology: The Journal of Pan African Studies, 9*(8), 9–25.

Bonilla-Silva, E. (2006). *Racism without racists: Color-blind racism and the persistence of racial inequality in the United States.* Rowman & Littlefield.

Brown, B. (2012). *Daring greatly: How the courage to be vulnerable transforms the way we live, love, parent, and lead.* Penguin.

Buchanan, N. T. (2020). Researching while Black (and female). *Women and Therapy, 43*(1–2), 91–111. https:// doi.org/10.1080/02703149.2019.1684681

Carlson, E. B. (1997). *Trauma assessments: Clinician's guide.* Guilford.

Carroll, G. (1998). *Environmental stress and African Americans: The other side of the moon.* Greenwood Press.

Carter, R. T. (2007). Racism and psychological and emotional injury: Recognizing and assessing race-based traumaticstress. *TheCounseling Psychologist, 35*(1), 13–105. https://doi.org/10.1177/0011000006292033

Carter, R. T., Kirkinis, K., & Johnson, V. E. (2020). Relationships between trauma symptoms and race-based traumatic stress. *Traumatology, 26*(1), 11–18. http://doi.org/10.1037/trm0000217

Clark, R., Anderson, N. B., Clark, V. R., & Williams D. R. (1999). Racism as a stressor for African Americans: A biopsychosocial model. *American Psychologist, 54*(10), 805–816.

Cokley, K. (2006). The impact of racialized schools and racist (mis) education on African American students' academic identity. In M. G. Constantine & D. W. Sue (Eds.), *Addressing racism: Facilitating cultural competence in mental health and educational settings* (pp. 127–144). Wiley.

Crenshaw, K. (1989). Demarginalizing the intersection of race and sex: A Black feminist critique of antidiscrimination doctrine, feminist theory and antiracist politics. *University of Chicago Legal Forum*, 139–168.

Felder, P. (2010). On doctoral student development: Exploring faculty mentoring in the shaping of African American doctoral student success. *The Qualitative Report, 15*(2), 455–474.

Franklin, J. (2016). Racial microaggressions, racial battle fatigue, and racism-related stress in higher education. *Journal of Student Affairs at New York University, 12*(44), 44–55.

Gasman, M., Hirschfeld, A., & Vultaggio, J. (2008). "Difficult yet rewarding": The experiences of African American graduate students in education at an ivy league institution. *Journal of Diversity in Higher Education, 1*(2), 126–138. https://doi.org/10.1037/1938-8926.1.2.126

Hall, J. M., & Fields, B. (2015). "It's killing us!" Narratives of adults about microaggression experiences and related health stress. *Global Qualitative Nursing Research, 2*, 1–14. https://doi.org/10.1177/2333393615591569

Harrell, S. P. (2000). A multidimensional conceptualization of racism-related stress: Implications for the well-being of people of color. *American Journal of Orthopsychiatry, 70*(1), 42–57.

Hemmings, C., & Evans, A. M. (2018). Identifying and treating race-based trauma in counseling. *Journal of Multicultural Counseling and Development, 46*(1), 20–39.

Jacobs, A. (2017). "I am not your mammy": Storm, uhura, and the unraveling of the archetypes of the mammy figure and the angry Black woman. *The Unbearable Humanities*, 68–79. http://vahumanitiesconference.org/wp-content/uploads/2019/10/22321368.pdf#page=74

Johnson-Bailey, J., Valentine, T. S., Cervero, R. M., & Bowles, T. A. (2008). Lean on me: The support experiences of Black graduate students. *The Journal of Negro Education, 77*(4), 365–381.

Jones, M. K., Harris, K. J., & Reynolds, A. A. (2021). In their own words: The meaning of the strong Black woman schema among Black US college women. *Sex Roles, 84*(5), 347–359. https://doi.org/10.1007/s11199-020-01170-w

Kirkinis, K, Pieterse, A. L., Martin, C., Agiliga, A., & Brownell, A. (2018). Racism, racial discrimination, and trauma: A systematic review of the social science literature. *Ethnicity & Health, 26*(3), 392–412. https://doi.org/ 10.1080/13557858.2018.1514453

McNair-Barnett, B. (1993). Invisible southern Black women leaders in the civil rights movement: The triple constraints of gender, race, and class. *Gender & Society, 7*(2), 162–182.

McWhorter, J. H. (2000). *Losing the race: Self-sabotage in Black America*. Simon and Schuster.

Pierce, C. (1970). Offensive mechanisms. In F. B. Barbour (Ed.), *The Black seventies* (pp. 265–282). Porter Sargent.

Pierce, C. M. (1975). The mundane extreme environment and its effect on learning. In S. G. Brainard (Ed.), *Learning disabilities: Issues and recommendations for research* (pp. 111–119). National Institute of Education, Department of Health, Education, and Welfare.

Pierce, C. M., Carew, J. V., Pierce-Gonzalez, D., & Wills, D. (1977). An experiment in racism: TV commercials. *Education and Urban Society, 10*, 61–87.

Pieterse, A. L., Carter, R. T., Evans, S. A., & Walter, R. A. (2010). An exploratory examination of the association among racial and ethnic discrimination, racial climate, and trauma-related symptoms in a college student population. *Journal of Counseling Psychology, 57*(3), 255–263.

Pizzaro, M., & Kohli, R. (2020). "I stopped sleeping": Teachers of color and the impact of racial battle fatigue. *Urban Education, 55*(7), 967–991. https://doi.org/10.1177/0042085918805788

Posselt, J. R. (2016). *Inside graduate admissions: Merit, diversity, and faculty gatekeeping*. Harvard University Press.

Pyke, K. D. (2018). Institutional betrayal: Inequity, discrimination, bullying, and retaliation in academia. *Sociological Perspectives, 61*(1), 5-13. https://doi.org/ 10.1177/0731121417743816

Ragland-Woods, C. C., Chronister, K. M., Perez Grabow, A., Woods, W. E., & Woodlee, K. (2021). Racial battle fatigue: The experiences of Black/African American, biracial Black, and multiracial Black identified graduate students. *Journal of Black Psychology, 47*(4–5), 219–243. https://doi.org/10.1177/00957984211002615

Renaud, B., & Renaud, C. (Directors). (2007). *Little Rock central: 50 years later* [Film]. Home Box Office.

Robinson, J. L. (2018). *Imposterized: The experiences of tenured and tenure-track black women instructional faculty at california community colleges* (Order No. 10825030). [Doctoral dissertation, California State University, Long Beach]. ProQuest Dissertations & Theses Global.

Sacks, T. K. (2018). Performing Black womanhood: A qualitative study of stereotypes and the healthcare encounter. *Critical Public Health, 28*(1), 56–69. https://doi.org/10.1080/09581596.2017.1307323

Smith, W. A. (2004). Black faculty coping with racial battle fatigue: The campus racial climate in a post-civil rights era. In D. Cleveland (Ed.), *A long way to go: Conversations about race by African American faculty and graduate students at predominately White institutions* (pp. 171–190). Peter Lang s.

Smith, W. A., Allen, W. R., & Danley, L. L. (2007). "Assume the position ... you fit the description" Psychosocial experiences and racial battle fatigue among African American male college students. *American Behavioral Scientist, 51*(4), 551–578. https://doi.org/10.1177/0002764207307742

Smith, W. A., Hung, M., & Franklin, J. D. (2011). Racial battle fatigue and the miseducation of Black men: Racial microaggressions, societal problems, and environmental stress. *The Journal of Negro Education, 80*(1), 63–82.

Smith, W. A., Yosso, T. J., & Solorzano, D. G. (2006). Challenging racial battle fatigue on historically White campuses: A critical race examination of race-related stress. In C. A. Stanley (Ed.), *Faculty of color: Teaching in predominately White colleges and universities* (pp. 299–327). Anker.

Stanton, A. G., Jerald, M. C., Ward, L. M., & Avery, L. R. (2017). Social media contributions to strong Black woman ideal endorsement and Black women's mental health. *Psychology of Women Quarterly, 41*(4), 465–478. https://doi.org/10.1177/0361684317732330

Stone, S., Saucer, C., Bailey, M., Garba, R., Hurst, A., Jackson, S. M., Krueger, N., & Cokley, K. (2018). Learning while Black: A culturally informed model of the impostor phenomenon for Black graduate students. *Journal of Black Psychology, 44*(6), 491–531. https://doi.org/10.1177/0095798418786648

Sue, D. W. (2010). *Microaggressions in everyday life: Race, gender and sexual orientation.* Wiley.

Sue, D. W., Capodilupo, C. M., Torino, G. C., Bucceri, J. M., Holder, A. M. B., Nadal, K. L., & Esquilin, M. (2007). Racial microaggressions in everyday life: Implications for clinical practice. *The American Psychologist, 62*(4), 271–286. https://doi.org/10.1037/0003-066X.62.4.271

Tucker, A. (2016). *Talkin' back and shifting Black: Black motherhood, identity development and doctoral study* [Doctoral dissertation, University of Wisconsin-Milwaukee]. Theses and Dissertations.

Williams, T. D., Shamp, L. M., & Harris, K. J. (2017). Microaggression in psychotherapy. *Psychotherapy Bulletin, 52*(4), 12–18 https://societyforpsychotherapy.org/wp-content/uploads/2018/04/Bulletin52-4.pdf

INDEX

ABOUT THE EDITOR

Kevin Cokley, Ph.D. holds the Oscar and Anne Mauzy Regents Professorship for Educational Research and Development in the College of Education at the University of Texas at Austin. He is a Fellow of both the University of Texas System and University of Texas Academy of Distinguished Teachers, Director of the Institute for Urban Policy Research & Analysis, and Professor of Educational Psychology and African and African Diaspora Studies. Dr. Cokley's research and teaching can be broadly categorized in the area of African American psychology with a focus on racial and ethnic identity and understanding the psychological and environmental factors that impact African American students' academic achievement. He studies the psychosocial experiences of students of color and is currently exploring the impostor phenomenon and its relationship to mental health and academic outcomes. Dr. Cokley's publications have appeared in professional journals such as the *Journal of Counseling Psychology*, *Cultural Diversity and Ethnic Minority Psychology*, *Journal of Black Psychology*, *Journal of Black Studies*, *Journal of Multicultural Counseling and Development*, and *Harvard Educational Review*. He is the past editor-in-chief of the *Journal of Black Psychology* and was elected to Fellow status in the American Psychological Association for his contributions to ethnic minority psychology and counseling psychology. He holds the title of Distinguished Psychologist in the Association of Black Psychologists and is the recipient of the 2014 Regents' Outstanding Teaching Award, the 2009 Charles and Shirley Thomas Award for mentoring ethnic minority students, the 2008 "10 Rising Stars of the Academy" award by *Diverse Issues in Higher Education*, the 2007 Association of Black Psychologists' Scholarship Award, and the 2004 co-recipient of the Emerging Professional Award given by the Society for the Psychological Study of Ethnic Minority Issues. He is author of the 2014 book *The Myth of Black Anti-Intellectualism*, which challenges the notion that African American students are anti-intellectual. He has written numerous op-eds in major media outlets on topics such as Blacks' rational mistrust of police, the aftermath of Ferguson, police and race relations, racism and White supremacy, the limitations of de-escalation training, and racial disparities in school discipline. His research has been recognized in media outlets including the *New York Times*, *USA Today*, and *Inside Higher Education*.

ABOUT THE CONTRIBUTORS

Marlon L. Bailey, LCSW, from Austin Texas, currently holds a Master of Science in social work and is a doctoral graduate student in the counseling psychology program at the University of Texas at Austin. He is a student, a therapist, and an athlete. He is very proud of his contribution to *Making Black Lives Matter: Confronting Anti-Black Racism*. His research interests include imposter phenomenon, news fatigue, social psychology, race, and racial violence. He is currently researching the psychological toll that news of racial violence may exact on viewers.

Pearis Bellamy, MS, is a counseling psychology doctoral candidate at the University of Florida. Peariss's research and clinical interests include trauma, specifically intimate partner violence, sexual violence, and racial trauma. In 2020, Pearis dreamed up Academics for Black Survival and Wellness, alongside her mentor, Dr. Della Mosley, in hopes of providing healing and support for Black people through collective action in academia. The initiative has garnered over 15,000 participants from across the world who are participating or have participated in antiracism trainings centered on accountability and action (non-Black participants) and healing and wellness workshops and experiences (Black participants).

Dawn T. Bounds, PhD, PMHNP-BC, is an assistant professor at the Sue and Bill Gross School of Nursing at the University of California, Irvine (UCI). She received her PhD in nursing as well as her clinical training as a psychiatric mental health nurse practitioner (PMHNP) from Rush University in Chicago. Her research is focused on the risk and resilience of youth generally and the prevention of risk behaviors (i.e., substance use), mental health symptoms, and sexual exploitation using community- and family-based interventions specifically. Bounds is an alumnus of the prestigious SAMHSA Minority Fellowship Program at the American Nurses Association, MacLean Center for Clinical Medical Ethics Fellowship at the University of Chicago, and an inaugural recipient of the Chancellor's Inclusive Excellence Award at UCI.

Carly Coleman, Ohio native, is a doctoral student in the counseling psychology department at the University of Texas at Austin. Her previous research examining the inequities of academic outcomes for young Black students has shaped her own research interests. Broadly, her research interests include community factors that influence Black adolescent development and academic achievement among Black students. She has served as an academic and professional development mentor for adolescents, with a focus on Black females. Her vehemence in developing strong, productive Black youth is how she makes Black lives matter.

Benson George Cooke, EdD, is professor of counseling and psychology, clinical coordinator for graduate mental health counseling, and the 2020 Faculty Excellence Award Recipient in Teaching at the University of the District of Columbia. He has authored books, book chapters, journals, and magazine articles. He has presented nationally and internationally, appeared on radio, cable network, television programs and documentaries. He is past national president of the Association of Black Psychologists, and the recipient of numerous awards including the ABPsi Distinguished Psychologist. He organized national guidelines for culturally competent therapeutic responses to Hurricane Katrina in 2005. Cooke earned degrees at Morehouse College and the University of Massachusetts, Amherst.

Shaina Hall is a 3rd-year doctoral student in counseling psychology at the University of Texas at Austin. She currently serves as the copresident of the Black Graduate Student Association at UT. Her experience as a student leader has facilitated her passion for advocacy, community building, and making Black lives and experiences matter. Her research interests are social justice advocacy, race-related stress, and cognitive emotional processes in Black women. Shaina also works at the community mental health center as a practicum student where she continues her work with Black students and helping them find their voices and meaning in their experiences.

Keoshia Harris, MA (she/her/hers), is a doctoral student at the University of Texas at Austin. Her lived experiences as a Black woman ignited her passion while complex interactions in the university setting strengthened her passion for uplifting disenfranchised communities. After obtaining her master's degree, Keoshia maintained this social justice orientation when serving at-risk youth and families as a licensed family therapist. She continues her advocacy work as Division 45 student representative and in research exploring race-related stress in addition to the lasting impact of racism among Black individuals. In each role, Harris aims to create a rhetoric that Black voices matter.

Marlie Harris is a graduate from the University of Texas at Austin with a bachelor's degree in human development and family sciences. Her research is built around a desire to destigmatize mental health care and raise awareness around mental health care access in marginalized communities. She has experience in a variety of disciplines, including multicultural psychology, human sexuality, and biology, and has plans to pursue her master's in mental health counseling.

Mercedes Holmes is an undergraduate philosophy and global management student of the University of Texas at Austin (at time of publication). Holmes is most proud to serve on the executive boards of various Black and historically Black organizations at UT Austin and has been awarded the Larry Temple Scholarship as an aspiring public servant. Holmes is currently researching post-Blackness in racial identity politics and critical race theory under the Ronald E. McNair Post-Baccalaureate Achievement Program and hopes to continue work within and for the Black community in her academic and professional future.

Maryam Jernigan-Noesi is a licensed psychologist, clinical researcher, and educator. Her professional training and work experiences include mental health, women's health, health disparities, and adult and family interventions. Clinically, Jernigan-Noesi has worked alongside a multidisciplinary team of health providers in mental health, community, medical, academic settings, and private practice. As a consultant, she works with organizations to implement equitable and culturally inclusive policies. Additionally, Dr. Jernigan-Noesi facilitates professional development training for a wide range of agencies, professional societies, corporations, legal professionals, mental health agencies, and community organizations.

Steven Jones (ABD), is a social psychology PhD candidate from Rutgers, the State University of New Jersey, and the 2021 predoctoral fellow at William Patterson University in New Jersey. He is a diversity scientist focused on investigating issues that impact equal opportunity. Specifically, he examines majority and minority perceptions of various phenomena, including in-group bias, sexism, and cronyism. His current research explores relationships between races and genders. He has earned degrees from Palm Beach State College, the University of the District of Columbia, and Rutgers, the State University of New Jersey.

Kuukuwa Koomson is a recent graduate from UT Austin. She majored in psychology with a minor in business administration. She lives in Dallas, but with her 4 years spent in Austin she's managed to be a part of and lead the Texas Student Circle of Black Psychologist, Texas Black Homecoming, Black Student Alliance, African Student Association, and a few other organizations. Koomson has a passion for finding ways to uplift and support the Black community. After graduation she plans on taking a gap year then pursuing a PsyD in hopes to either become a school psychologist or start her own practice working with youth.

Nolan Krueger is a Bay Area native. A multiracial-Black descendent of civil rights–oriented Black professionals, he found his calling at the intersection of race, higher education, and the criminal legal system. As a student, he witnessed the underrepresentation of Black collegians, and following a brief period of incarceration, he experienced the overrepresentation of Black men behind bars. Nolan—a Ford fellow—makes Black lives matter through research examining psychosocial stressors and resilience among Black collegians as well as multiracial mental health; through scholarship on the psychological impact of policing on Black collegians; and through scholar activism advocating prison abolition and accredited correctional education.

LaNya Lee is a Black, queer, nonbinary scholar completing their degree in psychology at the University of Florida. They are a research assistant with the WELLS Healing and Research Collective under the supervision of Dr. Della V. Mosley. Their current interests include alternative options to prisons that lead to healing and wellness, the healing and wellness of QTPOC communities with a specific focus on Black queer and/or transgender folks, and combatting anti-Black racism. They aspire to utilize and hold a Black feminist framework to work toward the healing and liberation of Black people and other marginalized communities.

Jioni Lewis is an associate professor of counseling psychology at the University of Maryland, College Park. Her research is focused on investigating the influence of discrimination on the health of people of color, with a specific focus on the impact of gendered racism on Black women's health and well-being as well as culturally relevant protective factors, such as racial identity, resistance, and radical healing. Dr. Lewis has received several national awards for her research, teaching/mentoring, and social justice advocacy, including the 2019 Emerging Professional Contributions to Research Award from the Society for the Psychological Study of Culture, Ethnicity, and Race.

Ricardo Henrique Lowe, Jr., is a research associate for the Institute of Urban Policy Research and Analysis (IUPRA) and a doctoral student in applied demography at the University of Texas at San Antonio. His research delves into the economic and residential incorporation of Afro-Caribbean immigrants in the Americas, including Costa Rica, Panamá, and the United States. Lowe also is a sociologist and holds membership with the Association of Black Sociologists (ABS), along with two nationally renowned Honor Societies—Alpha Kappa Delta and Alpha Chi.

Tracie A. Lowe is the assistant director of assessment with the Institute for Urban Policy Research and Analysis at the University of Texas at Austin. Her research focuses on the experiences of Black students in higher education with a particular emphasis on Black women graduate students. Additionally, she studies issues of equity in marginalized communities in Texas related to health, education, housing, income, and wealth. Lowe holds a doctorate in educational leadership and policy from the University of Texas at Austin, a master's degree in educational administration, and a bachelor's degree in interdisciplinary studies from Texas A&M University College Station.

Brianna McBride is a recent graduate of the University of Texas at Austin, earning two bachelor's degrees: communication and leadership and government. At UT Austin, she was involved in a multitude of Black organizations focused on uplifting the Black undergraduate community. Also, she worked in the Office of Admissions and spearheaded her own Black recruitment events. This fall, McBride will be staying in Austin, Texas, to attend the LBJ School of Public Affairs to pursue a master's in public affairs. Her interests include DEI work within recruitment, retention, and the success of Black and Brown students at institutions of higher education.

Sukyi McMahon is senior policy director, Austin Justice Coalition. McMahon provides strategic planning and direction for AJC's policy team, which develops and advocates for racial equity policies at the local, state, and national levels. Sukyi is the founding chair-woman of the board, and she has served in several fundamental roles throughout AJC's history to help bring the organization into its maturity. On the national scale, Sukyi is a senior consultant at Columbia University Justice Lab's Square One Project. She lends her expertise to local roundtables around the country that bring together community leaders, academics, and other experts to spark transformational thinking about racial reckoning and justice policy.

Jeannette Mejia experiences power, privilege, and oppression as a Black Dominican American cisgender woman from Lawrence, Massachusetts who is light, straight, fat, and working class. She's a first-generation college student with a bachelor's in psychology, a master's in critical ethnic studies from UMass Boston, and is a rising 3rd-year doctoral student in counseling psychology at the University of Florida. She is committed to working toward the liberation of all Black people. She aims to apply Black feminist/intersectional approaches to facilitate healing and survival from intersecting systems of oppression with Black and Brown communities with deep love and gratitude for her communities, ancestors, and family.

Isha Metzger is a first-generation American from Atlanta, Georgia, by way of Sierra Leone, West Africa. She is a licensed clinical psychologist with a PhD in clinical-community psychology from the University of South Carolina. As director of the EMPOWER lab and owner of Cultural Concepts, Dr. Metzger's career is aimed at taking a strengths-based, antideficit approach to reaching youth of color, and to standing against anti-Black racism through "Engaging Minorities in Prevention, Outreach, Wellness, Education, & Research." As an assistant professor of psychology, Metzger is invested in mentoring and training the next generation of community-based prevention scientists.

Norweeta G. Milburn, PhD, is a professor in residence in the Department of Psychiatry and Biobehavioral Sciences in the Division of Population and Behavioral Health. She received her PhD in community psychology from the University of Michigan (Ann Arbor). Her research interests include homelessness, substance abuse, mental health, and family-based behavioral interventions. She has led grants from the National Institute on Drug Abuse, the National Institute of Mental Health, the U.S. Department of Education, and the National Institute on Minority Health and Health Disparities. Dr. Milburn is a fellow in the American Psychological Association (APA). Her honors include being an inaugural member of the Leadership Institute for Women in Psychology, receiving the Community, Culture and Prevention Science Award from the Society for Prevention Research, and being an honorary professor in the Division of Psychotherapy and University of Cape Town's Department of Psychiatry and Mental Health in South Africa.

Chas Moore is an acclaimed activist and community organizer who has dedicated his life to helping Black, Indigenous, and people of color, impoverished communities, and those who suffer the brunt of systemic, institutional oppression. Under Moore's leadership, AJC has led local reform efforts such as creating the Austin Police Department's use of force policy, successfully fought against a faulty Austin Police Association Union contract, and successfully campaigned for the reallocation of $150 million from the Austin Police Department's budget to begin the process of creating public safety alternatives to traditional public safety methods. Moore's tenacity has garnered much recognition, including multiple awards, the 2019 Nathan Cummings Foundation Fellowship, and the 2019 Unlocked Futures Cohort backed by Academy award–winning artist John Legend.

Rico Mosby is a licensed psychologist in multiple states and is recognized by the National Register of Health Service Providers in Psychology. He performed his undergraduate studies at the University of Tennessee-Chattanooga and completed his doctoral work at Texas Tech University. He has over 20 years of experience in the mental health field, working in a variety of treatment venues. Dr. Mosby has worked to address the stigma associated with minorities seeking mental health services and currently provides brief and long-term therapy to individuals, couples, and families through his private practice, "The Victorious Mind, PLLC" in the Austin metro area.

Della V. Mosley is a Black, queer, cisgender woman and a healer-scholar-activist. She received her PhD in counseling psychology from the University of Kentucky. In 2018, Dr. Della developed the Wellness, Equity, Love, Liberation, and Sexuality Healing and Research Collective. In 2020, she cofounded Academics for Black Survival and Wellness, alongside the brilliant Pearis Bellamy. She is a proud member of the Psychology of Radical Healing Collective and an APA minority fellow. Her research, teaching, and service connect to her larger goal of enhancing the psychopolitical wellness of Black folx and of queer and/or transgender people of color.

Robert L. Muhammad, special assistant to the superintendent (2002–present), has been an integral part of Texas Empowerment Academy's staff since 2002. He started as the physical education teacher and after-school coordinator, and after his 1st year of service, Muhammad was promoted to be the office manager for the Texas Empowerment Academy due to his unwavering commitment to the institution and keen understanding of the school's mission. Muhammad currently serves as the special assistant to the superintendent, and he continues to use his organizational skills and leadership to interface with parents and mentor new leadership at the academy.

Edwin J. Nichols, PhD, is a clinical/industrial psychologist, and founding member of the Association of Black Psychologists. He was the first Black to head a center at the National Institute of Mental Health as chief of child and family mental health. He was a visiting professor at the University of Ibadan, Nigeria, and established the Child's Clinic for Psychological Assessment and Evaluation. His American and international I/O work is guided by his paradigm the Philosophical Aspects of Cultural Difference, first presented in 1976 at the World Psychiatric Conference, held at the University of Ibadan. He was educated at Assumption College, Canada; Tübingen Universität, Germany; and received his PhD in psychology and psychiatry, *cum laude*, Innsbruck Universität, Austria.

David Nowlin, superintendent, secondary principal (1999–present), is one of the founding TxEA members, and he has dedicated over 20 years in leading and providing initiatives for students to succeed, academically and personally. Over the years, Nowlin has grown TxEA from 7 to 377 students. Recently, his vision to serve high school students enabled TxEA to partner with Austin Community College (ACC) in the 2018–2019 school year. In 2021, TxEA will have its first graduating class of 16 students, and all have been accepted to three or more colleges or universities. Nowlin is a graduate of the University of Texas at Austin and has a bachelor's degree in history. Nowlin is originally from Abilene, Texas, but graduated from LBJ High School in Austin. Nowlin is a veteran, having spent 4 years in the U.S. Marines where he served in Desert Shield and Desert Storm. He has a passion for education and guiding students to fulfill their dreams.

Ifetayo Ojelade is a licensed psychologist, author, and executive director of A Healing Paradigm, based in Atlanta, Georgia. As an expert on trauma recovery, she works as a keynote speaker and workshop facilitator globally. Dr. Ojelade was initiated to Osun and Ifa in Osogbo, Nigeria. As an initiated ancestral priest of 20 years, she focuses on effective methods for integrating indigenous African healing practices into the therapy process. Her goal is to decolonize Western concepts of psychology by understanding how culture, indigenous African healing traditions, and spirituality can be used to heal people of African descent globally.

Annika Olson currently serves as the assistant director of policy research at the Institute for Urban Policy Research & Analysis, housed in the Black Studies Department at UT Austin. Olson is passionate about using research and legislative analysis to promote policy reform that betters the lives of vulnerable members of our community. Annika received two master's degrees in psychology and public policy from Georgetown University and her bachelors' in psychology from UMass Amherst. She has served as an AmeriCorps member in rural New Mexico working to address youth substance abuse and in Austin, Texas, teaching English and reading to K–2 students.

Carla Prieto is a rising 4th-year doctoral candidate in the University of Florida's counseling psychology program. She identifies as a cisgender, queer, White Latina who is proudly the daughter of immigrants. Prieto's research interests include the role of critical consciousness in contributing to the mental, physical, and vocational resilience of folx—especially Black and Brown folx—who experience systemic oppression, and she dreams of opening a holistic community mental health center for BIPOC in the future. Carla wholeheartedly believes that her liberation can be accomplished only when all Black, Brown, and Indigenous folx are truly free.

Garret Ross is a Black Korean with U.S. citizenship, who is upper middle class, 2.5 generation, and a queer, cisgender man who is light and thin. Ross recognizes how his simultaneous privilege and oppression of his positionality influences how he moves and what moves him. As a rising 3rd-year counseling psychology doctoral student at the University of Florida, Ross's investment in his niece's future (and futures of all Black people) ultimately grounds his work and commitment to Black liberation. Broadly, his work focuses on how anti-Blackness informs how Black people may navigate violence and accountability, personally and relationally.

LLyas Salahud-din, chief development officer (2018–present), brings a history of corporate, individual, and foundation fundraising to TxEA. Since his start at TxEA, Salahud-din has grown foundation funders from 0-16, raising millions for campus programs. In 2021 Salahud-din helped secure funding to purchase 20.5 acres to consolidate and build a new school. He has a master's in public administration with a concentration in nonprofit management. He is a 2017 Austin Area Research Organization (AARO) McBee fellow, a 2013 Leadership Austin Essential graduate, and the Austin, Texas 2021 Association of Fundraising Professionals (AFP) Fundraiser of the Year.

Sunshine (pronouns they/them) is a Black, queer, Afro-Latinx immigrant from São Paulo, Brazil. In 2021, they earned their master's degree at the Center of Gender, Sexuality, and Women Studies Research at the University of Florida. Currently, Sunshine acts as a project manager and an education and healing facilitator for Academics for Black Survival and Wellness, an initiative that aims to move academics toward taking action against anti-Black racism and promote wellness for Black folks. As a proud member of the WELLS Healing and Research Collective, they've continued to conduct research centering on the wellness of Black and Afro-diasporic communities.

Erlanger "Earl" Turner is a licensed psychologist and a tenure-track professor at Pepperdine University. He is also the executive director of Therapy for Black Kids, an organization that provides psychoeducational workshops and resources to help Black parents promote resilience and healthy emotional development among youth. Turner has over 15 years of experience in the field and has published several books, book chapters, and research on mental health among racial and ethnic communities. He is a nationally recognized mental health expert and past president of the Society for Child and Family Policy and Practice (Division 37 of the American Psychological Association).

Schuyler "Sky" C. Webb, PhD, MBA is a co-owner and principal consultant at McCray Webb & Associates in Arlington, Virginia. Webb conducted research program evaluations across six continents and authored over 230 publications, including peer-reviewed journal articles, scholarly papers, and technical reports. A coauthor and editor of six books, he conducted a wide range of research including psychopharmacology, undersea, hyperbaric and tropical medicine, human factors, allied health care professionals, epigenetics, sexual assault prevention, warriors' health care, Black and Latinx psychology, Asia-Pacific geo-military and international relations, and others. Webb earned degrees at Morehouse College, University of Massachusetts, National University, and Alliant International University.

Nia Williams is a licensed graduate professional counselor with a master's degree in clinical rehabilitation and mental health counseling from the University of the District of Columbia. She is also a maximizing access to research careers undergraduate student training in the Academic Research Scholarship Program where she explores and analyzes a variety of works from internal racism among African Americans and racial disparities within the community and assists in the analysis of generational trauma of African Americans.

TaShara Williams, MA, LPC-S, NCC, LVN (she/her/hers) served her country on active duty, in the U.S. Air Force, for 8 years. She served in OIF/OEF as well as several other amazing worldwide locations igniting her interest in multiculturalism. Immediately upon military separation, she began serving as a nurse while continuing lifelong learning educational dreams. After earning her master's degree from LA Tech University, she gained experiences as a mental health counselor working in school, inpatient/outpatient settings, and operates her own private practice while earning her PhD in counseling psychology. Research interests include race/culturally based trauma, and multicultural presentations of trauma symptomatology.

CPSIA information can be obtained
at www.ICGtesting.com
Printed in the USA
LVHW060150090122
708058LV00002B/10